Film Art: An Introduction

DAVID BORDWELL
KRISTIN THOMPSON

University of Wisconsin

Addison-Wesley Publishing Company

Reading, Massachusetts ■ Menlo Park, California ■
London ■ Amsterdam ■ Don Mills, Ontario ■ Sydney

*To our parents—Marjorie and Jay Bordwell
and Jean and Roger Thompson.*

This book is in the
ADDISON-WESLEY SERIES IN SPEECH,
DRAMA, AND FILM

Library of Congress Cataloging in Publication Data

Bordwell, David.
    Film art.

    (Addison-Wesley series in speech, drama, and film)
    Bibliography: p.
    Includes index.
    1. Moving-pictures--Aesthetics.   I. Thompson,
Kristin, 1950-   joint author. II. Title.
III. Series.
PN1995.B617   791.43'01   78-18633
    ISBN 0-201-00566-2

Second printing, February 1980

ISBN 0-201-00566-2
CDEFGHIJ-HA-8987654321

PREFACE

This book seeks to introduce the reader to the aesthetics of film. It assumes that the reader has no knowledge of cinema beyond the experience of moviegoing. Although some aspects of the book may prove useful for people with considerable knowledge of film, our aim is to survey the fundamental aspects of cinema as an art form.

By stressing film as art, we necessarily ignore certain aspects of the medium. Industrial documentaries, instructional filmmaking, propaganda, the social history of cinema or its impact as a mass medium—all these are important dimensions of film, and each would require a separate book for adequate treatment. Instead, this book seeks to isolate those basic features of film which can constitute it as an art. The book therefore directs itself at the person interested in how the film medium may give us experiences akin to those offered by painting, sculpture, music, literature, theater, architecture, or dance.

As we wrote this book, we envisioned readers of three particular sorts. First, there is the interested general reader, who wants to know a little more about the movies. Second, there is the student in a course in film appreciation, introduction to film, film criticism, or film aesthetics; for this reader, the book can function as a textbook. Third, there is the more advanced student of film, who may find here a convenient outline of principal issues and concepts and a set of suggestions for more specialized work.

Organizationally, *Film Art: An Introduction* offers a distinct approach to studying its topic. It might be possible to survey, willy-nilly, all contemporary approaches to film aesthetics, but we judged this to be too eclectic. Instead, we have sought an approach that would lead the reader in logical steps through various aspects of film aesthetics. Crucial to this approach is an emphasis on *the whole film*. Audiences experience entire films, not snippets. If the particular film is the irreducible center of our inquiry, we need an approach that will help us understand it. The approach we have chosen emphasizes the film as an artifact—made in particular ways, having a certain wholeness and unity, existing in history. We can outline the approach in a series of questions.

How is a film created? To understand film as art demands that we first understand how human labor creates the artifact. This leads to a study of *film production* (Part One).

How does an entire film function? This book assumes that like all artworks, a film may be understood as a *formal* construct. This leads to a consideration of what form is and how it affects us, of basic principles of film form, and of narrative and nonnarrative forms in cinema (Part Two). Matters of film form also demand that we consider the *techniques* which are characteristic of the film medium, for such techniques function within the form of the total film. Thus we will analyze the artistic possibilities of the four primary film techniques: mise-en-scene, cinematography, editing, and sound (Part Three).

How may we analyze a film critically? Armed with both a conception of film form and a knowledge of film technique, we can go on to analyze *specific films* as artworks. We analyze several such films as examples (Part Four).

How does film art change through history? Although a thorough history of cinema would require many volumes, here we can suggest how the formal aspects of film do not exist outside determinable historical contexts. We survey the most noteworthy *periods and movements in film history* to show how understanding form helps us locate films within history (Part Five).

It is worth noting that this approach to the entire film came from several years of teaching introductory film courses. As teachers, we wanted students to see and hear more in the films we studied, but it was evident that simply providing the "lecturer's view" would not teach students how to analyze films on their own. Ideally, we decided, students should master a repertory of *principles* which would help them examine films more closely. We became convinced that the best way to understand cinema is to use general principles of film form to help analyze specific films. Our success with this approach led us to decide that this book should be skills-centered. By learning basic concepts of film form and film technique, the reader can sharpen his or her perception of any specific film.

The stress on skills has another consequence. You will note that the book's examples and evidence are quite varied; we refer to a great many films. We expect that very few readers will have seen all of the films we mention, and certainly no teacher of a film course could possibly show every title. But we have varied our examples in the interests of clarity, vividness, and accessibility. If some titles seem unfamiliar, it is partly because film study over the past five years has opened up new areas of inquiry which any textbook must address. (Those areas, incidentally, are within the reach of film courses. Ozu's *The Only Son* is just as accessible as Bergman's *The Silence* and is in fact cheaper to rent; Antonioni's *Story of a Love Affair* is no harder to obtain than is his *Red Desert*. Almost every film we cite is available for rental or purchase or both.) Moreover, because the book stresses the acquisition of conceptual skills, the reader need not see all of the films we mention in order to grasp the general principles. Many other films can be used to make the same points. For instance, the possibilities of camera movement can be as easily illustrated with *La Ronde* as with *La Grande Illusion*; to exemplify narrative ambiguity, *Shadow of a Doubt* will serve as well as *Day of Wrath*. Indeed, although the book can serve as a syllabus for a course in cinema, it is also possible for a teacher to use different films to illustrate the book's ideas. (It would then be a useful exercise for the class to *contrast* the text example with the film shown, so as to specify even more clearly particular aspects of the film.) The book rests not on titles, but on concepts.

Film Art: An Introduction has certain unusual features. A book on film must be heavily illustrated, and most are. Virtually all film books, however, utilize so-called production stills—photographs taken during filming, but usually not from the position of the motion picture camera. The result is a picture that does not correspond to any image in the finished film. We have used very few production stills. Instead, the illustrations in this book are virtually all frame enlargements—magnified photographs from the actual film. Most of these illustrations come from 35-mm prints of the films, and with the exception of the shots from *Daisies*, all of the color illustrations are taken from 35-mm prints or negatives. Although obtaining access to 35-mm material has been tedious and costly, this book's emphasis on the film itself demands the finest photographic quality possible.

Another unusual feature is the Notes and Queries section at the end of almost every chapter. In these sections we attempt to raise issues, provoke discussion, and suggest further reading and research. As chapter supplements, the Notes and Queries sections constitute a resource for the advanced undergraduate, the graduate student, and the interested general reader.

In all, we hope that this book will help readers to watch a greater variety of films with keener attention and to ask precise questions about the art of cinema.

Thanks are in order to the many people who helped us prepare this book. The text was enormously improved by the suggestions and criticism of Michael Budd, Peter Bukalski, Don Fredericksen, J. Douglas Gomery, and Claudia Gorbman. We are grateful to our sponsoring editor, Damon Reed Gardner, our production editor, Evelyn Wilde, and to the Addison-Wesley staff for seeing a difficult project through to completion.

We must also thank the many people and institutions who helped us get access to images and get permission to reproduce them: David Allen; Tino Balio, Susan Dalton, and Maxine Fleckner of the Wisconsin Center for Film and Theater Research; Eileen Bowser, Mary Corliss, and John Gartenberg of the Museum of Modern Art; Martin Bresnick and Dorothy Desmond of MacMillan Audio-Brandon Films; Kent Carroll of Grove Press Films; Arnold Jacobs of Ajay Films; Janus Films; Jose Lopez of New Yorker Films; Roger L. Mayer of MGM, Inc.; Kazuto Ohira of Toho Films; Badia Rahman and Mary Agnes Beach of the University of Wisconsin—Madison Communication Arts Department; Leon Salzman of Bonded Storage; and Edith van Slyck of Pennebaker Films.

A final word of appreciation is due to Norman McLaren, Ernie Gehr, and Michael Snow, who kindly granted us permission to print frames from *Begone Dull Care*, *Serene Velocity*, and *Wavelength*, respectively.

Madison, Wisconsin   D. B.
January 1979   K. T.

The authors wish to express their appreciation to the following people, who reviewed the manuscript for *Film Art: An Introduction* and gave constructive comment and suggestions.

Michael Budd, Florida Atlantic University

Peter J. Bukalski, Southern Illinois University

Richard B. Byrne, The Annenberg School of Communications at the University of Southern California

Robert E. Davis, The University of Texas at Austin

Don Fredericksen, Cornell University

Douglas Gomery, The University of Wisconsin—Milwaukee

Claudia Gorbman, Indiana University

Ronald Gottesman, Center for the Humanities, University of Southern California

CONTENTS

Part One
Film Production

Part Two
Film Form

Part Three
Film Style

ix

**Part Four
Critical
Analysis
of Films**

Part Five
Film
History

Part One
Film
Production

CHAPTER 1

THE WORK OF FILM PRODUCTION

On sober reflection, we readily admit that films are like buildings, books, and symphonies—artifacts made by humans for human purposes. Yet as part of an audience watching an enthralling movie, we may find it difficult to remember that what we are seeing is not a natural object, like a flower or an asteroid. Cinema is so captivating that we tend to forget that movies are *made*. An understanding of the art of cinema depends initially on a recognition that a film is produced by both machines and human labor.

Technical Factors in Film Production ■

Watching a film differs from viewing a painting, a stage performance, or even a slide show. A film presents us with images in *illusory* motion. What creates this specific effect, this sense of "moving pictures"? For cinema to exist, a series of images must be displayed to a viewer by means of a mechanism which presents each image for a very short period and which inserts between successive images an interval of blackness. If a series of slightly different images of the same object is displayed under these conditions, physiological and psychological processes in the viewer will create the illusion of seeing a moving image. Such conditions for "moving pictures" exist only rarely in nature. Like most human artifacts, a film depends on particular technological factors.

First, the images must be capable of being displayed in a *series.* They might be on a row of cards, as in the Mutoscope (Fig. 1.1), and flipped past the viewer to create the illusion of movement. More commonly, the images are inscribed on a strip of some flexible material. Optical toys such as the Zoetrope put their images on strips of paper (Fig. 1.2), but cinema as we know it uses a strip of celluloid as support for the series of images, which are called *frames.* If the images are to be put on a strip of film, cinema usually requires three machines to create and display those images. All three share a basic principle: A mechanism controls how light is admitted to the film, advances the strip of film a frame at a time, and exposes it to light for the proper interval. The three machines are:

Figure 1.1

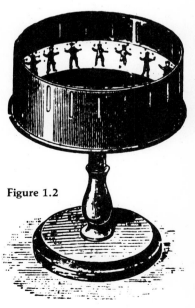

Figure 1.2

3

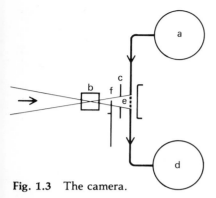

Fig. 1.3   The camera.

1. *The camera* (Fig. 1.3) In a light-tight chamber, a drive mechanism feeds the motion picture film from a reel (a) past a lens (b) and aperture (c) to a take-up reel (d). The lens focuses light reflected from a scene onto each frame of film (e). The mechanism moves the film intermittently, while a shutter (f) admits light through the lens only when each frame is unmoving and ready for exposure. The standard shooting rate for sound film is 24 frames per second.

2. *The printer.* Printers exist in various designs, but all consist of light-tight chambers which drive a negative or positive roll of film from a reel (a) past an aperture (b) to a take-up reel (c). Simultaneously, a roll of unexposed film (a′, c′) moves through the aperture (b or b′), either intermittently or continuously. By means of a lens (d), light beamed through the aperture prints the image (e) on the unexposed film (e′). The two rolls of film may come into contact and pass through the aperture simultaneously (Fig. 1.4 diagrams a contact printer). Or, light coming through the original may be beamed to the unexposed roll through lenses, mirrors, or prisms (as in (f), in the optical printer, Fig. 1.5).

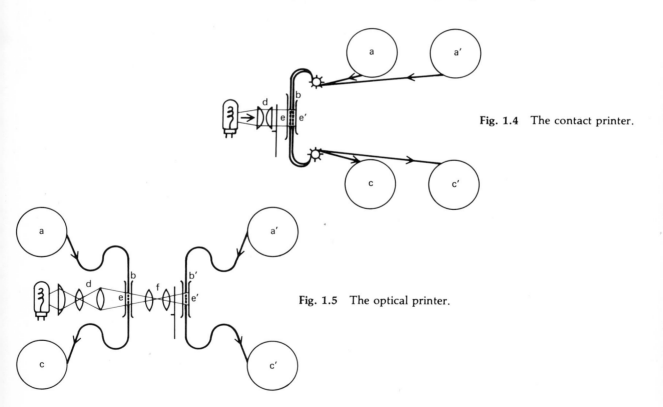

Fig. 1.4   The contact printer.

Fig. 1.5   The optical printer.

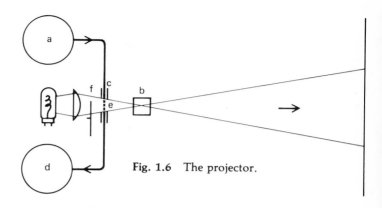

Fig. 1.6   The projector.

3.   *The projector* (Fig. 1.6). A drive mechanism feeds the exposed and developed film from a reel (a) past a lens (b) and aperture (c) to a take-up reel (d). Light is beamed through the images (e) and magnified by the lens for projection on a screen. Again, a mechanism moves the film inter-mittently past the aperture, while a shutter (f) admits light only when each frame is pausing. For the movement effect to occur, the film must display at least 12 frames per second; the shutter blocks and reveals each frame at least twice in order to reduce the flicker effect on the screen. The standard projection rate for sound film is 24 frames per second.

Camera, printer, and projector are all variants of the same basic machine. The camera and the projector both control the intermittent movement of the film past a light source. The crucial difference is that the camera gathers light from outside the machine and focuses it onto the film, whereas in the projector the reverse happens: The machine pro-duces the light which shines through the film onto a surface outside. The printer combines both other devices: Like a projector, it controls the passage of light through exposed film (the original negative or positive); like a camera, it gathers light to form an image (on the unexposed roll of film).

We think of cinema as a photographic medium, since its history is thickly intertwined with the history of still photography. Like photo-graphic film, motion picture film consists of a transparent *base* (formerly of nitrate, now of acetate) which supports a light-sensitive *emulsion* (a gelatin layer containing grains of silver halide). Light reflected from the environment strikes the silver compounds and registers a latent image. Chemical processing makes the latent image visible as a configuration of black grains on a white ground. From this image (usually a negative one) one or more copies (usually positive) may be printed photographical-ly. Although the filmmaker can create *non*photographic images on the film strip by drawing, cutting or punching holes, etching, or painting, most filmmakers have relied on the camera, the printer, and other photographic technology.

In order to run satisfactorily through camera, printer, and projector, the strip of film must have certain standardized features. The film strip is perforated along one or both edges, so that small teeth (sprockets) in the machines can seize the perforations (sprocket holes) and pull the film at a uniform rate and smoothness. Space is also reserved along one or both edges for an optical or magnetic sound track. The physical dimensions of the film have necessarily been standardized, with width being the crucial variable. Motion picture film widths, called *gauges*, are measured in millimeters. Although many gauges have been experimented with, the internationally standardized ones are 8 mm/super 8 mm, 16 mm, 35 mm, and 70 mm.

A popular gauge for both amateurs and experimentalists is 8 mm/super 8 mm (Fig. 1.7). Both 8 mm and super 8 mm are the same width, but perforations and screen area differ. Figure 1.8 shows 16-mm film, which is used for both amateur and professional film work. Most film study courses show 16-mm prints of films. The standard professional gauge is 35 mm. Most commercial theaters show 35-mm prints; Fig. 1.9 is a frame from *The Jazz Singer*. Another professional gauge is 70-mm film, which is used for "spectacular" projects (e.g., Fig. 1.10, a frame from *Lawrence of Arabia*).

Image quality varies directly with the width of the film; normally, the higher the gauge, the better defined and more detailed the image. The print we see of a film, however, may not be in the gauge of the original. Many films shot in 70 mm are also distributed in 35-mm prints, whereas most films studied in cinema courses were originally shot in 35 mm but are shown in 16 mm. A good general rule for the viewer is to try to see a film projected in the gauge in which it was shot. Thus a 35-mm print of Keaton's *The General* will almost certainly be photographically superior to a 16-mm or 8-mm print, whereas a film shot on super 8 mm will look fuzzy and grainy if printed and projected in 35 mm.

Running along the edges of the film strip there may also be a recording of the sound that accompanies the images. The sound track may be either *magnetic* or *optical.* In the magnetic type, a strip of magnetic recording tape runs along the film's edge; in projection, the film's track is "read" by a sound head similar to that on a tape recorder. The 70-mm frame in Fig. 1.10 has a magnetic sound track (running along both edges). An optical sound track encodes sonic information in the form of patches of light and dark in a parallel line running alongside the frames. During production, electrical impulses from a microphone are translated into pulsations of light which are photographically inscribed

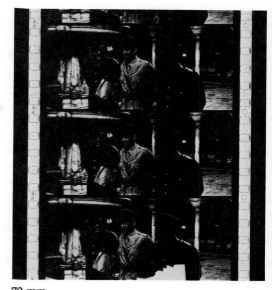

| 8 mm/super 8 mm | 16 mm | 35 mm | 70 mm |
| Figure 1.7 | Figure 1.8 | Figure 1.9 | Figure 1.10 |

on the moving film strip. (Modern optical sound recording usually records on magnetic tape initially, then transfers the taped sound onto film.) When the film is projected, the optical track produces varying intensities of light which are translated back into electrical impulses and then into sound waves. An optical sound track may encode the sound as *variable density* (gradations of black and white) or as *variable area* (a wavy contour of black and white within the sound image). The 16-mm frame in Fig. 1.8 has a variable area optical sound track; the 35-mm frame in Fig. 1.9 utilizes a variable-density optical track.

Specific machines, then, create a film from a raw material—a photochemically sensitive strip of perforated celluloid of a standardized gauge. Important as technology is, however, it is only part of the story.

Social Factors in Film Production ■

Machines don't make movies by themselves. Film production transforms raw materials into a product through the application of machinery *and* human labor. But human labor may be utilized in different ways, and those ways have to do with economic and social situations. How film work is financed, how decisions are made, how production tasks are assigned, and how different modes of production relate to the overall social context—a film is the result of all of these human factors.

Modes of Production

There are various ways of organizing the film-production process. It is one thing for you to make a film with your own money and equipment. It is another thing to participate in a filmmaking group which gives every member a say in the project. It is yet another thing to work as an assistant film editor for a film studio. Along these lines, we can distinguish three basic modes of production: individual, collective, and studio. Each mode operates on different principles.

In *individual* film production the filmmaker functions as an artisan. He or she may own the raw materials and the necessary equipment. Financial backing can be obtained on a film-by-film basis, and the production is generally on a small scale. There is very little division of labor: The filmmaker performs every production task, from obtaining financing to final editing. Though other people may be involved (e.g., as actors), the principal creative decisions rest with the filmmaker. Examples of individual film production include "home movie" filming, as well as much avant-garde filmmaking (e.g., the surrealists of the 1920s, the New American cinema of today, some documentary filming).

In *collective* film production several film workers participate equally in the project. Like individual filmmakers, the group may own its means of production; the production is often on a small scale, and money is supplied by investors or agencies for a specific project. But although there is a greater degree of division of labor (no one member performs all of the necessary tasks), production decisions are made collectively, and the group shares common goals. Examples are documentary groups such as the Maysles brothers (*Gimme Shelter, Grey Gardens)*, the Newsreel group, and the French collective SLON. Both individual and collective modes of production are sometimes known as "independent" production.

Studio film production operates on a much larger scale. A studio is a firm in the business of manufacturing films. As a corporate entity requiring a great deal of capital investment, the studio typically makes many films at one time. Studio workers do not own the means of production, and most do not participate in the decisions which determine the production process. Studio workers are employed on the basis of their ability to perform specific tasks (costume design, acting, photography, etc.). Thus a specific division of labor arises. In studio production, although the overall course of the production is surveyed by a producer, the labor creating the film is divided into many discrete tasks, each performed by a specialist.

Collective workers share common goals and decision-making powers, but studio workers usually have no vision of the project in its totality. Planning and execution phases are split. A scriptwriter might write one scene of one film and another scene of another film; the final cutting of the film might be done by someone who knows little of the project. The clearest analogy (though it is inadequate in many respects) is assembly-line manufacture; a manager supervises a number of workers, each trained in a particular task, functioning within a system of mass production. Examples of this mode of production are the Hollywood studios as they developed between 1920 and 1950 and the major firms of Europe, the Orient, and Scandinavia of the same period. Throughout film history, more films have probably been made independently (especially educational, propaganda, and publicity films), but in every major country studio film production has been the economically dominant form.

Recent years have seen a certain blending of independent and studio production in the figure of the free-lance film worker. Since the major Hollywood and European studios have become primarily distribution firms, filmmaking has proceeded along somewhat independent lines. Federico Fellini, Francis Ford Coppola, Alfred Hitchcock, Robert Altman, and similar filmmakers are famous examples of a practice that is now common. A director and a producer decide on a particular project and obtain financial backing (usually after a firm has agreed to distribute the film). The director or producer then hires personnel specifically for the film, permitting the concentration on a single project characteristic of independent filmmaking. Yet the practice is on the whole closer to a variant of the studio system, because it retains a specialized division of labor and because the workers usually have no common goals and have little part in decision making.

Stages and Roles in Production

Whatever the production organization, each mode goes through the same basic steps in creating a film. Moreover, each stage of film production involves a set of roles. In studio production each phase is supervised by a different person, and each role is assigned to one or more workers. In an individual production setup, on the other hand, the filmmaker may take the film through all of the stages and carry out all of the roles personally. Or, a group may decide collectively how to assign each member to several roles. Each role defined within film production may be occupied by several people, a few people, or one person.

There are three fundamental stages of film production: *preparation, shooting,* and *assembly*. Each of these can be subdivided into distinct phases and roles.

Preparation. Even the most improvised film must be planned to some degree. Money, time, equipment, and labor must be obtained. At this stage two roles emerge as critical: that of producer and that of writer.

The producer's role is chiefly financial and organizational. In the studio system the producer is a studio executive, but there have been independent producers as well, and the solitary filmmaker acts as his or her own producer. Some famous producers are Carlo Ponti, Walt Disney, and Irving Thalberg.

The producer oversees a portion of preparation we may call *the financial phase.* The producer obtains financial support for the film, arranges a schedule and a budget, and makes arrangements to get personnel. The producer also usually oversees a second phase we may call *the literary phase:* A writer enters the project. The writer's task is to prepare a script. This may mean adapting a text from another medium (such as a play or novel) or creating an original script. (At the height of the studio system writers were brought in solely to prepare a script and then had no control of how it changed once it left their hands. Today, writers with completed scripts often seek out producers.) The script may go through many stages, the most common of which are the *treatment* (a synopsis outlining the basic action) and the *shooting script* (a detailed "blueprint," complete with scenes and dialogue; a director may collaborate at this stage). Well-known screenwriters are Dudley Nichols, Ben Hecht, and Anita Loos; some authors who have done scriptwriting are William Faulkner, Ernest Hemingway, and Vladimir Nabokov. In theory the producer oversees all phases of production, and some producers (e.g., David O. Selznick) were famous for their deep involvement in various stages. In practice, though, the producer's energies are concentrated on the preparation phase. Large-studio production, which puts a single producer in charge of several films at the same time, made a practice of having a "unit production manager" represent the producer in subsequent phases.

Shooting. During this stage of production images and sounds are inscribed on the film. Many roles are defined here, but the chief one is that of the *director.* Traditionally, the director coordinates how all of the various elements of the film medium put the prepared material on film. Thus the director has extensive control over the look and sound of the film. The director often works with the *art director,* or set designer, for the film. If the production is a large one, the director may have assistants or "second-unit" directors assigned to particular scenes. Some famous directors are Orson Welles, Alfred Hitchcock, Andy Warhol, and John Ford. (All four also functioned as producers.) In Fig. 1.11 the Russian director Sergei Eisenstein looks through a camera mounted on a crane while making *Ivan the Terrible.*

Figure 1.11

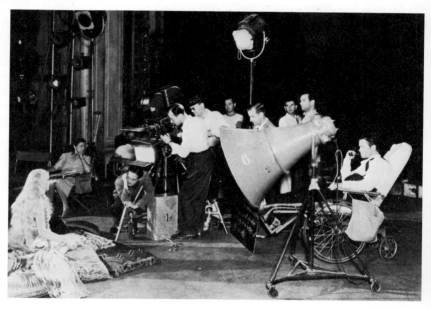

Figure 1.12

The director controls several units of production labor:

1. A *photography unit*, including:
   (a) a *cinematographer*, an expert on photographic imagery, light-
       ing, and camera manipulation, who consults with the director
       as to how a scene will be lit and filmed. Famous cinema-
       tographers include Gregg Toland (seen in Fig. 1.12 on the set of
       Citizen Kane; Welles directs from his wheelchair at the right,
       Toland crouches below the camera to line up the shot, and
       actress Dorothy Comingore sits at the left), Raoul Coutard

Figure 1.13

Figure 1.14

(films of François Truffaut and Jean-Luc Godard), Lee Garmes (several of Joseph Von Sternberg's films), and Giovanni di Venanzo (films of Luchino Visconti and Federico Fellini). The cinematographer supervises:

    (b) a camera operator, who runs the machine and who may also have assistants to load the camera, push a dolly, etc.;

    (c) a *key grip*, the head prop person, who may also have a staff;

    (d) a *gaffer*, the head electrician, who also has a staff.

2. A *sound unit*, including:

    (a) a *mixer*, whose role demands a knowledge of sound as sophisticated as the cinematographer's knowledge of imagery. The mixer supervises the recording of sound during shooting and during the assembly phase (Fig. 1.13 shows the mixer at work on the 1939 film *Juarez*, with the film's composer, Erich Korngold, at the right). The mixer's staff includes:

    (b) a *recordist*, who runs the sound equipment and may have a staff;

    (c) a mike person, who manipulates the microphone extension (*boom*), guiding the microphone where necessary.

3. In a fiction film, a *cast*. In the studio system stars would usually be under contract. Figure 1.14 shows Greta Garbo in a screen test (a procedure used to determine casting and try out lighting, costume, makeup, and camera positions in relation to the actor).

4. A miscellaneous unit including a makeup staff, a costume staff, a set design staff, hairdressers, carpenters, and others.

Figure 1.15

The solitary filmmaker may perform all of the relevant roles personally; the small crew may divide them somewhat. Figure 1.15, a posed shot from the 1937 production of *The Prisoner of Zenda*, illustrates studio division of labor during the shooting phase. In the foreground on the far left are two cast members (Douglas Fairbanks, Jr., and Ronald Colman); in the center, with hat and pipe, stands the director, John Cromwell; on the right stands the "script girl" (whose job it is to keep props and details continuous from scene to scene and to keep a record of the shots made). In the background, upper center, stands the cinematographer, James Wong Howe; behind him, the camera operator; and in the far right, a mike man and a grip.

The director, then, supervises the complex process of *shooting* the film. What this process produces is a set of *shots*. In production each uninterrupted inscription of an image on the film by the camera creates a shot: a strip of film containing one or more frames which present a spatial and temporal continuity. At the shooting stage the separate shots are often recorded "out of continuity." That is, to minimize costs, all shots using a certain setting or certain objects and costumes are usually filmed in one period—even if those shots will appear at very different points in the finished film. For example, a film's story might begin and end in a lavish mansion, but the intervening scenes might take place elsewhere. In most film production the first and last scenes would be filmed, say, in a week, to avoid having to rebuild the set and reestablish the lighting.

A more complicated example is the filming of the recent motion picture *Serpico*. In the finished film the protagonist develops from a clean-shaven police officer to a shaggy hipster. In production, however, the film was shot in *reverse* order. The star, Al Pacino, began with long hair and beard; then for each scene, his hair and beard were trimmed bit by bit until he became clean-cut. Thus the *last* episodes to be shot were the *first* the audience would eventually see. It is rare for shots to be filmed in exactly the order in which the audience sees them; even documentaries typically reedit the shots for specific effects.

Because shooting usually proceeds out of continuity, the director and crew must have some way of labeling each shot made. A *clapboard* is held up before the camera at the start of each shot. On the surface of the clapboard are noted the production, scene, shot, and *take* (the particular filming of each shot required); the hinged arm makes a distinct cracking sound that permits the editor to synchronize the sound and picture later (see Fig. 9.83). In this way each shot is tagged for future reference.

In the course of shooting, the director may shoot wholly "within the studio" (e.g., building a set of the Pyramids) or "on location" (e.g., going to film at the Pyramids). The director may call for a shot to be retaken several times. Particular scenes may require the use of special optical effects or the use of miniatures (see Fig. 1.16, a miniature used in the making of *The Comedians*), all of which the director must coordinate. In addition, the director and the crew have a chance to check the ongoing quality of their work by viewing *rushes*—the processed and printed shots they have already made.

Assembly. Even before shooting is completed, the task of assembling various shots and sounds has probably begun. At this stage the roles of *editor* (or cutter) and *sound mixer* become central—though these roles are usually still under the control of the roles of producer or director. Also, the editing and sound mixing often overlap, since editor and mixer make mutual adjustments of picture and sound relations.

The editor first assembles the shots into a rough cut—the film without sound, loosely strung in sequence. From this the editor builds toward a final cut, reordering and trimming the shots, perhaps adding images from a library of stock shots. At the same time, laboratory work (e.g., color printing) is done.

Meanwhile, the chief mixer assembles the film's sound track. Some sound (usually dialogue) has been recorded during filming. Now sound

Figure 1.16

effects, music, voice-over commentary, and perhaps some dialogue must be added. The mixer and staff are prepared to manufacture any sound needed—a pistol shot, a car crash, a steam whistle. If a line of dialogue was muffled or if it must be changed, an actor may return to rerecord or *dub* his or her voice in synchronization with the image. A composer will view the final cut and write and time a score for it. Usually, sounds are recorded on distinct tracks—voice tracks, effects tracks, and music tracks—which may number 20 or more. Finally, these are mixed and synchronized with the final cut. The resulting "married print" constitutes the finished film. When the original negative is cut and the sound track is printed on it, the laboratory produces positive prints for distribution and exhibition.

Film production has been our principal concern, but the social institution of cinema also depends on distribution and exhibition. In most countries studio production has tied its finances up with film rental firms and theater circuits. For example, in the late 1920s Paramount bought hundreds of theaters, thus guaranteeing itself a market for its product. United States courts declared such a practice monopolistic, but in this country distribution is still controlled by the major production firms.

Production has always affected distribution and exhibition. In the heyday of Hollywood, studios produced a variety of films (cartoons, comedy shorts, newsreels) which accompanied the feature film and made

Figure 1.17

up a package with specific exhibition appeal. (The theater marquee in Fig. 1.17 advertises an early sound film, *White Shadows in the South Seas*, with an accompanying Laurel and Hardy short and a newsreel.) Similarly, today an expensive film must make back its costs as soon as possible, so it will play first-run theaters for awhile before moving to second-run ones. A film, usually a cheaper one, may try for saturation, running in many theaters at once in hopes of a quick return. In such ways mass production determines a need for mass distribution and consumption.

Independent filmmakers, on the other hand, may try to break into the studio distribution/exhibition structure (as Emile de Antonio did with *Millhouse* and Andy Warhol has done with several films). More often independent filmmakers may seek to create alternative distribution/exhibition structures to reach particular audiences. For example, films of the New American cinema are distributed to campuses and museum audiences through agencies such as the Film-Makers' Cooperative.

Implications of Different Modes of Film Production

Since much of cinema's uniqueness rests on the technical and social factors that produce it, the modes and stages of film production have considerable implications for the study of film as an art. For one thing, a film is often classified on the basis of assumptions about how it was produced. How we think a film was made is relevant to how we categorize it. We often distinguish a *documentary* film from a *fiction* film on the basis of production. Typically, the documentary filmmaker controls only certain variables of preparation, shooting, and assembly; some variables (e.g., script, rehearsal) may be omitted, whereas others (e.g., setting, lighting, behavior of the figures) are present but often uncontrolled. For example, in interviewing an eyewitness to an event, the filmmaker will control lighting, camera work, and editing, but will not tell the witness what to say or how to act. The fiction film, on the other hand, is characterized by much more control over script and other aspects of the preparation and shooting phases.

Similarly, we identify the category of *compilation* film by the fact that such a film is produced primarily by assembling images that record certain historical evidence about a topic. Gathering visual and auditory material from archives and other sources, the compilation filmmaker may skip the shooting stage of production and simply assemble newsreel footage to create a film dossier on a given subject, e.g., television series such as "Victory at Sea" and "The World at War."

One more kind of film is distinguished by features of its production: the *animated* film. Here the film does not record an independent, continuously existing stream of action; Daffy Duck and Mickey Mouse do not exist to be filmed. An animated film is produced frame by frame. Either images are drawn right on the film itself, or, more often, the camera photographs a series of static drawings. In either case animation is characterized by unusual production work at the shooting stage.

Film production not only defines particular types of films, but is also tied to modes of production in the society as a whole. Because of the technological requisites of production, cinema began in the most highly industrialized societies—the United States, Germany, France, and England. In these countries filmmaking quickly became a business for both individual filmmakers and firms. Studio film production tends to occur when countries have achieved division of labor in other manufacturing industries. In American and European industry, for instance, the separation of production planning from execution had been accomplished by 1900, and the same separation was practiced in the film industry in the subsequent decade.

Once film and equipment become more widely available, minority modes of production are possible. With access to 8-mm and 16-mm cameras, film, and projectors, people can engage in individual and collective film production. But this access rests in turn on the existence of a leisure class that can afford to purchase such machines and that knows how to operate them. Just as MGM could not have developed in the

Middle Ages, so independent film production cannot indigenously spring up among the tribes of South Africa. Film production has historically modeled its practices on economic production in other industries, and the overall economic nature of a society constrains the modes of film production which can develop there.

Finally, the mode of film production affects how we view the filmmaker as artist. This is the issue of "authorship." Who, it is often asked, is the "author," the artist responsible for the film?

For some modes of film production, the question is easily answered. In individual production the author must be the solitary filmmaker—Stan Brakhage, Louis Lumière, yourself. Collective film production creates collective authorship; the author is the entire group (San Francisco Newsreel or SLON). The question of authorship becomes difficult only when asked of studio production.

In the earlier instances "authorship" is defined by control and decision making, whether by an individual or a collective. But studio film production delegates tasks to so many individuals that it is often difficult to determine who decides what. Is the producer the author? In the prime years of the Hollywood studio system, the producer might have had little or nothing to do with shooting. The writer? Again, in Hollywood, the writer's scripts might be completely transformed in filming. So is this situation like collective production, with "group authorship"? No, since studio division of labor denies film workers common goals and shared decision making. Moreover, if we consider not only control and decision making, but also "individual style," it must be admitted that certain studio workers leave recognizable and unique traces on the films they make. Cinematographers such as Hal Mohr and Gregg Toland, set designers such as Hermann Warm, choreographers such as Gene Kelly—the contributions of these people usually stand out within the films they made. So where does the studio-produced film leave the idea of authorship?

In recent years the most commonly accepted solution has been to regard the director as the "author" of most studio films. Although the writer prepares a script, that script does not define the finished film, since later phases of production can modify the script beyond recognition. (Indeed, writers are famous for complaining how directors mutilate scripts.) In general, the director's role comes closest to orchestrating all of those stages of production which most directly affect how a movie looks and sounds.

For a director to orchestrate the labor of shooting and assembly does not mean that he or she is expert at every job or even overtly orders this or that. Within the studio mode of production, the director can delegate tasks to trusted and competent personnel; hence the tendency of directors to work habitually with certain actors, cinematographers, composers, and so on. Alfred Hitchcock is said to sit boredly on the set during filming, never looking through the camera's viewfinder; yet he has sketched out every shot beforehand and thoroughly explained to his cinematographer what he wants. Even in the assembly phase, the director can exercise remote-control power. Often Hollywood studios would not permit the director to supervise the editing of the film. But John Ford, for example, got around this by simply making only one take of each shot whenever possible, with very little overlap of action from shot to shot. By precutting the film "in his head," Ford gave the editor the bare minimum and had no need to set foot in an editing room. Finally, the importance of the director's role is confirmed by the recent trend for the director to operate on a free-lance basis, organizing his or her chosen project.

For all of these reasons, in what follows we will generally identify the director as the author of the film in question. There are exceptions, but usually it is through the director's control of the shooting and assembly phases that the film's form and style crystallize. These two aspects of a film are central to film art and thus to the concerns of the rest of this book.

Notes and Queries ■

The Illusion of Movement in the Cinema

The motion of the film image is illusory, produced wholly by physiologically innate responses to certain stimuli. What causes the illusion? The traditional explanation is "persistence of vision," a concept proposed by Peter Mark Roget in 1824. But today this idea has no scientific status. At least three concepts of modern perceptual psychology are relevant to the explanation of film's illusion of movement:

1. *The phi phenomenon.* In 1912 the Gestalt psychologist Max Wertheimer discovered that when two side-by-side lights were flashed at certain intervals (25–400 milliseconds), viewers perceived not two lights flashing independently, but a single *moving* light. (The same effect can be seen on neon advertising signs that use arrows or "moving" lines of light.) Wertheimer dubbed this effect the "phi phenomenon."

2. *Masking.* If an image is presented briefly and another quickly interrupts it, recognition of the previous form is considerably reduced, or "masked." Since a viewer needs a certain amount of time to perceive a stimulus, the presentation of a series of images at high speed will affect how images are integrated into a clear, continuous vision.

3. *Flicker fusion.* If projected light is broken by a series of flickers at different rates, certain of those rates reach a point where viewers no longer perceive flicker but only constant light—a point of "flicker fusion."

No researcher has yet ascertained exactly how these processes shape our awareness of illusory movement, but plainly projection of a film at 12 to 24 frames per second (fps) establishes a rate at which all of these phenomena can operate. Engineers quickly discovered that perceived flicker was reduced if the projector shutter broke the light beam more often than once per frame; at 16 fps flicker fusion is more easily achieved by flashing each frame three times, at 24 fps by flashing each frame twice. Similarly, the overall similarity from frame to frame in most shots serves to eliminate masking. And the phenomenon of apparent motion on the screen seems to be a variant of the phi phenomenon. (It has even been suggested that Wertheimer conceived the experiment after considering the nature of cinema.)

The Technical Basis of Cinema

André Bazin suggests that humankind dreamed of cinema long before it actually appeared: "The concept men had of it existed so to speak fully armed in their minds, as if in some platonic heaven" (*What Is Cinema?*, Vol. 1, Berkeley: University of California Press, 1967, p. 17). But the fact of the matter is that whatever its antecedents in Greece and the Renaissance, the cinema became technically feasible only in the nineteenth century. Motion pictures depended on many discoveries in various scientific and industrial fields: optics and lens making, the control of light (especially by means of arc lamps), chemistry (involving particularly the production of cellulose), steel production, precision machining, and other areas. The cinema machine is closely related to other machines of the period. For example, engineers in the nineteenth century designed machines that could intermittently unwind, advance, perforate, advance again, and wind up a strip of material at a constant rate. The drive apparatus on cameras and projectors is a late development of a technology which had already made feasible the sewing machine, the telegraph tape, and the machine gun. The nineteenth-century origins of film are even more apparent today; compare cinema technology's mechanical and electrical basis with image systems (television, holography) which depend on electronics, computers, and lasers.

We lack a good history of film technology. Some engineering aspects are covered in Raymond Fielding, ed., *A Technological History of Motion Pictures and Television* (Berkeley: University of California Press, 1967). Gordon Hendricks has written several specialized, painstaking monographs on early inventions: *The Edison Motion Picture Myth* (Berkeley: University of California Press, 1961), *Beginnings of the Biograph* (New York: The Beginnings of the American Film, 1964), *The Kinetoscope* (New York: The Beginnings of the American Film, 1966), and *Eadweard Muybridge* (New York: Viking, 1975). See also Kemp Niver, "Motion-Picture Film Widths," *Journal of the Society of Motion Picture and Television Engineers* **77**, 8 (August 1968): 814–818. A promising start toward an economic history of cinema technology is Reese V. Jenkins's *Images and Enterprise: Technology and the American Photographic Industry 1839 to 1925* (Baltimore: Johns Hopkins University Press, 1975). In *Basic Motion Picture Technology* (New York: Hastings House, 1975), L. Bernard Happé includes some historical background; the book as a whole constitutes a superb introduction to the technical basis of cinema.

Modes of Film Production

Many "how-to-do-it" books discuss basic stages and roles of film production. Especially good are Raymond Spottiswoode, *Film and Its Techniques* (Berkeley: University of California Press, 1964); Lenny Lipton, *Independent Filmmaking* (San Francisco: Straight Arrow, 1972); and Edward Pincus, *Guide to Filmmaking* (New York: Signet, 1969). Titles in two excellent series specialize in certain production phases. The Tantivy/Barnes Screen Textbook series has Terence St. John Marner's *Film Design* (New York: Barnes, 1974) and *Directing Motion Pictures* (New York: Barnes, 1974) and Russell Campbell's *Practical Motion Picture Photography* (New York: Barnes, 1970) and *Photographic Theory* (New York: Barnes, 1970). The Focal Press series contains many useful titles, including Alec Nisbett's *The Technique of the Sound Studio* (New York: Hastings House, 1974) and L. Bernard Happé's *Your Film and the Lab* (New York: Hastings House, 1974). See also "Designed for Film," *Film Comment* **14**, 3 (May–June 1978): 25–60, on the set designer's role.

The broad aspects of film production have not been studied sufficiently; for instance, we still lack a satisfactory general account of studio production in any major country. For Hollywood we have Hortense Powdermaker's *Hollywood: The Dream Factory* (Boston: Beacon Press, 1950) and Ezra Goodman's *Fifty Year Decline and Fall of Hollywood* (New York: Signet, 1961), both quite jaundiced and somewhat casual. Better are economic accounts such as those by Howard T. Lewis, *The Motion Picture Industry* (New York: Van Nostrand, 1933); May Huettig, *Economic Control of the Motion Picture Industry* (Philadelphia: University of Pennsylvania Press, 1944); and Michael Conant, *Antitrust in the Motion Picture Industry* (Berkeley: University of California Press, 1960), which deal with production in relation to distribution and exhibition. There are also many anecdotal biographies and chatty memoirs of stars, directors, producers, and other personnel. We have no shortage of "case studies" of the making of particular films, of which the most acerbic remains Lillian Ross's *Picture* (New York: Avon, 1960), and the most useful remains François Truffaut's "Diary of the Making of *Fahrenheit 451*," in *Cahiers du Cinéma in English*, nos. 5, 6, and 7 (1966).

Types of films distinguished by their production practices include documentary, compilation, and animated films. For documentaries, see Richard Meran Barsam, *Nonfiction Film: A Critical History* (New York: Dutton, 1973), Erik Barnouw, *Documentary: A History of the Nonfiction Film* (New York: Oxford University Press, 1974), and John Grierson, *Grierson on Documentary* (London: Faber and Faber, 1966). A history of the compilation film may be found in Jay Leyda, *Films Beget Films* (New York: Hill and Wang, 1964). The standard works on film animation are John Halas and Roger Manvell, *The Technique of Film Animation* (New York: Hastings House, 1968) and Ralph Stephenson, *Animation in the Cinema* (New York: Barnes, 1967).

The relation of modes of film production to social practice as a whole has been explored very little and nowhere systematically. Ian Jarvie's *Movies and Society* (New York: Basic Books, 1970) compares methods of socialization in studio film production with those in other areas of life. A good introduction to twentieth-century modes of production is Harry Braverman's, *Labor and Monopoly Capital* (New York: Monthly Review Press, 1974).

Authorship

Among students of film, no question starts an argument faster than "Who is the author of a studio-produced film?" Many disputes arise because the concept of authorship has at least three different meanings.

Author as Production Worker. This is the concern of this chapter. For some film scholars, the director of a studio film cannot be the author unless he or she seeks to fulfill every role personally. (An example is Charles Chaplin, who was producer, writer, director, composer, and star of his late films.) Other scholars maintain that if the director cannot do all those tasks, he or she must at least have overt veto control at every stage of production (as, say, Jacques Tati and Federico Fellini do). In the view of still other scholars, the director's role provides the closest thing to a grasp of the totality of the shooting and assembly phases. Not that the director can do everything or make every choice. But the director's role is defined as a synthetic one, combining various contributions into a whole. This is the position we have taken in this book. Other statements of the "director as orchestrator" view may be found in V. F. Perkins's *Film as Film* (Baltimore: Penguin, 1972) and in Peter Wollen's *Signs and Meanings in the Cinema* (Bloomington: Indiana University Press, 1972).

Author as Personality. In France in the 1950s young writers grouped around the magazine *Cahiers du cinéma* began to discover traces of "personal style" in Hollywood films. Attributing this personality to the director, they stressed the "Howard Hawks" flavor (love of action and professional stoicism), the "Alfred Hitchcock" flavor (suspense but also a brooding Catholic guilt), etc. This became known as the *politique des auteurs*, the "position of being for authors." The idea was taken up by Andrew Sarris in a series of now famous essays. "The strong director imposes his own personality on a film. . . . The auteur theory values the personality of a director precisely because of the barriers to its expression." (*The American Cinema* [New York: Dutton, 1968], p. 31.) Auteurism also became an evaluative method, enabling the *Cahiers du cinéma* critics and Sarris to establish rankings of auteurs and non-auteurs. (Sarris: Fred Zinneman has only a superficial "personal commitment" to direction, David Lean's *Doctor Zhivago* is a work of "the most impeccable impersonality.") The *politique des auteurs* made a major step toward our understanding of film as art, but according to this conception, what constitutes "personality"? Film form and style? Certain preferred themes, stories, actors, genres? For an analysis of the Romantic assumptions underlying the idea of personality, see Edward Buscombe, "Ideas of Authorship," *Screen* **14**, 3 (Autumn 1973): 75–85.

Author as a Group of Films. In reaction to the fuzziness of the notion of "personality," some have suggested that we regard the idea of the "author" as simply a critical category. On this account, the critic would group films by *signature* of director, producer, screenwriter, or whatever. Thus *Citizen Kane* could belong to the "Orson Welles" group *and* to the "Herman Mankiewicz" group *and* to the "Gregg Toland" group, etc. The critic would then analyze the patterns of relations within a given group. This would mean that certain aspects of *Citizen Kane* interact with aspects of other films directed by Welles, or of other films written by Mankiewicz, or of other films photographed by Toland. The "author" is no longer a person, but, for the sake of analysis, a system of relations among several films bearing the same signature. Implications of this position are developed by Peter Wollen in *Signs and Meanings in the Cinema* (Bloomington: Indiana University Press, 1972): "Fuller or Hawks or Hitchcock, the directors, are quite separate from 'Fuller' or 'Hawks' or 'Hitchcock,' the structures named after them" (p. 168). This approach, of course, could be applied to independent works as well as to studio-produced films.

Distinctions among author as worker, personality, and group of films can help guide us through many disputes in film study. For instance, consider the argument in recent years between proponents of the "director as auteur," led by Andrew Sarris (in *The American Cinema* and elsewhere) and proponents of the "screenwriter as auteur," led by Richard Corliss (in *The Hollywood Screenwriters* [New York: Avon, 1972] and *Talking Pictures* [New York: Penguin, 1974]). The Sarris/ Corliss disputes do not distinguish among these three concepts of authorship; what sorts of problems arise as a result?

Part Two
Film Form

"How are films made?" is an ambiguous question. We have given one answer: Films are made by people working with technology. But the question can also mean "By what principles is a film put together? How do the various parts relate to one another to create a whole?" These questions will take us into problems of cinema as an art medium.

In the next two chapters we will start to answer such aesthetic questions. We assume that a film is not a random collection of elements. If it were, people would not care if they missed the beginnings or endings of films or if films were projected out of sequence. But they do care. When you describe a book as "hard to put down" or a piece of music as "absorbing" or "gripping," you are implying that a *pattern* exists there, that an internal system governs the relations among parts and engages your interest. This system of relationships among parts we shall call *form*. Chapter 2 examines form in film to see what makes that concept so important to the understanding of cinema as an art.

One formal feature that commonly seizes our interest while viewing a film is its "story." Chapter 3 examines different types of form that may occur in films—both *nonnarrative* and *narrative* form. We shall see there that not all films tell stories and that whether or not a film does, we can examine that film's form; we can, that is, analyze how its parts relate to one another in ways which fascinate us.

CHAPTER 2

THE SIGNIFICANCE OF FILM FORM

The Concept of Form in Film ■

Form is of central importance to any artwork, regardless of its medium. The entire study of the nature of artistic form is the province of the aesthetician; it is too large a question for us to deal with extensively here. (See the first part of the Notes and Queries to this chapter for pertinent readings.) But some ideas of aesthetic form are indispensible in analyzing films.

Form as System

We will consider a system as a specific set of interrelated elements that depend on and affect one another. The human body is one such system; if one component, the heart, ceases to function, all of the other parts will be in danger as well. Within the body there are individual, smaller systems, such as the nervous system or the optical system. Most of us are all too well aware that a single small malfunction in a car's workings may bring the whole machine to a standstill; the other parts may not need repair, but the whole system depends on the operation of each part. Other, more abstract sets of relationships also constitute systems: a body of laws governing a country, for example, or the ecological balance among the wildlife in a lake.

As with each of these cases, a film is not simply a random set of elements flung together. A film has form, and by film form, in its broadest sense, we mean the total system created by a given film. Form is *the overall system of relationships among elements that make up the whole film.* In this part of the book and also in Part Three (on film style), we shall be examining the types of elements a film may contain and how the film viewer can understand their interrelationships. We seek to understand how form as a total system works in films.

This definition of form is still very abstract, so let us draw our examples from one film that many people have seen. In *The Wizard of Oz* there are many interrelated elements. There is, most obviously, a set

27

of *narrative* elements; these comprise the film's story. Dorothy dreams that a tornado blows her to Oz, where she encounters certain characters, and the narrative continues to the point where Dorothy awakens from her dream to find herself home in Kansas. There is also a set of *stylistic* elements: the way the camera moves, the patterns of color in the frame, the use of music, and other devices.

Because *The Wizard of Oz* is a system and not just a hodgepodge, the elements within each set relate to one another. Recall that the colors in *The Wizard of Oz* are interrelated (the ruby slippers, the green-faced witch dressed in black, the Emerald City); so are the other stylistic elements (music, settings, etc.). The narrative elements also relate to one another: For example, the characters in Oz parallel characters in Dorothy's Kansas life. So each set of elements may be seen as a smaller system—a subsystem—within the larger system of the total film.

Moreover, each of these subsystems will relate dynamically to the others. In *The Wizard of Oz* the narrative subsystem is clearly tied to the stylistic subsystem. Film colors identify prominent landmarks, such as Kansas (in black and white) and the Yellow Brick Road. Movements of the camera call our attention to narrative action. And the music serves to describe certain characters and actions. It is this overall pattern of relationships among the various subsystems of elements that makes up the *form* of *The Wizard of Oz*.

"Form versus Content"

Very often people assume that "form" as a concept is the opposite of something called "content." This implies that a poem or a musical piece or a film is like a jug; an external shape, the jug, *contains* something that could just as easily be held in a cup or a pail. Under this assumption, form becomes less important than whatever it is presumed to contain.

We do not accept this assumption. Considering form as the total system of the film implies that there is no inside or outside. We assume that every component *functions within* the overall pattern. Thus we shall treat as formal elements many things that some people consider "content." From this standpoint, subject matter and abstract ideas all enter into the total system of the artwork. They become related to one another and interact dynamically. As a result, subject matter and ideas become somewhat different from what they might be outside the work.

For example, consider a historical subject, such as the United States Civil War. The real Civil War may be studied, its causes and consequences disputed. But in a film—say, D. W. Griffith's *The Birth of a Nation*—the Civil War is not neutral "content." It enters into relationships with other elements: a story about two families, political ideas about Reconstruction, and the epic film style of the battle scenes, to take just three instances. The form of Griffith's film emerges out of the relationship of the Civil War to the other elements in the film's overall system. A different film by another filmmaker might draw on the same subject matter, the Civil War, but there the subject would play a different role in a different formal system. For example, in *Gone with the Wind* the Civil War functions as a backdrop for the heroine's romance, whereas in *The Good, the Bad, and the Ugly* the war aids three cynical men in their search for gold. Thus subject matter is shaped by formal context.

Formal Expectations

Film form guides the audience's experience. Our experience of artworks is patterned and structured. Turning off a record before a song is over or discovering that the last few pages of a novel are missing brings frustration because of our urge for form; we realize that the system of relationships within the work has not yet been completed. Something more is needed to make the form whole and satisfying. We have been caught up in the interrelationships among elements and want to understand how the patterns develop and complete themselves.

How does form guide our experience of an artwork? For one thing, form creates the sense that "everything is there." Why is it satisfying when a character glimpsed early in a film reappears an hour later or when a shape in the frame is balanced by another shape? Because such relations among parts suggest that the film has its own organizing laws or rules—its own system.

For another thing, form intensely involves the audience. The appeal of form can be very great. Usually we perceive things around us in a practical way. But in a film the things that happen on the screen serve no such practical end for us. We can see them differently. In life if a person fell down on the street, we would probably hurry to help the person up. But in a film when Buster Keaton or Charlie Chaplin falls, we laugh. We shall see in Chapter 5 how even as basic an act of filmmaking as framing a shot creates a new way of seeing. We watch a pattern which is no longer just "out there" in the everyday world, but which has become a calculated part within a self-contained whole. Film form can even make us perceive things anew, shaking us out of our accustomed habits and suggesting fresh ways of hearing, seeing, feeling, and thinking.

Try the following experiment (suggested by Barbara Herrnstein Smith). Assume that "A" is the first letter of a series. What follows?

  1. AB

You probably made a *formal assumption*, i.e., that the letters would be in alphabetical order. Your expectation was correct. What follows AB?

Most people say "C." But form does not always gratify our initial expectation.

2. ABA

Here form takes us by surprise, puzzles us. If we are puzzled by a formal development, we readjust our expectations and try again. What follows ABA?

3. ABAC

Here the possibilities were chiefly two: ABAB or ABAC. (Note that your expectations *limit* possibilities as well as select them.) If you expected ABAC, your expectation was gratified and you can confidently predict the next letter. If you expected ABAB, you still should be able to make a strong hypothesis about the next letter.

4. ABACA

Simple as this game is, it illustrates the involving power of form. You as a viewer or listener don't simply let the artwork parade past you. You enter into an active participation with it, proposing and readjusting expectations about form as the experience develops.

Consider now a story in a film. A cowboy saunters into the town saloon. Immediately we form expectations—perhaps he will encounter some other character or get into a fight. Even such a stereotyped situation asks that the audience participate actively in the ongoing form by making certain hypotheses about "what will happen next" and readjusting expectations accordingly.

Expectation pervades our experience of art. In reading a mystery story we expect that a solution will be offered at some point, usually the end. In listening to a piece of music we expect repetition of melody or motif. Many musical pieces, in fact, follow the ABACA pattern we have just outlined; a refrain is followed by one verse, the refrain is repeated, a new verse follows, and so on. Similarly, in looking at a painting we glance first at what we expect to be the most prominent features, then scan the less prominent portions. From beginning to end, our involvement with a work of art depends largely on expectations.

Not that the expectations must be immediately satisfied. The satisfaction of our expectations may be *delayed,* as when crosscutting prolongs one event in a film by alternating shots of it with shots of another event. Often what we call "suspense" is no more than the delayed fulfillment of an expectation.

Expectations may also be "cheated." When we expect ABC but get ABA, the surprise is a result of our incorrect expectation. We do not expect that a gangster in 1930s Chicago will find a rocket ship in his garage; if he does, our reaction is based on the need to readjust our assumptions about what can happen in this story. (This immediately suggests that comedy often depends on the radical cheating of expectations.) In such ways expectation controls the audience's involvement in the form.

But artistic form also has the power to disturb our expectations. We often associate art with peace and serenity, but many artworks offer us conflict, tension, and shock. A form may even strike us as unpleasant because of its imbalances or contradictions. Many people find atonal music, abstract or surrealist painting, and experimental writing highly disturbing. Similarly, there are many important directors whose films jar rather than soothe us. As we shall see in examining the editing of Eisenstein's *October* or the ambiguous narrative in Resnais's *Last Year at Marienbad*, a film may rely on shifts, contradictions, and gaps. The point is not to condemn or wish away such films, but to understand that in disturbing us, such films still arouse *formal* expectations. Indeed, if we can adjust our expectations to a disturbing work, we may even become more deeply involved in our viewing of it than we would be with a work that gratifies our expectations easily. Such disturbing artworks may display new kinds of form to which we are not accustomed. Our initial disturbance may diminish as we grasp the work's unique formal system. Or, some of these disturbing works may become less coherent than more traditional ones, but they reward analysis partly because they reveal to us our normal, implicit expectations about form.

Conventions and Experience

Our ABAC example illustrates still another point. One guide to our hunches was prior experience. Our knowledge of the alphabet makes ABAX an unlikely alternative. This suggests how aesthetic form is not a pure activity isolated from other experiences. Important implications for artist and spectator flow from this.

First, precisely because artworks are human artifacts and because the artist lives in history and society, he or she cannot avoid relating the work, in some way, to other works and to aspects of the world in general. A tradition, a dominant style, a popular form—some such elements will be common to several different artworks. Such common traits are usually called *conventions.* For example, it is a convention of the musical film genre that characters sing and dance—a convention which (to return to our initial example) *The Wizard of Oz* firmly accepts. It is one convention of narrative form that the narrative solves the problems the characters confront, and the film likewise accepts this convention by letting Dorothy return to Kansas. Formal conventions are principal ways that artists relate their work to other works.

From the spectator's standpoint, his or her perception of artistic form will arise from both cues within the work and prior experiences. But although our *ability* to recognize formal cues may be innate, the *particular* habits and expectations we bring to the artwork will be guided by other experiences—experiences derived from everyday life and from other artworks. You were able to play the ABAC game because you had learned the English alphabet. You may have learned it in everyday life (in a classroom, from your parents) or from an artwork (as some children now learn the alphabet from television cartoons). Similarly, we are able to recognize the "journey" pattern in *The Wizard of Oz* because we have taken trips and because we have seen other films organized around this pattern (e.g., *Stagecoach* or *North By Northwest).* Our expectations are guided by our real-life experiences and our knowledge of formal conventions.

In recognizing film form, then, the audience must be prepared to understand formal cues through knowledge of life and of other artworks. But what if the two principles come into conflict? In ordinary life people don't simply start to sing and dance, as they do in *The Wizard of Oz.* Very often conventions demarcate art from life, saying implicitly, "In artworks of this sort the laws of everyday reality don't operate. By the rules of *this* game, something 'unreal' *can* happen." All stylized art, from opera, ballet,and pantomime to comedy and other genres, depends on the audience's willingness to suspend the laws of ordinary experience and to accept particular conventions. It is simply beside the point to insist that such conventions are unreal or to ask why Tristan sings to Isolde or why Buster Keaton doesn't smile. Very often the most relevant prior experience for perceiving form is not everyday experience, but previous encounters with works having similar conventions.

Form and Feeling

Certainly emotion plays a large role in our experience of form. To understand this role, let us distinguish between emotions *represented in* the artwork and an emotional *response felt* by the spectator. If an actor grimaces in agony, the emotion of pain is *represented within the film.* If, on the other hand, the viewer who sees the painful expression laughs out loud (as the viewer of a comedy might), the emotion of amusement is *felt by the spectator.* Both types of emotion have formal implications.

Emotions represented within the film interact as parts of the film's total system. For example, that grimace of pain might be reaffirmed by the contortions of the comedian's body. Or, a cheerful scene might stand in contrast to a mournful one. A tragic event might be undercut by humorous editing or music. All of the emotions present in a film may be seen as systematically related to one another through that film's form.

The spectator's emotional response to the film is related to form as well. We have just seen how cues in the artwork interact with our prior experience, especially our experience of artistic conventions. Often form in artworks appeals to ready-made reactions, already formulated emotions: fear of darkness or heights, or even stereotyped reactions to certain images (sexuality, race, social class). But form can create new responses as easily as it can harp on old ones. Just as formal conventions often lead us to suspend our normal sense of real-life experience, so form may lead us to override our everyday emotional responses. Why else would people whom we would despise in life become spellbinding as characters in a film? How can we watch a film about a subject that normally repels us and find it fascinating? The answer lies in the systematic quality of our involvement in form. In *The Wizard of Oz* we might, for example, find the land of Oz far more attractive than Kansas. But because the film's form leads us to sympathize with Dorothy in her desire to go home, we feel great satisfaction when she finally returns to Kansas.

It is first and foremost the dynamic process of form that engages our feelings. Expectation, for instance, spurs emotion. To make an expectation about "what happens next" is to invest some emotion in the situation. Delayed fulfillment of an expectation may produce anxiety, sympathy, concern, or suspense. (Will the detective find the criminal? Will boy get girl? Will the melody return?) Cheated expectations may produce puzzlement or keener interest. (So he isn't the detective? This isn't a romance story? Is there melody here at all?) Gratified expectations may produce a feeling of satisfaction or relief. (The mystery is solved, boy does get girl, the melody returns one more time.) Note that all of these possibilities *may* occur. There is no general recipe by which a novel or film can be concocted to produce the "correct" emotional response. It is all a matter of context—that is, of the individual system that is each artwork's overall form. All we can say for certain is that the emotion felt by the spectator will emerge from the totality of formal relationships in the work. This is one reason why we should try to perceive as many formal relations as possible in a film, for on this perception rests our reaction to that film.

Taken in context, the relations between the feelings represented in the film and those felt by the spectator can be quite complex. Many people believe that no more sorrowful event can occur than the death of a child. In most films this event would be represented so as to summon up the sadness we would also feel in life. But the power of artistic form can alter the emotional tenor of even this event. In Jean Renoir's *The Crime of M. Lange* the cynical publisher, Batala, rapes and abandons the young laundress, Estelle. After Batala disappears, Estelle becomes integrated into the courtyard community and returns to her former fiancé. But Estelle is pregnant by Batala and bears his child. The scene when Estelle's employer, Valentine, announces that the child was born dead is one of the most emotionally complex in cinema. The first emotions represented are solemn sorrow: The characters display grief. Suddenly Batala's cousin remarks, "Too bad. It was a relative." In the film's context this is taken as a joke, and the other characters break out in smiles and laughter. The shift in the emotion represented in the film catches us off guard. Since these characters are not heartless, we must readjust our reaction to the death and respond as they do—with relief. That Estelle has survived is far more important than the death of Batala's child. The film's formal development has rendered appropriate a reaction that might be perverse in ordinary life. This is a daring, extreme example, but it dramatically illustrates how both emotions onscreen and our responses are dependent on form.

Form and Meaning

Like feeling, meaning is important to our experience of artworks. Again, however, it may be useful to distinguish meanings *as components within the film* from the viewer's *analysis of meanings,* an activity usually called *interpretation.* This distinction will let us situate meaning within the overall system of an entire film.

Often in a film we will have a sense that a particularly significant meaning is being presented. For instance, Dorothy's final line in *The Wizard of Oz* is "There's no place like home," and we are strongly tempted to take that as a statement of the meaning of the entire film. But, first, *why* do we feel that as a strongly meaningful line? In ordinary conversation it is a cliché. In context, however, the line is uttered in close-up, it comes at the end of the film (a formally privileged moment), and it refers back to all of Dorothy's desires and ordeals, recalling the film's narrative development toward her achievement of her goal. It is the *form* of the film that gives the familiar homily an unfamiliar weight.

This means that we must examine how particular meanings in a film interact with other elements of the overall system. If "There's no place like home" adequately and exhaustively summarizes the meaning of *The Wizard of Oz,* no one need ever see the film; the summary would suffice. But like feelings, meanings are formal entities; they play a part along with other elements to make up the total system. We usually can't isolate a particularly significant moment and declare it to be *the* meaning of the whole film. Even Dorothy's "There's no place like home," however strong as a summary of *one* meaningful element in *The Wizard of Oz,* must be placed in the context of the film's entire beguiling Oz fantasy. If

"There's no place like home" were the whole point of the film, why is there so much that is pleasant in Oz? The explicit meanings of a film are situated within the *whole* film and set in dynamic formal relation to one another.

In trying to see the meaningful moments of a film as parts of a larger whole, it is useful to set individually significant moments against one another. Thus Dorothy's final line could be juxtaposed to the scene of the characters getting spruced up after their arrival at the Emerald City. We can try to see the film as not "about" one or the other, but rather about the relation of the two—the risk and delight of a fantasy world versus the comfort and stability of home. Thus the film's total system will be larger than any one meaning we find in it. Instead of asking, "What does this film mean?" we can often usefully ask, "How do *all* the film's meanings interrelate formally?"

One more implication of a film's meanings is worth mention. What is the nature of these meanings? Since films are human artifacts, meaning is a social phenomenon. The meanings in a film are ultimately *ideological*; that is, they spring from systems of *culturally specific beliefs about the world.* Religious beliefs, political opinions, conceptions of race or sex or social class, even our most unconsciously held, deep-seated notions of life—all these constitute our ideological frame of reference. Although we live as if our beliefs were the only true and real explanations of how the world is, we need only compare our own ideology with that of another group or culture or historical period to see how historically and socially shaped those views are.

Films, like other artworks, carry within themselves traces of ideological beliefs, and these traces can become a part of the film's meanings. For example, if *The Wizard of Oz* works on a tension between the dangerous appeal of fantasy and the drab stability of home, we can see that tension as resulting from specific, *socially defined* conceptions of fantasy, home, childhood, rural life, parents' roles, and so on. Ideologically, *The Wizard of Oz* represents, in complicated ways, problems of importance to American society. Again, however, these ideological conceptions are not simple beads to be strung together: A film *enacts* ideological meanings through its particular and unique formal system. We shall see in Part Four how the narrative and stylistic systems of *Meet Me in St. Louis, The Crime of M. Lange,* and *La Chinoise* can be analyzed for ideological implications.

In discussing the meaning and the ideological implications of *The Wizard of Oz,* we are already doing *interpretation*. How is interpretation related to film form? Some viewers approach a film expecting to learn great lessons about life. They may admire a film because it conveys a profound or relevant message. Important as meaning is, though, this attitude often errs by splitting the film into the content portion (the meaning) and the form (the vehicle for the content). This can lead to very abstract conceptions (often called *themes):* This film is "about courage," that film is "about love." Such descriptions have some value, but they are very general; hundreds of films fit them. To summarize *The Wizard of Oz* as about the virtues of home does not do justice to the specific qualities of the film as an experience. The search for general meanings often leaves behind the *particular and concrete* features of a film.

This is not to say that we should not interpret films. But we should strive to make our interpretations more precise by seeing how each film's thematic meanings are intimately and uniquely bound up with the film's total form. In a film meanings depend closely on the relations among the elements of narrative and stylistic form. In *The Wizard of Oz* the visual element called "the Yellow Brick Road" has no meaning in and of itself. But if we examine the function it fulfills in relation to the narrative, the music, the colors, and so on, we can see that the Yellow Brick Road does indeed function meaningfully. Dorothy's strong desire to go home makes the Road represent that desire. We want Dorothy to be successful in getting to the end of the Road, as well as in getting back to Kansas; thus the Road participates in the theme of the desirability of home.

But interpretation of meaning should not be an end in itself; it helps in understanding the overall form of the film. Nor does interpretation exhaust the possibilities of a device. We can say many things about the Yellow Brick Road other than how its meaning relates to the film's thematic material. We could analyze how the Road becomes the stage for dances and songs along the way; we could see how it is narratively important because an indecision at a crossroads delays Dorothy long enough to meet the Scarecrow; we could work out a color scheme for the film, contrasting the yellow road, the red slippers, the green Emerald City, and so forth. From this standpoint, interpretation may be seen as one kind of formal analysis, one that seeks to analyze a film's meanings. But those meanings should be constantly tested by reimmersing them in the concrete texture of the whole film.

Films mean. But in analyzing film art, we cannot regard meaning as a simple product to be extracted from the film; interpretation is only one kind of analysis. As the most abstract statements we can make, thematic descriptions of films may carry us away from the concrete texture of the film experience. In the chapters that follow, that concrete texture—narrative versus nonnarrative forms, style as a formal system—will claim our primary attention. Nonetheless, everything that follows has implications for filmic meaning, and we will often point those implications out. We will postpone full-blown interpretative analysis until Part Four, because there we shall be dealing in detail with *entire* films. At that point interpretation will take its place within our analysis of a film's total system.

Evaluation

In talking about an artwork, people often *evaluate* it, that is, they make claims about its goodness or badness. Reviews in popular magazines exist almost solely to tell us whether a new film is worth seeing; our friends often urge us to go to their latest favorite. But all too often we discover that the film that someone else esteemed appears only mediocre to us. At that point we may bemoan the fact that most people evaluate films only on the basis of their own, often idiosyncratic, tastes.

How, then, are we to evaluate films with any degree of objectivity? We can start by realizing that there is a difference between personal taste and evaluative judgment. To say "I like this film" or "I hated it" is not equal to saying "It's a good film" or "It's wretched." There are very few people in the world whose enjoyment is limited only to the greatest works. Most people can enjoy a film they know is not particularly good. This is perfectly reasonable—unless they start trying to convince people that these pleasant films actually rank among the undying masterpieces. At that point others will probably stop listening to their judgments at all.

We may set aside, therefore, personal preference as the sole basis for judging a film's quality. Instead, the critic who wishes to make a relatively objective evaluation will use specific *criteria*. A criterion is a standard which can be applied in the judgment of many works; in this way, the critic gains a basis for comparing films for relative quality.

There are many different criteria. Some people evaluate films on "realistic" criteria, that is, whether the film conforms to their view of reality. War buffs, for example, might judge a film entirely on whether the right kinds of airplanes or guns were used in the battle scenes; the narrative, editing, characterization, sound, and visual style might be of little interest to them. Other people condemn films because they don't find the action plausible; they will dismiss a scene by saying, "Who'd really believe that X would meet Y just at the right moment?" But we have already seen that artworks often violate laws of reality and operate by their own conventions and internal rules. We suggest that the viewer ought to look for criteria which are appropriate to a view of films as formal systems.

Nor will moral criteria help us much here. For some viewers, any film with nudity or certain language could be judged bad, whatever the role played in the film's formal system by these things. Members of the local Playboy Club might apply just the opposite criteria.

All of these criteria may be suited to the purposes of the people who use them. But this book will suggest criteria that can deal with films as artistic, formal constructs. Such criteria should allow us to take each individual film's form into account as much as possible; we can see whether it succeeds, *on its own terms,* in creating a set of formal relationships.

One such criterion is *complexity.* We can argue that complex films (*not* simply complicated films) are good insofar as they engage our perception on many levels, create a multiplicity of relations among many separate formal elements, and tend to create interesting formal patterns. A second formal criterion might be *originality.* Originality for its own sake is pointless, of course; just because something is different does not mean that it is good. But if an artist takes a familiar convention and uses it in a way that makes it fresh again or creates a new set of formal possibilities, then (all other things being equal) the resulting work may be considered good from an aesthetic standpoint.

Evaluation can serve many useful ends. It can call attention to neglected artworks or make us rethink our attitudes toward accepted classics. But just as the discovery of meanings is not the end point of formal analysis, we ought not to see ourselves as primarily setting out to establish what the great films are. General statements ("This is a masterpiece") seldom enlighten us very much. Usually an evaluation interests us insofar as it points to aspects of the film and shows us relations and qualities we have hitherto missed. Like interpretation, evaluation is most useful when it drives us back to the film itself as a formal system, helping us to understand that system better.

In reading this book, you will find that we have generally minimized evaluation. We think that most of the films and sequences we analyze are more or less good on the criteria of complexity and originality, but the purpose of this book is not to persuade you to accept a list of cinema masterpieces. Rather, we believe that if we show in detail how films may be understood as artistic systems, you will have an informed basis for whatever evaluations you wish to make.

Summary

If one issue has governed our treatment of aesthetic form, it might be said to be *concreteness.* Form is a concrete system of patterned relationships—in any artwork, in any medium. Such a concept lets us see how even elements of what is normally considered "content"—subject matter, or abstract ideas—take on specific and unique functions within any artwork. Our experience of an artwork is also a concrete one. We create specific expectations which are aroused, guided, delayed, cheated, satisfied, or disturbed. We compare the particular aspects of the artwork with general conventions which we know from life and from art. Abstract emotions and meanings become specified and qualified through the concrete context of the artwork. And even when we apply general criteria in evaluating artworks, we ought to use those criteria to help us discriminate more, to penetrate more deeply into the particular aspects of the artwork. The rest of this book is devoted to studying these properties of aesthetic form in cinema.

Principles of Film Form ■

Because film form is a system—that is, a unified set of related, interdependent elements—there must be some principles which help create the relationships among the parts. In disciplines other than the arts, principles may be sets of rules. In the physical sciences principles may take the form of mathematical propositions. For example, the design of an airplane must take into account principles of aerodynamics. Its designer needs to determine the plane's form in relation to his or her knowledge of these principles.

In the arts, however, there are no absolute principles of form which all artists must follow. Artworks are products of culture; hence many of the principles of artistic form are matters of social convention. (For example, films that follow one particular set of formal principles are widely recognized as "Westerns.")

But within these social conventions, each artwork tends to set up its own specific formal principles. The forms of different films can vary enormously. We can distinguish, however, five general principles at work in the operation of a film's formal system: function; similarity and repetition; difference and variation; development; and unity/disunity.

Function

If form in cinema is the overall interrelations among various systems of elements, we assume that every element in this totality has one or more *functions.* That is, every element will be seen as fulfilling one or more roles within the whole system.

Of any element within a film we can ask: What are its functions? Recall our example of *The Wizard of Oz.* Every element in the film fulfills one or more roles. For instance, Miss Gulch, the woman who wants to take Toto from Dorothy, reappears in the Oz section as the Witch. In the opening portion of the film Miss Gulch causes Dorothy to run away from home; in Oz the Witch seeks to prevent Dorothy from returning home by keeping her away from the Emerald City and by trying to take the ruby slippers. Even an element as apparently minor as the dog Toto serves many functions: The dispute over Toto causes Dorothy to run away from home and to miss getting back in time to take shelter from the cyclone; and later Toto's chasing of a cat makes Dorothy jump out of the ascending balloon and miss her chance to go back to Kansas. Even Toto's gray color, set off against the brightness of Oz, creates a link to the black and white of the Kansas episodes at the film's beginning. Functions, then, are almost always multiple; both narrative and stylistic elements have functions.

One useful way to grasp the function of an element is to ask what other elements demand that it be present. Thus the narrative requires that Dorothy run away from home, so Toto is made to fulfill this function. Or, to take another example, Dorothy must be distinguished from the Wicked Witch, so costume, age, voice, and other characteristics function to contrast the two. Finally, the switch from black and white to color film functions to signal the arrival at the bright fantasy land of Oz.

Note, finally, that the concept of function does not depend on the filmmaker's intention. Often discussions of films get bogged down in the question of whether the filmmaker "knew what he or she was doing" in including this or that element. In asking about function, we do not ask for a production history. From the standpoint of intention, Dorothy may sing "Over the Rainbow" because singing that song was in Judy Garland's MGM contract. But from the standpoint of function, we can say that Dorothy's singing that song fulfills certain narrative and stylistic functions. (It establishes her desire to leave home, its reference to the rainbow foreshadows the colored Oz sequences, etc.) In asking about formal function, therefore, we ask not, "How did this element get there?" but rather, "What is this element *doing* there?"

Similarity and Repetition

In our example of the ABAC pattern, we saw how we were able to predict the next steps in the series. One reason for this was that there was a regular pattern of repeated elements. Like beats in music or meter in poetry, the repetition of the A's in our pattern established and satisfied formal expectations. Similarity and repetition, then, comprise an important principle of film form.

Much of our correctly perceiving a film depends on the ability to recognize pertinent similarities. For instance, we must be able to remember and identify characters and settings when they reappear; we would not get very far in *The Wizard of Oz* if we could not remember from scene to scene who Dorothy is. More subtly, film form plays with general similarities as well as exact duplication. It is important to the understanding of *The Wizard of Oz* that we see the similarities between the three Kansas farmhands and the three figures Dorothy meets along the Yellow Brick Road and the similarity between the itinerant Kansas fortune-teller and the old charlatan posing as the Wizard in Oz. The duplication is not exact, but the similarity is very strong. Likewise, the viewer will notice the repetition of the manner in which Dorothy meets the three

Oz characters and the way in which each meeting is climaxed by singing, "We're off to see the Wizard." Throughout any film we can observe similarities and repetitions of everything from lines of dialogue and bits of music to camera positions, characters' behavior, and story action. Our recognition of these similarities and repetitions provides part of our pleasure in viewing the film, much as the repetitive sounds of rhymes contribute to our pleasure in reading poetry.

It is useful to have a term to help describe formal repetitions, and the most common is the term *motif.* We shall call *any significant repeated element in a film* a motif. A motif may be an object, a color, a place, a person, a sound, or even a character trait. We may call a pattern of lighting or camera position a motif if it is repeated through the course of a film. The form of *The Wizard of Oz* utilizes all of these kinds of motifs, as we have seen. Even in such a relatively simple film, we can see the pervasive presence of similarity and repetition as formal principles.

Difference and Variation

The form of a film could hardly be comprised only of repetitions. AAAAAA is pretty boring. There must also be some changes or variations, however small. Thus difference is another fundamental principle of film form.

We already know the need for variety, contrast, and change in films. Characters must be distinguished, environments must be delineated, different times or activities must be established. Even within the image, we must distinguish differences in tonality, texture, direction and speed of movement, and so on. Form needs its stable "background" of similarity and repetition, but it also demands the establishment of differences.

This means that although motifs (scenes, settings, actions, objects, stylistic devices) may be repeated, those motifs will seldom be repeated *exactly.* Variation will appear. In our chief example, *The Wizard of Oz,* the three Kansas hired hands are not exactly the same as their "twins" in Oz. (The Oz characters are more stylized fantasy figures.) Nor is the repeated motif of Toto's disruption of a situation always functioning in the same way: In Kansas it disturbs Miss Gulch and induces Dorothy to take Toto away, but in Oz Toto's disruption *prevents* Dorothy from going away. Even though Dorothy's determination to return home is a stable and recurrent motif, it expresses itself in varied ways because of the different obstacles she encounters.

Differences among the elements may often sharpen into downright opposition among them. We are most familiar with formal oppositions as conflicts among characters. It is true that character conflict is an important formal phenomenon, but we can situate it within the larger formal principle of difference. Thus not only characters but also settings, actions, and other elements may be opposed. In *The Wizard of Oz* Dorothy's desires are opposed, at various points, by the differing desires of Aunt Em, Miss Gulch, the Wicked Witch, and the Wizard, so that the film's formal system derives many dynamics from characters in conflict. But there are also color oppositions: black-and-white Kansas versus colorful Oz, Dorothy in red-white-and-blue versus the Witch in black, and so on. Settings are opposed as well—not only Oz versus Kansas, but also the various locales within Oz and especially the Emerald City versus the Witch's castle. Voice quality, musical tunes, and a host of other elements play off against one another, demonstrating that any motif may be opposed by any other motif.

Repetition and variation are two sides of the same coin. To notice one is to notice the other. In analyzing films we ought to look for similarities *and* differences. Constantly poised between the two, we can point out motifs *and* contrast the changes they undergo.

Development

One way to keep ourselves aware of how similarity and difference operate in film form is to look for principles of development from part to part of the film. Development will constitute some patterning of similar and differing elements. Our pattern ABAC is based not only on repetition (the recurring motif of A) and difference (the varied insertion of B and C), but also on a principle of *progression* which we could state as a rule (alternate the first letter of the alphabet with successive letters in alphabetical order). Though simple, this is a principle of *development,* governing the form of the whole series.

Think of formal development as *a progression moving from X through Y to Z.* For example, the story of *The Wizard of Oz* shows development in many ways. It is, first, a *journey:* from Kansas through Oz to Kansas. Many films possess such a journey-plot. *The Wizard of Oz* is not only a journey, but also a *search* beginning with an initial separation from home, tracing a series of efforts to find a way home (e.g., to convince the Wizard to help), and ending with the object (Kansas, home) being found. Within the film there is also a pattern of *mystery,* which usually has the same from-X-through-Y-to-Z pattern: We begin with a question (Who is the Wizard of Oz?), pass through attempts to answer it, and conclude with the question answered (The Wizard is a fraud). Thus even such an apparently simple film is composed of several developmental patterns.

One way to size up how a film develops formally is to *compare the beginning with the ending.* By looking at the similarities and differences between the beginning and ending, we can start to understand the overall pattern of the film. We can test this advice on *The Wizard of Oz*. A comparison of the beginning and ending on the level of narrative reveals that the journey on which Dorothy initially sets out ends with her return home; the journey has been a search for an ideal place "over the rainbow" and has turned into a search for a way back to Kansas. The final scene repeats and develops the narrative elements of the opening. Stylistically, the beginning and ending are the only parts that use black-and-white film stock. This supports the contrast the narrative creates between the dreamland of Oz and the bleak landscape of Kansas. The fortune-teller, Prof. Marvel, comes to visit Dorothy, reversing the situation of her visit to him when she had tried to run away. At the beginning he had convinced her to return home; then, as the Wizard in the Oz section, he had also represented her hopes to return home. Finally, when she recognizes Prof. Marvel and the farmhands as the basis of the characters in her dream, she remembers how much she had wanted to come home from Oz.

Earlier, we suggested that film form engages our emotions and expectations in a *dynamic* way; now we are in a better position to see why. The constant interplay between similarity and difference, repetition and variation, engenders an active, developing awareness of the film's formal system. The film's development may be visualized in static terms (a diagram often helps), but we ought not to forget that formal development is a *process*.

Unity/Disunity

All of the relationships among elements in a film create the total filmic system. Even if an element seems utterly out of place in relation to the rest of the film, we can't really say that it "isn't part of the film." At most, the unrelated element is enigmatic or incoherent; it may be a flaw in the otherwise completely integrated system of the film—but it *does affect* the whole film.

When all of the relationships within a film are clear and economically interwoven, we say that the film has *unity*. We call a unified film "tight," because there seem to be no gaps in the formal relationships. Every element present has a specific set of functions, similarities and differences are determinable, the form develops logically, and there are no superfluous elements.

Unity is a matter of degree. Almost no film is so tight as to leave no end dangling, but if a film largely manages to create clear relations throughout its form, we generally find it unified.

But films may introduce a degree of disunity. Some films simply fail to achieve unity; such a film's formal system introduces elements and then fails to create clear relationships between them and the rest of the film. Such disunities are particularly noticeable when the filmic system as a whole is striving for unity. One element in *The Wizard of Oz* remains dangling at the end, for example. We never find out what happens to Miss Gulch; presumably she still has her legal order to take Toto away, but no one refers to this in the last scene. Here the film leaves one line of expectations unfulfilled, leaving itself less unified than it might at first appear.

But suppose we saw a film in which several characters die mysteriously, and we never find out how or why. This film leaves a number of loose ends, but the repetition suggests that the omission of clear explanations is not just a mistake. Our impression of a deliberate disunity would be reinforced if other elements of the film also failed to relate clearly to one another. Some films, then, create disunity as a positive quality of their form. This does not mean that these films become incoherent. Their disunity is *systematic*, and it is brought so consistently to our attention as to constitute a basic feature of the film. Inevitably such films will be formally disunified only to a relative degree; they have less unity than we may be used to, but do not simply fall apart before our eyes. Later we shall see how films such as *Innocence Unprotected, Last Year at Marienbad,* and *La Chinoise* utilize formal disunity.

Summary

We can summarize the principles of film form as a set of questions which you can ask about any film.

1. Of any element in the film, you can ask: What are its functions in the overall form?

2. Are elements or patterns repeated throughout the film? If so, how and at what points?

3. How are elements contrasted and differentiated from one another? How are different elements opposed to one another?

4. What principles of progression or development are at work throughout the form of the film? More specifically, how does a comparison of the beginning and ending reveal the overall form of the film?

5. What degree of unity is present in the film's overall form? Is disunity subordinate to the overall unity, or does disunity dominate?

In this chapter we have examined some very abstract principles of film form. Armed with these general principles, we can press on to distinguish more specific types of form, the recognition of which is important for understanding film art.

Notes and Queries ■

Form in Various Arts

Many of the ideas in this chapter are based on ideas of form to be found in other arts. All of the following constitute helpful further reading: Monroe Beardsley, *Aesthetics* (New York: Harcourt Brace and World, 1958), especially Chapters IV and V; Rudolf Arnheim, *Art and Visual Perception* (Berkeley: University of California Press, 1974), especially Chapters II, III, and IX; Leonard Meyer, *Emotion and Meaning in Music* (Chicago: University of Chicago Press, 1956) and *Music, the Arts, and Ideas* (Chicago: University of Chicago Press, 1967); Rene Wellek and Austin Warren, *Theory of Literature* (New York: Harcourt Brace and World, 1956); Victor Erlich, *Russian Formalism: History, Doctrine* (The Hague: Mouton, 1965); E. H. Gombrich, *Art and Illusion* (Princeton, N. J.: Princeton University Press, 1961).

The Concept of Form in Film

Some film theorists have addressed themselves to the problem of defining form in the cinema. Provocative ideas on the *systematic* quality of film form may be found in Lev Kuleshov, *Kuleshov on Film* (Berkeley: University of California Press, 1974) and Sergei Eisenstein, *The Film Sense* (New York: Harvest, 1942). These theorists also help erase the awkward form/content dichotomy. For a critical discussion of these and other theorists of film form, see J. Dudley Andrew, "The Formative Tradition," *The Major Film Theories* (New York: Oxford University Press, 1975), pp. 11–101.

On the relation of form to the audience, see the books by Meyer mentioned above. The ABAC example is borrowed from Barbara Herrnstein Smith's excellent study of literary form, *Poetic Closure* (Chicago: University of Chicago Press, 1968). Compare Kenneth Burke's claim: "Form is the creation of an appetite in the mind of the auditor and the adequate satisfying of that appetite." (See Kenneth Burke, "Psychology and Form," *Counter-Statement* [Chicago: University of Chicago Press, 1957], pp. 29–44.) Gestalt psychology posited that the mind has innate form-making capacities, and this has made Gestalt thinkers strong contributors to theory of film form in terms of audience response. See Rudolf Arnheim, *Film as Art* (Berkeley: University of California Press, 1957).

"Aggressive" Forms

Unusual as it may seem, many films seek to disturb the viewer, and we should try to understand how this happens. Our study must go beyond a form/content conception, e.g., "graphic depiction of sex or violence," to examine how a film's total system may deeply affect the viewer. Surrealist cinema offers one alternative, and its conception of cinematic form is discussed in J. H. Matthews, *Surrealism and Film* (Ann Arbor: University of Michigan Press, 1971) and in the numerous biographies of Luis Buñuel. The Surrealists' own writings on cinema are available in Paul Hammond, ed., *The Shadow and Its Shadow* (London: British Film Institute, 1978). Current avant-garde work has made displeasure an important goal; see Annette Michelson, ed., *New Forms in Film* (Montreux, 1974) and Peter Gidal, ed., *Structural Film Anthology* (London: British Film Institute, 1976). Some current conceptions of aggressive form are discussed in Gregory Battcock, ed., *The New American Cinema* (New York: Dutton, 1967) and in Susan Sontag, "The Aesthetics of Silence," *Styles of Radical Will* (New York: Delta, 1970), pp. 3–34. More generally, the definitive study of "aggressive form" in film remains Chapters 7 and 8 of Noël Burch's *Theory of Film Practice* (New York: Praeger, 1973).

Similarity and Difference

No systematic study has been made of how films may be based on repetitions and variations, but most critics implicitly recognize the importance of the processes. A valuable exercise would be to read a critical essay on a film you have seen and to ask how the critic points out similarities and differences in the filmic system.

Some theorists have pointed out the play of similarity and difference much more explicitly. After an analysis of one sequence from *The Big Sleep*, Raymond Bellour ("The Obvious and the Code," *Screen* **XV**, 4 [Winter 1975]: 7–17) concludes that a specific pattern of similarities and differences of shots makes the narrative intelligible to us. Stephen Heath attributes a great importance to the "rhyming" effect of certain scenes in *Jaws* ("*Jaws*, Ideology, and Film Theory," *Times Higher Education Supplement*, No. 231 [March 26, 1976]: 11).

The strangeness of some films may come from their playing up of *differences* within their formal systems. Two theorists have devoted considerable attention to the functions of tension and conflict in cinematic form. See Sergei Eisenstein's *Film Form* (New York: Harvest, 1949) and Noël Burch's *Theory of Film Practice*, mentioned above. Both theorists use the term *dialectics* of form, but in different ways. How would you define the differences between these theorists?

CHAPTER 3
NARRATIVE AND NONNARRATIVE FORMAL SYSTEMS

Film form is important; how do we begin to understand it? Two important subsystems within any film are its *narrative or nonnarrative form* and its *style.* The rest of this book will examine those subsystems. This chapter will show how narrative and other types of form can shape the overall film. In Part Three (Chapters 4–8), we shall examine how a film's use of the cinema medium makes its style a formal system. After we have delineated these two systems, we shall go on, in Parts Four and Five, to analyze how the two sorts of systems work in particular films. Throughout, we will rely on those principles (outlined in Chapter 2) which are basic to all formal systems: function, similarity and repetition, difference and variation, development, and unity and disunity. Our first step is straightforward. Some films don't tell stories; others do. This commonsensical distinction opens up the very interesting problem of nonnarrative versus narrative form.

Nonnarrative Forms ■

The simplest type of film form is *categorical* form. Here the filmmaker presents a subject by cataloguing a set of conceptual types. This principle of formal organization is appropriate to a documentary film which attempts to show the viewer the different kinds of, say, butterflies. Such a film might show one type of butterfly, giving information about its habits, then show another, with more information, and so on.

Here the form is relatively straightforward. Repetition structures the film, since each new example shows the same basic type of creature, a butterfly. Variation enters because each butterfly belongs to a new species. The filmmaker might introduce a pattern of development into such a film by progressing from small butterflies to large ones or from drab to colorful ones.

In some films categorical form appears only at the beginning, to introduce the film. Dziga Vertov's *A Sixth Part of the World* and Frank Capra's *The Battle of Russia* both begin with segments which present a series of shots of the different peoples who live in the Soviet Union.

Another type of film form is *rhetorical* form, in which the filmmaker presents a logical or persuasive argument. This type of form goes beyond the categorical type in that it tries to convince the viewer of some quality about the subject; it does not simply provide information about it.

Rhetorical form creates its development by comparing reasons, evidence, and arguments. Rhetorical form is extremely common on television: Commercials use rhetorical form to persuade viewers to buy products or to vote for candidates, whereas a documentary program may use rhetorical form to convince the audience that a situation needs changing. Rhetorical form is common in film documentaries as well. In 1937 Pare Lorentz made *The River* for the United States government; the purpose was to convince the public that the Tennessee Valley Authority was a necessary government program. The film begins by outlining the history of the depletion of the valley's resources. What resulted, the film goes on to show, was flooding, loss of property, and human misery. Finally, the film shows how TVA dams help control flooding and provide electricity to rural communities. This is a standard developmental pattern for rhetorically organized film and television documentaries: from the exposition of a situation through an explanation of its effects to a final argument about action that should be taken.

The third type of form is *abstract* form. Here the separate elements of the film organize according to "pure" formal principles. That is, the filmmaker chooses some trait of the film medium itself and constructs the form of the film around it. Frequently this trait is the patterns of the graphic composition on the flat screen. The filmmaker may create a series of changing shapes and colors which have their own interest for the spectator, without necessarily representing any objects from the real world. Oskar Fischinger is a filmmaker whose career has been devoted to making abstract films; his *Motion Painting No. 1* (Fig. 3.1) presents the constantly appearing and shifting strokes of colored paint in patterns juxtaposed with a musical track.

Indeed, many abstract films build their forms around quasimusical principles. The play of filmic techniques against one another becomes like the combination of individual notes into a passage of music. The filmmaker may imbue the editing with a noticeable rhythm; the change of graphic patterns may be rhythmic as well.

Not all abstract films are drawings or paintings of shapes. Some filmmakers photograph real objects, but transform them via filmic technique into patterns of abstraction. Fernand Léger and Dudley Murphy's *Ballet Mécanique* photographs such mundane things as pot lids and

Figure 3.1

Christmas-tree ornaments. This silent film relies on the play of light and movement to create a fascinating pattern from shot to shot. The film includes shots of people, but they do not serve as characters in a narrative. Instead, *Ballet Mécanique* combines the back-and-forth movement of a woman in a swing with shots of other swinging objects; at one point the film even shows an upside-down shot of the woman in the swing.

The basic quality of abstract films is that they rely on the viewer's attention to similarities and differences in material qualities of the film medium: color, graphic compositions, movement, editing, sounds, and all of the other techniques we will be examining in more detail in Part Three. The formal development of abstract films can become very complex, depending on the types of techniques chosen and on the intricacy of the principles used to create relationships among these techniques. A film that uses a complex principle for combining several elements, such as rhythmic editing, movements of colors and shapes, and superimposed images, can engage us in a playful struggle to adjust our expectations to its novel form.

If we were setting out to make a film about, say, our local grocery store, we might choose to use any of these three types of film form. We could go through the store and film each portion, to show what sorts of things the store contains. We might show the meat section, the produce section, the checkout counters, and so forth. This film would utilize categorical form.

But we might instead set out to convince our audience of something about this grocery store: that, for example, a locally owned grocery store gives its customers better service than does a chain store. This would lead us to make a rhetorical film. For this version, we might film the owner of the store giving customers personal help; we might interview him about the services he tries to provide for them and interview customers about their opinions of the store; we might try to show that the food carried by the store is of superior quality. Overall, we would try to give our audience reasons to believe our main point, that this locally owned store is a better place to shop.

We might decide on a third alternative, to make an abstract film using the objects in the store. In this case we would try to film the store, which most people would consider quite mundane, in interesting and striking ways. Unusual camera positions could distort the shapes of cans and boxes on the shelves, close framings could bring out bright colors, an incongruous musical track could affect the audience's reaction to the images, and so on.

These three approaches would lead to very different films, even though the original subject, the store, would remain the same in each case. But there is yet another basic way we might choose to structure our film about this grocery store. We might tell a story about it. If we went through a "typical day" in the store, we would now be utilizing a fourth type of film form, *narrative*. Narrative form is so important that it deserves a separate look.

Narrative Form ■

Perhaps narrative films are not, strictly speaking, the kind of film the average spectator sees most often. After all, most people are constantly surrounded by rhetorically organized films in the shape of television commercials. But when we speak of "going to the movies," we almost invariably mean that we are going to see a narrative film. Since most of the narratives we see are fictitious, we will concentrate on fictional narratives. Much of what follows, however, also applies to factual narratives—for example, documentary films which choose narrative rather than rhetorical form.

A narrative is *a chain of events in cause-effect relationship occurring in time.* (Narrative is not the same as narra*tion;* "narration" usually refers to the voice-over commentary sometimes used in films to describe situations and events.) A narrative is what we usually mean by the term "story," though we shall try to define that term more precisely later. A narrative begins with one situation; a series of changes occurs according to a pattern of causes and effects; finally, a new situation arises which brings about the end of the narrative.

Events in a narrative must relate causally and occur in time; a random set of events cannot be a story. Consider the following series of events: "A man tosses and turns, unable to sleep. A mirror breaks. A telephone rings." We would not consider this a narrative, for we don't know of any causal or temporal relationships among these events.

But consider now a new description of these same events. "A man has a fight with his boss; he tosses and turns that night, unable to sleep. In the morning, he is still so angry that he smashes the mirror while shaving. Then his telephone rings; his boss has called to apologize." Now we have a narrative. We can understand that the three events are part of a series of causes and effects: The argument with the boss causes the sleeplessness and the broken mirror. A phone call from the boss resolves the conflict; the narrative ends. In this example time is also important. The sleepless night occurs before the breaking of the mirror, which in turn occurs before the phone call; all of the action runs from one day to the following morning. The narrative develops from an initial situation of no conflict between employee and boss, through a series of events caused by the conflict, to the resolution of the conflict.

This narrative is not a very complex or interesting one; it fulfills only the barest requirements. Most narratives are far more substantial. (Note, however, that many jokes we tell are tiny narratives, often no more complex than the one we have just constructed.) Simple as it is, though, our sample shows how important causality and time are to narrative form. In the next sections we shall look in more detail at these essential features.

Cause and Effect

If narrative depends so heavily on cause and effect, what kinds of things can function as causes in a narrative? Usually the agents of cause and effect are *characters*. Characters in narratives are *not* real people (even when the characters are based on historical personages, as with Napoleon in *War and Peace*). Characters are constructed in a narrative; they are collections of character *traits*. When we say that a character in a film was "complex" or "well developed," we really mean that the character was a collection of several or varying traits. A rich character such as Sherlock Holmes is a mass of traits (his love of music, his addiction to cocaine, his ability at disguises, and so on). On the other hand, a minor character may have only one or two traits.

In general, a character will have the number and kind of traits needed to function adequately in the narrative. The second scene of Alfred Hitchcock's *The Man Who Knew Too Much* shows that the heroine, Jill, possesses the trait of being an excellent shot with a rifle. For much of the film, this trait seems incidental to the narrative, but in the last scene Jill is able to shoot one of the villains when a police marksman cannot do it. This skill with a rifle is not a natural part of a person named Jill; it is a trait that helps make up a character named Jill, and it serves a specific narrative function (as well as other functions that we shall examine later). Character traits can involve attitudes, skills, preferences, psychological drives, details of dress and appearance, and any other specific quality the film creates for a character.

But some causes and effects in narratives do not originate with characters. Causes may be supernatural. In the book of Genesis, God causes the earth to form; gods bring about events in Greek plays. Causes may also be natural. In the so-called disaster movies, an earthquake or tidal wave may be the cause that precipitates a series of actions on the parts of the characters. The same principle holds when wild animals, like the shark in *Jaws*, terrorize a community. (The film may tend to anthropomorphize these natural causes by assigning human traits, e.g., malevolence, to them.) But once these natural occurrences set the situation up, human desires and goals usually enter the action to develop the narrative. For example, a man escaping from a flood may be placed in the situation of having to decide whether to rescue his worst enemy.

Time: Story and Plot

Causes and their effects are the basis of narrative, but they don't occur in a void; they take place in time. As we watch a film, we do not always see the events in chronological order, in accurate duration, or in exact frequency. Instead, the film may present later events first; only toward the end of the film might we discover that certain events came earlier and caused the ones we have already seen. Moreover, the film may eliminate days or years of narrative action. Finally, we may see the same event many times even though it happens only once; or, we may see only once an event that we know happens frequently. So a narrative really has two aspects, which we shall call its *story* and its *plot*.

The *story* is the series of causal events as they occur in chronological order and presumed duration and frequency. Usually the events are not presented in exact chronological order; the order in which they occur in the actual film is their *plot* order. The duration of story events is also altered in the plot's presentation. And the plot may show one event and imply that it happens regularly in the story; less frequently, the plot shows the same event over again. The story, then, is a mental reconstruction *we* make of the events in their chronological order and in their presumed duration and frequency. The plot is the way in which these events are actually presented in the film.

Temporal Order. This distinction may sound difficult, but actually we are quite accustomed to watching films that present events out of order. A flashback is a simple example of a portion of a story that is presented out of chronological order. Suppose we see a shot of a woman thinking about her childhood, then a second shot depicting her as a girl; we understand that the second shot actually shows an earlier time in the story events than the first. This doesn't confuse us, because we mentally rearrange the events into the order in which they would logically have to occur: Childhood comes before adulthood. From the plot order, we infer the story order.

Nor are flashbacks the only way in which plot and story orders may differ. Most detective films, for example, start quite late in the story, in order to conceal the killer and create a mystery. A detective film's story might involve a quarrel between killer and victim, the killing, the killer's flight, the discovery of the body, the calling in of the detective, the detective's investigation, the detective's accusation of the suspect, and the suspect's confession. Yet the film's plot might start at the discovery of the body or at the moment when the detective is called in on the case. The investigation then attempts to discover what the earlier story events were. In the last few scenes of detective films the detective and the killer often give lengthy summaries of events that occurred before the first events depicted in the plot.

Temporal Duration. Similarly, story duration is seldom respected in plot treatment. Usually the amount of time an action takes is reduced. Titles such as "two years later" or a one-minute sequence concisely depicting the rise of a politician or film star—these are traces of the elimination of portions of story duration. The story action may consume days, years (e.g., *Gone with the Wind*), or eons (*2001*), but the plot will simply eliminate or compress this time span. It is also possible for the plot to *expand* story duration. In cinema the most famous example is that of the raising of the bridges in Sergei Eisenstein's *October*. Here, an event that takes only a few moments in the story is stretched out to several minutes in the plot presentation (by means of film editing). As a result, this action gains a tremendous emphasis, especially because its slowness contrasts with the quicker pace of the scene's earlier events.

Temporal Frequency. A film's plot may change story frequency in several ways. If the story contains a habitual action that must happen several times, the plot will present *one or a few* occurrences and let these sum up the rest. In Buster Keaton's *Battling Butler*, the unathletic hero is mistaken for a famous boxer and has to train for a big fight. The training period is a month, but we see only a few grueling exercise sessions and sparring matches; these serve to suggest the many repeated ordeals the hero must undergo during that month.

Occasionally, a single *story* event may appear twice or even more in the *plot* treatment. If we see an event early in a film and then there is a flashback to that event later on, we see that same event twice. Some films use multiple narrators, each of whom describes the same event; again, we see it occur several times. This may allow us to see the same action from different viewpoints; the plot may also provide us with more information, so that we understand the event in a new context when it reappears. We shall see an example of this in *Citizen Kane*.

Story and plot are, then, useful categories for examining narrative order, duration, and frequency. As we shall see with *Citizen Kane*, a film may fascinate its audience by making its plot vary considerably from its implicit story.

Other Narrative Features

Causality and temporal relations are essential to narrative form. In analyzing narrative films, however, we will also find it useful to apply three other concepts. These concepts are motivation, parallelism, and patterns of development between openings and closings.

Motivation. A narrative is not a natural object; its events do not take place in the same real world in which we exist. Instead, a narrative is a human artifact, a construct. Therefore, we should avoid saying, "It is *natural* that X happens in that narrative." Events that occur in narrative films have a *function* in the overall system of the plot. Therefore, we should ask, "What is X *doing* in this narrative? How does X function?" (As we saw with *The Wizard of Oz*, many narrative elements have several functions.)

Because narrative films are human constructs rather than natural objects, we can expect that any one element in a film will have some logical justification for being there. This justification is the *motivation* for that element. Sometimes people use the word "motivation" to apply only to reasons for characters' actions, e.g., a murderer acts from "motives" such as hatred or jealousy. Here, however, we will use "motivation" to apply to any filmic element that is justified by the film's overall form.

A costume, for example, needs motivation. If we see a man in beggar's clothes in the middle of an elegant society ball scene, we will ask why he is dressed in this way. He could be the victim of practical jokers who have deluded him into believing that this is a masquerade. He could be an eccentric millionaire out to shock his friends. Such a scene does occur in *My Man Godfrey*. The motivation for the beggar's presence at the ball is a scavenger hunt; the young society people have been assigned to bring back, among other things, a beggar. An event, the hunt, *motivates* the presence of an inappropriately dressed character.

Motivation is so common in films that spectators tend to take it for granted. The presence of a candle in a room motivates the fact that we can see the characters. (We may be aware that the source of the light is actually not just the candle, but the candle is the ostensible source and motivates the light.) The movement of a character across a room may motivate the moving of the camera to follow the action and keep the character within the frame.

Narrative motivation often involves the "planting" of information in advance of a scene. In one film we shall be examining, *Stagecoach*, there is a last-minute rescue from Indians by a cavalry troop. If these soldiers appeared from nowhere, we would most likely find the rescue a weak resolution to the battle scene. But *Stagecoach* begins with a scene of the cavalry discovering that Geronimo is on the warpath. Several later scenes involve the cavalry, and the passengers on the coach learn that the soldiers at one of their stops have had a skirmish with the Indians. These previous scenes of cavalry troops motivate their appearance in the final rescue scene.

In order to discover the motivation for an element, we should ask: What justifies this being in the film? Some narrative films tend to motivate all of their elements very thoroughly. Very few elements play no part in the narratives of such films. On the other hand, films that do introduce elements without narrative motivation tend to depart from this norm of unified, closed narrative. An element without narrative motivation may produce ambiguity; we are not sure why something happens or how it relates to other elements in the overall system. A series of elements without narrative motivation may create its own systematic pattern of repetitions and variations; in this case systematic uses of disunity or of ambiguity may result. Such ambiguous or disunified films challenge our normal perceptions of films. (We shall examine several such films in Part Four.)

Parallelism. A narrative film can create patterns of similarity and difference by means of *parallelism*. Here two narrative motifs or events are compared in order to point up how they are alike in some respects while differing in others. Two characters' actions may parallel each other; we see scenes involving the first character, then scenes involving the second. For example, D. W. Griffith's *A Corner in Wheat* shows a businessman who has cornered the wheat market celebrating at a lavish dinner party. From this scene, the locale shifts to a bakery where hungry people are denied bread because the price of wheat has been driven up. Here a causal connection motivates the juxtaposition of the two scenes; the businessman's financial success (which allows him to feast) has created the poor people's hunger.

But the parallel elements need not have any causal, spatial, or temporal connection; the simple pattern of juxtaposing them invites us to compare them. Vera Chytilova's feminist film *Something Different* bases its narrative form entirely on an extended parallel. It depicts the lives of two women in modern society: one a gymnast, the other a housewife. The two women never meet; we never know if the events of their lives are taking place concurrently and in the same city. (The closest connection ever made is when the gymnast appears on the housewife's television in one scene.) By paralleling the two chains of actions, Chytilova develops a thematic comparison. The gymnast's active life points up the domestic oppression of the housewife; on the other hand, we see also that the gymnast has not entirely escaped male dominance—in her case by her trainer.

Parallelism, with or without a causal connection between the elements, is common in films. A parallel may involve more than two elements; Griffith's *Intolerance* weaves four individual stories together into one main plot. Again, these stories have no causal connections, and they take place in widely separate time periods: the fall of Babylon, the crucifixion of Christ, the St. Bartholemew's Day Massacre, and a contemporary romance. What motivates the interweaving of these stories is their parallel concentration on the idea of intolerance through the ages.

Parallelism can organize whole films or can motivate the presence of a subplot within a larger narrative structure. The romance of two secondary characters may have similarities to that of the hero and heroine, thereby deepening our understanding of the main plot events. As we shall see later, the repetition of a stylistic technique such as camera movement or editing may create a parallelism connecting one scene of a film with another. Parallelism creates unity between parts and helps motivate the presence of elements.

Openings, Closings, and Patterns of Development

In Chapter 2 our discussion of formal development suggested that it is often useful to compare beginnings and endings. This holds true for narrative form as well, since a narrative's cause-effect logic usually involves a change from an initial situation to a final situation.

A film doesn't just start; it *begins*. The opening provides us with a basis for what is to come; it integrates us into the film. Causes of subsequent narrative events, significant motifs, and important features of the initial plot situation are all laid out in the opening. We know that if we come in late, we have missed experiencing the totality of the film; even staying to watch the beginning will not make up for it. Thus the opening of a film sets up a certain range of possibilities, raising our expectations about what is to come.

No film can explore all of the possibilities hovering at its opening. As the narrative proceeds, the causes and effects will define narrower patterns of development. One common pattern of progression, for example, is a journey. In *The Wizard of Oz* Dorothy starts in Kansas, and her overall journey through Oz takes her back there. The trip through Oz is not simply a sightseeing tour. Each smaller step of the journey (to the Emerald City, to the Witch's castle, to the Emerald City again) is governed by the same principle—her desire to go home. Later we shall analyze several films with journey structures, including *Our Hospitality* and *Stagecoach*.

Search patterns govern the plots of many films. In a mystery tale the characters may search for the solution to the problem, for a vital clue, or for a missing character. In René Clair's *Le Million* a character gives away a coat that turns out to have a winning lottery ticket in its pocket; the rest of the film involves the comic search for the missing coat.

Almost any situation can furnish a pattern for the development of a narrative. A romantic triangle may cause characters to try to outmaneuver one another, as we shall see in *His Girl Friday*. Jacques Tati's film *Mr. Hulot's Holiday* patterns its narrative development around the seven days of a vacation; each day Mr. Hulot progressively alienated the other guests at a beach resort by his eccentricities and mistakes. By the end of the narrative, almost no one will speak to him; the comic development of the film depends on this progression. Such principles of development organize the parts of a narrative into a coherent whole rather than just a random collection of events.

A film also does not simply stop; it *ends*. By the time we reach the end, there may be very few possibilities for further development. In a mystery, for instance, the clues may eliminate all but a few suspects. Or, the climax of a Western may involve a shootout in which we know that one of the two participants will die. Very often the ending will resolve, or "close off," the chains of cause and effect—the hero wins, everyone lives happily ever after. But not all films have such a sense of finality. An ending can be relatively ambiguous, or "open." In other words, the plot presents story events which leave us uncertain as to the nature of the final consequences. If in a mystery film we learn who the criminal is, the film has closure; but if it leaves a doubt about that person's guilt, it remains relatively open.

The Classical Hollywood Cinema

The number of possible narratives is unlimited. Historically, however, the cinema has tended to be dominated by a single mode of narrative form. In the course of this book we shall refer to this dominant mode as the "classical Hollywood cinema"—"classical" because of its wide and long history, "Hollywood" because the mode assumed its definitive shape in American studio films (although the same mode governs many narrative films made in other countries). What are the typical traits of this narrative mode?

This conception of narrative depends on the assumption that the action will spring primarily from *individual characters as causal agents*. Natural causes (floods, earthquakes) or societal causes (institutions, wars, economic depressions) may serve as catalysts or preconditions for the action, but the narrative invariably centers on personal psychological causes: decisions, choices, and traits of character.

Often an important trait that functions to get the narrative moving is a *desire*. The character wants something. The desire sets up a goal, and the course of the narrative's development will most likely involve the process of achieving that goal. In *The Wizard of Oz* Dorothy has a series of goals, as we have seen: first to save Toto from Miss Gulch, then to get home from Oz. This latter goal involves smaller goals along the way: getting to Oz and then killing the Witch. We shall see in *Stagecoach* how the central character has a goal of revenge, whereas the subsidiary characters have goals of their own.

If this desire to reach a goal were the only element present, there would be nothing to stop the character from achieving the goal immediately. But there is a counterforce in the classical narrative: an opposition that creates conflict. The protagonist comes up against a character whose traits and goals are opposed to his or hers. As a result, the protagonist must seek to change the situation so that he or she can achieve the goal. Dorothy's desire to return to Kansas is opposed by the Wicked Witch, whose goal is to obtain the ruby slippers. Dorothy must eventually eliminate the Witch before she is able to use the slippers to go home. In *Stagecoach* the protagonist, who is under arrest by the marshal, has to prove himself trustworthy before the marshal finally allows him to participate in the shootout that finally gains him his revenge.

Cause and effect imply *change*. If the characters didn't desire something to be different from the way it is at the beginning of the narrative, change wouldn't occur. Therefore, characters and their traits, particularly desire, are a strong source of causes and effects.

But don't all narratives have protagonists of this sort? Actually not. In 1920s Soviet films, such as Sergei Eisenstein's *Potemkin, October,* and *Strike,* no *individual* acts as protagonist. More recently, Jacques Rivette's *Out One Spectre* and Robert Altman's *Nashville* experiment with eliminating protagonists. In films like those of Eisenstein and Yasujiro Ozu, many events are seen as caused not by characters, but by larger forces (social dynamics in the former, an overarching Nature in the second). In many other narratives the protagonist is not active but passive. So the active, goal-oriented protagonist, though common, does not appear in every narrative film.

In the classical Hollywood narrative mode the chain of actions that results from predominantly psychological causes tends to motivate most or all other narrative events. Time is subordinated to the cause-effect chain in a host of ways. The plot will omit insignificant durations in order to show only events of causal importance. (The hours Dorothy and her entourage spend walking on the Road are omitted, but the moments during which she meets a new character are presented.) The plot will order story chronology so as to present the cause-effect chain most strikingly. Thus if a character acts peculiarly, we may get a flashback to reveal the cause of the odd behavior. Special devices weld plot time to the story's cause-effect chain: the appointment (which motivates characters encountering each other at a specific moment) and the deadline (which makes plot duration dependent on the cause-effect chain). Motivation in the classical narrative film will strive to be as clear and complete as possible—even in the fanciful genre of the musical, in which song and dance numbers become motivated as either expressions of the characters' emotions or stage shows mounted by the characters.

Finally, most classical narrative films display strong degrees of closure at the end. Leaving no loose ends unresolved, these films seek to cap their causal chains with a final effect. We usually learn the fate of each character, the answer to each mystery, and the outcome of each conflict.

Again, none of these features is necessary to narrative form in general. There is nothing to prevent a filmmaker from presenting the "dead time" or narratively unmotivated intervals between more significant events. (François Truffaut, Jean-Luc Godard, Carl Dreyer, and Andy Warhol do this frequently, albeit in very different ways.) The filmmaker's plot can also reorder story chronology to make the causal chain *more* perplexing. For example, Jean-Marie Straub and Danièle Huillet's *Not Reconciled* moves back and forth among three widely different time periods. Dusan Makavejev's *Love Affair, or the Case of the Missing Switchboard Operator* uses flash-forwards interspersed with the main plot action; only gradually do we come to understand the causal relations of these flash-forwards to the "present-time" events. The filmmaker can also include material that is unmotivated by narrative cause and effect, such as the chance meetings in Truffaut's films, the political monologues and interviews in Godard's films, the "intellectual montage" sequences in Eisenstein's films, the transitional shots in Ozu's work, and so on. Finally, the filmmaker need not resolve all of the action at the close; films made outside the classical tradition tend to have quite "open" endings.

We shall see in Chapter 6 how the classical Hollywood mode also makes cinematic space subservient to causality by means of continuity editing. For now it suffices to note how the classical mode tends to treat narrative cause and effect in specific and unique ways. This mode is, however, only one system among many that have been and could be used for constructing films.

Dividing a Film into Parts ■

At this point, you may be asking a question. If film form is the systematic relation of parts to create a whole, how may a narrative or nonnarrative film be divided into parts? What parts may constitute a film?

Any film may be divided into various sections—e.g., ten-minute intervals or 100-foot chunks—but the most common subdivision is the *sequence*. A sequence is a major part of a film, consisting of at least one shot and usually more than one shot. The sequence is not an arbitrary division, but rather is demarcated by certain cinematic devices (cuts, fade-ins and -outs, dissolves, optical effects, changes from color to black and white, sound shifts, etc.). Moreover, a sequence has a conceptual coherence: It is a *meaningful* part. In different sorts of films we might find different sorts of sequences: categories for a film in categorical form, stages of an argument for a film in rhetorical form, or material categories (e.g., dark/light, movement/stillness) for a film whose form is abstract. A narrative film is divisible into sequences, according to phases of the narrative action. Many narrative-film sequences are called *scenes*. Here the term is used in its theatrical sense, to refer to distinct phases of the action occurring within a relatively unified time and space. When a critic divides a film into parts, the activity is often called *segmentation*. Our analysis of *Citizen Kane* will depend on segmenting the film into its sequences and scenes.

Narrative Form in Citizen Kane ■

Citizen Kane is a useful film with which to begin film analysis, because it is unusual in form and varied in style. In what follows we shall examine *Citizen Kane* to discover how principles of narrative form may function in a particular film. *Kane*'s investigation-plot carries us toward analyzing how causality and goal-oriented characters may operate in narratives. The film's manipulations of our knowledge shed light on the story/plot distinction. *Kane* also helps define how ambiguity may arise when certain elements are not clearly motivated. Finally, the comparison of *Kane*'s beginning with its ending shows how a film may deviate from the patterns of classical Hollywood narrative construction.

Citizen Kane's Causality

Citizen Kane has two distinct sets of characters who cause events to occur. On the one hand, a group of reporters seeks information about Kane; on the other hand, Kane and the characters who know him provide the subject of the reporters' investigations. The initial causal connection between the two groups is Kane's death, which leads the reporters to make a newsreel summing up his career. But the newsreel is already finished when the plot introduces the reporters; the boss, Rawlston, supplies the cause that initiates the investigation of Kane's life. Thompson's newsreel fails to satisfy him; Rawlston's desire for "an angle" for the newsreel gets the search for "Rosebud" under way. Thompson thus gains a goal, which sets him delving into Kane's past. His investigation constitutes one main line of the plot.

But another line of action, Kane's life, has already taken place in the past. There too a group of characters has caused actions to occur. Many years before, a poverty-stricken boarder at Kane's mother's boarding house has paid her with a supposedly worthless deed to a silver mine. The wealth provided by this mine causes Mrs. Kane to appoint Thatcher as young Charles's guardian; Thatcher's guardianship results (in somewhat unspecified ways) in Kane's growing up into a spoiled, rebellious young man, and so on.

Citizen Kane is an unusual film in that the object of the investigator's search is a set of character traits. Thompson seeks to know what traits in Kane's personality led him to say "Rosebud" on his deathbed; this "mystery" motivates Thompson's detectivelike investigation. Kane, a very complex character, has many traits that influence the other characters' actions. As we shall see, however, *Citizen Kane*'s narrative does not ultimately define all of Kane's character traits.

Kane himself has a goal; he too seems to be searching for a something related to "Rosebud." At several points characters speculate that Rosebud was something that Kane lost or never was able to get. Again, the fact that Kane's goal remains so vague makes this an unusual narrative.

Other characters in Kane's life provide causal material for the narrative. The presence of several characters who knew Kane well makes Thompson's investigation possible, even though Kane himself has died. Note too how the characters provide a range of information that spans Kane's entire life. This is important if we are to be able to reconstruct the progression of story events in the film. Thatcher knew Kane as a child; Bernstein, his manager, knew his business dealings; his best friend, Leland, knew of his personal life (his first marriage in particular); Susan Alexander, his second wife, knew him in middle age; and the butler, Raymond, managed Kane's affairs during his last years. Each of these characters has a causal role in Kane's life, as well as in Thompson's investigation. Note that Kane's wife, Emily, does not tell a story, since Emily's story would simply duplicate Leland's and would contribute no additional information to the "present-day" part of the narrative, the investigation; hence the plot simply eliminates her (via a car accident).

Story and Plot

The order, duration, and frequency of story events differ greatly from the presentation of those events in the plot of *Citizen Kane*. Indeed, much of the film's power arises from the transformation of these events from story to plot. The earliest *story* event about which we learn is the giving of the deed to Mrs. Kane; the second sequence in the film, the newsreel, gives us this information. But the first event in the *plot* of *Citizen Kane* is Kane's death. Here is a linear segmentation summing up the plot events of the film. (Long vertical lines indicate major sequences; short vertical lines mark off shorter scenes within these sequences. Locales are written above the horizontal line; actions, below it.)

Xanadu	Projection room	
Kane's death 1	Newsreel 2	Reporters' discussion

El Rancho	Thatcher Library	├——1st Flashback——┤				Bernstein's office
Conversation with Alexander 3	Thompson reads 4	Kane as a boy	*Inquirer* campaign	Depression	Thompson stops reading	Conversation with Bernstein 5

├——2nd Flashback——┤				Leland's nursing home	├——3rd Flashback——┤	
Takeover of *Inquirer*	Party	Engagement	Conversation	Conversation with Leland 6	Breakfast table sequence	Conversation

├—3rd Flashback resumes——┤		El Rancho	├——4th Flashback——┤	
Alexander, political campaign, opera career	Conversation	Conversation with Alexander 7	Opera career, Xanadu	Conversation

Xanadu	├—5th Flashback——┤			
Conversation with Raymond 8	Destruction of room	Reporters talk and leave	Kane's possessions	Exterior of house

This plot takes about a week or less (the amount of time Rawlston gives Thompson to do the investigation); the story covers the approximately 75 years of Kane's life, plus the week after his death, during which Thompson works on his newsreel.

In the course of this plot we learn a great deal about Kane's character traits. The only time we see Kane in "the present" is in the first scene, when he dies; all other scenes in which he appears occur in the flashbacks. (We cannot call the newsreel an actual appearance of the character, but rather images of the character.)

The spectator's understanding of the story in its chronological order and assumed duration and frequency involves following a complex tapestry of plot events. For example, in the first flashback Thatcher's diary tells of a scene in which Kane loses control of his newspapers during the Depression; by this time Kane is a middle-aged man. Yet in the second flashback Bernstein describes Kane's youthful arrival at the *Inquirer* and his engagement to Emily. We mentally reverse these plot events into a correct chronological (story) order, then continue to rearrange other events as we learn of them.

This process of mentally rearranging plot events into story order might be quite difficult in *Citizen Kane* were it not for the presence of the "News on the March" newsreel. The first sequence in Xanadu disorients us, for it shows the death of a character about whom we so far know almost nothing. But the newsreel gives us a great deal of information quickly. Moreover, the newsreel uses a narrative parallel to give us a miniature introduction to the plot of the ensuing film. Here is a linear diagram of the newsreel sequence:

Shots of Xanadu	Funeral/ headlines	Growth of financial empire	Silver mine, Mrs. Kane's boarding house	Thatcher testimony	Political career
A	B	C	D	E	F

"Private life"— weddings, divorces	Opera house, Xanadu	Political campaign	Depression	1935: Kane's old age	Isolation at Xanadu	Death announced
G	H	I	J	K	L	M

A comparison of this diagram with the one for the whole film shows some striking formal similarities. "News on the March" begins by emphasizing Kane as "Xanadu's Landlord"; a short segment (A) presents shots of the house, its grounds, and its contents. This is a variation on the opening of the whole film (1), which consisted of a series of shots of the grounds, moving progressively closer to the house. That opening sequence had ended with Kane's death; now the newsreel follows the shots of the house with Kane's funeral (B). Next comes a series of newspaper headlines announcing Kane's death. In a comparison with the plot diagram of *Citizen Kane*, these headlines occupy the approximate formal position of the whole newsreel itself (2). Even the title card that follows the headlines ("To forty-four million U.S. news-buyers, more newsworthy than the names in his own headlines was Kane himself . . . ") is a brief parallel to the scene in the projection room, in which the reporters decide that Thompson should continue to investigate Kane's "newsworthy" life.

The order of the newsreel's presentation of Kane's life roughly parallels the order of scenes in the flashbacks related to Thompson. "News on the March" moves from Kane's death to summarize the building of Kane's newspaper empire (C), with a description of the boarding house deed and the silver mine (including an old photograph of Charles with his mother, as well as the first mention of the sled). Similarly, the first flashback (4) tells how Thatcher took over the young Kane's guardianship from his mother and how Kane first attempted to run the *Inquirer*. The rough parallel continues: The newsreel tells of Kane's political ambitions (F), his marriages (G), his building of the opera house (H), his political campaign (I), and so on. In the main plot Thatcher's flashback describes his own clashes with Kane on political matters. Leland's flashback (6) covers the first marriage, the affair with Susan, the political campaign, and the premiere of *Salammbo*. These are not all of the similarities between the newsreel and the overall film; you can tease out many more by comparing the two closely.

In general, the newsreel provides us with a "map" at the beginning of the investigation into Kane's life. As we see the various scenes of the flashbacks, we already expect certain events and have a rough chronological basis for fitting them into our story reconstruction.

Citizen Kane also provides a clear demonstration of how events that occur only once in the story may appear multiple times in the plot. In their respective flashbacks, both Leland and Susan Alexander describe the latter's debut in the Chicago premiere of *Salammbo*. Watching Leland's account (6), we see the performance from the front; we witness the audience reacting with distaste. Susan's version (7) shows us the performance from behind and on the stage, to suggest her humiliation. This repeated presentation of Susan's debut in the plot does not confuse us, for we recognize the two scenes as depicting the same story event. ("News on the March" also refers briefly to Susan's opera career, in parts G and H.)

Overall, *Citizen Kane*'s narrative is relatively complex, for its plot plays a great deal with story events. Yet *Citizen Kane* succeeds in presenting an intricate plot without becoming confusing.

Motivation

Some critics have argued that Welles's use of the search for "Rosebud" is a flaw in *Citizen Kane*, because the identification of the word proves it to be a trivial gimmick. If indeed we assume that the whole point of *Citizen Kane* is really to identify "Rosebud," this charge might be valid. But in fact, "Rosebud" serves a very important motivating function in the film; it serves to create Thompson's goal and to focus our attention on his delving into the lives of Kane and his associates. *Citizen Kane* becomes a mystery story; but instead of investigating a crime, the reporter investigates a character. So the "Rosebud" clues provide the basic motivation necessary for the plot to progress. (Of course, the "Rosebud" device serves other functions as well; for instance, the little sled provides a transition from the boarding house scene to the cheerless Christmas when Thatcher gives Charles a new sled.)

Citizen Kane's narrative revolves around an investigation into traits of character; as a result, these traits provide many of the motivations for events. (In this respect, the film obeys principles of the classical Hollywood narrative model.) Kane's desire to prove that Susan is really a singer and not just his mistress motivates his manipulation of her opera career. His mother's overly protective desire to remove her son from what she considers to be a bad environment motivates her appointment of Thatcher as the boy's guardian. The interested reader will be able to find in the film dozens of actions that are motivated by character traits and desires.

At the end of the film, Thompson gives up his search for the meaning of "Rosebud," saying he doesn't "think any word can explain a man's life." Thompson's statement motivates his acceptance of his failure, of course. But if we as spectators are to accept this idea that no key can unlock the secrets of a life, we need further motivation, and the film provides this. In the scene in the newsreel projection room, Rawlston suggests that "maybe he told us all about himself on his deathbed"; one of the reporters says, "Yeah, and maybe he didn't." Already the suggestion is planted that "Rosebud" may not provide any adequate answers about Kane. Later Leland scornfully dismisses the "Rosebud" issue and goes on to talk of other things. These brief references to "Rosebud" help justify Thompson's pessimistic lines in the final sequence.

The presence of the scene in which Thompson first visits Susan Alexander at the El Rancho nightclub (3) might seem puzzling at first. Unlike the other scenes in which he visits people, no flashback occurs here. Thompson learns from the waiter that Susan knows nothing about

"Rosebud"; he could easily learn this on his second visit to her. So why should the film include the scene at all? One reason lies in the fact that Susan's story, when she does tell it, covers events relatively late in Kane's career. As we have seen, the flashbacks go through Kane's life roughly in order. If Susan had told her story first, we would not have all of the material necessary to understand it. But it is narratively logical that Thompson should start his search with Kane's ex-wife, presumably the surviving person closest to him. In Thompson's first visit, Susan's drunken refusal to speak to him motivates the fact that her flashback comes later; by that point, Bernstein and Leland have filled in enough of Kane's personal life to prepare the way for Susan's flashback. This first scene functions partly to provide this motivation for postponing Susan's flashback until a later part of the plot.

Motivation makes us take things for granted in narratives. Mrs. Kane's desire for her son to be rich and successful motivates her decision to entrust him to Thatcher, a powerful banker, as his guardian. We may be inclined to think it is just natural that Thatcher is a rich businessman; this fact, however, in turn provides several important motivations. It motivates Thatcher's presence in the newsreel; he is powerful enough to have been asked to testify at a congressional hearing. More important, Thatcher's success motivates the fact that he has kept a journal now on deposit at a memorial library that Thompson visits. This in turn justifies the fact that Thompson is able to find information from a source who knew Kane as a child.

But *Citizen Kane* departs somewhat from the usual practice of the classical Hollywood narrative by leaving some motivations ambiguous. The ambiguities relate primarily to Kane's character. The other characters who tell Thompson their stories all have definite opinions of Kane, but these don't always tally. Bernstein still looks on Kane with sympathy and affection, whereas Leland is cynical about his own relationship with Kane. The reason for some of Kane's actions remains unclear. Does he send Leland the $25,000 check in firing him because of a lingering sentiment over their old friendship or from a proud desire to prove himself more generous than Leland? Why does he insist on stuffing Xanadu with hundreds of artworks which he never even unpacks?

Parallelism

Parallelism does not provide the entire basis of *Citizen Kane*'s narrative form, but several parallel structures are present. We have already seen important formal parallels between the newsreel and the film's plot as a whole. We have also noticed a parallel between the two major lines of action: Kane's life and Thompson's search. "Rosebud" serves as a summary of the things Kane strives for through his adult life; we see him repeatedly fail to find love and friendship, living alone at Xanadu in the end. His inability to find happiness parallels Thompson's failure to locate the significance of the word "Rosebud." This parallel does not imply that Kane and Thompson share similar character traits. Rather, it allows both lines of action to develop simultaneously in similar directions.

Another narrative parallel juxtaposes Kane's political campaign as he runs for governor with his attempt to build up Susan's career as an opera star. In each case he seeks to inflate his reputation by influencing public opinion. In trying to achieve success for Susan, Kane forces his newspaper employees to write favorable reviews of her performances; this parallels the moment when he loses the election and the *Inquirer* automatically proclaims fraud at the polls. In both cases Kane fails to realize that his power over the public is not great enough to hide the flaws in his projects: first his affair with Susan, which ruins his campaign, then her lack of singing ability, which Kane refuses to admit. Here the parallel points up how Kane continues to make the same kinds of mistakes throughout his life.

Patterns of Development

The progression from beginning to ending in *Citizen Kane* leads us through two lines of action, as we have seen: Thompson's search for a key to explain Kane's life on the one hand and Kane's life on the other. Each of Thompson's visits in his investigation leads to a flashback that gives us a further look at Kane. The order of Thompson's visits allows the series of flashbacks to have a clear pattern of progression.

Even though the flashbacks do not present events in their exact chronological order, they do progress. Thompson moves from people who knew Kane early in his life to those who knew him as an old man. Moreover, each flashback contains a distinct type of information about Kane. Thatcher establishes Kane's political stance; next Bernstein gives an account of the business dealings of the newspaper. These provide the background to Kane's early success and lead into Leland's stories of Kane's personal life, where we get the first real indications of Kane's failure. Susan continues the description of his decline with her account of how he had manipulated her life. Finally, in Raymond's flashback Kane becomes a pitiable old man.

Thus even though the order, duration, and frequency of events in the story vary greatly from those in the plot of *Citizen Kane*, the film presents Kane's life through a steady pattern of development. The "present-day" portions of the narrative—Thompson's scenes—also follow their own pattern of a search. By the ending this search has failed (as Kane's own search for happiness or personal success had also failed).

Because of this failure, the ending of *Citizen Kane* remains somewhat more open than was the rule in Hollywood in 1941. True, Thompson does resolve the question of "Rosebud" for himself by saying that it would not have explained Kane's life. But in most classical narrative films the main character reaches his or her goal (and Thompson is the main character of this one line of action).

The line of action involving Kane himself has even less closure. Not only does Kane apparently not reach his goal, but also the film never specifies what that goal is to start with. Most classical narratives create a situation of conflict. The character must struggle with a problem and solve it by the ending. Kane begins his adult life in a highly successful position (happily running the *Inquirer*), then gradually falls into a lonely, failed existence. (This reversal is one reason why we must see Kane's death at the *beginning* of the film; we must anticipate his eventual lonely end if the narrative is to introduce conflict and tension into the early scenes.) We are never sure exactly what, if anything, it would take to make Kane happy. *Citizen Kane*'s lack of closure in this line of action made it a very unusual narrative for its day.

The search for "Rosebud" does lead to a certain resolution at the end: We the audience discover what "Rosebud" was. The ending of the film, which follows this discovery, strongly echoes the beginning. The beginning had moved past fences toward the house; now a series of shots takes us away from the house and back outside the fences, with their "No Trespassing" sign and large K insignia.

But even at this point, when we learn the answer to Thompson's question, a degree of uncertainty remains. Just because we have learned what Kane's dying word meant, do we now have the key to his entire character? Or is Thompson's final statement *correct*—that no one word can explain a person's life? It is tempting to declare that all of Kane's problems arose from his loss of his sled and home life as a child, but the film also suggests that this is too easy a solution. It is the kind of solution that the slick editor Rawlston would pounce on as an "angle" for his newsreel.

For years critics have debated whether "Rosebud's" solution does give us a key that resolves the entire narrative. This debate should suggest the ambiguity at work in *Citizen Kane*. The film itself provides evidence for both views and hence avoids complete closure. (You might contrast this slightly open ending with the tightly closed narratives of *His Girl Friday*, *The Man Who Knew Too Much*, and *Stagecoach*, in Part Four. You might also compare *Citizen Kane*'s narrative with two other films that contain ambiguities: *Day of Wrath* and *Last Year at Marienbad*, also in Part Four.)

Conclusion

Not every narrative analysis goes through the categories of cause-effect, story/plot differences, motivations, parallelism, and progression from opening to closing in that exact order, as we have done here. Our purpose in this examination of *Citizen Kane* has been as much to illustrate these concepts as to analyze the film's narrative. With practice, the critic becomes more familiar with these analytical tools and can use them flexibly, suiting his or her approach to the specific film at hand.

A thorough understanding of these principles of narrative analysis is particularly important as we move into a consideration of film techniques, for narrative and cinematic techniques function together to create the overall formal system of a film. Narrative may motivate a stylistic device; a specific stylistic technique may alter story/plot relationships (as we shall see with such techniques as elliptical editing). The analytical tools presented here in Part Two, in combination with an ability to analyze the function of the techniques to be defined in Part Three, should help us discuss whole filmic systems. At the end of our survey of film techniques, we shall return to *Citizen Kane* to analyze how its use of the film medium is related to its narrative form.

Notes and Queries ∎

Types of Form

A good introduction to the concept of rhetorical form is Stephen Toulmin's *The Uses of Argument* (Cambridge: Cambridge University Press, 1958). Do some films have a "layout of arguments" similar to Toulmin's? Abstract form is often best examined in the light of principles of musical form; see Parts III and IV of William S. Newman's *Understanding Music* (New York: Harper, 1967).

Narrative form is currently undergoing sophisticated and subtle research in many fields. The concepts we discuss in this chapter are drawn primarily from Russian Formalist literary criticism. See Lee T. Lemon and Marion J. Reis, eds., *Russian Formalist Criticism: Four Essays* (Lincoln: University of Nebraska Press, 1965); Ladislav Matejka and Krystyna Pomorska, eds., *Readings in Russian Poetics* (Cambridge, Mass.: MIT Press, 1971); Tzvetan Todorov, "Some Approaches to Russian Formalism," *Twentieth Century Studies*, no. 7/8 (December 1972): 6–19; and Victor Erlich, *Russian Formalism* (The Hague: Mouton, 1965). Similar approaches may be found in Roland Barthes, "An Introduction to the Structural Analysis of Narrative," *New Literary History* 6, 2 (Winter 1975): 237–272; Tzvetan Todorov, *The Poetics of Prose* (Ithaca:

Cornell University Press, 1977); and Jonathan Culler, *Structuralist Poetics* (Ithaca: Cornell University Press, 1976).

The various aspects of narrative form have been analyzed individually. Most theorists agree that cause-effect relations and chronology are central to narrative. In a traditional narrative, the French novelist Alain Robbe-Grillet asserts, "the succession of facts, the narrative concatenation, as is said today, is based entirely on a system of causalities: what follows phenomenon A is phenomenon B, the consequence of the first; thus, the chain of events in the novel" ("Order and Disorder in Film and Fiction," *Critical Inquiry* 4, 1 [Autumn 1977]: 5). A good analysis of causality and temporality may be found in Roland Barthes, "Action Sequences," in Joseph Strelka, ed., *Patterns of Literary Style* (University Park: University of Pennsylvania Press, 1971). Our discussion of story/plot and time is based on Boris Tomashevsky, "Thematics," in Lemon and Reis, pp. 61–78, and on Gerard Genette, "Time and Narrative in *A la Recherche du Temps Perdu*," in J. Hillis Miller, ed., *Aspects of Narrative* (New York: Columbia University Press, 1971), pp. 93–118, and Genette, *Figures III* (Paris: Seuil, 1972). On motivation, see Tomashevsky's distinction of three types (compositional, realistic, and artistic) in Lemon and Reis, pp. 78–87. Frank Kermode has written a book on narrative closings, *The Sense of an Ending* (New York: Oxford University Press, 1968).

Linear Segmentation and Diagramming

Dividing a film into sequences in order to analyze its form is usually called *segmentation*. It is not difficult to do, though most often we do it intuitively. Recent film theory has devoted some consideration to the principles by which we segment a film. See Raymond Bellour, "To Analyze, to Segment," *Quarterly Review of Film Studies* 1, 3 (August 1976): 331–354.

The most influential explanation of how to segment a narrative film has been Christian Metz's famous "Grand Syntagmatic of the Image Track." Metz suggests that there are eight basic sorts of sequences (with some subdivisions and exceptions). See Christian Metz, *Film Language*, trans. M. Taylor (New York: Oxford University Press, 1974) and Stephen Heath, "Film/Cinetext/Text," *Screen* 14, 1/2 (Spring/Summer 1973): 102–127.

Usually a feature-length film will have no more than 40 sequences and no fewer than 5, so if you find yourself dividing the film into tiny bits or huge chunks, you may want to shift to a different level of generality. Of course, sequences and scenes can also be further subdivided into subsegments. As a tool for segmenting any film, a linear diagram like ours for *Citizen Kane* is of great help. Stretching the parts out like clothes on a line lets you visualize formal relations (beginnings and endings, parallels, patterns of development, etc.).

Narrative Analyses of Films

Sample narrative analyses of films may be found in Alan Williams, "Narrative Patterns in *Only Angels Have Wings*," *Quarterly Review of Film Studies* **1**, 4 (November 1976): 357–372; Kristin Thompson, "The Duplicitous Text: An Analysis of *Stage Fright*," *Film Reader* **2** (1977): 52–64, and "Parameters of the Open Film: *Les Vacances de M. Hulot*," *Wide Angle* **3**, 1 (Spring 1978); Joyce Nelson, "*Mildred Pierce* Reconsidered," *Film Reader* **2** (1977): 65–70; Robin Wood, *Hitchcock's Films* (New York: Barnes, 1969) and "Dusan Makavejev," in Ian Cameron *et al.*, *Second Wave* (New York: Viking, 1970), pp. 7–33; Maureen Turim, "Gentlemen Consume Blondes," *Wide Angle* **1**, 1 (Spring 1976): 68–77. The Indiana University Press Filmguide series tended to emphasize narrative form, and these monographs are often good introductions to problems of film analysis. Typical are these: James Naremore, *Filmguide to Psycho* (Bloomington: Indiana University Press, 1973); E. Rubinstein, *Filmguide to The General* (Bloomington: Indiana University Press, 1973); Ted Perry, *Filmguide to 8½* (Bloomington: Indiana University Press, 1975); and David Bordwell, *Filmguide to La Passion de Jeanne d'Arc* (Bloomington: Indiana University Press, 1973).

For advanced study, a difficult but rewarding analysis of Welles's *Touch of Evil* has been done by Stephen Heath in "Film and System: Terms of Analysis," *Screen* **16**, 1 (Spring 1975): 7–77, and **16**, 2 (Summer 1975): 91–113.

"Rosebud"

Critics have scrutinized few films as closely as *Citizen Kane*. For a sampling, see Joseph McBride, *Orson Welles* (New York: Viking, 1972); Charles Higham, *The Films of Orson Welles* (Berkeley: University of California Press, 1970); David Bordwell, *"Citizen Kane,"* in Bill Nichols, ed., *Movies and Methods* (Berkeley: University of California Press, 1976); and Robert Carringer, "Rosebud, Dead or Alive: Narrative and Symbolic Structure in *Citizen Kane*," *PMLA* (March 1976): 185–193.

Pauline Kael, in a famous essay on the making of the film, finds "Rosebud" a naive gimmick. Interestingly, her discussion emphasizes *Citizen Kane* as part of the journalist-film genre and tends not to go beyond the detective-story aspect. See *The Citizen Kane Book* (Boston: Little, Brown, 1971), pp. 1–84. In contrast, other critics find "Rosebud" an incomplete answer to Thompson's search; compare particularly the Bordwell and Carringer analyses above. Another account of the making of the film is offered by Peter Bogdanovich, in "The Kane Mutiny," *Esquire* **78**, 4 (October 1972): 99–105, 180–190. For a balanced account of *Kane*'s classical and modern features, see Peter Wollen, "Introduction to *Citizen Kane*," *Film Reader* **1** (1975): 9–15. Half of this issue of *Film Reader* is devoted to analyzing *Citizen Kane*.

Part Three
Film Style

We are still seeking to understand the principles by which a film is put together. Chapter 2 showed that the concept of film form offers a way to do this. We went on to look at one important formal distinction operating in films—narrative or nonnarrative systems. Chapter 3 suggested some ways to understand such systems. Our analysis of *Citizen Kane* exemplified how we can grasp the narrative form of a film.

But when we see a film, we don't engage with only a narrative or nonnarrative system. We see a *film*—not a play or a painting or a novel. Analyzing a painting demands a knowledge of color, shape, and composition; analyzing a novel demands knowledge of language; analyzing music requires knowlege of sound. In sum, to understand form in any art, we need to be familiar with the specific medium in which that art exists. Similarly, our understanding of a film's form must also consider features of the *film medium*.

Part Three of this book investigates the film medium. We shall look at four sets of techniques characteristic of cinema: two techniques of the shot, mise-en-scene and cinematography; the technique that relates shot to shot, editing; and the relation of sound to film images. We shall survey the various opportunities and choices that each technique offers to the filmmaker. More important, we shall concentrate on the *formal functions* of each technique. How may a film technique guide our expectations in a given film? How may it furnish motifs for the overall film? How may a technique develop across a film? How may one technique reinforce another? In Part Three we will discover that in any one film, certain techniques tend to create a formal system of their own. That is, a film will tend to repeat and develop specific techniques in patterned ways. This unified, repeated, developed, and significant use of specific film techniques we shall call *style*. In our study of particular films (Keaton's *Our Hospitality*, Renoir's *Grand Illusion*, Bresson's *A Man Escaped*, Huston's *Maltese Falcon*, and Eisenstein's *October)*, we shall see how each filmmaker creates a distinctive stylistic system.

The use a film makes of the medium—the film's style—does not, however, exist in antiseptic isolation from its use of narrative or nonnarrative form. We shall find, again and again, that *film style interacts with film narrative* in many ways. Often film techniques support and enhance narrative form. Mise-en-scene, camera framing and movement, continuity editing, and other devices can function to advance the cause-effect chain, create parallels, or manipulate story/plot relations. But also, film style may become separated from narrative form, attracting our attention in its own right. Unusual camera movements, discontinuity editing, and other uses of film technique can call our attention to the techniques as a somewhat independent system. In either event, the four chapters that follow will continually return to the problem of the relations—sometimes peaceful, sometimes antagonistic—between the formal system of narrative and the formal system of style.

CHAPTER 4

THE SHOT: MISE-EN-SCENE

Of all the techniques of cinema, mise-en-scene is the one with which we are most familiar. After seeing a film, we may not recall the cutting or the camera movements, the dissolves, or offscreen sound, but we will almost surely recall items of mise-en-scene. We remember the costumes in *Gone With the Wind* or the bleak, chilly lighting in Charles Foster Kane's Xanadu. We retain vivid memories of the rainy, gloomy settings in *The Big Sleep* or the cozy family home in *Meet Me in St. Louis*. We recall Harpo Marx clambering over Edgar Kennedy's peanut wagon *(Duck Soup)* and Katharine Hepburn defiantly splintering Cary Grant's golf clubs *(The Philadelphia Story).* In short, many of our most sharply etched memories of the cinema turn out to be of this or that element of mise-en-scene.

What Is Mise-en-Scene? ■

In the original French, the term means "having been put into the scene," and it was first applied to the practice of stage direction. Film scholars, extending the term to film direction as well, use the term to signify the director's control over what appears in the film frame. As you would expect from the term's theatrical origins, mise-en-scene includes those aspects that overlap with the art of the theater: setting, lighting, costume, and the behavior of the figures. In controlling the mise-en-scene, the director *stages the event* for the camera.

Realism ■

Before we analyze mise-en-scene in detail, one preconception must be brought to light. Just as viewers often remember this or that bit of mise-en-scene from a film, so viewers often judge mise-en-scene by standards of "realism." A car seems to be "realistic" for the period the film depicts, or a gesture doesn't seem realistic because "real people don't act that way."

But realism as a standard of value involves several problems. Concepts of realism become quite elusive, varying across cultures, through time, and even among individuals. Marlon Brando's acclaimed "realist" performance in the 1954 film *On the Waterfront* looks stylized today. To some contemporary American critics, William S. Hart's Westerns seem realistic, but to French critics of the 1920s, the same films seemed as artificial as a medieval epic. Moreover, realism has become one of the most problematic issues in the philosophy of art. (See Notes and Queries for examples.) Most important, to rigidly insist on realism for all films can blind us to the great range of mise-en-scene possibilities.

Look, for instance, at the picture from *The Cabinet of Dr. Caligari* (Fig. 4.32). The contorted trees, and the stylized slump of the sleepwalker as he falls certainly don't accord with our conception of normal reality. Yet to condemn the film on grounds of realism would be foolish, for the film uses stylization to present a madman's fantasy.

It is better, then, to examine the *functions* of mise-en-scene than to dismiss this or that element that happens not to match our conception of realism. This means that the filmmaker may use *any* system of mise-en-scene and that we should analyze its functions in the total film—how mise-en-scene is motivated, how it varies or develops, how it works in relation to narrative and nonnarrative forms.

The Power of Mise-en-Scene ■

To confine the cinema to some notion of realism would indeed impoverish mise-en-scene. For mise-en-scene has the power to transcend normal conceptions of reality, as we can see from a glance at the cinema's first master of the technique, Georges Méliès. Méliès's mise-en-scene enabled him to create a totally imaginary world on film.

A caricaturist and magician, Méliès became fascinated by the Lumière brothers' demonstration of their short films in 1895. After building a camera copied from the Lumière machine, Méliès began filming unstaged street scenes and moments of passing daily life. One day, the story goes, he was filming at the Place de l'Opéra and his camera jammed as a bus was passing. After some tinkering, he was able to resume filming, but by this time the bus had gone and a hearse was passing in front of his lens. When Méliès screened the film, he discovered something totally unexpected: A moving bus seemed to transform itself instantly into a hearse! Whether apocryphal or not, the tale at least dramatically illustrates Méliès's recognition of the magical powers of mise-en-scene. He would devote most of his efforts to cinematic conjuring.

But to do so would require preparation, since Méliès could not count on lucky accidents like the bus/hearse transformation. He would have to plan and stage action for the camera. Drawing on his experience in theater, Méliès built one of the first film studios—a small, crammed affair bristling with theatrical machinery, balconies, trapdoors, and sliding backdrops. His cartoon talent enabled him to sketch detailed shots beforehand and to design sets and costumes. Figures 4.1 and 4.2 illustrate the close correspondence between his planning drawings and the finished shots. As if this weren't enough, Méliès starred in his own films (often in several roles per film). His desire to create magic effects led Méliès to control the mise-en-scene of his films down to the last detail.

Such control was necessary to create the fantasy world he envisioned. Only in a studio could Méliès produce *The Mermaid,* in which an undersea world is created out of an actress in costume, a fishtank placed in front of the camera, some sets, and "carts for monsters" (see Fig. 4.3). Only by careful preparation and setting design could he present the illusion of *The Man with the Rubber Head,* wherein Méliès inflates the disembodied head of Méliès! Figures 4.4 and 4.5 show that the trick depended on double exposure and Méliès in a cart rolling toward the camera.

Méliès's "Star-Film" studio made hundreds of short fantasy and trick films based on such a control over every element in the frame, and the first master of mise-en-scene demonstrated the great range of technical possibilities it offers. The legacy of Méliès's magic is a delightfully unreal world wholly obedient to the whims of the imagination.

Figure 4.1

Figure 4.2

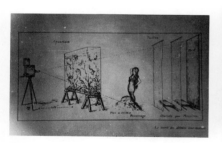

Figure 4.3

Figure 4.4

Figure 4.5

Aspects of Mise-en-Scene ■

What possibilities for selection and control does mise-en-scene offer the director? We can mark out four general areas and indicate some potential uses of each.

Setting

Since the earliest days of cinema, critics and audiences have understood that setting plays a more active role in cinema than in most theatrical styles. André Bazin writes:

> The human being is all-important in the theatre. The drama on the screen can exist without actors. A banging door, a leaf in the wind, waves beating on the shore can heighten the dramatic effect. Some film masterpieces use man only as an accessory, like an extra, or in counterpoint to nature, which is the true leading character.

Cinema setting, then, can come to the forefront; it need not be only a container for the action, but can dynamically enter into the narrative action.

Figure 4.6

The filmmaker may control setting in many ways. One way is to select an already existing locale in which to stage the action, a practice stretching back to the earliest films. Louis Lumière shot his short comedy, *L'Arroseur Arrosé* (Fig. 4.6) in a garden, and Victor Sjöstrom filmed *The Outlaw and His Wife* in the splendor of the Swedish countryside (production still, Fig. 4.7). Similarly we see the desert in *Lawrence of Arabia*, Gaudi buildings in Antonioni's *The Passenger*, and Times Square in *The French Connection*.

Figure 4.7

On the other hand, the filmmaker may choose to construct the setting. Méliès understood the increased control yielded by shooting in a studio, and many subsequent filmmakers followed his lead. In France, Germany, and especially the United States, the ability to create a wholly artificial world on film led to the development of several approaches to constructing setting. Some directors have emphasized historical authen-

Figure 4.8

ticity. For example, Erich Von Stroheim prided himself on meticulous research into details of locale, as the production still from *Greed* illustrates
(Fig. 4.8). Even so recent a film as *All the President's Men* took a similar
tack, seeking to duplicate the Washington *Post* office on a sound stage
by reproducing every detail of the original newsroom; even waste paper
from the office was scattered around the set.

Other films have not been so committed to historical verisimilitude.
Though D. W. Griffith studied the various historical periods presented in
Intolerance, his Babylon—part Assyrian, part Egyptian, part American
—constitutes a personal image of that city (production still, Fig. 4.9).
Similarly, in *Ivan the Terrible* Sergei Eisenstein freely stylized the decor
of the Czar's palace to harmonize with the lighting, costume, and figure
movement, so that characters crawl through doorways that resemble
mouseholes and stand frozen before allegorical murals.

Setting can crowd the actors, as in the cluttered production still
from *The Scarlet Empress* (Fig. 4.10), or it can be reduced to zero, to a
striking *absence*, as in many animated films and in Godard's *Le Gai
Savoir* and Dreyer's *La Passion de Jeanne d'Arc* (Figs. 4.11 and 4.12). Setting can be convulsed and contorted, as in the angular streets and tilting
buildings of *The Cabinet of Dr. Caligari* (a film heavily influenced by
German Expressionist painting). Whether selected or constructed, histor-

Figure 4.9

Figure 4.10

Figure 4.11

Figure 4.12

ically authentic or stylized, setting can function in a virtually infinite number of ways.

The manipulation of a shot's setting for narrative functions also implies that the setting may create "props"—another term indicating the overlap between cinematic and theatrical mise-en-scene. When part of the setting is motivated to operate actively within the ongoing action, we are justified in calling it a prop. Needless to say, films teem with examples: the snowstorm paperweight that shatters at the beginning of *Citizen Kane*, the little girl's balloon in *M*, the cactus rose in *The Man Who Shot Liberty Valance*, Cesare's coffin in *The Cabinet of Dr. Cali-*

gari. In the shower murder in *Psycho* the shower curtain is at first an innocuous part of the setting, but when the killer enters the bathroom, the curtain functions to screen her (him?) from our sight. Later, after the murder, Norman Bates uses the curtain to wrap up the victim's body. In *The Crime of M. Lange* a poster outside Batala's publishing house advertises its new dime-novel series "Javert," but after Batala has left the company, Lange and his associates pull the poster down to reveal the window and room that have for so long been blocked from sunlight. Later we shall examine in more detail how elements of setting can weave through an entire film to form motifs within the narrative.

Costume

Like setting, costume can have specific functions in the total film, and the range of possibilities is huge. Erich Von Stroheim, for instance, was as passionately committed to authenticity of dress as of setting, and he was said to have created underwear that would instill the proper mood in his actors even though it was never to be seen in the film. One shot of Griffith's *Musketeers of Pig Alley* shows Lillian Gish in a faded and threadbare dress, which summarizes the poverty in which the character lives. Costumes may, on the other hand, be quite stylized, calling attention to their purely graphic qualities. In *The Cabinet of Dr. Caligari* the somnambulist Cesare wears a jet-black leotard, whereas the woman he abducts wears a white nightgown. Throughout *Ivan the Terrible* costumes are carefully orchestrated with one another in their colors, their textures, and even their movements. Note, for instance, the plastic sweep and dynamism of the robes in the shot of Ivan and Philip (Fig. 4.13). In *Meet Me in St. Louis* characters become associated with specific costume colors. And costume may in fact be so sparse as to bleed into the setting: In one scene of *THX 1138* George Lucas strips both locale and clothing to stark white on white.

Figure 4.13

Just as settings may furnish props for the film's ongoing narrative system, so may costume. To think of Dracula is to think of how his billowing cape enwraps him, unfolds, and closes decisively around a victim. To recall the film director Guido in Fellini's *8½* is to recall those sunglasses which he persistently uses to shield himself from the world outside. In cinema any portion of a costume may become a prop: a pince-nez (*Potemkin*), a pair of shoes (*Strangers on a Train, The Wizard of Oz*), a cross pendant (*Ivan the Terrible*), a jacket (*Le Million*). When Hildy Johnson, in *His Girl Friday*, switches from her role of aspiring housewife to that of reporter, her stylish hat with its low-dipping brim is replaced by a "masculine" hat with its brim pushed up, journalist-style (Figs. 4.14 and 4.15). Film genres make extensive use of costume props—the six-gun, the automatic pistol, the top hat and cane. Every major film come-

Figure 4.14

Figure 4.15

Figure 4.16

Figure 4.17

Figure 4.18

Figure 4.19

dian has turned a specific costume into a panoply of props: Chaplin's cane and derby, Fields's cigar and top hat, Laurel and Hardy's derbies and too-tight suits, Harpo Marx's capacious pockets, Jacques Tati's pipe, raincoat, and "hush-puppy" shoes. Examples could be multiplied indefinitely, but the crucial point is that costume motifs may function to unify the film's overall form.

Lighting

The manipulation of an image's lighting controls much of its impact. In cinema, lighting is more than just illumination that permits us to see the action. Lighting can define the space of the frame, separating foreground from background or linking up areas of the composition. Lighting can articulate the textures of a face, a piece of wood, a spiderweb, a girder, rain speckling a pane of glass. Lighting can mold and shape. It can reveal (a spotlight can zero our attention toward a person or object) and can conceal (a shadow may shield a figure or object). A few shadows imply an entire prison in one shot from De Mille's *The Cheat* (Fig. 4.16). Josef von Sternberg, one of the cinema's great masters of lighting, wrote that "the proper use of light can embellish and dramatize every object." For our purposes, we can isolate three major features of film lighting: its *quality*, *direction*, and *source*.

Lighting *quality* refers to the relative intensity of the illumination. "Hard" lighting creates clearly defined shadows, whereas "soft" lighting creates a diffused illumination. The terms are relative, and many lighting situations will fall in between the extremes, but we can in practice easily recognize the differences. Hard lighting creates bold shadows and crisp textures and edges. The veins in the hand are emphasized by the hard lighting in Fig. 4.17, a close-up from Robert Bresson's *Pickpocket*. In Fig. 4.18, a shot from *Ivan the Terrible*, softer lighting blurs contours and textures and makes for more diffusion and gentler contrasts between light and shade.

The *direction* of lighting in a shot refers to the path of light from its source(s) to the object lit. "Every light," writes von Sternberg, "has a point where it is brightest and a point toward which it wanders to lose itself completely. . . . The journey of rays from that central core to the outposts of blackness is the adventure and drama of light." For convenience we can distinguish among frontal lighting, side lighting, back lighting, under lighting, and top lighting.

Frontal lighting can be recognized by its tendency to eliminate shadows. In Plate 1, a shot from Godard's *La Chinoise*, the result of such frontal lighting is a fairly flat-looking image.

In *Touch of Evil* Welles uses a hard *sidelight* to sculpt the characters' features. Note the sharp shadows cast by noses, cheekbones, and lips, as well as the shadows cast on the left wall (Fig. 4.19).

The illumination of only the edges of the figure is characteristic of *backlighting*. In Fig. 4.20, a frame from *Citizen Kane*, the figure is almost a silhouette. Backlighting defines depth by sharply distinguishing an object from its background.

Underlighting suggests that the light comes from below the subject. In Fig. 4.21 (from Abel Gance's *La Roue*), the underlighting situates an offscreen fireplace.

Rare in its pure state, *top lighting* usually appears along with light coming from other directions. In the shot from Ivan Mosjoukin's *Le Brasier Ardent* shown in Fig. 4.22, the spotlight shines from above.

Figure 4.20

Figure 4.21

Figure 4.22

Figure 4.23

As these later photos suggest, seldom will a shot have only one *source* of light. Lighting specialists have developed a versatile range of standardized sources, but two will suffice for our purposes: the *key light* and the *fill light*. The key light is the primary lighting source of the image, providing the dominant illumination and casting the dominant shadows. A fill light may then be used to "fill in," to soften or eliminate shadows cast by the key light. Through a combination of the two, the exact degree of lighting can be controlled.

Figure 4.24

In Fig. 4.23 the key light is hard and comes from the side. No fill light softens the shadows, as is often the case in this film, Welles's *Touch of Evil*.

Figure 4.24 shows a frame from Gance's *La Roue*. Note that the bold backlighting is complemented by a key light from the left and a fill light from the right.

Figure 4.25 shows a shot from *Bezhin Meadow*, in which Eisenstein uses a number of light sources and directions. The key light falling on the figures comes from the left side, but it is hard on the face of the old woman in the foreground and softened on the face of the man by a fill light from the right. The thin rim of light on the old woman's shoulder indicates some backlighting from the doorway as well.

Figure 4.25

Figure 4.26

Figure 4.27

Figure 4.28

Hollywood filmmaking developed the custom of using at least *three* light sources per shot: key light, fill light, and backlight. In Fig. 4.26, a shot from William Wyler's *Jezebel*, the heroine is lit from the right (key), the left (fill), and the rear. This practice came to be known as "three-point lighting." Usually a fourth, less intense light would be applied to the background.

All of these examples illustrate the cinema's ability to control the look and function of a shot through light quality, direction, and source. No component of mise-en-scene is more important than "the drama and adventure of light."

Figure Expression and Movement

The director may also control the behavior of various figures in the mise-en-scene. Here the word "figures" covers a wide range of possibilities, since the figure may represent a person but could also be an animal (Lassie, the donkey Balthasar, Donald Duck), an object (as in *Ballet Mécanique's* choreography of bottles, straw hats, and kitchen utensils), or even a pure shape (as in an abstract film). Mise-en-scene can give such figures the power to express feelings and thoughts; it can also dynamize them to create various kinetic patterns.

In Fig. 4.27 (from *Seven Samurai*) the samurai have won the battle with the bandits. Virtually the only movement in the frame is the driving rain, but the slouching postures of the men leaning on their spears express their tense weariness.

In *White Heat* figure expression and movement cooperate to present an image of psychotic rage. In Fig. 4.28 Cody Jarrett (James Cagney), after learning of his mother's death, flings himself furiously at a guard.

In Oskar Fischinger's *Motion Painting #1* (see Fig. 3.1) abstract shapes move in time to accompanying music.

Although abstract shapes can become a part of the mise-en-scene, we usually think of figure expression and movement as "acting." Too often viewers (and critics) tend to treat actors as representing real people in a story. Yet as we have seen, filmmakers who control mise-en-scene do not "capture" already existing events; rather, they create the event to be filmed. An actor's performance in a film consists of visual elements (appearance, gestures, facial expressions) and sound (voice, effects). At times, of course, an actor may contribute only visual aspects, as in the silent period of film history. Similarly, an actor's performance may sometimes exist only on the sound track of the film; in *A Letter to Three Wives*, Celeste Holm's character, Addie Ross, speaks a narration over the images, but never appears on the screen.

Since the character the actor creates is in part a figure in the mise-en-scene, films may contain a wide variety of acting styles. It is not always fruitful to judge an actor's performance by its "believability" in relation to some view we may have of reality. In a very stylized film an attempt to give a "realistic" performance would make the character stand out as inappropriate to his or her place in the context of the film's total mise-en-scene.

This fact indicates a clue for analyzing actors' performances. If the actor looks and behaves in a manner *appropriate* to his or her character's *function* in the context of the film, the actor has given a good performance—*whether or not* he or she has behaved as a real person might in such circumstances.

A few examples will serve to demonstrate how many acting styles can exist. Each may be appropriate to its context because cinema itself has so many different styles of mise-en-scene. A film may strive for a certain resemblance to "realistic" behavior by attributing character behavior to psychological motivation. Thus in *Winchester 73* James Stewart plays a man driven by a desire for revenge that borders on psychosis; his extremes of gesture and facial expression are acceptable because they fit the traits which have been assigned to his character earlier in the film (see Fig. 4.29).

Psychological motivation is less important in a film like *Trouble in Paradise*, a sophisticated comedy of manners in which the main concern is with broad character *types* in a comic situation. In Fig. 4.30 two rivals for the affections of the same man pretend to be friends, although they actually wish to trick each other. Their exaggerated smiles and postures are amusing because we know the underlying situation. Again, the performances are perfectly appropriate to the style of the film.

Comedy doesn't provide the only motivation for stylization. *Ivan the Terrible* is a film that heightens every element—music, costume, setting—to create a larger-than-life portrait of its hero; Nikolai Cherkasov's broad, abrupt gestures fit in perfectly with all of these other elements to create an overall unity of composition (Fig. 4.31).

The actor is always a graphic element in the film, but some films underline this fact. In *The Cabinet of Dr. Caligari* Conrad Veidt's portrayal of the somnambulist resembles a dance; his behavior blends in with the graphic elements of the setting—his body echoes the tilted tree trunks, his arms and hands their branches and leaves (Fig. 4.32). As we shall see in our examination of the history of film styles, the graphic design of this scene in *Caligari* typifies the systematic distortion characteristic of German Expressionism.

In *Breathless,* director Jean-Luc Godard juxtaposes Jean Seberg's face with a print of a Renoir painting (Fig. 4.33). We might think that Seberg is giving a wooden performance, for she simply poses in the frame and turns her head; indeed, her acting in the entire film is not conven-

Figure 4.29

Figure 4.30

Figure 4.31

Figure 4.32

Figure 4.33

tionally expressive. Yet as Fig. 4.33 points up, her face and general appearance are visually appropriate for her function in the film.

As with every element of a film, acting cannot be judged on some universal scale separate from the concrete context. We must understand the function of the figure's expression and movement within the film's overall formal system.

Mise-en-Scene in Space and Time ■

Setting, costume, lighting, and figure expression and movement—these are the elements of mise-en-scene. Yet one seldom appears in isolation. Each element usually combines with others to create a specific system in every film. The general formal principles of unity/disunity, similarity, difference, and development will guide us in analyzing how specific elements of mise-en-scene can function together. What are some ways in which mise-en-scene affects our attention? What pulls our eye to a portion of the frame at a given moment?

Looking is purposeful; what we look *at* is guided by our hunch about what to look *for*. In viewing an image we make hypotheses on the basis of many factors. One general factor is the total form of the film, especially if the form is narrative. As a powerful cue for our attention, narrative often steers us through the image: If the shot shows a crowd, for example, we scan the faces in search of our hero. Another controlling factor is sound. As we shall see in Chapter 7, sound can draw attention to areas of the image in many ways. A third source of control is written language, as when a title cues us what to look for in the following frame. Fourth, mise-en-scene creates purely spatial and temporal factors that may guide our viewing of the image.

Space

Figure 4.34

One important pictorial factor that guides our attention is the overall relation of foreground to background. Lighting, setting, costume, and figure behavior may be organized to present a flat space, a shallow space, or a deep space, depending on what *depth cues* are present. Depth cues pick out different planes in the shot and thus enable us to distinguish foreground from background.

Purely flat space is very rare, but in Fig. 4.34, a frame from Norman McLaren's *Begone, Dull Care,* there are few cues for depth. The space has only two planes, as in an abstract painting.

In *La Passion de Jeanne d'Arc*, the shots often suggest only two planes—a foreground (occupied by a face) and a neutral background (a wall or the sky). In Fig. 4.35 the only depth cue is *overlap* of edges—the face's edge stands out against the setting.

Figure 4.35

Plate 2, a shot from *La Chinoise*, adds one more plane—drifting cigarette smoke—to the other two (face and setting). This illustrates that in cinema *movement* is an important depth cue (the shifting smoke indicates another plane in the foreground). Note also the *cast shadow* in the background, which is yet another depth cue.

Aerial perspective, or the hazing of more distant planes, is another depth cue; we tend to see clearer elements as belonging to the foreground. In William Wyler's *Jezebel*, as in many Hollywood films, lighting (and lens focus) blur the setting to make the closer objects stand out more (Fig. 4.36).

Figure 4.36

In Straub and Huillet's *Chronicle of Anna Magdalena Bach* the mise-en-scene provides several depth cues: overlap of edges, cast shadows, and *size diminution*. That is, figures and objects farther away from us are seen to get proportionally smaller; the smaller the figure appears, the farther away we believe it to be (Fig. 4.37). This reinforces our sense of there being a deep space with considerable distances between the various planes.

At this point, you might want to return to shots illustrated earlier in this chapter to compare how different images use depth cues in the mise-en-scene to create different foreground/background relations.

Though the foreground/background relations in the mise-en-scene often guide our "reading" of the shot, they aren't the only pictorial factors at work. Lines and shapes, light/dark patterns, and expressive movement also play a part. To see how such factors work together to guide our attention, let's examine two examples from Carl Dreyer's film *Day of Wrath*.

In the first shot, Anne is standing before a grillwork panel (Fig. 4.38). She is not speaking, but since she is a major character in the film, the narrative already directs us to her. Setting, lighting, costume, and

Figure 4.37

Figure 4.38

Figure 4.39

figure expression create pictorial cues that confirm our expectations. The setting yields a network of intersecting lines against which the delicate curves of her face and shoulders stand out for our notice. The lighting creates a patch of brightness on the right half of the frame and a patch of darkness at the left. Anne's face is precisely at the intersection of these two areas, and her face becomes sculpted by their interplay.

Coordinated with the lighting in creating the pattern of light and dark is Anne's costume—black dress punctuated by white collar, black cap edged with white—which again emphasizes her face. Given the two major planes of the shot, the geometrical background distinguishes the more important foreground element, Anne. Moreover, Anne's slightly sad face, the most expressive element in this frame, ensures that our scanning of the frame will pause there. Thus although there is no motion in the frame, Dreyer has controlled our attention through the lines and shapes, the lights and darks, and the foreground and background relations set up by the overall mise-en-scene.

In the second shot, Dreyer sets up a to-and-fro movement of our eye from the couple to the cart (Fig. 4.39). Again, the plot helps us, since the characters and cart are crucial narrative elements. Sound helps too, since Martin is at the moment explaining to Anne the function of the cart. But mise-en-scene also plays a role. The foreground/background relations set up a unified interplay between Anne and Martin on the front plane and the cart of wood on the rear plane. The prominence of the couple and the cart is reinforced by line and shape, light and dark: The elements are defined by hard-edged lines rather than by soft blurring of the trees and by dark costumes within the predominantly bright lighting and setting.

Although all of our examples in this chapter have been in black and white, the principles of mise-en-scene hold for color as well. Settings, costumes, lighting, and figure behavior can have prominent functions in a color film. Most of Jacques Tati's *Playtime* utilizes settings and costumes that are gray, brown, and black—cold, steely colors (see Plate 3). In the latter part of the film, however, beginning in the restaurant scene, the characters' costumes start to sport gay reds, pinks, and greens (see Plate 4). This color change supports a development in the narrative action from an inhuman city landscape to one based on human pleasures.

In *Ivan the Terrible* color is integrated with lighting. As Vladimir stares, the lighting changes from a neutral white to a startling blue (see Plates 5 and 6). Interestingly, this change is not motivated realistically (say, by showing a new source of blue light) but psychologically, to express Vladimir's sudden panic.

Similarly, all of the elements of mise-en-scene can utilize color to create graphic patterns of movements, foreground and background relations, line and shape, and light and dark. Color can assist lighting in defining texture and movement. Color can also become a depth cue, especially if bright, saturated colors are set against more muted ones. In one shot from Ozu's *An Autumn Afternoon* (Plate 7), many depth cues are at work—overlap, aerial perspective, movement, and perspective diminution—but more striking is the bright gold, red, and silver bridal costume in the foreground. In fact, red and silver hues form a motif that starts in the very first shot of the film (Plate 8).

The graphic configurations of color need not be narratively motivated, however—even if they occur in a narrative film. Robert Bresson's *Lancelot du Lac* uses a very sparse and muted color scheme throughout, and brighter colors tend to stand out by their relative *lack* of narrative motivation (Plate 9).

Time

So far we have examined some spatial factors that guide our viewing of an image. But our viewing takes time, too. Only a very short shot forces us to grasp the image "all at once." In most shots we get an initial overall impression that creates formal expectations. These expectations are quickly modified as our eye roams around the frame. A static composition, such as our first shot from *Day of Wrath* (Fig. 4.38), may keep pulling our eye back to a single element (here, Anne's face). A composition emphasizing movement becomes more "time-bound" because our glance may be directed from place to place by various speeds, directions, and rhythms of movements. In the second image from *Day of Wrath* (Fig. 4.39) Anne and Martin are turned from us (so that expression and gesture are minimized), and they are standing still. Thus the single movement in the frame—the cart—catches our attention. But when Martin speaks and

Figure 4.40

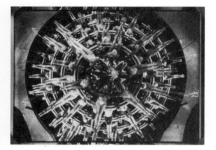

Figure 4.41

Figure 4.42

turns, we look back at the couple, then back at the cart, and so on, in a shuttling, dynamic shift of attention. In such ways mise-en-scene can control not only *what* we look at, but also *when* we look at it.

Indeed, a film's mise-en-scene may set up its own unique sense of movement in time. Normally, for instance, we ignore the movement of scratches and dust on a film. But in David Rimmer's *Watching for the Queen*, in which the first image is an absolutely static photograph, the jumping bits of dust on the film draw our attention. Consider the varying qualities of movement in these three films.

1. Stasis dominates Fig. 4.40, a shot from Ozu's *Diary of a Tenement Gentleman*. Only the slight flapping of a crumpled newspaper blowing in the wind catches our eye. In the absence of other motion, even such a minimal movement can become very striking.

2. In Fig. 4.41, a shot from Busby Berkeley's *Footlight Parade*, there are strongly opposed movements in foreground and background: alternating tiers of bodies swing their legs in opposite directions.

3. In Fig. 4.42, a shot from Jacques Tati's *Playtime*, the frame contains movements of differing speeds and directions. Various actions compete for our attention, forcing us to scan the frame in order to notice as much as possible.

Mise-en-scene as a whole, then, helps compose the film shot in space and time. Setting, lighting, costume, and figure behavior interact to create patterns of foreground and background, line and shape, light and dark, and movements. These patterns are systems—unified, developing systems that not only guide our perception from frame to frame, but also help create the overall form of the film.

Narrative Functions of Mise-en-Scene: <u>Our Hospitality</u> ■

Like all film techniques, mise-en-scene has various functions in various contexts. First are *pictorial functions*. At the minimum, mise-en-scene provides the shot with graphic elements, which in addition to their own intrinsic appeal can develop into formal patterns. A totally abstract film, such as John Whitney's *Permutations* or Hans Richter's *Rhythmus 21*, will present its "setting" and "figure behavior" as highly stylized designs. Alternatively, most films seek to represent three-dimensional objects and space on the screen; in these representational films the mise-en-scene elements will present identifiable locales, figures, costumes, etc., but the graphic functions of mise-en-scene will still be present. As we saw in the two examples from *Day of Wrath*, every shot in every film may be examined as a set of shapes, tonalities, and movements in space and time.

(Chapter 6 will show how editing may develop these patterns from shot to shot.)

Second are *narrative functions*. In most films graphic functions of mise-en-scene are accompanied by narrative functions. Mise-en-scene can obviously affect the narrative of a film: We compare and contrast locales, identify salient characters, and follow developing actions as the mise-en-scene presents them to us. It is, then, often useful to ask how any aspect of mise-en-scene functions in relation to the film's narrative system. More specifically, we can ask how any aspect of mise-en-scene unifies the narrative through becoming a *motif*—an element that recurs significantly throughout the film. Through the fundamental formal principles of unity, function, similarity, difference, and development, mise-en-scene may furnish motifs for the overall form of the film.

Let us look at how mise-en-scene could function in relation to the narrative system of an entire film. *Our Hospitality*, like most films of Buster Keaton, exemplifies how mise-en-scene can economically advance the narrative and create a pattern of motifs. And since the film is a comedy, we shall find that the mise-en-scene also creates gags. *Our Hospitality*, then, exemplifies what we shall find in our study of every film technique: An individual element will almost always have *several* functions, not just one.

Consider, for example, how the settings function within *Our Hospitality*'s narrative. The film begins with a Prologue showing how the feud between the McKays and the Canfields results in the deaths of the young Canfield and of Willie McKay's father. Willie's mother flees with her baby from their Southern home to the North. The main action begins with the now-adult Willie McKay, in New York, receiving word of his inheritance; he then takes a train south to claim his estate. Once Willie returns to the South, we see a continuous shift in setting as he travels from the town street, then to his "estate," then to the river, and so on. Thus the action depends heavily on shifts of setting that establish Willie's two journeys, as baby and as man, and later his wanderings around town.

More specifically, certain settings fulfill distinct narrative functions. The McKay "estate," which Willie envisions as a mansion, turns out to be a tumbledown shack. The McKay place is paralleled to (contrasted with) the Canfields' palatial plantation home. In narrative terms the Canfield home gains even more functional importance when the Canfield father forbids his sons to kill Willie on the premises: "Our code of honor forbids us to shoot him while he is a guest in our house." (Once Willie overhears this, he determines *never* to leave.) Thus, ironically, the home of Willie's enemies becomes the only safe spot in town, and many scenes are organized around the Canfield brothers' attempts to lure Willie out. At the end of the film another setting takes on significance: the meadows,

Figure 4.43

Figure 4.44

Figure 4.45

Figure 4.46

mountains, river banks, rapids, and waterfalls across which the Can-fields pursue Willie. In such ways every setting becomes highly motivated by the narrative cause-effect chain and parallels.

The same narrative motivation marks the film's use of costume. Willie is characterized as a city boy through his dandified suit, whereas the Southern gentility of the elder Canfield is represented through his white planter's suit. Props become important here: Willie's suitcase and umbrella succinctly summarize his role as visitor and wanderer, and the Canfields' ever-present pistols remind us of their goal of continuing the feud. Note also that it is a change of costume (Willie's disguising himself as a woman) that enables him to escape from the Canfield household.

Like setting, lighting in *Our Hospitality* has both general and specific functions. The film systematically alternates scenes in darkness with scenes in daylight. The feuding in the Prologue takes place at night; Willie's trip South and wanderings through the town occur in daylight; that night Willie comes to dinner at the Canfields' and stays as a guest; next day, the Canfields pursue him; and the film ends that night with the marriage of Willie and the Canfield daughter. More specifically, the somber action of the Prologue is distinguished from the rest of the film by its hard, side key lighting. When the elder McKay flings off his hat to douse the lamp, the illumination changes from a soft blend of key, fill, and backlight to a stark key light from the fireplace (see Figs. 4.43 and 4.44). Later, the murder scene is played out in flashes of light—lightning, gunfire—which fitfully punctuate the overall darkness. The bulk of the film, however, is evenly lit in the three-point method.

Most economically of all, virtually every bit of the behavior of the figures functions to support and advance the cause-effect chain of the narrative. The way Canfield sips and savors his julep establishes his Southern ways; his Southern hospitality in turn will not allow him to shoot a guest in his house. Similarly, Willie's every move expresses his diffidence or resourcefulness. Even more concise is the way in which the film uses the arrangement of figures and setting in depth to present two narrative events simultaneously. While the engineer drives the locomotive, the other cars pass him on a parallel track (Fig. 4.45). Or, in another shot, the Canfield boys in the foreground make plans to shoot Willie, while in the background Willie overhears them and starts to flee (Fig. 4.46). In yet another shot, while Willie ambles along unsuspectingly in the background, one Canfield waits in the foreground to ambush him (Fig. 4.47). Thanks to depth in the spatial arrangement, Keaton is able to pack together and connect two story events, resulting in a tight narrative construction.

All of these devices for narrative economy considerably unify the film, but some other elements of mise-en-scene function as specific

motifs. For one thing, there is the repeated squabble between the anony-
mous husband and wife. On his way to his "estate" Willie passes a husband beating his wife; Willie intervenes to protect her; the wife proceeds
to thrash Willie for butting in. On Willie's way back, he passes the same
couple, still fighting, but studiously avoids them; nevertheless, the wife
aims a kick at him as he passes. The mere repetition of the motif
strengthens the film's narrative unity, but it functions thematically, too,
as another joke on the contradictions surrounding the idea of hospitality.

Figure 4.47

Other motifs recur. Willie's first hat is too tall to wear in a jouncing
railway coach. (When it gets crushed, he trades it for the familiar Keaton
trademark, a porkpie hat.) Willie's second hat serves to distract the Canfields when Willie coaxes his dog to fetch it. There is also a pronounced
water motif in the film. Water as *rain* conceals from us the murders in the
Prologue and later saves Willie from leaving the Canfield home after
dinner ("It would be the death of anyone to go out on a night like this!").
Water as a *river* functions significantly in the final chase. And water as a
waterfall appears early in the film, when the demolition of a dam
showers Willie; later, a ravine waterfall becomes the setting for Willie's
rescue of the Canfield daughter. (Compare Fig. 4.48 with Fig. 4.56.)

Figure 4.48

Two specific motifs of setting powerfully unify the narrative. First
there is the recurrence of an embroidered sampler hanging on the Canfield wall: "Love Thy Neighbor." It appears initially in the Prologue of
the film, when seeing it motivates Canfield's attempt to stop the feud.
The sampler reappears at the end when Canfield, enraged that Willie has
married his daughter, glances at the wall, reads the inscription, and resolves to end the years of feuding. His change in attitude is motivated by
the earlier appearance of the sampler motif. There is also a "gun rack"
motif. In the Prologue each feuder goes to his fireplace mantlepiece to get
his pistol. Later, when Willie arrives in town, the Canfields hurry to their
gun rack and begin to load their pistols. Near the end of the film, when
the Canfields return home after failing to find Willie, one of the sons
notices that the gun rack is now empty. And in the final shot, when the
Canfields accept the marriage and lay down their arms, Willie produces
from all over his person a staggering assortment of pistols taken (as a
precaution) from the Canfields' own supply. Thus mise-en-scene motifs
unify the film through their repetition, variation, and development.

Yet *Our Hospitality* is more than a film whose narrative system
relates economically to patterns of mise-en-scene. It is a comedy, and one
of the funniest. We should not be surprised to find, then, that Keaton
uses mise-en-scene for gags. Indeed, so unified is the film that most of the
elements that create narrative economy also yield comic effects.

The mise-en-scene bristles with many individually comic elements.
Settings are exploited for amusement—the ramshackle McKay estate, the

Figure 4.49

Figure 4.50

Figure 4.51

Figure 4.52

Broadway of 1830, the specially cut train tunnel (Fig. 4.49). Gags of costume also stand out. Willie's disguise is divulged by a gap in the rear of his skirt; later, Willie puts the same costume on his horse to distract the Canfields. Most strongly, comedy arises from the behavior of the figures. The railroad engineer's high kick unexpectedly swipes off his conductor's hat. (Keaton's father, Joe, played this role and in Fig. 4.50 demonstrates one of his famous vaudeville stunts.) The elder Canfield sharpens his carving knife with ferocious energy, just inches from Willie's head. When Willie lands at the bottom of the river, he stands there looking left and right, his hand shading his eyes, before he realizes where he is. Later, Willie scuds down the river, leaping out of the water like a fish and skidding across the rocks.

Perhaps the only aspect of mise-en-scene that competes with the comic brilliance of the figures' behavior is the film's use of deep space for gags. Many of the shots we've already examined function to create comedy as well: The engineer stands firmly oblivious to the separation of train cars from engine (see Fig. 4.45), just as Willie is unaware that the Canfield boy is lurking murderously in the foreground (see Fig. 4.47).

Even more striking, though, is the deep-space gag that follows the demolition of the dam. The Canfield boys have been searching the town for Willie. In the meantime, Willie sits on a ledge, fishing. As the water bursts from the dam and sweeps over the cliff, it completely engulfs Willie (Fig. 4.51). At that very instant, the Canfield brothers step into the foreground, still looking for their victim (Fig. 4.52). The water's conceal-ment of Willie reduces him to a neutral background for the movement of the Canfields. Keaton's erasure of the background plane and the sudden revelation of a new foreground plane confirms André Bazin's observation that slapstick comedy succeeded because "most of its gags derived from a comedy of space, from the relation of men to things and to the surrounding world."

However appealing the individual gags are, *Our Hospitality* patterns its comic motifs as strictly as it does its other motifs. The film's journey-pattern often arranges a series of gags according to a formal principle of "theme and variations." For instance, during the train trip south, a string of gags is based on the idea of people encountering the train: Several people turn out to watch it pass, a tramp rides the rods, and an old man chunks rocks at the engine. Another swift series of gags takes the train tracks themselves as its "theme": The variations include a humped track, a donkey blocking the tracks, curled and rippled tracks, and finally no tracks at all.

Figure 4.53

But the most complex theme-and-variations series can be seen in the motif of "the fish on the line." Early in *Our Hospitality* Willie is angling and hauls up a miniscule fish. Shortly afterward, a huge fish yanks him into the water (Fig. 4.53). Later in the film, through a series of mishaps, Willie becomes tied by a rope to one of the Canfield sons. A great many gags arise from this umbilical-cord linkage, especially one that results in Canfield's being pulled into the water as Willie was earlier.

Figure 4.54

Perhaps the single funniest moment in the film occurs when Willie realizes that since the Canfield boy has fallen off the rocks, so must he (see two phases of this shot in Fig. 4.54 and 4.55). But even after Willie gets free of Canfield, the rope remains tied around him. So in the film's climax Willie is dangling from a log over the waterfall like the fish on the end of his fishing pole (Fig. 4.56). Here again, one element fulfills multiple functions: The fish-on-the-line device advances the narrative, becomes a motif unifying the film, and takes its place in a pattern of parallel gags involving variations of Willie on the rope. In such ways *Our Hospitality* becomes an outstanding example of the integration of cinematic mise-en-scene with narrative form.

Figure 4.55

Summary ■

The viewer who wants to study mise-en-scene should look for it systematically. Watch, first of all, for how setting, costume, lighting, and the behavior of the figures present themselves in a given film. (As a start, try to trace only one sort of element—say, setting, or lighting—through an entire film.) We should also reflect on the patterning of mise-en-scene elements: How do they function? How do they constitute motifs that weave their ways through the film? In addition, we should notice how mise-en-scene is patterned in space and time to attract and guide the viewer's attention through the process of watching the film. Finally, we should try to relate the system of mise-en-scene to the narrative system of the film. Hard-and-fast prejudices about realism are of less value here than an openness to the great variety of mise-en-scene possibilities. Awareness of

Figure 4.56

those possibilities will better help us to determine the narrative functions of mise-en-scene.

Notes and Queries ■

On "Realism" in Mise-en-Scene

Many film theorists have seen film as a realistic medium par excellence. For such theorists as Siegfried Kracauer, André Bazin, and V. F. Perkins, cinema's power lies in its ability to present a recognizable reality. The realist theorist thus often values authenticity in costume and setting, "naturalistic" acting, and unstylized lighting. "The primary function of decor," writes V. F. Perkins, "is to provide a believable environment for the action" (*Film as Film,* Baltimore: Penguin, 1972, p. 94). André Bazin praises the Italian neorealist films of the 1940s for "faithfulness to everyday life in the scenario, truth to his part in an actor" (*What Is Cinema?*, Vol. II, Berkeley: University of California Press, 1970, p. 25).

Though mise-en-scene is always a product of selection and choice, the realist theorist may value the filmmaker who creates a mise-en-scene that *appears* to be reality. Kracauer suggests that even apparently "unrealistic" song and dance numbers in a musical can seem impromptu (*Theory of Film*, New York: Oxford University Press, 1965), and Bazin considers a fantasy film such as *The Red Balloon* realistic because here "what is imaginary on the screen has the spatial density of something real" (*What Is Cinema?*, Vol. I, Berkeley: University of California Press, 1966, p. 48).

These theorists, then, set the filmmaker the task of representing some historical, social, or aesthetic reality through the selection and arrangement of mise-en-scene. Though this book postpones the consideration of this problem—it lies more strictly in the domain of film theory—the "realist" controversy is worth your examination. For arguments against a realist theory of mise-en-scene, see Noël Burch, *Theory of Film Practice* (New York: Praeger, 1973) and Sergei Eisenstein, *Film Form* (New York: Harvest, 1949) and *The Film Sense* (New York: Harvest, 1942).

The Staged and the Unstaged in Mise-en-Scene

The distinction between "documentary" and "fiction" films often rests on the difference between the staged and the unstaged. In a fiction film the filmmaker controls the mise-en-scene completely, but the documentary film purports to present unstaged events. For example, in *A Hard Day's Night* Richard Lester staged a Beatles concert and was able to control setting, lighting, costumes, and figure behavior. But in *Monterey Pop* and *Woodstock* the filmmakers had no such control over the event and exercised their control by means of other techniques—editing, camera work, and sound. Does the concept of documentary assume that the filmed event retains at least some of its "rawness" as an unstaged part of the world?

Interestingly, disputes periodically arise about faked documentaries, which use actors, rehearse shots, or falsify time and place. These disputes often revolve around the assumption that documentary should not rely on mise-en-scene. The most famous "borderline" documentary is Leni Riefenstahl's *Triumph of the Will*. Controversy still rages as to whether the film simply documented the 1934 Nazi Party Congress or whether the event was staged especially for the film. If the latter is true, the film would be the most stupendous effort of mise-en-scene in film history.

Most films we see, however, utilize mise-en-scene, and the technique is used not only in live-action films, but also in animated and abstract films. Indeed, the animated film constitutes the extreme limit of the director's control of mise-en-scene—the most controlled sort of film there is. A good introduction to the subject is John Halas and Roger Manvell, *The Technique of Film Animation* (London: Focal Press, 1968).

Lighting

One of the most fascinating aspects of mise-en-scene is lighting. John Alton's *Painting With Light* (New York: Macmillan, 1949) and Gerald Millerson's *Technique of Lighting for Television and Motion Pictures* (New York: Hastings House, 1972) are excellent surveys of the techniques as practiced in the Hollywood cinema. See also James Wong Howe, "Lighting" and Victor Milner, "Painting with Light," in *Cinematographic Annual* I (1930) (New York: Arno Press, 1972), pp. 47–60 and 91–108 for older but informative discussions.

One of the cinema's masters of lighting, Josef von Sternberg, has much to say on the subject in his entertaining autobiography, *Fun in a Chinese Laundry* (New York: Macmillan, 1965). Raoul Coutard discusses a different notion of lighting in "Light of Day," in Toby Mussmann, ed., *Jean-Luc Godard* (New York: Dutton, 1968), pp. 232–239. Hollywood cinematographers recall their lighting experiments in Charles Higham, *Hollywood Cameramen* (London: Thames and Hudson, 1970). Detailed studies of the history of film lighting may be found in Patrick Ogle, "Technological and Aesthetic Influences upon the Development of Deep Focus Cinematography in the United States," *Screen* XIII, 1 (Spring 1972): 45–72 and in Peter Baxter, "On the History and Ideology of Film Lighting," *Screen* XVI, 3 (Autumn 1975): 83–106.

Depth

Though film directors have of course manipulated depth and flatness of
the shot since the beginning of cinema, critical understanding of these
spatial qualities did not emerge until the 1940s. It was then that André
Bazin called attention to the fact that certain directors staged their shots
in unusually deep space. Bazin singled out F. W. Murnau (for *Nosferatu*
and *Sunrise*), Orson Welles (for *Citizen Kane* and *The Magnificent
Ambersons*), William Wyler (for *The Little Foxes* and *The Best Years of
Our Lives*), and Jean Renoir (for practically all of his 1930s work). Today
we would add Kenji Mizoguchi (for *Osaka Elegy, Sisters of Gion,* and
others) and even Sergei Eisenstein (for *Old and New, Ivan the Terrible,*
and the unreleased *Bezhin Meadow*). By offering us depth and flatness as
analytical categories, Bazin increased our understanding of mise-en-
scene. (See "The Evolution of the Language of Cinema," in *What Is
Cinema?* Vol. I.) See also V. F. Perkins, *Film as Film.*

Guiding the Viewer's Eye

Not surprisingly, it was also Bazin who suggested that shots staged in
depth and shot in deep-focus give the viewer's eye greater freedom than
do flatter, shallower shots: The viewer's eye can roam across the screen.
(See Bazin, *Orson Welles* [New York: Harper & Row, 1978].) Noël Burch
takes issue: "All the elements in any given film image are perceived
as equal in importance" (*Theory of Film Practice,* p. 34). Psychological
research on pictorial perception suggests, however, that viewers do
indeed scan images according to specific cues. A good review of the subject, with bibliography, may be found in Julian Hochberg, "The
Representation of Things and People," in E. H. Gombrich *et al., Art,
Perception, and Reality* (Baltimore: Johns Hopkins University Press,
1972), pp. 47–94. In cinema, static visual cues for "when to look where"
are reinforced or undermined by movement of figures or of camera, by
sound track and editing, and by the overall form of the film.

CHAPTER 5

THE SHOT: CINEMATOGRAPHIC PROPERTIES

Mise-en-scene is at bottom a theatrical notion: The filmmaker stages an event to be filmed. But a total account of cinema as an art cannot stop with simply what is put in front of the camera. The "shot" does not exist until patterns are inscribed on a strip of film. The filmmaker also controls what we will call the *cinematographic* qualities of the shot—not only what is filmed but also *how* it is filmed. This consists of control over three features: (1) the photographic qualities of the shot; (2) the framing of the shot; and (3) the duration of the shot. This chapter surveys these three areas of control.

The Photographic Image ■

Cinematography (literally, "writing in movement") depends to a large extent on photography ("writing in light"). Sometimes the filmmaker will eliminate the camera and simply work on the film itself, but even when drawing, painting, or scratching directly on film, punching holes in it, or growing mold on it, the filmmaker is carving patterns of light onto celluloid for the eye of the viewer. Most often the filmmaker uses a camera to regulate how light from some object will be photochemically registered on the sensitized film. In any event, the filmmaker can select the range of tonalities, manipulate the speed of motion, and transform perspective.

The Range of Tonalities

Whether an image seems all grays or stark black and white, what range of colors is present in an image, whether textures stand out clearly or recede into a haze—all of these factors lie within the filmmaker's control. The handling of film stock and the exposure can alter the subtlest visual qualities of the shot.

Figure 5.1

Figure 5.2

Film *stocks*, or the different types of photographic film, vary in their light sensitivity. Some are "slow"—that is, are not as sensitive to light as are "faster" film stocks. This means that more light is needed to produce an image on a slower stock than is needed to produce an equally bright image on a faster stock.

The choice of film stock has many artistic implications, for the relative "speed" of the stock affects the image's appearance. A slower black-and-white film stock will usually produce a larger range of grays, more detail in textures, and softer contrasts. A faster black-and-white film stock tends toward a narrower gray range, less well-defined details, and a more contrasty look. In *Les Carabiniers* (Fig. 5.1), Jean-Luc Godard chose a very fast film stock, which yielded a grainy, contrasty, almost bleached-out look. But in *The Crime of M. Lange* (Fig. 5.2), Jean Renoir used a significantly slower film stock, which rendered many more grays as well as details of line and texture.

The choice of film stock need not work only with blacks, whites, and shades of gray. As everyone knows, color film stocks may produce a wider range of the spectrum. In fact, different color film stocks yield different color qualities. Technicolor (as used in *Meet Me in St. Louis*, Plates 10 and 11), the Agfa color stock which Eisenstein used to film part of *Ivan the Terrible* (Plates 5 and 6), DeLuxe, Eastmancolor (Plates 1, 2, 3, 4, and 9), "Trucolor," and others—all have different visual features, and filmmakers working in color tend to select film stocks with great care.

The tonalities of the image can also be affected by the control of how the film is developed in the laboratory. Historically, the earliest film stocks ("orthochromatic") were fairly slow and sensitive only to certain frequencies of light. But when the filmmaker wanted darker scenes to be well exposed, the laboratory could develop the footage to compensate for the comparative slowness of the film. In the mid-1920s, however, orthochromatic film began to be replaced by the faster panchromatic stock, which was sensitive to a wider range of colors of light. The gain in flexibility meant a loss of the rich image quality of orthochromatic stock. And, expectably, soon laboratories were "pushing" panchromatic in the developing process to make the film even faster.

Today, the filmmaker can control laboratory development to achieve particular effects. A good example is the *Les Carabiniers* frame (Fig. 5.1); its "newsreel" quality is heightened by both the film stock and lab work that "pushed" the film stock. "The positive prints," Godard has explained, "were simply made on a special Kodak high contrast stock. This treatment was necessary to obtain, rightly or wrongly, the same photographic quality as the early Chaplin films, with the black and white contrasts of the old orthochromatic stock. Several shots, intrinsically too gray, were duped again sometimes two or three times, always to their highest contrast."

Needless to say, the laboratory process of developing and printing may alter the tonalities of the color stock just as it alters black and white. (Early Technicolor films are now often printed on Eastmancolor stock, which results in a slight loss of brightness in the hues.) But various procedures may also add color to footage originally shot in black and white. *Tinting* casts a uniform hue of any chosen color over the image. *Toning* (see Plate 12, from Vera Chytilova's *Daisies*) reproduces the image's gray scale in the desired color (the whites are white, the grays slightly colored, the blacks heavily colored). Both tinting and toning were common in the silent cinema. Night scenes were colored blue, firelight red, and so on.

Rarest of all is the difficult process of *hand-coloring*, whereby portions of black-and-white images are painted in colors, frame by frame. The ship's flag in Eisenstein's *Potemkin* was originally hand-colored red against a blue sky. A recent use of hand-coloring may be seen in Makavejev's *Innocence Unprotected* (see Plate 13). Other color laboratory possibilities include developing a film in a solution intended for another film stock or exposing a film to light during development (the latter process being called solarization). One result of such laboratory manipulations of color can be seen in Plate 16, from Chytilova's *Daisies*.

The range of tonalities in the image is also affected by the *exposure* of the image in the course of the photographic process. The filmmaker usually controls exposure by regulating how much light passes through the camera lens, though images shot with "correct" exposure can also be overexposed or underexposed in developing and printing. We commonly think that a photograph should be "well exposed"—neither underexposed (too dark, not enough light admitted through the lens) or overexposed (too bright, too much light admitted through the lens). But even "correct exposure" usually offers some latitude for choice; it is not an absolute. Moreover, the filmmaker can use overexposure or underexposure for specific effects. In *Ordet* Carl Dreyer has deliberately overexposed the windows, washing out the upper portion of the image (Fig. 5.3). And in the American *films noirs* of the 1940s, the cinematographer sometimes underexposed the image to increase the pervasive darkness.

Figure 5.3

Exposure can in turn be affected by *filters*—slices of glass or gelatin put in front of the lens of camera or printer to reduce certain frequencies of light reaching the film. Filters thus alter the range of tonalities in quite radical ways. A filter can make footage shot by sunlight seem to be shot by moonlight (so-called "day-for-night" filming). Hollywood cinematographers during the 1930s sought to add glamor to close-ups of women by means of diffusion filters and silks. Filters applied during shooting or during printing can drastically alter the color image. In all, in both filming and in laboratory work the choice of both film stock and exposure powerfully affects the image that we see on the screen.

Speed of Motion

A gymnast's performance seen in slurred slow-motion, ordinary action accelerated to comic speed, a tennis serve stopped in a freeze-frame—we are all familiar with the effects of the control of the speed of motion. Of course, the filmmaker who stages the event to be filmed can (within limits) dictate the pace of the action. But that pace can also be controlled by a photographic power unique to cinema: the control of the depicted speed of movement.

The speed of the motion we see on the screen depends on the relation between the rate of the film as shot and printed and the rate of projection. Both rates are calculated in frames per second. The standard rate of shooting and projection for the sound cinema is 24 frames per second. This means that during shooting, the camera will normally expose 24 separate frames per second, that that rate will not be changed during printing, and that in theaters the projector will show the film at the same rate. Hence the depicted movement will look "normal."

But as far as speed of movement is concerned, any particular rate of shooting and projection is less important than the *uniformity* between shooting, printing, and projection rates. It would not affect speed of movement if a film were shot and printed at 16 frames per second, as long as it was also projected at 16 frames per second. For example, we are so used to seeing silent films with jerky, accelerated movements that we assume that the films always looked that way. But before 1930 or so, standards for shooting and projection rates were simply different from those now. A film might be shot at 16 or 18 or 20 frames per second. As long as projectors had variable-speed controls, the projectionist could match the rate of projection to the original shooting rate.

If naturalness of depicted movement depends on uniformity among shooting, printing, and projection rates, the speed of that depicted movement can be altered by varying any of the three factors. We are most used to projection's effects on movement speed, because although most silent projectors could vary their speeds, most contemporary film projectors cannot. Thus a film shot at 16 frames per second will often be shown at 24 frames per second ("sound speed"), accelerating the action with adverse results. Projection can, of course, also affect depicted movement through freeze-framing or through running the film in reverse.

Projection usually lies outside the filmmaker's control, but he or she can control the rate of the film during shooting and laboratory printing. The camera's drive mechanism can be adjusted to vary the shooting rate. Assuming a constant projection speed, the fewer frames per second shot, the greater the acceleration of the screen action. The more frames per second shot, the slower the screen action. This may sound inconsistent, but it makes sense. Filming at 12 frames per second yields only those 12 frames for every second the action lasts. If we project that film at the standard 24 frames per second, the 12 frames will be onscreen for only half a second—the action will seem twice as fast as it originally was. Such "fast-motion" effects are achieved by slowing the rate of the film passing through the camera. In the silent era the cameraperson simply cranked the camera drive handle fewer times per second. The result was often a comic effect; the chief experiment in the use of undercranking for noncomic purposes occurs in F. W. Murnau's *Nosferatu,* in which the vampire's accelerated motion represents supernatural power.

On the other hand, if we film a one-second action at 48 frames per second and project it at 24 frames per second, the event the audience sees will consume two seconds onscreen—it will be slowed down. Overcranking, or cranking quite quickly, was used notably in Dziga Vertov's *Man with a Movie Camera* to render sports events in detailed slow motion, a function that of course persists today.

When cameras became motorized, most still had a variable-drive control. In Rouben Mamoulian's *Love Me Tonight* the members of a hunt decide to ride quietly home to avoid waking the sleeping deer; their ride is filmed in slow motion to create a comic depiction of quietness. By knowing the final projection speed, the filmmaker can vary the shooting speed and create a wide range of depicted speeds of action.

Although 24 frames per second became the normal shooting speed, special cameras were designed to accomplish specialized tasks. For *time-lapse* cinematography, which permits us to see the sun set in seconds or a flower sprout, bud, and bloom in a minute, a very low shooting speed is required—perhaps one frame per minute, hour, or even day. For *high-speed* cinematography, which may seek to record a bullet shattering glass, the camera may expose more than 1000 frames per second! A common range on cameras today is between 8 and 64 frames per second.

After filming, the filmmaker can still control movement speed on the screen through various laboratory procedures. The most common means used is the optical printer (see Fig. 1.5), which rephotographs an already processed film, copying all or part of each original frame onto another reel of film. Still assuming a constant speed of projection, the filmmaker can use the optical printer to skip frames (accelerating the action when projected), reprint a frame at desired intervals (slowing the action by *stretch-printing*), stop the action (repeat a frame over and over, to freeze the image for seconds or minutes), or even reverse the action. Nowadays some silent films are stretch-printed with every other frame repeated, so that they may run more smoothly at sound speed. We are familiar with freeze-framing, slow-motion, and reverse-motion print-ing effects from the "instant replays" of sports films and investigative documentaries. Many experimental films have made striking use of the optical printer's possibilities, especially Dziga Vertov's *Man with a Movie Camera* and Ken Jacobs's *Tom Tom the Piper's Son.*

Perspective Relations

You are standing on railroad tracks, looking toward the horizon. The tracks not only recede, but also seem to meet at the horizon. You glance at the trees and buildings along the tracks. They diminish by a simple, systematic rule: The closer objects look larger, the farther objects look smaller—even if they are actually of uniform size. The optical system of your eye, registering light rays reflected from the scene, supplies a host of information about scale, depth, and spatial relations among parts of the scene. Such relations are called *perspective* relations.

The lens of a photographic camera does roughly the same thing. It gathers light from the scene and transmits that light onto the flat surface of the film to form an image that represents size, depth, and other dimen-sions of the scene. One difference between the eye and the camera, though, is that photographic lenses may be changed and each type of lens will render perspective relations in different ways. If two different lenses photograph the same scene, the perspective relations in the resulting image could be drastically different. A wide-angle lens could exaggerate the depth you see down the track or could make the trees and buildings seem to bulge; a telephoto lens could drastically reduce the depth, mak-ing the trees seem very close together and nearly the same size. (Compare the visual effects on the faces in Figs. 5.5 and 5.6.)

Control of perspective relations in the image is obviously very important to the filmmaker. The chief variable in the process is the *focal length* of the lens. In technical terms the focal length is the distance from the center of the lens to the point where light rays converge to a point of focus. The focal length of the lens can affect perspective relations in several ways.

The focal length alters the perceived magnification, depth, and scale of things in the image. We usually distinguish three sorts of lenses on the basis of their effects on perspective.

1. *The wide-angle, or short focal-length, lens.* (In 35-mm cinema-tography a wide-angle lens today is usually about 25 mm.) Depending on aperture setting, the focal length, and subject-to-camera distance, this lens tends to distort straight lines toward the edges of the screen, bulging them outward. Depth is also exaggerated. Two drastic examples of wide-angle lens effects may be found in Jean-Luc Godard's *Pierrot le Fou* (Fig.

5.4) and Orson Welles's *Touch of Evil* (Fig. 5.5). Note how shape is distorted and scale exaggerated in both shots.

2. *The normal, or middle focal-length, lens.* (Today the average is around 50 mm.) The medium focal-length lens seeks to minimize perspective distortion.

Figure 5.4

3. *The telephoto, or long focal-length, lens.* (Today telephoto lenses range from 75 mm to 200 mm or longer.) The onscreen effects of longer lenses are usually as noticeable as those of wide-angle lenses. Generally, the space of the shot is flattened; depth is reduced and the planes seem squashed together. The most familiar uses of telephoto lenses are in the filming or televising of sports events. In a baseball game there will invariably be shots taken from almost directly behind the umpire. You have probably noticed that such telephoto shots make catcher, batter, and pitcher look unnaturally close to one another. Akira Kurosawa was famous for introducing extensive use of telephoto lenses into his films, as Fig. 5.6, a still from *Seven Samurai*, shows. Note how the figures seem very close together and almost the same size, even though the two facing front are actually quite far behind the third.

Figure 5.5

There is one sort of lens that offers the director a chance to manipulate focal length and hence transform perspective relations during a single shot. This lens is the zoom lens. A zoom lens is optically designed to permit the continuous varying of focal length. Zoom lenses were originally designed for aerial and reconnaissance photography; they gradually became a standard tool for newsreel filming. It was not, however, the general practice to zoom during shooting. The cameraperson varied the focal length as desired and then started filming. In the late 1950s, however, the increased portability of cameras led to a trend toward zooming while filming. Now the zoom lens is commonly used to substitute for moving the camera forward or backward. Onscreen, the zoom shot gives several cues for moving toward or away from a figure, chiefly by magnifying or demagnifying the objects filmed and by including or excluding surrounding space. The zoom, however, is not a genuine movement of the camera, since the camera remains stationary and the lens simply increases or decreases its focal length. Nevertheless, the zoom can produce very interesting and peculiar transformations of scale and depth, as demonstrated in a film such as Michael Snow's *Wavelength*; another example occurs in the opening scene of Francis Ford Coppola's *The Conversation*.

Figure 5.6

The impact that focal length can have on the image's perspective qualities is dramatically illustrated in Ernie Gehr's *Serene Velocity*. The scene is an empty corridor. Gehr shot the film with a zoom lens, which permitted him to change the len's focal length. Gehr explains that he:

Figure 5.7

Figure 5.8

Figure 5.9

divided the mm range of the zoom lens in half and starting from the middle I recorded changes in mm positions. . . . The camera was not moved at all. The zoom lens was not moved during recording either. Each frame was recorded individually as a still. Four frames to each position. To give an example: I shot the first four frames at 50 mm. The next four frames I shot at 55 mm. And then, for a certain duration, approximately 60 feet, I went back and forth, four frames at 50 mm, four frames at 55 mm; four frames at 50 mm, four frames at 55 mm; etc. . . . for about 60 feet. Then I went to 45–60 [mm] and did the same for about 60 feet. Then to 40–65, and so on.

The resulting film presents an image whose perspective relations pulsate rhythmically—first with little difference in size and scale (see Figs. 5.7 and 5.8), but gradually with a greater tension between a telephoto image and a wide-angle one. In a sense *Serene Velocity* takes as its subject the effect of focal length on perspective.

Focal length not only affects how shape and scale are magnified or distorted, but also determines the lens's depth of field. Depth of field is the range of distances before the lens within which objects can be photographed in sharp focus. Thus a lens with a depth of field of ten feet to infinity will render any object in that range clearly, but sharpness will decrease when the object moves closer to the lens (say, to four feet). A wide-angle (short focal-length) lens has a relatively greater depth of field than does a telephoto (long focal-length) lens.

Depth of focus should not be confused with the concept of deep space, used in Chapter 4. "Deep space" is a term for the way the filmmaker has established the action of the scene as taking place on several different planes, *regardless of whether or not all of these planes are in focus.* In the case of *Our Hospitality* those planes usually *are* in sharp focus, but in other films not every plane of deep space is in focus. Consider Fig. 5.9. In this shot from *The Crime of M. Lange*, the action is staged in three planes of deep space: Valentine in the foreground, Batala going out the door, and the concierge passing in the distance. But the shot does not display great depth of field, since the foreground plane (Valentine) is out of focus, whereas the two more distant planes are in focus. Deep space is a property of mise-en-scene, affecting how the image is staged; depth of field is a property of the photographic lens, affecting what planes of the image are in focus.

If depth of field controls perspective relations by choosing what planes will be in focus, what choices are open to the filmmaker? He or she may opt for what is usually called *shallow focus*—choosing to focus on only one plane and letting the other planes blur. Before 1940 it was common practice to shoot close-ups in shallow focus, making the faces sharp and the background hazy. Sometimes objects near the camera were thrown out of focus so that the sharper middle ground would claim the viewer's attention. But in the 1940s, partly due to the influence of *Citizen Kane*, Hollywood filmmakers began using faster film, shorter focal-length lenses, and more intense lighting to yield a greater depth of field. The contract-signing scene from *Citizen Kane* (Fig. 5.10) offers a famous example: From one plane near the lens (Bernstein's head) through several planes in the middle ground to the wall far in the distance, everything is in sharp focus. This practice came to be called *deep focus*.

Figure 5.10

Since the lens may be refocused at various points, the filmmaker may also adjust perspective relations while filming by *racking* or *pulling* focus. It is a cliché of contemporary cinema that a shot may begin on an object close to the lens—say, a tree branch—and rack-focus so that the branch blurs and the lovers in the distance spring into crisp focus. One shot in Chytilova's *Daisies* focuses initially on burning streamers in the foreground (Fig. 5.11) and then racks focus (and tilts down) to the women behind them (Fig. 5.12). Thus the lens can transform the depth, scale, and shapes within the scene to control our perception of space.

Figure 5.11

The image's perspective relations may also be affected by special procedures worth a brief mention. The grab bag of techniques known as "special effects" contains several ways that the filmmaker can manipulate spatial relations. There are *superimpositions* (produced either through double-exposure during filming or later in laboratory printing), wherein one image rests "on top of" another. Separately photographed planes of action may also be combined onto the same film to create the illusion that the two planes are adjacent; the various techniques for achieving this illusion are called *process shots*. For example, the filmmaker may project a film presenting one plane of action while photographing another plane—say, an actor—against that projection. This is what is being done in Fig. 5.13, a production still from *The Sands of Iwo Jima*. This is usually called *back projection*.

Figure 5.12

Figure 5.13

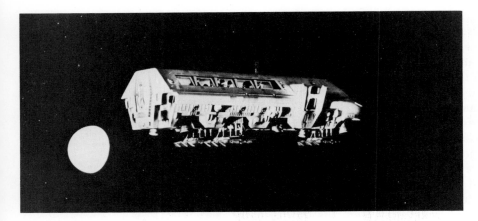

Figure 5.14

Figure 5.15

Figure 5.16

Or, the filmmaker may print two images together to represent two separate planes; such shots are called *matte* shots. Figure 5.14, a production still from *2001*, is composed of several images: one of the outer-space background, one of the spacecraft with blank portholes, and one of the portions inside the craft visible through the portholes. In printing, the ship was matted onto the sky, and the porthole views were matted onto the ship. Still other special-effects techniques include split-screen and multiple-frame techniques, whereby we see one or more separate images—each with its own separate perspective relations—side by side within the larger frame.

Like other film techniques, photographic manipulations of the shot are not ends in themselves. They function within the overall context of the film. Specific treatments of tonalities, speed of motion, or perspective should be judged less on criteria of "realism" than on criteria of function. For instance, many Hollywood filmmakers strive to make their back-projection shots unnoticeable. But in Jean-Marie Straub and Danièlle Huillet's *The Chronicle of Anna Magdalena Bach*, the perspective relations are yanked out of kilter by an inconsistent back-projection (Fig. 5.15). Since the film's other shots have been filmed on location in correct perspective, this blatantly artificial back-projection calls our attention to the visual style of the entire film. Similarly, Fig. 5.16, a shot from *Daisies*, looks unrealistic (unless we posit the man as being about two feet long), but Chytilova has used setting, character position, and deep focus to make a comic point about the two women's treatment of men. The filmmaker chooses not only how to register light and movement photographically, but also how those photographic qualities will function within the overall formal system of the film.

Figure 5.17

Figure 5.18

Framing ■

Important as they are, the photographic qualities of the image do not overshadow the act of framing the image. It may seem tenuous to talk of something as elusive as the border of the image, since it may seem a sheerly negative feature, a simple edge or break. (After all, literary critics don't talk of the margins of the pages in *Moby Dick*.) But in a film, the frame is not simply a neutral border; it produces a *certain vantage point* onto the material within the image. In cinema the frame is important because it actively *defines* the image for us.

If proof were needed of the power of framing, we need only turn to the first major filmmaker in history, Louis Lumière. An inventor and businessman, Lumière and his brother Auguste devised one of the first practical cinema cameras (Fig. 5.17). The Lumière camera, the most flexible of its day, doubled as a projector and as a developing tank. Whereas the bulky American camera invented by W. K. L. Dickson was about the size of an office desk (Fig. 5.18), the Lumière camera weighed only 12 pounds and was small and portable. As a result of its lightness, the Lumière camera could be taken outside and could be simply and quickly set up. Louis Lumière's earliest films presented simple events—workers leaving his father's factory, a game of cards, a family meal. But even at so early a stage of film history, Lumière was able to use framing to transform everyday reality into cinematic events.

Consider one of the most famous Lumière films, *The Arrival of a Train at La Ciotat Station* (1895). Had Lumière followed theatrical practice, he might have framed the shot by setting the camera perpendicular to the platform, letting the train enter the frame from one side, broadside to the spectator. But instead, Lumière positioned the camera at an oblique angle. The result is a dynamic composition, with the train arriv-

Figure 5.19

Figure 5.20

ing on a diagonal (Fig. 5.19). If the scene had been shot perpendicularly, we would have seen only a string of passengers' backs climbing aboard, but the oblique angle brings out many aspects of the passengers' bodies and several planes of action. We see some figures in the foreground, some in the distance. Simple as it is, this single-shot film, less than a minute long, aptly illustrates how choosing a position for the camera makes a drastic difference in the framing of the image and hence how we perceive the filmed event.

Consider another Lumière short, *Baby's Meal* (1895) (Fig. 5.20). Lumière selected a camera position that would emphasize certain aspects of the event. A long shot would have situated the family in its garden, but Lumière frames the figures at a medium distance, which downplays the setting but emphasizes the family's gestures and facial expressions. The frame's control of the scale of the event has also controlled our understanding of the event itself.

Framing can powerfully affect the image by means of: (1) the size and shape of the frame; (2) the way the frame defines onscreen and off-screen space; (3) the way framing controls the distance, angle, and height of a vantage point onto the image; and (4) the way framing can be mobile in relation to the mise-en-scene.

Frame Dimensions and Shape

We are so accustomed to the frame as a rectangle that we should remember that it need not be one. In painting and photography, of course, images have frames of various sizes and shapes: narrow rectangles, ovals, vertical panels, even triangles and parallelograms. In cinema the choice has been more limited.

The ratio of the length of one side of the frame to the length of the top or bottom is called the *aspect ratio*. The rough dimensions of this ratio were set quite early in the history of cinema by Edison, Dickson, Lumière, and other inventors. The film frame was to be rectangular, its aspect ratio approximately two to three. Nonetheless, there was no absolute agreement as to the exact dimensions. Many early sound films (e.g., F. W. Murnau's *Sunrise*, René Clair's *Le Million*) were shot in an almost square frame. Some silent filmmakers adventurously experimented with aspect ratios. Abel Gance shot and projected sequences of *Napoleon* (1927) in a format he called "triptychs." This was a wide-screen effect composed of three normal frames side by side. Gance sometimes used the effect to show a single huge expanse, sometimes to put three distinct images side by side (Fig. 5.21). In contrast, in 1930 the Soviet director Sergei Eisenstein argued for a square frame, which would make compositions along horizontal, vertical, and diagonal directions equally feasible. But in the early 1930s the Hollywood Academy of Motion Picture Arts and Sciences established the so-called Academy ratio of 1:1.33

Figure 5.21

Figure 5.22

Figure 5.23

(for reasons of sound and exhibition conditions). This was standardized throughout the world, and most of the frames reproduced in this book are in Academy ratio.

But the 1:1.33 ratio has not been unchallenged; several other aspect ratios have been used. The most common are *wide-screen* ratios, which make the frame a narrower rectangle. One frequently used process, CinemaScope, requires a special lens (the anamorphic lens) to produce its wide-screen effect. The CinemaScope ratio is 1:2.35. Figure 5.22, from *High and Low*, is a squeezed image on the strip of film, whereas Fig. 5.23 is the image as projected on the screen. (*High and Low* was shot in Toho-Scope, the Japanese equivalent of CinemaScope.)

Other wide-screen processes rely on masking the camera or projector lens to change the dimensions of the frame. Common masked ratios are 1:1.65 and 1:1.85. Figure 5.24 shows the viewfinder of a camera shooting in Panavision. The two black horizontal lines show the area of the image as it will be projected in a theater. But the portions at the top and bottom of the viewfinder will also be recorded on the film. This is because the film will eventually be shown on television, which has a different aspect ratio (about 1:1.33, the old Academy ratio). The viewfinder markings permit the camera operator to compose for several ratios.

Figure 5.24

Figure 5.25

Figure 5.26

Figure 5.27

Perhaps the ultimate extension of the rectangular aspect ratio comes with various experiments in 360° cinema (seen at various world's fairs and international expositions). In wraparound cinema ratios, the frame runs in a complete circle around the audience.

The rectangular frame, while by far the most common, has not prevented filmmakers from experimenting with other frame shapes. This has usually been done by attaching variously shaped masks over either the camera's or the printer's lens to block the passage of light. Masks have been of a variety of shapes and were quite common in the silent cinema. A moving circular mask that opens to reveal or closes to conceal a scene is called an *iris*. In *La Roue* Gance experimented with a variety of circular and oval masks (Fig. 5.25). In Fig. 5.26, a shot from Griffith's *Intolerance*, most of the frame is boldly blocked out to leave only a thin vertical slice, emphasizing the soldier's fall from the tower. A number of directors in the sound cinema have revived the use of irises and masks. In *The Magnificent Ambersons* (Fig. 5.27), Orson Welles uses an iris to close a scene; the old-fashioned device adds a nostalgic note to the sequence.

Masking is not the only way in which filmmakers have sought to alter the shape of the screen. Cinerama, introduced commercially in 1952, presents us with the rectangular screen slightly curved on the edges, a tactic that increases our sense of immersion in the image. Originally a process involving three separate frames projected side by side, Cinerama later became another anamorphic process, with the image squeezed onto a single frame.

Finally, mention should be made of those infrequent experiments with multiframe imagery. In this process several different images, each with its own size and shape of frame, appear within a larger frame. Recent films have experimented with this—the most commercially successful have been *The Boston Strangler* and *Sisters*—but it was not unknown to the silent cinema (Griffith and Gance sometimes employed such devices), and in the sound cinema it was sometimes used to present scenes of telephone conversations and the like. Since multiframe imagery permits a complex interaction among different graphic, spatial, and temporal properties, as well as between sizes and shapes of the various frames, it deserves more extended exploration by both filmmakers and film students.

Onscreen and Offscreen Space

Whatever its shape, the frame makes the image finite. The film image is bounded, limited. From an implicitly continuous world, the frame selects a slice to show us. Even in those early films so heavily dependent on theater, the characters enter the image *from* somewhere and go off *to* someplace else—*offscreen space*. Even in an abstract film we cannot resist the sense that the shapes and forces that burst into the frame come from somewhere. If the camera leaves an object or person and moves elsewhere, we will assume that that object or person is still there, outside the frame.

Noël Burch has pointed out six zones of offscreen space: the space beyond each of the four edges of the frame, the space behind the set, and the space behind the camera. It is worth considering how many ways a filmmaker can imply the presence of things in these zones. A character can direct looks or gestures at something offscreen. As we shall see in Chapter 7, sound can offer potent clues about offscreen space. And of couse something from offscreen can protrude part way into the frame. Virtually any film could be cited for examples of all these possibilities, but attractive instances are offered by films that utilize offscreen space for surprise effects.

In William Wyler's *Jezebel* the heroine, Julie, greets some friends in medium-shot (Fig. 5.28), when suddenly a huge fist holding a glass appears in the center foreground (Fig. 5.29). Julie looks off at it and

Figure 5.28

Figure 5.29

Figure 5.30

Figure 5.31

Figure 5.32

Figure 5.33

comes forward, the camera following her to frame her with the man who had toasted her (Figs. 5.30 and 5.31). The intrusion of the hand abruptly signals us of the man's presence; Julie's glance, the camera movement, and the sound track confirm our new awareness of the total space. The director has used the selective powers of the frame to exclude something of great importance and then introduced it with startling effect.

More systematically, D. W. Griffith's *Musketeers of Pig Alley* makes use of sudden intrusions into the frame as a motif developing across the whole film. When a gangster is trying to slip a drug into the heroine's drink, we are not aware that the Snapper Kid has entered the room until a plume of his cigarette smoke wafts into the frame (Fig. 5.32). At the film's end, when the Snapper Kid receives a payoff, a mysterious hand thrusts into the frame to offer him money (Fig. 5.33). Griffith has thus exploited the surprise latent in our sudden awareness that figures are offscreen.

The use of the fifth zone of offscreen space, that behind the set, is of course common; characters go out a door and are now concealed by a wall or a staircase. Somewhat rarer is the sixth zone—the offscreen space behind and near the camera. One famous example occurs in Jean Renoir's *Rules of the Game*, in the context of a shot in which characters virtually explode into the frame from offscreen space. André and Robert

Figure 5.34   Figure 5.35

are embroiled in a fistfight; during the melee, André is flung back onto and over a divan (Fig. 5.34). Then magazines start flying at him from over the top of the frame, from "behind us," as it were (Fig. 5.35). In such ways the director can turn the necessary limitations of the frame edge to advantage.

Angle, Level, Height, and Distance of Framing

The frame implies not only space outside itself, but also a position from which the material in the image is viewed. Most often, of course, such a position is that of the camera filming the event, but this need not always be true. In an animated film the position implied by the drawn frames is not necessarily the same position that the camera occupies during the making of the film; shots in an animated film may be framed as high or low angles, or long shots or close-ups, all of which simply result from the drawings selected to be photographed. Still, in what follows, we shall continue to speak of "camera angles," "camera level," "camera height," and "camera distance," with the understanding that these terms refer simply to what we see on the screen and need not always conform to what occurred during production.

Angle. The frame implies an *angle of vision* with respect to what is shown. It thus positions us at some angle onto the shot's mise-en-scene. The number of such angles is infinite, since there is an infinite number of points in space that the camera might occupy. In practice, we typically distinguish three general categories: the straight-on angle, the high angle, and the low angle. The straight-on angle is the most common. Figure 5.36 shows a straight-on angle from Straub and Huillet's *Chronicle of Anna Magdalena Bach.* The high angle positions us "looking down" at the material within the frame, as in Fig. 5.37, a shot from *Ivan the Terrible.* The low-angle framing positions us as "looking up" at the framed material (as in Fig. 5.38, again from *Ivan the Terrible).*

Figure 5.37

Figure 5.36

Figure 5.38

Figure 5.39

Level. We can also distinguish the degrees to which the framing is "level." This ultimately bears on the sense of gravity governing the filmed material and the frame. Assume that we are filming telephone poles. If the framing is level, the horizontal edges of the frame will be parallel to the horizon of the shot and perpendicular to the poles. If horizon and poles are at diagonal angles, the frame is *canted* in one manner or another. The canted frame is relatively rare, although a few films make heavy use of it, such as Carol Reed's *The Third Man* (see Fig. 5.39).

Height. Sometimes it becomes important to specify the sense that the framing gives us of being stationed at a certain *height*. Camera angle is, of course, related to height in a certain sense (to frame from a high angle entails being at a higher vantage point than the material in the image),

Figure 5.40

Figure 5.41

Figure 5.42

but camera height is not simply a matter of camera angle. For instance, the Japanese filmmaker Yasujiro Ozu often positions his camera only about three feet above the ground to film characters or objects on the floor (see Plates 7, 14, and 15). Note that this is not a matter of camera angle, for the angle is a straight-on one. Filming from such a low height with a straight-on angle is an important quality of Ozu's visual style.

Distance. Finally, the framing of the image stations us not only at a certain angle and height and on a level plane or at a cant, but also with respect to distance. Framing supplies a sense of being far away from or close to the mise-en-scène of the shot. This aspect of framing is usually called camera distance. In what follows, we shall use the standard measure—the scale of the human body—but any other filmed material would do as well. The examples are all from Carol Reed's *The Third Man*.

Figure 5.43

In the *extreme long shot*, the human figure is barely visible (Fig. 5.40). This is the framing for landscapes, bird's-eye views of cities, and other extensive entities. In the *long shot*, figures are more prominent, but the background still dominates (Fig. 5.41). The so-called *plan américain* ("American shot") is very common in the Hollywood cinema. For example, in Fig. 5.42 the human figure is framed from the knees up. This shot permits a nice balance of figure and surroundings. Shots at the same distance of nonhuman subjects are called medium long shots.

The *medium shot* frames the human body from the waist up (Fig. 5.43). Gesture and expression now become more visible. The *medium close-up* frames the body from the chest up (Fig. 5.44). The *close-up* is traditionally the shot emphasizing facial expression, the details of a gesture, or a significant object (Fig. 5.45). The *extreme close-up* singles out a portion of the face (eyes or lips), isolates a detail, magnifies the minute (Fig. 5.46).

Figure 5.44

Note that the scale of the photographed material within the frame is as important as any real "camera distance." From the same "camera distance," you could film a long shot of a person or of King Kong's elbow.

Figure 5.45

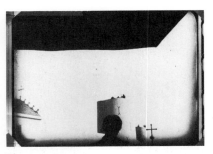

Figure 5.46   **Figure 5.47**

We would not call the shot in Fig. 5.47 (from *La Passion de Jeanne d'Arc*) a close-up just because only Jeanne's head appears in the frame; the framing is that of a long shot because in scale her head is relatively small. (If the framing simply adjusted downward, her whole body would be visible.) In judging camera distance, the relative proportion of the material framed provides the basic determinant.

Common confusions exist about framing. First, categories of framing are obviously matters of degree. There is no universal measure of camera angle or distance; no precise cut-off point distinguishes between a long shot and an extreme long shot, or a slightly low angle and a straight-on angle. Moreover, filmmakers are not bound by terminology; they rightly do not worry if a shot doesn't fit into traditional categories. Nevertheless, the overall concepts are clear enough to be workable. It is not of great importance whether the shot that cuts John Wayne off slightly above his waist is to be called a "true" medium shot or a "true" medium close-up. What is important is that we recognize how that framing functions in that particular film and that we notice when it reappears.

Functions of Framing. Another problem is more important. Sometimes we are tempted to assign absolute meanings to angles, distances, and other qualities of framing. It is tempting to believe that framing from a low angle automatically "says" that a character is powerful and that framing from a high angle presents him or her as dwarfed and defeated. Verbal analogies are especially seductive: A canted frame seems to mean that "the world is out of kilter."

The analysis of film as art would be a lot easier if technical qualities automatically possessed such hard-and-fast meanings, but individual films would thereby lose much of their uniqueness. The fact is that framings have no absolute or general meanings. In *some* films angles and distances carry such meanings as mentioned above, but in other films— probably most films—they do not. To rely on such formulas is to forget that meaning and effect always stem from the total film, from its opera-

Figure 5.48

Figure 5.49

Figure 5.50

Figure 5.51

tion as a system. The context of the film will determine the function of the framings, just as it determines the function of mise-en-scene, photographic qualities, and other techniques. Consider three examples.

At many points in *Citizen Kane*, low-angle shots of Kane do convey his looming power, but the lowest angles in the film occur at the point of Kane's most humiliating defeat—his miscarried gubernatorial campaign. In this context the low angle functions to isolate Kane against an empty background (Fig. 5.48). Note that angles of framing affect not only our view of the main figures, but also the background against which those figures may appear.

If the cliché were correct, Fig. 5.49, a shot from *North by Northwest*, would express the powerlessness of Van Damm and Leonard. In fact, Van Damm has just decided to eliminate his mistress by pushing her out of a plane, and he is saying: "I think that this is a matter best disposed of from a great height." The angle and distance of Hitchcock's shot wittily prophesy how the murder is to be carried out.

The world is hardly out of kilter in the shot from Eisenstein's *October* shown in Fig. 5.50. The canted frame dynamizes the effort of pushing the cannon.

These three examples should demonstrate that we cannot reduce the richness of cinema to a few recipes. We must, as usual, look for the *functions* the technique performs in the particular *context* of the total film.

Camera distance, height, level, and angle often take on clear-cut narrative functions. Camera distance can establish or reestablish settings and character positions, as we shall see when we examine the editing of the first sequence of *The Maltese Falcon*. A framing can isolate a narratively important detail—the tears of Henriette in *A Day in the Country* (Fig. 5.51), the snips of Jeanne's hair in *La Passion de Jeanne d'Arc* (Fig. 5.52).

Figure 5.52

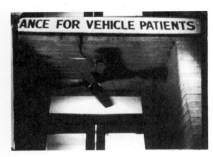

Figure 5.53

Figure 5.54

Figure 5.55

Framing also contributes to our grasping a given shot as "subjective" or not; in Fig. 5.53, a shot from *Possessed*, the distance and the angle furnish cues which impel us to read the shot as through the eyes of a patient being brought into a hospital on a stretcher. Less obviously, camera distance and angle can situate us in one area of the narrative's space. The angle and distance of Fig. 5.54, a shot from *Sergeant York*, do not show the preacher from any specific character's vantage point, but we are generally situated in the congregation's position. (An alternative distance and angle might view the preacher from a high angle and from the rear.) A canted framing may serve the narrative function of marking certain shots or sequences as distinctly different from the rest of the film: Note the canted framings in Fig. 5.55, a shot from a montage sequence in *The Roaring Twenties*.

Framings may serve the narrative in yet other ways. Across an entire film the repetitions of certain framings may associate themselves with a character or situation. That is, framings may become motifs unifying the film. In *The Maltese Falcon* Casper Gutman is frequently photographed from a low angle, emphasizing his obesity. Throughout *La Passion de Jeanne d'Arc* Dreyer returns obsessively to extreme close-up shots of Jeanne.

Or, certain framings in a film may stand out by virtue of their rarity. The ominously calm effect of the shot of the birds descending on Bodega Bay (in Hitchcock's *The Birds)* arises from the abrupt shift from straight-on medium shots to an extreme long shot from very high above the town (see Figs. 6.26 and 6.27). In a film composed primarily of long shots and medium shots, an extreme close-up will obviously have considerable force. Similarly, *Rio Bravo* is so full of nonsubjective straight-on angles that the very early shot of John Chance observed from the low-angle subjective viewpoint of Dude sharply marks Chance as the protagonist.

Even within a single sequence, we can note how camera angle, level, and distance change significantly. In the final sequence from Hitchcock's *Saboteur,* at the top of the Statue of Liberty, the hero is holding the coat-sleeve of the saboteur, who dangles precariously. The sleeve's stitching starts to tear. Hitchcock cuts from extreme long shots, high- and low-angled, canted this way and that, of the statue to extreme close-ups of the threads ripping out one by one. The scene's suspense derives principally from the drastic difference between the broad view (emphasizing the saboteur's danger) and the near-microscopic enlargement (his fate literally hangs by a thread).

But framings do not function only to emphasize narrative form. They can have their own intrinsic interest as well. Close-ups can bring out textures and details we might otherwise ignore. We can see the smallest surreptitious gestures of a pickpocket in the medium close-up from Robert Bresson's *Pickpocket* (Fig. 5.56); a series of similar close shots makes up a dazzling, balletlike scene in this film. Long shots can permit us to explore expansive spaces; part of the visual delights of Westerns, of *2001*, or of *Seven Samurai* result from long shots that make huge spaces manifest.

Figure 5.56

Our eye also enjoys the formal play presented by unusual angles on familiar objects, as when René Clair in *Entr'acte* frames a ballerina from straight below, transforming the figure into an expanding and contracting flower (Fig. 5.57). In *La Passion de Jeanne d'Arc* the upside-down framings (Fig. 5.58) are not motivated as a character's point of view; they exist as an exploration of framing in its own right. "By reproducing the object from an unusual and striking angle," writes Rudolf Arnheim, "the artist forces the spectator to take a keener interest, which goes beyond mere noticing or acceptance. The object thus photographed sometimes gains in reality, and the impression it makes is livelier and more arresting."

Figure 5.57

Framing may be used for comic effect, as Charlie Chaplin, Buster Keaton, and Jacques Tati have all shown. We have seen how in *Our Hospitality*, Keaton stages many gags in depth; now we can see that well-chosen camera angles and distances are also vital to the gags' success. Likewise, in Tati's *Playtime* mise-en-scene and camera position cooperate to create humorous visual patterns. At one point, M. Hulot turns around to discover that a doorman locking a door has suddenly sprouted "horns" (the door handles; see Plate 3). The visual pun issues from the precisely chosen camera angle and distance. Later in the film, a waiter is pouring champagne for a group of ladies (see Plate 4). But the camera angle and the positions of the figures carefully conceal most of the glasses, so that the waiter seems to be watering the flowers on the ladies' hats. We cannot classify all the nonnarrative functions of framing; we can only suggest that camera distance, angle, height, and level have the constant possibility of sharpening our perception of purely visual qualities.

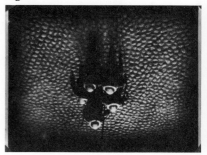

Figure 5.58

The Mobile Frame

All of the features of framing we have examined are present in every framed image. Paintings, photographs, comic strips, and other images all furnish instances of aspect ratios, in-frame and out-of-frame relations, angle, height, level, and distance of the frame's vantage point. But there is one resource of framing that is specific to cinema (and television). In film it is possible for the frame to *move* with respect to the framed material. *"Mobile framing"* means that within the confines of the image we see, the framing of the object changes. Since the framing orients us to the

Figure 5.59

Figure 5.60

Figure 5.61

Figure 5.62

material in the image, we often see ourselves as moving *along with* the frame. Through such framing we may approach the object or retreat from it, circle it or move past it. The mobile frame may thus produce changes of camera height, distance, angle, or level *within* the shot.

Types of Mobile Framing.   We usually refer to the ability of the frame to be mobile as "camera movement." Very often the term is accurate, for usually mobility of framing is achieved through the camera's being physically moved during production. The camera, as we know, is usually attached to a support while filming, and this support may be designed to move the camera. There are several kinds of camera movement, each one of which creates a specific effect onscreen.

The *pan* (short for "panorama") movement rotates the camera on a vertical axis. The camera as a whole does not displace itself. Onscreen, the pan gives the impression of a frame horizontally scanning space from left to right or right to left. In Figs. 5.59 and 5.60, shots from Dreyer's *Ordet*, the camera pans right to keep the figures in frame as they cross a room.

The *tilt* movement rotates the camera on a horizontal axis. Again, the camera as a whole does not change its placement. Onscreen, the tilt movement yields the impression of unrolling a space from top to bottom or bottom to top (see Figs. 5.11 and 5.12).

In the *tracking* (or *dolly* or *trucking*) shot the camera as a whole does change position, traveling in any direction along the ground—forward, backward, circularly, diagonally, or from side to side. Figures 5.61 and 5.62 show two stages of a tracking shot in Welles's *Magnificent Ambersons;* note how the figures have remained in the same basic relationship to the frame, while the background has shifted.

In the *crane* shot the camera leaves the ground and can travel not only forward and backward, in and out, but also up and down. Variations of the crane shot are helicopter and airplane shots, which allow the camera to travel great distances above the ground. The funeral scene in *Ivan the Terrible* begins with a crane down from a high view of the coffin (Fig. 5.63) to a lower position, ending with a framing on Ivan seated at the coffin's base (Fig. 5.64).

Such framing movements are the most common, but virtually any kind of camera movement can be imagined (somersaulting, rolling, gyroscopic, etc.). Only a few camera movements might be mistaken for each other. The pan resembles a lateral tracking shot, and the tilt resembles a vertical crane shot. But a little practice makes the differences easy to spot. In both the pan and the tilt, the body of the camera does not change position; it simply rotates, as if you were swiveling your head left or right, up or down. In the lateral tracking shot and the vertical crane shot, the camera is moved horizontally or vertically, as if you watched the countryside from a moving car or a city from a moving glass elevator. As we shall see, types of camera movements can be combined.

Figure 5.63

Camera movements have held an appeal for filmmakers and audiences since the beginnings of cinema. Why? Visually, camera movements have several arresting effects. They tend to increase information about the space of the image. Objects' positions become more vivid and sharp than in stationary framings. New objects or figures are usually revealed. Tracking shots and crane shots supply continually changing perspectives on passing objects as the frame continually shifts its orientation. Objects appear more solid and three-dimensional when the camera arcs (i.e., tracks along a curved path) around them. Pan and tilt shots present space as continuous, both horizontally and vertically.

Moreover, it is usually impossible not to see camera movement as a substitute for *our* movement. It is not just that objects swell or shrink; we seem to approach or retreat from them. This is not, of course, the case in a literal sense: We never forget that we are watching a film in a theater. But camera movement provides several powerful cues for a convincing substitute movement. Indeed, so powerful are these cues that filmmakers often make camera movements *subjective*—motivated narratively to represent the view through the eyes of a moving character. Narratively subjective or not, the roving camera eye, the mobile framing of the shot, acts as a surrogate for our eye and our attention. Camera movement illustrates very well how the image frame defines our view of a scene.

Figure 5.64

In certain circumstances our view may be explicitly identified with that of the camera itself. A bumpy, jiggling image usually implies that the camera was *handheld*, that the operator did not anchor the machine on a tripod, but instead trusted his or her body to act as the support. In Fig. 5.65 Don Pennebaker handholds the camera during the filming of his

Figure 5.65

Figure 5.66

Figure 5.67

Figure 5.68

Keep on Rocking. This sort of camera movement became common in the late 1950s, with the growth of the cinéma-vérité documentary, although the device soon appeared in fiction filmmaking. Often the handheld camera functions as either a special form of subjective point of view or a reminder of the presence of the camera filming the scene.

Camera movement is the most common way of making the frame mobile, but it is not the only way. In animation filming the camera seldom moves from one position, but through the drawing of individual "cels" frame by frame, the animator can create the effect of camera movement, as in this pan shot from *The Old Grey Hare* (Figs. 5.66, 5.67, and 5.68). Alternatively, a mobile frame effect can be achieved by photographing a still picture or a stopped frame of film and gradually enlarging or reducing any portion of that image, as is frequently done in optical printing. Iris masking can open up to reveal a vista or close down to isolate a detail. Finally, the zoom lens, as we've already mentioned, can be used to provide a mobile framing.

The differences between the laboratory or zoom sorts of mobile framing and some kinds of mobile framing created by camera movement during filming are difficult to illustrate on the printed page. No one will think an iris-in or a circular tracking shot is a zoom. But how, for instance, can we as viewers distinguish between a zoom-in and a forward tracking shot, a crane shot back and a change in framing created on the optical printer? In general, animation, special effects, and the zoom lens make the frame mobile by reducing or blowing up some portion of the image. Although the tracking shot and the crane shot do enlarge or reduce portions of the frame, this is not *all* that they do. In the genuine camera movement static objects in different planes pass one another at different rates, displaying *different aspects* to us; backgrounds gain depth. In general, the space is rounder and more solid in a camera movement than in a zoom, as these two pairs of frames from Alain Resnais's *La Guerre Est Finie* illustrate. Figures 5.69 and 5.70 are both portions of a tracking shot. With the zoom and its kin, however, static objects display the *same* aspects and remain in the same positions relative to each other. Perspective relations change, too: Backgrounds look flatter and more squeezed (Figs. 5.71 and 5.72). In sum, when the camera moves, we sense our own movement through the space; when the lens zooms, a bit of the image is magnified or demagnified.

Figure 5.69

So far, we've isolated these different sorts of mobile framings in fairly pure states. But filmmakers frequently combine such framings within a single shot: The camera may track and pan at the same time or crane up while zooming. Still, every instance can be identified as a combination of the basic types.

Figure 5.70

Functions of Frame Mobility. Our catalog of the types of mobile framings is of little use without a consideration of how such framing strategies function systematically within films. How does mobile framing relate to cinematic space? To cinematic time? How do mobile framings create certain patterns of their own? Such questions demand that we look for how mobile framing interacts with the form of the film.

Figure 5.71

1. *The mobile frame and space.* The mobile frame has enormous impact on space, considerably affecting onscreen and offscreen space. A forward tracking shot or zoom makes onscreen space offscreen. Other camera movements and optical effects may reveal fresh offscreen areas. In many films the camera moves back from a detail and brings something unexpected into the shot's space. This is what happens in our earlier example from *Jezebel;* after the hand with the glass intrudes into close-up, the camera moves back to frame the man standing in the foreground. The mobile frame also continually affects the distance, angle, height, and level of the framing. A track-in may change the distance from long shot to close-up; a crane up may change the angle from a low one to a high

Figure 5.72

Figure 5.73

Figure 5.74

Figure 5.75

one. It is useful to think of frame mobility as a way of controlling *spatial changes.*

We can, in general, ask several questions of how the mobile frame relates to space. Are the frame's movements dependent on figure movement? For example, one of the commonest functions of camera movement is *reframing.* If a character moves in relation to another character, very often the frame will slightly adjust to the movement. In *Open City,* when Ricci is in Pina's apartment, he changes position slightly as he sits on the table edge, and the frame shifts slightly to accommodate his movement. Reframing can be an art unto itself, as in *His Girl Friday,* which strives to balance its compositions through reframing. When Hildy moves, the camera pans right to reframe her; when Walter swivels in his chair, the camera reframes leftward—each time guiding our attention and maintaining a balanced composition (see Figs. 5.73, 5.74, and 5.75). Since reframings are motivated by figure movement, they tend to be relatively unnoticeable; practice is needed to spot them. When you do start to notice them, you may be surprised at how frequently they appear; the classical narrative cinema uses them continually.

Reframing is only one way that the mobile frame may be dependent on figure movement. The camera may also move to follow figures or moving objects. A pan may keep a racing car centered; a tracking shot may follow a character from room to room; or a crane shot may pursue a rising balloon. In such cases frame mobility functions primarily to keep our attention fastened on the subject of the shot, and it subordinates itself to that subject's movement.

Such following shots can become quite complex. Michelangelo Antonioni's *Cronaca di un Amore (Story of a Love Affair)* contains many scenes in which several characters are present. Typically the camera follows one figure moving to meet another, then follows the second character's movement to another spot, where he or she meets someone else, then traces the third character's movement, etc. The card-party sequence in *Cronaca* is a superb example of the camera's restlessly following character after character in rapid succession.

But the mobile frame need not be subordinate to the movement of figures at all: It can move independently of them, too. Often, of course, the camera moves away from the characters to reveal something of significance to the narrative. The most banal examples are movements that point out an overlooked clue, signs that comment on the action, or unnoticed shadows or "clutching hands."

But frame mobility independent of the characters can be much more subtle. The moving camera can establish a locale the characters will eventually enter. This is what happens at the start of Otto Preminger's *Laura,* when the camera glides through Waldo Lydecker's sitting room,

Figure 5.76

Figure 5.77

Figure 5.78

Figure 5.79

Figure 5.80

Figure 5.81

establishing him as a man of wealth and taste, before fastening on the detective MacPherson. In Renoir's *The Crime of M. Lange* the moving camera characterizes Lange by leaving him and panning around to survey the objects in his room (Figs. 5.76–5.81).

Sometimes, though, we can be thrown off guard by a movement that only *apparently* establishes a space for action, as in the opening of Kenji Mizoguchi's *The Forty-Seven Ronin*. After a static shot of the courtyard of a castle, the camera cuts to another view of the courtyard, now seen from within the corridor of the castle. The camera inches laterally along the corridor, its gaze fastened on the utterly empty courtyard. Surely, we expect, someone or something will enter that courtyard. Sure enough, voices are heard as the camera continues slowly to track right. But then, after what seems like minutes, the camera pans right to reveal men standing in the corridor and talking. We have been misled; the real action was occurring in the corridor, offscreen, and the camera's sidewise trajectory deliberately excluded the action. Moreover, this camera movement establishes sheerly empty space as important to the film, as it will prove in ensuing scenes.

Whether dependent on figure movement or independent of it, the mobile frame can profoundly affect how we perceive the space within the frame and offscreen. Different sorts of camera movements create different conceptions of space. In *Last Year at Marienbad* Resnais often employs a rectilinear tracking shot that moves into corridors and through doorways, turning a fashionable resort hotel into a maze. Alfred Hitchcock has produced some of the most famous single camera movements in film history: a track-and-crane shot that moves from a high-angle long shot of a ballroom over the heads of the dancers to an extreme close-up of a drummer's blinking eyes *(Young and Innocent)*, an especially tricky combination track-*in* and zoom-*out* to plastically distort the shot's perspective (used in *Marnie* and *Vertigo*). (The device reappears in *Jaws* by Stephen Spielberg, when Sheriff Brody at the beach

Figure 5.82

suddenly realizes that a child has been killed.) In films such as *The Red and the White, Agnus Dei,* and *Red Psalm* Miklos Jancso has specialized in very lengthy camera movements that roam among groups of people moving across a plain. His shots use all of the resources of tracking, panning, craning, zooming, and racking focus, to guide our perception of spatial relations.

For his film *La Région Centrale* Michael Snow built the machine pictured in Fig. 5.82. Since all of the moving arms could pivot the camera in several ways, the machine produced a varied series of rotational camera movements—everything from elaborate corkscrew spirallings to huge, Ferris-wheel spins. Snow set up his machine in a barren Canadian landscape, and the film that resulted transforms that landscape into a series of uniquely mobile views.

All of these examples illustrate various ways in which frame mobility affects our perception of space. Of any mobile framing we can ask: How does it function to reveal or conceal offscreen space? Is the frame mobility dependent on figure movement or independent of it? What particular trajectory does the camera pursue? Such questions will best be answered by considering how spatial effects of the camera movement function with respect to narrative or nonnarrative form.

2. *The mobile frame and time.* Since frame mobility is a kind of movement, it involves time as well as space, and filmmakers have realized that our senses of duration and rhythm are affected by the mobile frame. The importance of duration in camera movement, for example, can be sensed by comparing two Japanese directors, Yasujiro Ozu and Kenji Mizo-

guchi. Ozu prefers short, abrupt camera movements, as in *Early Summer* and *The Flavor of Green Tea Over Rice.* Mizoguchi, on the other hand, cultivates the leisurely, drawn-out tracking shot in his films. That camera movements simply take less time in Ozu's films than in Mizoguchi's constitutes a major difference between the two directors' styles. Shortly we shall see a major example of how duration is controlled by a long-take camera movement in the opening of Welles's *Touch of Evil.*

The velocity of frame mobility is important, too. A zoom or a camera movement may be relatively slow or fast. Richard Lester started a fad in the 1960s with the use of very fast zoom-ins and -outs. In comparison, one of the most impressive early camera movements, D. W. Griffith's monumental crane shot into Belshazzar's feast in *Intolerance,* gains majesty through its inexorable slowness. Obviously, narrative factors may motivate the velocity of a mobile framing: A quick track-in to a significant object or a slow craning out from figures in a landscape can underline significant narrative qualities.

Sometimes the speed of the mobile framing functions rhythmically. In Will Hindle's *Pastorale d'été* a gentle, bouncing rhythm is created by zooming in and slightly tilting up and down in time to Honegger's music. Often musical films make use of the speed of camera movement to underline qualities of a song or dance. During the "Broadway Rhythm" number in *Singin' in the Rain,* the camera cranes quickly back from Gene Kelly several times, and the speed of the movement is timed to match the rhythm of the lyrics. In short, the duration and velocity of the mobile frame can significantly control our perception of the time of the shot.

3. *Patterns of mobile framing.* The mobile frame can create its own specific motifs within a film. Consider, for example, how Alfred Hitchcock's *Psycho* begins and ends with a forward movement of the frame. At the beginning, the camera pans right and zooms in on a building in a cityscape; repeated forward movements finally carry us under a window blind and into the darkness of a cheap hotel room. The camera's movement inward, the penetration of an interior, is repeated throughout the film, often motivated as subjective point of view as various characters move deeper and deeper into Norman Bates's mansion. The next-to-last shot of the film shows Norman sitting against a blank white wall, while we hear his interior monologue; the camera again moves forward into a close-up of his face. This shot is the climax of the forward movement initiated at the start of the film; the film has traced a movement into Norman's mind. Another film that relies heavily on a pattern of forward, penetrating movements is *Citizen Kane,* which depicts the same inexorable drive toward the revelation of a secret.

Other kinds of movements can repeat and develop across a film. Max Ophuls's *Lola Montès* uses both 360-degree tracking shots and constant upward and downward crane shots to contrast the circus arena with the world of Lola's past. Films as otherwise different as Jean Renoir's *Grand Illusion* and Fritz Lang's *The Big Heat* share the habit of beginning a sequence on a relatively close shot of an object and then tracking back to situate that object in a dramatic context—sometimes with startling results. In Michael Snow's ——— (usually called *Back and Forth)* the constant panning to and fro across a classroom, ping-pong fashion, determines the basic formal pattern of the film; it comes as a surprise when near the very end, the movement suddenly becomes a repeated tilting up and down. In these and many other films the mobile frame sets up marked repetitions and variations.

In these examples, repetitions and variations of camera-movement motifs interact with the film's narrative or nonnarrative form. By way of summary, we can look at two films that illustrate possible relations of the mobile frame to narrative form. These two films constitute a pertinent contrast in that one uses the mobile frame in order to strengthen and support the narrative, whereas the other—paradoxical as it sounds—subordinates narrative form to an overall frame mobility.

Jean Renoir's *Grand Illusion* is a war film in which we almost never see the war. The staples of the genre—heroic charges, doomed battalions—are absent; World War I remains permanently offscreen. Instead, Renoir concentrates on how national and social-class relations are affected by war. Marechal and Boeldieu are both French; Rauffenstein is a German. Yet the aristocrat Boeldieu has more in common with Rauffenstein than with the mechanic Marechal. The film's narrative form traces the death of the Boeldieu/Rauffenstein upper class and the precarious survival of Marechal and his pal Rosenthal—their flight to Elsa's farm, their interlude of peace there, and their final escape back to France and presumably back to the war as well. Within this framework, camera movement has several functions, all directly supportive of the narrative. First, and least unusual, is its tendency to adhere to figure movement: When a character or vehicle moves, Renoir often pans or tracks to follow. The camera follows Marechal and Rosenthal walking together after their escape; it tracks back when the prisoners are drawn to the window by the sound of marching Germans below. But it is the movements of the camera *independent* of figure movement that make the film more unusual.

When the camera moves on its own in *Grand Illusion,* we are conscious of it as actively interpreting the action, often giving us information of which the characters are ignorant. For example, when a prisoner is digging in the escape tunnel and pulls on the string to signal to be pulled out, the camera frames the can being tugged over (Fig. 5.83), then pans left to reveal that the characters do not notice it (Figs. 5.84 and

Figure 5.83

Figure 5.84

Figure 5.85

Figure 5.86

Figure 5.87

5.85). Sometimes, in fact, the camera is such an active agent that Renoir will use repeated camera movements to create specific patterns of narrative significance.

One such pattern is the movement to link characters with details of their environment. Sometimes a sequence begins on a close-up of some detail, and the camera moves back to anchor this detail in its larger spatial and narrative context. When Renoir begins the scene of Boeldieu and Marechal's discussion of escape plans with a close-up of a caged squirrel (Fig. 5.86) before tracking back to reveal the men (Fig. 5.87), the narrative parallel is apparent.

Figure 5.88

More complicated is the scene of the Christmas celebration at Elsa's, which begins on a close-up of the crêche and tracks back to show, in several stages, the interplay of reactions among the characters. Such camera movements are not simply decoration; their habit of beginning on a scenic detail before moving to the larger context makes narrative points economically, constantly emphasizing relationships among elements of Renoir's mise-en-scene. So does the rarer track-*in* to a detail at the *end* of a scene, as when after Boeldieu's death, Rauffenstein goes to cut the geranium, the one flower in the prison (Fig. 5.88), and Renoir tracks in to a final close shot of the flower pot (Fig. 5.89).

Figure 5.89

Figure 5.90

Figure 5.91

Figure 5.92

Figure 5.93

Figure 5.94

Figure 5.95

Characters are tied to their environment by some even more ambitious moving-camera shots; these shots function to stress important narrative parallels. In the first scene, as Marechal leaves the officers' bar (Fig. 5.90), Renoir pans and tracks left from the door to reveal pinups and a cynical poster (Figs. 5.91 and 5.92). One scene later, in the German officers' bar, a similar camera movement (this time in the opposite direction) leaves the characters and explores, on its own, a similar collection of decorations (Figs. 5.93, 5.94, and 5.95). Through camera movement Renoir indicates a similarity between the two warring sides, blurring their national differences and stressing common desires. The camera movements *as movements,* repeated in a systematic pattern, create the narrative parallel.

Or, consider how two parallel tracking shots compare the war of the aristocrats and the war of the lower-class people. We are introduced to Rauffenstein's new position as commander of a prisoner-of-war camp through a lengthy tracking shot that begins on a cross (ironic, since the chapel has been commandeered as a bivouac) and tracks along whips, spurs, weapons, and gloves to a servant preparing Rauffenstein's gloves and finally to Rauffenstein himself (Figs. 5.96 through 5.103). In this shot Renoir presents, wordlessly, the military mystique of grace on the battlefield that characterizes the aristocrats' war. But late in the film a parallel shot criticizes this. Again the shot begins on an object—a picture

Figure 5.96

Figure 5.97

Figure 5.98

Figure 5.99

Figure 5.100

Figure 5.101

Figure 5.102

of Elsa's dead husband (Fig. 5.104)—and tracks back to reveal pictures of other of Elsa's relatives as she recites offscreen where they were killed; the camera tracks left (Fig. 5.105) to the kitchen table, where the child Lotte sits alone (Fig. 5.106) as Elsa explains offscreen: "Now the table is too large." That Elsa's war has none of Rauffenstein's glory is conveyed chiefly through a parallel created by the repeated camera movement.

Another function of moving the camera independently of figure movement is to link characters with one another. Again and again in the prison camps, the camera moves to join one man to another, spatially indicating their shared condition. When the prisoners ransack the collec-

Figure 5.103

Figure 5.104

Figure 5.105

Figure 5.106

tion of women's clothes, one man decides to dress up in them, and when he appears, a stillness falls over the men; Renoir tracks silently over the prisoners' faces, each one registering a reticent longing. In the scene of the prison vaudeville show, the men learn that the French have recaptured a city; the camera moves among them as they begin defiantly to sing the "Marseillaise." Renoir presents the shot as a celebration of spatial unity, tracking right from the musicians (Fig. 5.107) along the singing performers (Figs. 5.108 and 5.109) to a pair of worried German guards (Fig. 5.110); the camera then pans left to reveal a row of the audience of prisoners on their feet, singing (Fig. 5.111); the camera tracks forward past the musicians again (Fig. 5.112), then pans quickly left to face the entire audience (Fig. 5.113). This very complex camera movement circulates among the prisoners as they join together in defiance of their captors.

In Elsa's cottage as well as in the prison, camera movement links characters: Recall the shot that moves from Elsa and Rosenthal inside through the window to Marechal outside. The culmination of the linking movement comes near the film's end, when Renoir pans from the Germans on one side of the border (Fig. 5.114) to the distant French escapees on the other (Figs. 5.115 and 5.116); even on this scale, Renoir's camera refuses to honor national divisions.

A remark of André Bazin's is pertinent here: "Jean Renoir found a way to reveal the hidden meaning of people and things without destroying the unity that is natural to them." In such ways as these, camera movement in *Grand Illusion* functions as an active agent in creating the film's drama; in its ability to place emphasis and make associations, the camera work is as important as is the mise-en-scene. The camera carves into space to create connections that enrich the film's narrative form. Renoir has found imaginative ways to make the mobile frame sustain and elaborate a system of narrative relationships within his films.

Figure 5.107

Figure 5.108

Figure 5.109

Figure 5.110

Figure 5.111

Figure 5.112

Figure 5.113

Figure 5.114

Figure 5.115

Figure 5.116

Figure 5.117

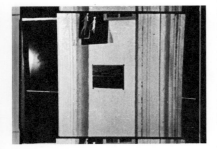

Figure 5.118

Figure 5.119

In Michael Snow's *Wavelength* the relation of narrative to the mobile frame is almost exactly the inverse. Instead of supporting narrative form, frame mobility dominates narrative, even deflecting our attention from narrative. The film begins with a long-shot framing of a loft apartment, facing one wall and window (Fig. 5.117). In the course of the film the camera zooms in abruptly a short distance, then holds that framing; it zooms in a bit more, then holds that (Fig. 5.118); and so on. By the end of the film a photograph of ocean waves on the distant wall fills the frame in close-up.

Thus *Wavelength* is structured primarily around a single kind of frame mobility—the zoom-in. Its pattern of progression and development is not a narrative one, but that of an exploration, through deliberately limited means, of how the zoom transforms the space of the loft. The sudden zooms create frequent abrupt shifts of perspective relations. In excluding parts of the room, the zoom-in also magnifies and flattens what we see; every change of focal length gives us a new set of spatial relations. The sound track, for the most part, reinforces the basic formal progression by emitting a single humming tone that rises consistently in pitch as the zoom magnifies more and more.

Within *Wavelength*'s basic pattern, though, there are two contrasting subsystems. The first is a series of colored tints that plays across the image as abstract blocks of color; these tints often work against the depth represented in the shot of the loft. The second subsystem is a narrative one. At various intervals characters enter the loft and carry on certain activities (talking, listening to the radio, making phone calls). There is even a mysterious death, possibly a murder (note the body on the floor, Fig. 5.119). But the narrative events remain unexplained in cause-effect terms and inconclusive as to closure (although at the film's end we do hear a sound that resembles a police siren). Furthermore, none of these actions swerves the mobile framing from its predetermined course. The jerkily shifting and halting zoom continues, even when it will exclude important narrative information; the continuing trajectory of the framing remains central. Thus *Wavelength* pulls in bits and pieces of narrative, but these fragments of action remain secondary; they function within the temporal progression of the zoom.

Grand Illusion and *Wavelength* illustrate, in different ways, how frame mobility can guide and shape our perception of a film's space and time. Frame mobility may be motivated by larger formal concerns, as in Renoir's film, or it may itself become the principal formal concern, motivating other systems, as in Snow's film. What is important to realize is that by attention to how filmmakers utilize the mobile frame within specific contexts, we can gain a fuller understanding of how our experience of a film is created.

Duration of the Image: The Long Take ■

In our consideration of the film image, we have emphasized spatial qualities—how photographic transformations can alter the properties of the image, how framing defines the image for our attention. But cinema is an art of time as well as of space, and we have seen already how mise-en-scene and frame mobility operate in temporal as well as spatial dimensions. What we need to consider now is how the duration of the shot affects our understanding of it.

There is a tendency to consider the shot as recording "real" duration. A runner takes three seconds to clear a hurdle; if we film the runner, our projected film will also consume three seconds—or so the assumption goes. One film theorist, André Bazin, made it a major tenet of his aesthetic that cinema records "real time." (See Notes and Queries for a discussion of Bazin's position.) What must be noted, though, is that the relation of shot duration to the time consumed by the filmed event is not so simple.

First, obviously, the duration of the event on the screen may be manipulated by adjustments in the camera's or printer's drive mechanism, as we discussed earlier in this chapter. "Slow motion" or "fast motion" may present the runner's jump in twenty seconds or two. Second, more complex cases—such as narrative films—permit no simple equivalence of "real duration" with screen duration. The difference between story and plot—between the inferred narrative action and the presentation of that action—introduces complications.

Consider a shot from Ozu's *Her Only Son.* It is well past midnight, and we have just seen a family awake and talking; this shot shows a dim corner of the family's apartment, with none of the characters onscreen. But soon the light changes. The sun is rising. By the end of the shot it is morning. This transitional shot consumes about a minute of screen time. It plainly does not record the "real" duration of the story events—that duration would be at least five hours. To put it another way, the film's plot has condensed a story duration of several hours into the minute or so of this one shot. In the next chapter we shall examine how editing one shot with another can expand or contract duration, but we ought to recognize that it is just as possible to manipulate duration *within a single shot* as well. There need be no one-to-one correspondence between the onscreen duration of the shot and the duration of the story events represented.

The Long Take

Every shot has some measurable screen duration, but in the history of cinema, directors have varied considerably in their choice of short or lengthy shots. In general, early cinema (1895–1905) tended to rely on shots of relatively longer duration; with the growth of continuity editing (from around 1905 to 1935) shots tended to be shorter. But throughout the history of the cinema, some filmmakers have consistently preferred to utilize shots of greater duration than the average. The average shot length in American films of the 1930s is said to be around seven seconds. In various countries in the mid-1930s there was a tendency to increase the length of the shots, and this tendency continued throughout the next 20 years. The causes of this change are complex and not fully understood, but film scholars agree that the use of unusually lengthy shots—*long takes,* as they are called—constitutes a major resource for the filmmaker. Indeed, in the films of Jean Renoir, Kenji Mizoguchi, Orson Welles, Carl Dreyer, Andy Warhol, or Miklos Jancso a shot may go on for several minutes, and it would be impossible to analyze these films without an awareness of how the long take can contribute to a film's form and style. ("Long take" is not the same as "long shot"; the latter term refers to the apparent distance between camera and object.)

Formally, it is often useful to consider the long take as a large-scale part of a film. In a film with 500 shots, each shot is part of a sequence, which in turn belongs to a larger whole—as a brick is part of a wall, a wall is part of a whole building. But in a film consisting of 14 shots, things are different; the shot becomes a major part within the whole, as, say, a wall of poured concrete is a large-scale, complete unit of the entire building. The long take promotes the single shot to a role of great formal significance.

Because of this promotion, film critics and theorists often regard the long take as an alternative to a series of shots. The director may choose to present a scene in one or a few long takes or to present the scene through several shorter shots. Sometimes a director builds the entire film out of long takes, as Miklos Jancso frequently does. His films (e.g., *Winterwind, Agnus Dei, Red Psalm*) often present an entire scene in only one shot—a device known by the French term *plan-séquence,* or "shot sequence." Other directors choose to present certain scenes through long takes and other scenes through sequences composed of shorter shots. Within the context of a film built on long takes, editing can have a considerable force. André Bazin pointed out that *Citizen Kane* oscillates between quite lengthy shots (many of the dialogue scenes) and very short ones (in the "News on the March" sequence and other sequences). Hitchcock, Mizoguchi, Renoir, and Dreyer often change shot duration, depending on the scene's function in the entire film. Thus a film may present a rich interplay between the long take and editing.

If the long take often replaces editing, it should surprise no one that the long take is frequently allied to the mobile frame. The long

Figure 5.120

Figure 5.121

Figure 5.122

Figure 5.123

Figure 5.124

Figure 5.125

take may use panning, tracking, craning, or zooming to present continually changing vantage points that are comparable in some ways to the shifts of view supplied by editing from shot to shot. With the possible exceptions of Louis Feuillade and Andy Warhol, the masters of the long take tend to be also masters of camera movement. Very often frame mobility breaks the long-take shot into significant smaller units. In Mizoguchi's *Sisters of Gion,* one long take begins with Omocha and the older man seated (Fig. 5.120). Preparing to lure him into becoming her patron, she moves to an opposite end of the room, the camera following her (Figs. 5.121 and 5.122). Now a second phase of the scene occurs: She starts to appeal to his sympathy. He comes over to console her (Figs. 5.123 and 5.124); the camera moves into a tighter shot of the two as he succumbs to her advances (Fig. 5.125). Though there is no cutting, the camera and figure movements have demarcated important stages of the scene's action.

This example also illustrates perhaps the most important consequence of the long take. The Mizoguchi shot reveals a complete internal logic—a beginning, middle, and end. As a large-scale part of a film, the long take can have its own formal pattern, its own development, its own trajectory and shape. Suspense develops; we start to ask how the shot will continue and when it will end.

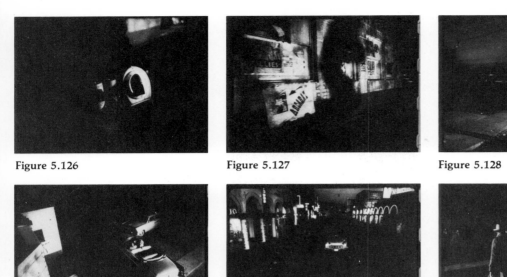

Figure 5.126

Figure 5.127

Figure 5.128

Figure 5.129

Figure 5.130

Figure 5.131

Figure 5.132

Figure 5.133

Figure 5.134

Figure 5.135

Figure 5.136

Figure 5.137

The classic example of how the long take can constitute a formal pattern in its own right is the opening sequence of Welles's *Touch of Evil* (Figs. 5.126 through Fig. 5.137). The shot begins with a close-up of a hand setting the timer of a bomb (Fig. 5.126). The camera tracks immediately right to follow the unknown assassin planting the bomb in a car (Figs. 5.127 and 5.128).

The camera cranes up to a high angle as the assassin flees and the victims arrive and set out in the car (Fig. 5.129). As the car goes around the corner, the camera circles the block, rejoins the car, and tracks back to follow it (Fig. 5.130).

The car passes Vargas and his wife, Susan, and the camera starts to follow them. The camera loses the car and tracks back with the couple as they move through the crowd (Fig. 5.131).

The shot continues as the camera tracks back until both the occupants of the car and Susan and Vargas again meet, this time at the border post. A brief scene with the border guard ensues (Figs. 5.132 and 5.133).

After tracking left with the car, the camera again encounters Susan and Vargas (Fig. 5.134). The shot ends as Susan and Vargas are about to kiss (Fig. 5.135). Their embrace is interrupted by the offscreen sound of an explosion. The couple turns to stare (Fig. 5.136). The next shot shows the car in flames (Fig. 5.137).

This opening shot makes plain most of the features of the long take: It offers an alternative to building the sequence out of many shots; it stresses the cut that finally comes (the sudden cut on the sound of the explosion to the burning car); the camera moves constantly. Most important, the shot has its own internal pattern of development. We expect that the bomb shown at the beginning will explode at some point, and we wait for that explosion through the duration of the long take. The shot establishes the geography of the scene (the border between Mexico and the United States), and the camera movement, alternately picking up the car and Vargas and Susan, weaves together two separate lines of narrative cause and effect that intersect at the border station. Vargas and Susan are thus drawn into the action involving the bombing. Our expectation is fulfilled when the end of the shot coincides with the explosion (offscreen) of the bomb. The shot has guided our response by taking us through a suspenseful process of narrative development. The long take's ability to present, in a single chunk of time, a complex pattern of events moving toward a goal makes shot duration as important to the image's effect as are photographic qualities and framing.

Summary ■

The film shot, then, is a very complex formal unit. Mise-en-scene fills the image with material, arranging setting, lighting, costume, and figure behavior within the formal context of the total film. Within that same formal context, the filmmaker also controls the cinematographic qualities of the shot—how the image is photographed and framed, how long the image lasts on the screen.

You can sensitize yourself to these cinematographic qualities in much the same way that you worked on mise-en-scene. Trace the progress of a single technique—say, camera angle—through an entire film. Become conscious of when a shot begins and ends, observing how the long take may function to shape the film's form. Watch for camera movements, especially those that follow the action (since those are usually the hardest to notice). In short, once we are aware of cinematographic qualities, we can move to an understanding of their various possible functions within the total film.

Yet film art offers still other possibilities for choice and control. Chapters 4 and 5 have focused on the shot. The filmmaker may also juxtapose one shot with another through editing, and that is the subject of Chapter 6.

Notes and Queries ■

General Works

If you are interested in cinematography, you might follow up these sources: Carl L. Gregory's *Motion Picture Photography* (New York: New York Institute of Photography, 1920; rev. ed., 1927) is a comprehensive work on silent cinematography techniques. The standard contemporary references are *The American Cinematographer Manual* (Hollywood: A.S.C., 1966); H. Mario Raimondo Souto, *The Technique of the Motion Picture Camera* (New York: Hastings House, 1967); Russell Campbell, *Photographic Theory for the Motion Picture Cameraman* (New York: Barnes, 1970) and *Practical Motion Picture Photography* (New York: Barnes, 1970). *American Cinematographer* and *The Journal of the Society of Motion Picture and Television Engineers* continually publish articles on studio filmmaking. A detailed introduction to lens optics is Sidney Ray's *The Lens in Action* (New York: Hastings House, 1976). Laboratory work is discussed in L. Bernard Happé's *Your Film and the Lab* (New York: Hastings House, 1974). Alternative points of view on cinematography may be found in Stan Brakhage "A Moving Picture Giving and Taking Book," *Film Culture,* 41 (Summer 1976): 39–57; Dziga Vertov, "The Vertov Papers," *Film Comment* **8**, 1 (Spring 1972): 46–51; and Maya Deren, "An Anagram of Ideas on Art, Form, and Film," and "Cinematography," in George Amberg, ed., *The Art of Cinema* (New York: Arno, 1972).

Color versus Black and White

Though today most films are shot on color stock and most viewers have come to expect that movies will be in color, color enjoys no absolute superiority over black and white. At many points in film history, each type of film stock has been used to carry different meanings. In 1930s and 1940s American cinema, color tended to be reserved for fantasies (e.g., *The Wizard of Oz*), historical films or films set in exotic locales *(Becky Sharp, Blood and Sand)*, or very lavish musicals *(Meet Me in St. Louis)*. Black and white was then believed to be more "realistic." But now that most films are in color, filmmakers can call on black and white to suggest a historical period (as witnessed by two such different films as Straub and Huillet's *Chronicle of Anna Magdalena Bach* and Bogdanovich's *Paper Moon*). Such rules of thumb as "color for realism" have no universal validity; as always, it is a matter of context, the function of color or black-and-white tonalities within a specific film.

For more data on the principles of color photography, see De Maré, *Color Photography* (Baltimore: Penguin, 1968); Joseph S. Friedman, *The History of Color Photography* (London: Focal Press, 1968); and Andreas Feininger, *Successful Color Photography* (Englewood Cliffs, N.J.: Prentice-Hall, 1969). Color in the cinema has not received as much discussion as it should. A brief but well-illustrated history of color in motion pictures may be found in Roger Manvell, ed., *The International Encyclopedia of Film* (New York: Crown, 1972); this article demonstrates conclusively that radically different color ranges can all be accepted as "realistic." Journals publishing articles on color cinematography include *The Journal of the Society of Motion Picture and Television Engineers* and *American Cinematographer*. Film theorists have debated whether color film is artistically more impure than black and white. One argument against color may be found in Rudolf Arnheim, *Film as Art* (Berkeley: University of California Press, 1967). How is Arnheim's argument disputed by V. F. Perkins in *Film as Film* (Baltimore: Penguin, 1972)?

Filmmakers have discussed the relative advantages and disadvantages of color. Believing that color evokes definite emotions, Rouben Mamoulian has claimed that the director must develop "a complete chromatic plan for the film." (See Rouben Mamoulian, "Color and Light in Films," *Film Culture*, 21 [Summer 1960]: 68–79.) Carl Dreyer agreed, stressing the necessity for the director to plan the color scheme to flow smoothly, "which creates the effect of persons and objects being in constant motion and causes the colors to glide from one place to another in changing rhythms, creating new and surprising effects when they collide with other colors or melt into them." ("Color Film and Colored Films," *Dreyer in Double Reflection* [New York: Dutton, 1973], pp. 168–173).

For Stan Brakhage, cinema must break down our normal sense of color, as "closed-eye vision" produces purely subjective tonalities: "I am stating my given ability, prize of all above pursuing, to transform the light sculptured shapes of an almost dark-blackened room to the rainbow-hued patterns of light without any scientific paraphenalia." (Brakhage, *Metaphors on Vision* [New York: Film Culture, 1963]). The filmmaker who theorized most extensively about color was Sergei Eisenstein. See especially "Color and Meaning," in *The Film Sense* (New York: Harcourt, Brace, 1947), pp. 113–153.

For general discussion of the aesthetics of film color, see: Raymond Durgnat, "Colours and Contrasts," *Films and Filming* **15**, 2 (November 1968): 58–62; and William Johnson, "Coming to Terms with Color," *Film Quarterly* **20**, 1 (Fall 1966): 2–22. Two essays on Jean-Luc Godard exemplify how the analyst can examine a film's color system: Paul Sharits, "Red, Blue, Godard," *Film Quarterly* **19**, 4 (Summer 1966): 24–29; and Edward Branigan, "The Articulation of Color in a Filmic System," *Wide Angle* **1**, 3 (1976): 20–31. The latter contains an excellent bibliography.

The Darkened Chamber

When an artist wants to produce an image of a scene, it is useful to have a systematic method of transcribing features of the scene onto paper, canvas, or whatever. In the fourteenth century painters and architects devised a mathematical system for reproducing spatial relations in a scene onto canvas: This became generally known as *geometrical perspective.* Assuming that the light rays from a scene gather at a point––the eye of the beholder—the artist used simple geometrical projection to reckon such a point and then design the picture as a grid or window interposed between the scene and the viewer. If the painter's geometry was correct, a viewer looking at the picture through a single peephole would see exactly what he or she would see if viewing the actual scene from a proportionate distance. Because of the importance of the viewer's station-point, this system is also called *monocular* ("single-eye") perspective. (There are other perspective systems as well, notably in the Orient.)

What does all this have to do with the photographic qualities of the film image? The crucial link is a mechanical device known as the *camera obscura* ("darkened chamber"). Originally used by the ancient Arabs and Greeks for viewing eclipses, the *camera obscura* became for the artists of the Renaissance a mechanical aid to correct perspective drawing. It was, originally, literally a chamber, a dark room with light entering so manipulated as to cast an inverted image on the opposite wall. In the mid-sixteenth century Italian experimenters attached lenses to the hole, added a diaphragm to sharpen the resulting image, and finally turned the image rightside up by means of another lens or a concave mirror. Later experimenters added focusing screens and viewing systems. Soon the darkened chamber became more portable—as a tent, a carriage, a sedan chair, a table, or a small box—and by the eighteenth century the *camera obscura* was small enough to be carried in the pocket or in the form of a book or walking stick. The purpose was to help a person draw accurate geometrical perspective. In the light of this, the camera became not only an artistic and scientific tool, but also a toy to satisfy a culture's desire for making images of the world. When it became possible to fix and permanently hold the camera's image on a chemically sensitized surface (plate, paper, or film), photography and cinematography began to be born.

We have already seen how the motion-picture camera can transform the filmed scene in ways that manipulate perspective. Today film theorists are asking to what extent the medium of cinema is necessarily bound up with that system of monocular perspective that gave birth to the camera. Some argue that Renaissance perspective issues from a specific social and political conception of the world—an ideology—that makes the world seem neatly objectified for the eye of the independent observer. If this is valid, the cinema may be in similar ways tied to a social and ideological position by the very nature of its machinery.

To analyze this position takes us beyond the scope of an introductory text. Yet since the issue is important to contemporary thinking about cinema, the interested reader can go to several places to find the argument set out in more detail. The crucial sources in English are Jean-Pierre Baudry, "Ideological Effects of the Basic Cinematographic Apparatus," *Film Quarterly* **28**, 2 (Winter 1974–75): 39–47; Daniel Dayan, "The Tutor-Code of Classical Cinema," *Film Quarterly* **28**, 1 (Fall 1974): 22–31; Stephen Heath, "Narrative Space," *Screen* **17**, 3 (Autumn 1976): 68–112. Students who read French will find in *Cahiers du Cinéma* since 1970 an ongoing debate on the subject. Do contemporary arguments about the perspective bias of the *camera obscura* take into account all of the different perspective systems developed since the Renaissance?

For the history of perspective in painting, see John White, *The Birth and Rebirth of Pictorial Space* (New York: Harper, 1972), E. H. Gombrich, *Art and Illusion* (Princeton, N.J.: Princeton University Press, 1969), Lee Baxandall, *Painting and Experience in Fifteenth Century Italy* (New York: Oxford, 1972), William Ivins, *On the Rationalization of Sight* (New York: Da Capo, 1973) and *Art and Geometry* (New York: Dover, 1964), and Fred Leeman, *Hidden Images* (New York: Abrams, 1976).

"Special Effects"

Part of the reason that major film studios tout themselves as "the magic factories" is that special-effects cinematography demands the complexity and expense that only a big firm can support. Special effects—rear projection, matte work, superimposition, and other procedures—require the time, patience, and rehearsal afforded by control over mise-en-scene. It is, then, no surprise that Méliès, the first person to exploit fully the possibilities of studio filmmaking, excelled at special-effects cinematography. Nor is it surprising that when UFA, the gigantic German firm of the 1920s, became the best-equipped film studio in Europe, many new special-effects processes were started there. Similarly, as Hollywood studios grew from 1920 on, so did their special-effects departments. Engineers, painters, photographers, and set designers collaborated to contrive fantastic visual novelties. In these "magic factories" most of the history of special effects has been made.

But such firms were not motivated by sheer curiosity. The costs of elaborate back projection and matte work were usually investments. First, expensive as they were, such tricks often saved money in the long run. Instead of building a huge set, one could photograph the actors through a glass with the setting painted on it. Instead of taking cast and crew to the North Pole, one could film them against a back projection. Second, special effects made certain film genres possible. The historical epic—whether set in Rome, Babylon, or Jerusalem—was unthinkable unless special effects were devised to create huge vistas and crowds. The fantasy film, with its panoply of ghosts, talking mules, and men invisible or incredibly shrinking, demanded the perfection of superimposition and matte processes. The science fiction genre simply could not exist without a barrage of special effects. It is not accidental that science fiction films have produced many of the newest special-effects innovations (*Metropolis*'s Schüfftan process, *2001*'s front projection and multiple mattes). For the major studios the "factory" principle was responsible for the "magic."

The definitive work on the subject is Raymond Fielding's *The Technique of Special Effects Cinematography* (New York: Hastings House, 1974). John Brosman's *Movie Magic* (New York: Plume, 1976) is a serviceable history. Articles on particular films' use of special effects appear regularly in *American Cinematographer* and *Filmmakers' Newsletter*.

Aspect Ratio

In Jean-Luc Godard's film *Contempt*, the director Fritz Lang (playing himself) laments that "CinemaScope is good only for filming funerals and snakes." *Contempt*, of course, is a CinemaScope film.

The aspect ratio of the film image has been debated since the inception of cinema. The Edison-Lumière ratio (1:1.33) was not generally standardized until 1911, and even after that other ratios were explored. Many cinematographers believed that 1:1.33 was the perfect ratio (perhaps not aware that it harks back to the "golden section" of academic painting). With the large-scale innovation of wide-screen cinema in the early 1950s, cries of distress were heard. Most camerapersons hated it: Lenses often were not sharp, lighting became more complicated, and as Lee Garmes put it: "We'd look through the camera and be startled at what it was taking in." Yet some directors—Nicholas Ray, Akira Kurosawa, Samuel Fuller, François Truffaut, Jean-Luc Godard—created unusual and fascinating compositions in the wide-screen ratio. Various wide-screen systems are surveyed in Michael Z. Wygotsky's *Wide-Screen Cinema and Stereophonic Sound* (New York: Hastings House, 1971). The most detailed defense of the aesthetic virtues of the wide-screen image remains Charles Barr's "Cinemascope: Before and After," *Film Quarterly* 16, 4 (Summer 1963): 4–24. To what extent does Barr's argument rest on an assumption that new technological possibilities create new formal and functional possibilities?

The Subjective Shot

In films we sometimes find the camera, through its positioning and movements, inviting us to see events "through the eyes" of a character. Some directors (Howard Hawks, John Ford, Kenji Mizoguchi, Jacques Tati) seldom use the subjective shot, but others (Alfred Hitchcock, Alain Resnais) use it constantly. The first scene of Samuel Fuller's *The Naked Kiss* starts with shocking subjective shots:

> We open with a direct cut. In that scene, the actors utilized the camera. They held the camera; it was strapped on them. For the first shot, the pimp has the camera strapped on his chest. I say to [Constance] Towers, 'Hit the camera!' She hits the camera, the lens. Then I reverse it. I put the camera on her, and she whacks the hell out of him. I thought it was effective. (Quoted in Eric Sherman and Martin Rubin, *The Director's Event* [New York: Signet, 1969], p. 189.)

Often the very first film a filmmaker conceives will be a subjective one. In his youth, Joris Ivens was fascinated by what he called "the I film" (*The Camera and I* [New York: International Publishers, 1969], p. 41).

Historically, filmmakers began experimenting with the "first-person camera" or the "camera as character" quite early. *Grandma's Reading Glasses* (1900) features subjective point-of-view shots. Keyholes, binoculars, and other apertures were often used to motivate optical point of view. In 1917 Abel Gance used many subjective shots in *J'Accuse*. The

1920s saw many filmmakers taking an interest in subjectivity, seen in such films as Jean Epstein's *Coeur Fidèle* (1923) and *La Belle Nivernaise* (1923), E. A. Dupont's *Variety* (1924), F. W. Murnau's *The Last Laugh* (1924), with its famous drunken scene, and Abel Gance's *Napoléon* (1928). Some believe that in the 1940s the subjective shot—especially the subjective camera movement—got completely out of hand in Robert Montgomery's *Lady in the Lake* (1946). For almost the entire film the camera represents the vision of the protagonist; we see him only when he glances in mirrors. "Suspenseful! Unusual!" proclaimed the advertising. "YOU accept an invitation to a blonde's apartment! YOU get socked in the jaw by a murder suspect!"

The history of the technique has teased film theorists into speculating about whether the subjective shot evokes identification from the audience. Do we think we *are* Robert Montgomery? Theorists in the silent era thought that we might tend to identify with that character whose position the camera occupies. But recent film theory is reluctant to make this move. *The Lady in the Lake* fails, Albert Laffay claims, because "by pursuing an impossible perceptual assimilation, the film in fact inhibits symbolic identification" (quoted in Christian Metz, "Current Problems in Film Theory," *Screen* **14**, 1/2 [Spring/Summer 1973]: 47). François Truffaut claims that we identify with a character not when we look *with* the character, but when the character looks *at us.* "A subjective camera is the negation of subjective cinema. When it replaces a character, one cannot identify oneself with him. The cinema becomes subjective when the actor's gaze meets that of the audience" (in Peter Graham, *The New Wave* [New York: Viking, 1968], p. 93). All of these claims remain murky; we need to study more seriously how the subjective shot functions within the film. A start is made in Edward Branigan's "The Point-of-View Shot," *Screen* **16**, 3 (Autumn 1975): 54–64, and Nick Browne, "The Spectator-in-the-Text," *Film Quarterly* **19**, 2 (Winter 1975–76): 26–44.

Camera Movement and Zoom

The visual effects of camera movement have been discussed in Raymond Durgnat, "The Restless Camera," *Films and Filming* **15**, 3 (December 1968): 14–18; and David Bordwell, "Camera Movement and Cinematic Space," *Ciné-Tracts* **1**, 2 (Summer 1977): 19–26.

A statement of the classical Hollywood cinema's position on camera movement may be found in Herb A. Lightman, "The Fluid Camera," *American Cinematographer* **27**, 3 (March 1946): 82, 102–103: "The intelligent director or cinematographer moves the camera only when the demands of the filmic situation motivate that movement." Compare the Soviet filmmaker Dziga Vertov: "I am eye. I am a mechanical eye. . . . I free myself from today and forever from human immobility. I am in con-

Plate 1 *La Chinoise*

Plate 2 *La Chinoise*

Plate 3 *Playtime*

Plate 4 *Playtime*

Plate 5 *Ivan the Terrible*

Plate 6 *Ivan the Terrible*

Plate 7 *An Autumn Afternoon*

Plate 8 *An Autumn Afternoon*

Plate 9   *Lancelot du Lac*

Plate 10   *Meet Me in St. Louis*

Plate 11   *Meet Me in St. Louis*

Plate 12   *Daisies*

Plate 13   *Innocence Unprotected*

Plate 14   *Ohayu*

Plate 15   *Ohayu*

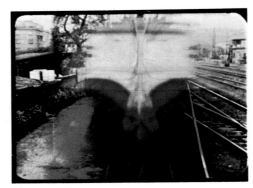

Plate 16   *Daisies*

stant movement" ("Kinoks-Revolution," in Harry M. Geduld, ed., *Film Makers on Film Making* [Bloomington: Indiana University Press, 1969], p. 85).

Since creating frame mobility by means of the zoom lens has become a common shooting technique today, recent discussions have compared zooming (usually unfavorably) with camera movement. See Arthur Graham, "Zoom Lens Techniques," *American Cinematographer* **44**, 1 (January 1963): 28–29; Paul Joannides, "The Aesthetics of the Zoom Lens," *Sight and Sound* **40**, 1 (Winter 1970–71): 40–42; and Stuart M. Kaminsky, "The Use and Abuse of the Zoom Lens," *Filmmakers' Newsletter* **5**, 12 (October 1972): 20–23. To what extent do these three authors agree about the "proper" utilization of the zoom?

"Real Time" and the Long Take

When the camera is running, does it record "real time"? If so, what artistic implications follow from that?

It was André Bazin who took the theoretical initiative in viewing cinema as an art which depends on "real time." Like photography, Bazin argued, cinema is a *recording process:* The camera registers, photochemically, the light reflected from the object. Like the still camera, the movie camera recorded space. But unlike the still camera, the movie camera could also record *time.* "The cinema is objectivity in time. . . . Now, for the first time, the image of things is likewise the image of their duration, change mummified as it were" (*What Is Cinema?* Vol. I [Berkeley: University of California Press, 1966], pp. 14–15). On this basis, Bazin saw editing as an intrusive interruption of the "natural" continuity of duration. He thus praised long-take directors such as Jean Renoir, Orson Welles, William Wyler, and Roberto Rossellini as artists whose styles respected concrete moment-to-moment life.

Bazin should be praised for calling our attention to the possibilities latent in the long take at a time when other film theorists considered it "theatrical" and "uncinematic." Yet the problem of "real time" in film seems more complicated than Bazin thought. The most productive avenues which Bazin's ideas opened up have involved the analysis of different directorial *styles* rather than analysis of the most "realistic" ways to shoot a scene. That is, analysts no longer tend to ask whether Renoir's long takes are more faithful to reality than Eisenstein's short shots; we ask instead about the shots' different formal functions in each director's films. Incidentally, Eisenstein himself—*before* Bazin—proposed shooting an entire scene from *Crime and Punishment* in one long take. See "Mise-en-shot" in Vladimir Nizhny, *Lessons with Eisenstein* (New York: Hill and Wang, 1969), pp. 93–139. Representative stylistic analyses include V. F. Perkins, "*Rope,*" *The Movie Reader* (New York: Praeger, 1972), pp. 35–37; David Thomson, *Movie Man* (New York: Stein and Day, 1967); Brian Henderson, "The Long Take," *Film Comment* **7**, 2 (Summer 1967): 6–11; and Barry Salt, "Statistical Style Analysis of Motion Pictures," *Film Quarterly* **28**, 1 (Fall 1974): 13–22.

CHAPTER 6

THE RELATION OF SHOT TO SHOT: EDITING

Since the 1920s, when film theorists began to realize what editing can achieve, it has been the most widely discussed film technique. This has not been all to the good, for some writers have mistakenly found in editing the key to good cinema (or even *all* cinema). Yet not all films use editing, and those that don't are none the less "cinematic" for that. In experimental filmmaking the absence of editing is common. For instance, films of Michael Snow (e.g., *La Région Centrale*) and of Andy Warhol (e.g., *Eat, Sleep, Empire*) consciously avoid editing. Likewise, many films of the pre-1910 period achieve their effects wholly by means of mise-en-scène or camera work. Thus the use of editing, though important, is wholly at the discretion of the filmmaker.

Still, one can see why editing has exercised such an enormous fascination for film aestheticians, for as a technique it is very powerful. The ride of the Klan in *The Birth of a Nation*, the Odessa Steps sequence in *Potemkin*, the "degradation of the gods" episode in *October*, the shower murder in *Psycho*, the train crash in *La Roue*, the diving sequence of *Olympia*, the "News on the March" reel of *Citizen Kane*—all of these celebrated moments derive much of their effect from editing. Perhaps more important, however, is the power of editing to pervade an entire film's system, becoming a key to the film's overall construction and effect: This is true of not only the films already mentioned, but also hundreds of others. If editing is not the most important film technique, it contributes considerably to the form and effect of a film.

What Editing Is ■

Editing may be thought of as the coordination of one shot with the next. We need to distinguish how editing is done in production from how editing appears on the screen to viewers. As we have seen, in film production

Figure 6.1

Figure 6.2

Figure 6.3

Figure 6.4

a shot is one or more frames in series on a continuous length of film stock. The film editor joins shots, the end of one to the beginning of another.

This junction may be made in several ways. A *fade-out* may gradually darken the end of shot A to black, and a *fade-in* may accordingly lighten shot B from black. A *dissolve* may briefly super-impose the end of shot A and the beginning of shot B (Figs. 6.1, 6.2, and 6.3). A *wipe* may peel off shot A and reveal shot B underneath, as in *Seven Samurai* (Fig. 6.4). The most common means of joining two shots, however, is the *cut*, which in production is usually made by splicing two shots together by means of cement or tape. Some filmmakers "cut" during shooting by planning or trusting that the film will emerge from the camera ready for final showing; in such cases the physical junction from shot to shot is accomplished in the act of filming. Such "editing in the camera," however, is rare; cutting after shooting is the norm.

As viewers, we perceive a shot as an uninterrupted segment of screen time, space, or graphic configurations. Fades, dissolves, and wipes are perceived as *gradually* interrupting one shot and replacing it with another. Cuts are perceived as instantaneous changes from one shot to another. Consider as an example of cutting, four shots from the first attack on Bodega Bay in Alfred Hitchcock's *The Birds* (see Figs. 6.5 through 6.8):

1. *Medium-long shot, straight-on angle.* Melanie, Mitch, and the Captain standing by the restaurant window talking. Melanie on extreme right, bartender in background (Fig. 6.5).

2. *Medium close-up.* Melanie looking to screen left by Captain's shoulder. She looks to right (out offscreen window) up, as if following with eyes. Pan right with her as she turns to the window and looks out (Fig. 6.6).

3. *Extreme long shot.* Melanie's point of view. Gas station across street, phone booth in left foreground. Birds dive-bomb attendant, right to left (Fig. 6.7).

4. *Medium close-up*. Melanie, profile. Captain moves right into shot, blocking out bartender; Mitch moves right into extreme foreground. All in profile look out window (Fig. 6.8).

Each of these four shots presents a different segment of time, space, and graphic materials. The first shot shows three people talking. An instantaneous change—a *cut*—shifts us to a medium shot of Melanie. (Hitchcock could have utilized a fade, dissolve, or wipe instead—with a slower change from shot to shot, or he could have handled the scene as one continuous shot, as we shall see presently.) In the second shot, space has changed (Melanie is isolated and larger in the frame), time is continuous, and the graphic configurations have changed (the arrangements of the shapes and colors vary). Another cut takes us instantly to what she sees. The gas station shot (Fig. 6.7) presents a very different space, a successive bit of time, and a different graphic configuration. Another cut returns us to Melanie (Fig. 6.8), and again we are shifted instantly to another space, the next slice of time, and a different graphic configuration. Thus the four shots are joined by three cuts.

Now let us consider alternative ways of presenting the *Birds* scene without editing. Imagine a camera movement that frames the four people talking, tracks in to Melanie as she turns, pans to the window to show the dive-bombing gull, and pans back to catch Melanie's expression. This would constitute one shot, for we would not have the disjunctions afforded by editing; the camera movements, no matter how fast, would not present the marked and abrupt shifts that cuts produce. Now imagine a deep-space composition that presents Mitch in the foreground, Melanie and the window in the middle ground, and the gull attack in the distance. Again, the scene could now be played in one shot, for we would have no abrupt change of time or space or graphics; the movements of the figures would not yield that disjunction of the screen material that is provided by editing. In this sequence, then, Hitchcock could have presented the action in a single shot (e.g., through a camera movement or a deep-space composition). Instead, he presents it in *more* than one shot—that is, through editing.

Once you become aware of editing, it is easy to notice, not only because it is such a prevalent technique, but also because the disjunctions of space, time, and graphics wrought by editing leap to the attentive eye. Both the instantaneous disjunction of the cut and the more gradual disjunction of the fade, dissolve, or wipe usually mark off shots quite plainly.

Dimensions of Film Editing ■

What is the scope of this technique? Editing offers the filmmaker four basic areas of choice and control:

Figure 6.5

Figure 6.6

Figure 6.7

Figure 6.8

1. Graphic relations between shot A and shot B.
2. Rhythmic relations between shot A and shot B.
3. Spatial relations between shot A and shot B.
4. Temporal relations between shot A and shot B.

Graphic and rhythmic relationships are present in the editing of any film. Spatial and temporal relationships are not usually present in the editing of abstract or "nonfigurative" films, but are present in the editing of films built out of nonabstract images (that is, the great majority of motion pictures). Let us trace the range of choice and control in each area. In each case the discussion will apply to all means of joining shots, but most of our examples will be drawn from the most common editing technique— cutting.

Graphic Relations Between Shot A and Shot B

The four shots from *The Birds* may be considered purely as graphic configurations, as patterns of light and dark, line and shape, volumes and depths, movement and stasis—*independent of* the shot's relation to the time and space of the story. For instance, Hitchcock has not drastically altered the overall brightness from shot to shot. But he could have cut from the uniformly lit second shot (Melanie turning to the window) to a shot of the gas station swathed in darkness. Moreover, Hitchcock has usually kept the most important part of the composition in the center of the frame (compare Melanie's position in the frame with that of the gas station attendant). He could, however, have cut from a shot in which Melanie was in, say, upper frame left to a shot locating the station attendant in the lower right of the frame.

Hitchcock has also played off a certain color difference: Melanie's hair and outfit make her a predominantly yellow and green figure, whereas the shot of the gas station is dominated by drab bluish grays set off by touches of red in the gas pumps. Alternatively, Hitchcock could have cut from Melanie to another figure composed of similar colors. Furthermore, the movement in Melanie's shot—her turning to the window—does not blend into the movements of either the attendant or the gull in the next shot, but Hitchcock could have echoed Melanie's movement in speed, direction, or frame placement by movement in the next shot. In short, editing together any two shots permits the interaction, through similarity and difference, of the *purely pictorial* qualities of those two shots. All of the aspects of mise-en-scene—lighting, setting, costume, and the behavior of the figures in space and time—and most cinematographic qualities—photography, framing, and camera mobility—all furnish potential graphic elements. Thus every shot provides possibilities for purely graphic editing.

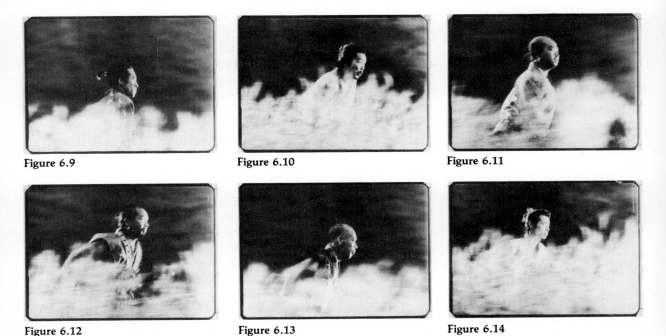

Figure 6.9   Figure 6.10   Figure 6.11

Figure 6.12   Figure 6.13   Figure 6.14

Though abstract films depend heavily on the graphic dimension of editing, most filmmaking has subordinated it to other areas of control. Yet at one level we perceive all film images as configurations of graphic material, and every film manipulates those configurations. Indeed, even in a film that is not pure abstraction, graphic editing can be a source of profound interest to filmmaker and audience.

Graphics may be edited to achieve smooth continuity or abrupt contrast. The filmmaker may link shots by graphic similarities, thus making what we can call a *graphic match*. Shapes, colors, tones of light or dark, or the direction or speed of movement in shot A may be picked up in the composition of shot B. For example, in *Seven Samurai*, after the samurai have first arrived at the village, an alarm sounds and they race to discover its source. The director, Akira Kurosawa, cuts together six shots of different running samurai, which he dynamically "matches" by means of composition, lighting, figure movement, and camera movement (Figs. 6.9–6.14). In the "Beautiful Girl" song in Stanley Donen and Gene Kelly's *Singin' in the Rain* there are amusing graphic matches achieved through dissolves from one fashionably dressed woman to another, each figure posed and framed quite similarly from shot to shot. Such precise graphic matching is, of course, relatively rare, but a general graphic continuity from shot A to shot B (keeping the center of interest at frame cen-

Figure 6.15

Figure 6.16

ter, retaining the overall lighting level, avoiding strong color clashes from shot to shot) is typical of the classical narrative cinema.

Yet shots need *not* be graphically continuous, if the filmmaker so chooses. Orson Welles frequently strives for a clash from shot to shot, as in *Citizen Kane* when the dark long shot of Kane's bedroom is followed by the bright opening title of the "News on the March" reel. Similarly, in *Touch of Evil* Welles dissolves from a shot of Menzies looking out a window on frame right (Fig. 6.15) to a shot of Susan Vargas looking out a different window on frame left (Fig. 6.16); the clash is further accentuated by contrasting screen positions of the window reflections. Alain Resnais's *Night and Fog* began something of a fad by utilizing an extreme but apt graphic conflict: Color footage of an abandoned concentration camp is cut together with black-and-white newsreel shots of the camps in the period 1942–1945. (Even here, though, Resnais found striking graphic similarities in shape, as when a tracking shot of fenceposts graphically matches a low-angle shot of marching Nazi legs.)

Later in this sequence from *The Birds*, Hitchcock puts graphic conflict to good use. Gasoline spurting from the pump has flowed across the street to a parking lot, and Melanie, along with several other people at the restaurant window, has seen a man accidentally set the gasoline alight. His car ignites, and an explosion of flame engulfs him. What we see next is Melanie watching helplessly as the flame races along the trail of gas toward the station. Hitchcock cuts the shots as shown in Figs. 6.17–6.27:

30.	(ls)	High angle. Melanie's viewpoint: flaming car, spreading flames.	73 frames
31.	(mcu)	Straight-on angle. Melanie, immobile, looking off left, mouth open.	20 frames
32.	(ms)	High angle, Melanie's viewpoint. Pan with flames moving from lower right to upper left of trail of gasoline.	18 frames
33.	(mcu)	as 31. Melanie, immobile, staring down (center).	16 frames
34.	(ms)	High angle, Melanie's viewpoint. Pan with flames moving from lower right to upper left.	14 frames
35.	(mcu)	as 31. Melanie, immobile, looking off right, staring, aghast.	12 frames
36.	(ls)	Melanie's viewpoint. Gas station. Flames rush in from right. Mitch, sheriff, and attendant run out left.	10 frames
37.	(mcu)	as 31. Melanie, immobile, stares off extreme right.	8 frames
38.	(ls)	as 36. Melanie's viewpoint. Cars at station explode.	34 frames
39.	(mcu)	as 31. Melanie covers her face with her hands.	33 frames
40.	(els)	Extreme high angle on city, flaming trail in center. Gulls fly into shot.	

Graphically, Hitchcock has exploited two possibilities of contrast. First, although each shot's composition centers the action (Melanie's

Figure 6.17

Figure 6.18

Figure 6.19

Figure 6.20

Figure 6.21

Figure 6.22

Figure 6.23

Figure 6.24

Figure 6.25

Figure 6.26

Figure 6.27

head, the flaming trail), the movements thrust in different directions. In shot 31 Melanie looks to the lower left, whereas in shot 32 the fire moves to the upper left; in shot 33 Melanie is looking down center, whereas in the next shot the flames still move to the upper left; and so on. More important—and what makes the sequence impossible to recapture on the printed page—is the crucial contrast of mobility and stasis. The shots of the flames present movement of both subject (the flames rushing along the gas) and of the camera (which pans to follow). But the shots of Melanie could almost be "stills," since they are absolutely static; she does not turn her head within the shots, and the camera does not move in or away from her. Interestingly too, instead of showing her turning to watch the flames, Hitchcock presents only static stages of her action, and so we must infer the progress of her attention. Such clashes of one direction with another and of movement with stasis constitute very powerful means of utilizing the graphic possibilities of editing. We shall examine some other means later.

Rhythmic Relations Between Shot A and Shot B

Each strip of film—each shot—is necessarily of a certain length. That length can be determined by the filmmaker. When we consider the absolute lengths of shot A and shot B, measured in frames, feet, or meters, we are considering the most basic *rhythmic* potential of editing. The physical length of any shot corresponds to a measurable duration onscreen. As we know, at "sound speed" 24 frames last one second in projection. A shot can be as short as a frame, or it may be thousands of frames long, running for many minutes when projected. This opens the possibility of controlling the rhythmic succession of the shots. The filmmaker may construct a steady rhythm by making all of the shots approximately the same length. An accelerating rhythm may arise from successively shorter shots; a spasmodic, irregular rhythm may be produced by a combination of shots of widely different lengths. Now these cases are somewhat oversimplified, since cinematic rhythm as a whole derives from not only editing, but other film techniques as well. The filmmaker also relies on mise-en-scene, camera position and movement, and the overall context to determine the editing rhythm. Nevertheless, the lengths of the successive shots contribute considerably to what we intuitively recognize as a film's tempo, or "pace."

Consider how Hitchcock handles the rhythm of the first gull attack in *The Birds*. Shot 1, the medium shot of the group talking (Fig. 6.5), consumes 996 frames, or about 41 seconds. But shot 2 (Fig. 6.6), which shows Melanie looking, is much shorter—309 frames (almost 13 seconds). Even shorter is shot 3 (Fig. 6.7), which is only 55 frames (about 2⅓ seconds). The fourth shot (Fig. 6.8)—of Melanie joined by Mitch and the Captain—lasts only 35 frames (about 1½ seconds). Clearly Hitchcock is accelerating the rhythm at the beginning of what will be a tense sequence. In what follows, Hitchcock makes the shots fairly short, but subordinates the length of the shot to the internal rhythm of the dialogue and the movement in the images. As a result, shots 5 through 29 (not illustrated here) have no fixed pattern of lengths. But once the essential components of the scene have been established, Hitchcock again manipulates rhythm, as can be seen in shots 30 through 40 (Figs. 6.17 through 6.27). In presenting Melanie's horrified realization of the flames racing from the parking lot to the gas station, this series of shots climaxes the rhythmic acceleration of the sequence. As the description on p. 156 shows, after the shot of the spreading flames (no. 30, Fig. 6.17), each shot decreases in length by two frames, from 20 frames to 8. Shot 38 (Fig. 6.25), a long shot that lasts over 600 frames, brakes this acceleration by functioning as both a pause and a suspenseful preparation for the next savage bird attack. In this scene variations in rhythm lead us to expect changes in narrative action.

What is the point of all these numbers? The theater viewer cannot, of course, count frames, but he or she does *feel* and *recognize* the accelerating cutting in this sequence. Through his editing, Hitchcock impels the viewer's perception to move at an increased pace, and this pace is an essential component in the excitement of the scene.

Hitchcock is not, of course, the only director to utilize rhythmic editing. Such possibilities were initially explored before 1920 by such directors as D. W. Griffith (especially in *Intolerance*), Abel Gance, and Lev Kuleshov. In the 1920s the Hollywood cinema, the Soviet montage school, and the French "impressionist" filmmakers developed complementary approaches to the matter of rhythm. When sound films became the standard, pronounced rhythmic editing survived not only in musical comedies and fantasies such as René Clair's *A Nous la Liberté* and *Le Million*, Rouben Mamoulian's *Love Me Tonight*, and Busby Berkeley's dance sequences in *42nd Street* and *Footlight Parade*, but also in dramatic films such as Lewis Milestone's *All Quiet on the Western Front*. In classical Hollywood cinema the rhythmic use of dissolves became crucial to the "montage sequence," which we shall discuss shortly. To this day, rhythm is recognized as a fundamental resource of the editor, as witness not only the vogue of fast cutting in the 1960s (e.g., Richard Lester's Beatles films), but also the ubiquitous television soft drink commercials cut to the beat of the song on the sound track.

Spatial Relations Between Shot A and Shot B

Editing may not only control graphics and rhythm, but may construct film space as well. Exhilaration in this newly discovered power can be sensed in the writings of such filmmakers as the Soviet director Dziga Vertov: "I am eye. I am builder. I implanted you, a most remarkable chamber which did not exist until I created it today. In this chamber there are 12 walls, photographed by me in various parts of the world. Manipulating shots of walls and details, I have succeeded in arranging them in an order which pleases you." Such elation is understandable, since editing permits the filmmaker to relate through similarity, difference, or development, *any* two points in space, for whatever purpose she or he chooses.

One may, for instance, start with a shot that establishes a spatial whole and follow this with a shot of a part of this space. This is what Hitchcock does in shot 1 and shot 2 of the sequence described above: a medium-long shot of the group of people followed by a medium shot of only one, Melanie. Such analytical breakdown is a very common editing pattern, especially in classical continuity editing.

One may, alternatively, construct a whole space out of component parts, as Hitchcock also does in the *Birds* sequence. Note that we do not see a single establishing shot including Melanie *and* the gas station. In production the restaurant window need not be across from the station at all; they could be in different cities or countries. (It is likely that, shooting "out of continuity," Hitchcock filmed the restaurant shots on a sound stage and the gas station shots in an outdoor set.) Yet we are compelled to see Melanie as being across the street from the gas station. The bird cry offscreen and the mise-en-scene (the window and Melanie's sidewise glance) contribute considerably, but it is primarily the editing that creates the spatial whole of restaurant-and-gas-station.

Such spatial manipulation through cutting is fairly common. In films compiled from newsreel footage, for example, one shot might show a cannon firing, and another shot might show a shell hitting its target; we infer that the cannon fired the shell (though the shots may show entirely different battles). Again, if a shot of a speaker is followed by a shot of a cheering crowd, we assume a spatial coexistence. The possibility of such spatial manipulation was examined by the Soviet filmmaker Lev Kuleshov, who came up with a series of "experiments" in constructing spatial relations by eliminating establishing shots. The most famous of these involved the cutting of neutral shots of an actor's face with other shots (variously reported as shots of soup, nature scenes, a dead woman, a baby). The result was that the audience immediately assumed not only that the actor's expression changed, but also that the actor was reacting to things present in the same space as himself. Similarly, Kuleshov cut together shots of actors "looking at each other" but on Moscow streets miles apart, then meeting and strolling together—and looking at the White House in Washington! Though films' use of such cutting predates Kuleshov's work, his study of this possibility has caused film scholars to call "the Kuleshov effect" any series of shots that *in the absence of an establishing shot* creates a spatial whole by joining disparate spatial fragments.

In contrast to such types of editing that build up a single locale, editing can also juxtapose two or more distinctly separate locales. In *Intolerance* D. W. Griffith cuts from Babylon to Gethsemane, from France to America. Such parallel editing, or *crosscutting*, is a common way films construct heterogeneous spaces.

More radically, the editing can present spatial relations as being ambiguous and uncertain. In Carl Dreyer's *La Passion de Jeanne d'Arc*, for instance, we know only that Jeanne and the priests are in the same room; because the neutral white backgrounds and the numerous close-ups provide no orientation to the entire space, we can seldom tell how far apart the characters are or precisely who is beside whom. We shall see later how *October* and *Last Year at Marienbad* create similar spatial discontinuities.

Temporal Relations Between Shot A and Shot B

Like the other film techniques, editing can control the time of the action denoted in the story. As the *Birds* example suggests, several areas of time are open to the filmmaker's manipulation.

First, there is the *order* of presentation of events. The men talk, then Melanie turns away, then she sees the gull swoop, then she responds. Hitchcock's editing presents these story events in the 1-2-3-4 order of his shots. But he could have shuffled the shots into a different order: Transposing shot 2 and shot 3 would be least unusual, but it is possible to put them in any order at all, even reverse (4-3-2-1). This is to say that the filmmaker may control temporal succession through the editing; as we saw in Chapter 3, such manipulation of events leads to changes in story-plot relations. We are most familiar with such manipulations as *flashbacks*, which juxtapose shots taken out of their presumed story order. In *Hiroshima Mon Amour*, for instance, Resnais cuts from a shot of the hand of the protagonist's Japanese lover to a shot of the hand of her German lover years earlier (with memory motivating the violation of temporal order). The rarer *flashforward* also breaks the presumed order of story events, by juxtaposing a shot of the "present" with a shot of a future event before returning to the present (as in the foreshadowings of death in *Love Affair, or the Case of the Missing Switchboard Operator* and *Don't Look Now*). Such edited manipulations of temporal order can become very complex, as in Straub's *Not Reconciled* and Resnais's *Last Year at Marienbad*, which interweave several different time schemes. We may assume, then, that if a series of shots traces a 1-2-3 order in the presentation of story events, it is because the filmmaker has chosen to do that, not because of any natural necessity of following this order.

Editing also offers ways for the filmmaker to alter the "natural" *duration* of story events as presented in the film's plot. In our sample sequence, it is true, the duration of the story events is presented whole: Melanie's act of turning consumes a certain length of time, and Hitchcock does not alter the duration of the event in his editing. Nevertheless, he could have omitted any or all of the duration of the event. Imagine cutting from shot 1 (the men talking and Melanie standing by) to a shot of Melanie already turned and looking out the window. The time it took her to turn to the window would be eliminated by the cut. Thus editing can create a temporal *ellipsis.* This is familiar to all of us. A film's plot may take two hours and yet cover several days, months, or years in the story; cuts, fades, dissolves, and wipes are crucial in elliding such time. For example, in *Citizen Kane* Charles responds to Thatcher's greeting with "Merry Christmas"; Welles cuts to Thatcher, somewhat older, saying, "And a happy new year" in dictating a letter to the 21-year-old Kane. Though seldom this flashy, ellipses abound in films: the time it takes to climb a stair, eat a meal, get dressed, or dial a telephone is frequently abridged by cuts, fades, dissolves, or wipes.

But Hitchcock could have altered the duration of the action in an opposite way—by *expansion*. For example, he might have extended shot 1 so as to include the beginning of Melanie's act of turning, then shown her beginning to turn in shot 2 as well. This would have prolonged the action, stretching it out past its story duration. The Russian filmmakers of the 1920s made frequent use of temporal expansion through such *overlapping* editing, and no one mastered it more thoroughly than Sergei Eisenstein. In *Strike,* when factory workers bowl over a foreman with a large wheel hanging from a crane, three shots expand the action; in *October* Eisenstein overlaps several shots of rising bridges in order to stress the significance of the moment; in *Ivan the Terrible* friends pour golden coins down on the newly crowned Ivan in a torrent that seems never to cease—in all of these sequences the duration of the action is prolonged through noticeably overlapping the movements from shot to shot.

Returning once more to the temporal relations in the *Birds* segment, we note that in the story Melanie turns to the window only once and the gull swoops only once. And Hitchcock presents these events on the screen the same number of times that they occur in the story. But of course Hitchcock could have repeated any of these shots. Melanie could have been shown turning to the window several times; this would be not merely overlapping a phase of an action, but rather full-scale repetition.

If this sounds peculiar, it is doubtless because we are overwhelmingly accustomed to seeing a shot present the action only once. Yet its very rarity may make repetition a powerful editing resource. In Bruce Conner's *Report* there is a newsreel shot of John and Jacqueline Kennedy riding a limousine down a Dallas street; the shot is systematically repeated, in part or in whole, again and again. We shall see a similar strategy of repetition at work in segments of *Last Year at Marienbad*. Thus *frequency* is another area of choice and control that, like order and duration, gives the filmmaker considerable temporal possibilities in editing.

Graphics, rhythm, space, and time, then, are at the service of the filmmaker through the technique of editing. Our brief survey should suggest that the potential range of these areas of control is virtually unlimited. Yet most films we see make use of a very narrow set of editing possibilities—so narrow, indeed, that we can speak of a dominant editing style throughout Western film history. This is what is usually called *continuity editing*, and because of its prevalance we will examine it. But the most familiar way to edit a film is not the only way to edit a film, and so we will also consider some alternatives to continuity editing.

Continuity Editing ■

Editing might appear to present a dilemma to the filmmaker. On one hand, it disunifies. The physical break between one shot and another may seem to have a disturbing effect, interrupting the viewer's flow of attention. But on the other hand, editing is undeniably a primary means for constructing a film. How can one use editing and yet control its potentially disruptive force? This problem (though not stated in these terms) first confronted filmmakers around 1900–1910. The solution eventually adopted was to plan the cinematography and mise-en-scene with a view to editing the shots according to a specific system. The purpose of the system was *to tell a story* coherently and clearly, to map out the chain of characters' actions in an undistracting way. Thus editing, supported by specific strategies of cinematography and mise-en-scene, was used to ensure *narrative continuity*. So powerful is this style that even today, a director or editor in narrative filmmaking is expected to be thoroughly familiar with it. How does this stylistic system work?

The basic purpose of the continuity system is to control the potentially disunifying force of editing by establishing a smooth flow from shot to shot. All of the possibilities of editing we have already examined are bent to this end. Graphics are kept roughly similar from shot to shot: The figures are balanced and symmetrically deployed in the frame; the overall lighting tonality remains constant; the action occupies the central zone of the screen. The rhythm of the cutting is usually made dependent on the camera distance of the shot: Long shots are left on the screen longer than medium shots are, and medium shots are left on longer than close-ups are. (Sometimes, in scenes of physical action, markedly accelerated editing rhythms may be present, regardless of the shot scale.) Since the continuity style seeks to present a narrative action, however, it is chiefly through the handling of space and time that editing furthers narrative continuity.

Spatial Continuity: The 180° System

In the continuity style the space of a scene is constructed along what is called variously the "axis of action," the "center line," or the "180° line." The scene's action—a person walking, two people conversing, a car racing along a road—is assumed to project along a straight line. Consequently, the filmmaker will plan, film, and edit the shots to establish this center line as clearly as possible. The camera work and mise-en-scene in each shot will be manipulated to establish and reiterate the 180° space. A bird's-eye view (Fig. 6.28) will clarify the system.

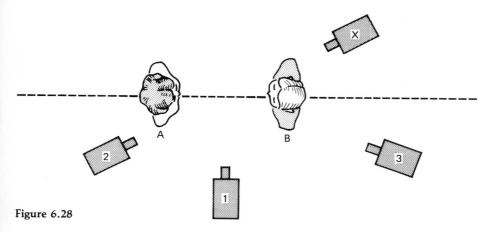

Figure 6.28

This bird's-eye view shows A and B conversing. The axis of action is that imaginary line connecting the two people. Under the continuity system, the director would arrange the mise-en-scene and camera placement so as to establish and sustain this line. The camera can be put at any point as long as it stays on the same *side* of the line (hence the 180° term). A typical series of shots would be: (1) a long shot of A and B; (2) a shot over A's shoulder, "favoring" B; (3) a shot over B's shoulder, favoring A. But to cut to a shot from camera position "x" would be considered a violation of the system because it *crosses* the axis of action. Indeed, one handbook on film directing calls shot x flatly "wrong." To see why, we need to examine what this 180° system does.

It ensures some common space from shot to shot. As long as the axis of action is not crossed, portions of the space will tally from shot to shot. In our example, assume that there is a wall with pictures and shelves behind A and B. If we follow shot 1 with shot 2, not only will one side of B reappear as a common factor, but so will at least part of the wall, the pictures, and shelves. We are thus oriented to the space presented in shot 2: It is simply part of the space of shot 1, observed from a new position. But if we follow shot 1 with shot x, we see both a new side of B and an entirely different background (another wall, a door, or whatever). A defender of traditional continuity would claim that this disorients us; has B moved to another locale? Thus the 180° rule generates a common area from shot to shot, which stabilizes space and orients the viewer within the scene.

It ensures constant screen direction. Assume now that A is walking left to right; A's path constitutes the axis of action. As long as our shots do not cross this axis, cutting them together will keep the screen direction of A's movement constant, from left to right. But if we *cross* the axis and film a shot from the other side, not only will the background change, but also A will now appear on the screen as moving from *right to left*. Such a cut could be disorienting.

Consider the standard scene of two cowboys meeting for a shootout on a town street. The hero and villain form the 180° line; the hero is walking from left to right, and the villain is approaching from right to left. But now imagine cutting in a shot of the hero taken from the *opposite* side of the line. He is now seen as moving from right to left. Has he taken fright and turned around while the villain was onscreen? Under these circumstances, a break in continuity could be quite confusing. Even more disorienting would be crossing the line while establishing the same shootout situation. If the first shot of the whole scene shows the hero walking left to right and the second shot shows the villain (from the other side of the line) also walking left to right, we would probably not be able to tell whether they were walking toward each other. The two men would seem to us to be walking in the same direction at different points on the street; we would be likely to be startled if they suddenly came face to face within the same shot. Though we shall examine some strategems for getting "across the line," it is enough for now to see that adhering to the 180° system ensures consistent screen direction from shot to shot. (We shall see in our examination of *Stagecoach* in Part Four that not all violations of screen direction are necessarily confusing.)

It should be obvious that the 180° system prides itself on delineating space clearly. The viewer always knows where the *characters* are in rela-

Figure 6.29   Shot 1a

Figure 6.30   Shot 1b

Figure 6.31   Shot 2

Figure 6.32   Shot 3

Figure 6.33   Shot 4

tion to one another and to the setting. More important, the viewer always knows *where he or she is* with respect to the story action. The space of the scene, cleanly and unambiguously unfolded, does not jar or disorient, because such disorientation, it is felt, will distract the viewer from the material at hand: the narrative chain of causes and effects. We saw in Chapter 3 that the classical Hollywood mode of narrative subordinates time, motivation, and other factors to the cause/effect sequence. We also saw how mise-en-scene and camera position and movement may function to present narrative material. Now we can note how continuity editing also works to subordinate space to causality. On the basis of the 180° principle, the continuity style has developed a repertory of tactics for building a smoothly flowing space subordinate to the narrative. Let us consider a concrete example, the opening of John Huston's *The Maltese Falcon*.

The action begins in the office of Sam Spade. Note that in the first two shots this space is established in several ways. First, there is the office window (shot 1a, Fig. 6.29) from which the camera pans down to reveal Spade (shot 1b, Fig. 6.30) rolling a cigarette. As Spade says, "Yes, sweetheart?" shot 2 (Fig. 6.31) appears. This is important in several respects. It is what would be called an *establishing* shot, delineating the overall space of the office: the door, the intervening area, the desk, and Spade's position. Note also that shot 2 establishes a 180° line between Spade and his secretary, Effie; we will always be on the same side of this 180° line.

Once laid out for us in the first two shots, the space is analyzed into its components. Shots 3 (Fig. 6.32) and 4 (Fig. 6.33) show Spade and Effie talking. Because the 180° line established at the outset is adhered to (each shot presents the two from the same side), we know their location and spatial relationships. In cutting to medium shots of the two, however, Huston relies on two other common tactics within the 180° system. The first is the *shot/reverse shot*. Once the 180° line has been established, we can show first one end point of the line, then the other, cutting back and forth (here from Effie to Spade).

The second tactic Huston uses here is the *eyeline match*. That is, shot A presents someone looking at something offscreen; shot B shows us what is being looked at. In neither shot are *both* looker and object present. (The shots from *The Birds* of Melanie watching the bird attack and the fire create eyeline matches.) This is a simple idea but a powerful one, since the *directional* quality of the eyeline creates a strong spatial continuity. To be looked at, an object must be near the looker. (It is probably the eyeline match that created the effects Kuleshov identified in his construction of false spaces through editing. That is, the expressionless actor seems to be looking at whatever is in the next shot, and the audience assumes that the actor is reacting accordingly.)

Figure 6.34   Shot 5a

Within the 180° system, the eyeline match, like constant screen direction, can stabilize space. Note how in shot 3, Effie's glance off right reiterates Spade's position even though he is not onscreen. And though Spade does not look up and create another eyeline match in shot 4, the camera position remains adamantly on the same side of the axis of action (indeed, the position is identical to that in shot 1b). Thus the breakdown of the scene's space is completely consistent, this consistency ensured by adherence to the 180° system. Thanks to the shot/reverse shot pattern and the eyeline match, even though the two characters are not in the same frame, we are always certain of their whereabouts.

Figure 6.35   Shot 5b

Such spatial clarity is reaffirmed in shot 5, which presents the same space as in shot 2. The office is thus shown again (shot 5a, Fig. 6.34), when the new character, Brigid O'Shaughnessy, enters (shot 5b, Fig. 6.35). Shot 5 is what is called a *reestablishing shot*, since it reestablishes the overall space that was analyzed into shots 3 and 4. The pattern, then, has been *establishment/breakdown/reestablishment*—one of the most common patterns of development of space in the classical continuity style.

Let us pause to examine how this pattern has functioned to advance the narrative. Shot 1 has partially established the space of the office, but has, more important, emphasized the protagonist of the story by linking him to the sign on the window. Offscreen sound and Spade's "Yes, sweetheart?" motivate the cut to shot 2. This establishing shot firmly anchors shot 1 spatially. It also introduces the source of the offscreen sound—the new character, Effie. The cut has occurred at precisely the moment when Effie enters. We are thus unlikely to notice the cut, because our expectations lead us to want to see what happens next. The space near the door has been shown when the cause-effect chain makes it important, not before and not after. Shots 3 and 4 present the conversation between Spade and Effie, and the shot/reverse shot and the eyeline match reassure us as to the characters' locations. We may not even notice the cutting, since the style works to emphasize the dramatic flow of the scene—what Effie says and how Spade reacts. In shot 5 the overall view

Figure 6.36   Shot 6a

Figure 6.37   Shot 6b

of the office is presented again, precisely at the moment when a new character is about to enter the scene, and this situates *her* firmly in the space. Thus the narrative—the dialogue, the entrance of new characters—is emphasized by adhering to the 180° system. The editing subordinates space to action.

We can trace the same procedures—with one additional variation—in the following shots. In shot 5 Brigid O'Shaughnessy enters Spade's office. Shot 6 presents another angle on the two of them as she comes toward him (shot 6a, Fig. 6.36) and sits down by his desk (shot 6b, Fig. 6.37). Again, the 180° line is observed, though the line no longer runs from Spade to the doorway; it now runs from Spade to the client's chair by his desk. Once established, this new line will not be violated.

The one extra factor here is a third tactic for ensuring spatial continuity—the *match on action*, a very powerful device. Assume that a figure starts to stand up in shot A. We can wait until the character is standing up and has stopped moving before cutting to shot B. But we can instead show the figure's movement *beginning* in shot A, and then we can cut to shot B, which shows the continuation of the movement. We would then have a match on action, the editing device that carries a movement across the break between two shots. In *The Maltese Falcon* scene the cut from shot 5 to shot 6 uses a match on action, the action being Brigid's walk toward Spade's desk. Again, the 180° system aids in concealing the match, since it keeps screen direction constant. As one would expect, the match on action is a tool of narrative continuity. It takes a practiced eye to spot a smooth match on action; so powerful is our desire to follow the action flowing across the cut that we ignore the cut itself. The similarity of movement from shot to shot holds our attention more than the differences resulting from the cut.

Except for the match on action, the editing in the rest of the scene uses the same tactics we have already seen. A new axis of action has been *established* (shot 6b), which enables Huston to break down the space into closer shots (shots 7–13, Figs. 6.38 through 6.44). All of these shots use the shot/reverse shot tactic: first one point on the 180° line, then the other. (Note the shoulders in the foreground of shots 7, 8, and 10—Figs. 6.38, 6.39, and 6.41.) Here again, the editing of space presents the dialogue action simply and unambiguously. Beginning with shot 11, Huston's cuts also create eyeline matches: Brigid looks off right at Spade (shot 11, Fig. 6.42); Spade looks off left at Brigid (shot 12, Fig. 6.43); Brigid looks off left toward the door (shot 13, Fig. 6.44); Archer, just coming in, looks off right at them (shot 14, Fig. 6.45); and they both look off at him (shot 15, Fig. 6.46). The 180° rule permits us always to know who is looking at whom.

When Archer enters, the breakdown of the space ceases momentarily, and Huston *reestablishes* the space with a long shot (shot 16a, Fig.

Figure 6.38 **Shot 7**

Figure 6.39 **Shot 8**

Figure 6.40 **Shot 9**

Figure 6.41 **Shot 10**

Figure 6.42 **Shot 11**

Figure 6.43 **Shot 12**

Figure 6.44 **Shot 13**

Figure 6.45 **Shot 14**

Figure 6.46 **Shot 15**

Figure 6.47   Shot 16a

Figure 6.48   Shot 16b

Figure 6.49   Shot 17

Figure 6.50

Figure 6.51

6.47) that integrates Archer into it (shot 16b, Fig. 6.48). (Compare shots 16b and 6a [Figs. 6.48 and 6.36] to see how almost exactly the same camera position earlier established Brigid's entrance.) Archer sits down on Spade's desk, establishing a new axis of action which governs the cut to the next shot (shot 17, Fig. 6.49; here Brigid is on one end of the axis, Spade and Archer on the other). The rest of the scene's editing analyzes this newly established set of relationships without ever crossing the line.

The viewer does not notice all this; indeed, he or she is not *supposed* to. Throughout, the shots present space to emphasize the cause-and-effect flow—the characters' actions, entrances, dialogue, reactions. The editing has economically organized space to convey narrative continuity.

There are other refinements of the 180° system, but one is worth brief mention: the so-called *cheat cut*. Sometimes a director may not have perfect continuity from shot to shot because he or she has composed each shot for specific reasons. Must the two shots match perfectly? Again, narrative motivation decides the matter. Given that the 180° system emphasizes narrative causality, the director has some freedom to "cheat" mise-en-scene from shot to shot. Consider two shots from William Wyler's *Jezebel*. Neither character moves during either shot, but Wyler has blatantly cheated the position of Julie: In the first shot the top of her head is even with the man's chin (Fig. 6.50), but in the second shot she seems to have grown several inches (Fig. 6.51). Yet the great majority of viewers would not notice the discrepancy, since it is the dialogue that is of paramount importance in the scene; here again, the similarities between shots outweigh the differences of position. There is, in fact, a cheat in the *Maltese Falcon* scene, too, between shots 6b and 7; in 6b (Fig. 6.37), as Spade leans forward, the back of his chair is not anywhere near him, yet in shot 7 (Fig. 6.38), it has been cheated to be just behind his left arm. Here again, the primacy of the narrative flow overrides such a cheat cut.

Can the director ever legitimately cross the axis of action? Yes. A scene occurring in certain settings—in a doorway or on a staircase, for instance—may "break the line." Also, having the actors or the camera move across the line may create a new axis of action that permits the filmmaker to cut to shots that would normally be out of continuity. (Since a violation of continuity can occur *only* at a cut, a camera movement cannot break continuity.) But the most usual way of crossing the line is by taking one shot from *on the line itself* and using that as a transition. If, say, in shot A a car is moving from left to right, shot B could be a *head-on* or *tails-on* shot (i.e., the car would be moving directly toward or directly away from the viewer). Then one could cut to shot C, showing the car moving from right to left. Without the shot taken *on* the axis of action, a cut from A to C would violate continuity, but shot B serves as a transition to permit the crossing of the line. This is relatively rare in a dialogue scene, but is more common in sequences of chases and outdoor physical action.

Finally, we may note how the continuity system has absorbed within itself one potentially jarring spatial possibility. If shot A presents one space (say, a living room) and shot B presents a totally different space (say, a prairie), the discontinuity could be quite disturbing. The continuity system has, however, controlled this device by harnessing it to the causal chain of characters' actions within the narrative. If the bandits are menacing the woman in the living room and if her husband is riding home, the spatial discontinuity is no longer jarring. The clear relationship between the two actions motivates the cutting together of two spaces. This is the famous *parallel editing*, or *crosscutting*, first extensively explored by D. W. Griffith in films such as *The Lonely Villa* and *The Lonedale Operator*. Crosscutting thus juxtaposes shots of two distinct spaces by cutting back and forth. Used in hundreds of films, the device is particularly powerful in Hitchcock's *Strangers on a Train*, where it engenders not only suspense but also a set of narrative parallels between the protagonist and the psychotic murderer. Whatever other functions it may have, though, crosscutting remains primarily a means of presenting narrative actions occurring in several locales.

Temporal Continuity: Order, Frequency, Duration

In the classical continuity system, time, like space, is organized according to the development of the narrative. We know that the plot's presentation of the story typically involves considerable manipulation of time. Continuity editing seeks to support and sustain this temporal manipulation.

Recall, to get specific, our distinction among temporal order, frequency, and duration. Continuity editing typically presents the story events in a 1-2-3 order (e.g., Spade rolls a cigarette, then Effie comes in, then he answers her, etc.). The only violation of this order is a flashback, signaled by a cut or dissolve. Furthermore, classical editing also typically presents only *once* what happens *once* in the story; in continuity style, it would be a gross mistake for Huston to repeat the shot of, say, Brigid sitting down (Fig. 6.37). (Only a flashback would motivate the repetition of a scene already witnessed.) So chronological sequence and "one-for-one" frequency are the most common methods of handling order and frequency in the continuity style of editing. What of duration?

In the classical continuity system, story duration is seldom expanded (screen time being greater than story time). Usually, duration is in complete continuity (plot time equaling story time) or is ellided (story time being greater than plot time). Let us first consider complete continuity, the most common possibility. Here a scene occupying five minutes in the story also occupies five minutes when projected on the screen. In the first scene of *The Maltese Falcon* there are three cues for such temporal continuity. First, the narrative progression of the scene has no gaps: Every move to a new position and every line of dialogue is presented. There is also the sound track. Sound issuing from the story space (what we shall later call "diegetic" sound) is a standard indicator of temporal continuity, especially when (as in this scene) the sound "bleeds over" each cut. Finally, there is the match on action between shots 5 and 6. So powerful is the match on action that it creates both spatial *and* temporal continuity. The reason is obvious: If an action carries across the cut, the space and time are assumed to be continuous from shot to shot. (Our look at *Last Year at Marienbad* in Chapter 9 will show that this is only an assumption, not a universal truth.) In all, an absence of ellipses in the story action, diegetic sound overlapping the cuts, and matching on action are three primary indicators that the duration of the scene is continuous.

Sometimes, however, a second possibility will be explored: *temporal ellipsis*. The ellipsis may, of course, omit seconds, minutes, hours, days, years, or centuries. Some ellipses are of no importance to the narrative development and so are concealed. To take a common example: A classical narrative film typically does not show the entire time it takes a character to dress, wash, and breakfast in the morning. Shots of the character going into the shower, putting on shoes, or frying an egg might be edited so as to eliminate the unwanted bits of time, with the plot presenting in seconds a process that might have taken an hour in the story. The *cut-in* (a shot presenting a detail of the previous shot) and the *cutaway* (a shot presenting some element in the scene but off-screen in the previous shot) are frequently used to cover short temporal ellipses.

But other ellipses are important to the narrative: The viewer must recognize that time has passed. For this task the continuity style has built up a varied repertory of devices. Most often, dissolves, fades, or wipes are used to indicate an ellipsis between shots. Thus from the last shot of one scene we dissolve or fade or wipe to the first shot of the next scene. (The Hollywood "rule" is that a dissolve indicates a brief time lapse and a fade indicates a much longer one.) In some cases contemporary practice substitutes a cut for such transitions. For example, in *2001* Kubrick cuts directly from a bone spinning in the air to a nuclear weapon orbiting the earth; not only one of the boldest graphic matches in recent narrative cinema, the cut also eliminates eons of story time.

In other cases it is necessary to show a large-scale process or very lengthy period—a war, a child growing up, the rise of a singing star. Here classical continuity uses another device for temporal ellipsis: the so-called *montage sequence.* (This should not be confused with the concept of "montage" in Sergei Eisenstein's film theory.) Brief portions of a process, informative titles (e.g., "1865" or "San Francisco"), stereotyped images (e.g., the Eiffel Tower), newsreel footage, newspaper headlines, and the like could be swiftly joined by dissolves and music to compress a lengthy series of actions into a few moments. We are all familiar with the most clichéd montage ellipses—calendar leaves fluttering away, newspaper presses churning out an Extra, clocks ticking portentously—but in the hands of deft editors such sequences become small virtuoso pieces in themselves. Slavko Vorkapich's montages of Americana in *Mr. Smith Goes to Washington,* Jack Killifer's tracing of a society across two decades in *The Roaring Twenties,* and Edward Curtis's brutal depictions of a gangster's rise in *Scarface* illustrate the powers of the device. Although currently the montage sequence is rare, the continuity style used such ellipses so frequently for 30 years that montages were widely parodied, in such films as Jean Renoir's *The Crime of M. Lange,* Orson Welles's *Citizen Kane,* and Frank Tashlin's *Will Success Spoil Rock Hunter?*

It is clear that the continuity style utilizes the temporal dimension of editing primarily for narrative purposes. Presenting the story chronologically means arranging events in order, "flashing back" when necessary to prior events. Presenting the story clearly demands that events be presented onscreen only as many times as they occurred in the story. And telling a story economically demands that the action be presented in its story duration or abridged by judicious ellipses. At least, this is how the classical Hollywood continuity system has conceived storytelling. Like graphics, rhythm, and space, time is organized to permit the smooth unfolding of narrative cause and effect. But there are some alternatives to the continuity style of editing.

Alternatives to Continuity Editing ■

Graphic and Rhythmic Possibilities.   Powerful and pervasive as it is, the continuity style remains only *one* style, and many filmmakers have explored other editing possibilities. One alternative to such emphasis is

Figure 6.52

to grant the graphic and rhythmic dimensions greater weight. That is, instead of joining shot A to shot B primarily on the basis of the spatial and temporal functions that the shot fulfills in presenting a story, you could join them on the basis of purely graphic or rhythmic qualities—independent of the time and space they represent. In the nonnarrative film of abstract form, graphic and rhythmic dimensions come to the fore. In films such as *Anticipation of the Night, Scenes from Under Childhood, Western History*, and others, Stan Brakhage has explored purely graphic means of joining shot to shot: Continuities and discontinuities of light, texture, and shape motivate the editing. Interested in the very surface of the film itself, Brakhage has scratched, painted on the image, even taped moth wings to it, in search of abstract graphic combinations. Similarly, parts of Bruce Conner's *Cosmic Ray, A Movie*, and *Report* cut together newsreel footage, old film clips, leader, and blank frames on the basis of graphic patterns of movement, direction, and speed. Many filmmakers have completely subordinated the space and time presented in each shot to the rhythmic relations among shots. "Single-frame" films (in which each shot is only one frame long) are the most extreme examples of this overriding rhythmic concern; two famous examples are Robert Breer's *Fist Fight* and Peter Kubelka's *Schwechater*.

The preeminence of graphic and rhythmic editing in nonnarrative cinema is not, however, as recent a phenomenon as these examples might suggest. As early as 1913, many painters were contemplating the pure-design possibilities offered by film, and many works of the European avant-garde movements of the 1920s combined an interest in abstract graphics with a desire to explore rhythmic editing. The results were as diverse as Man Ray's *Emak Bakia*, Henri Chomette's *Cinq Minutes de Cinéma Pur*, Germaine Dulac's *Thème et Variations*, Hans Richter's *Ghosts Before Breakfast*, and Walter Ruttmann's *Berlin: Symphony of a Great City*. Perhaps the most famous of these is Fernand Léger-Dudley Murphy's film *Ballet Mécanique* (Fig. 6.52). Shots of everyday objects (hats, bottles, Christmas-tree ornaments, kitchen utensils) are juxtaposed not for narrative purposes, but on the basis of similarity or difference of shape, placement within the frame, and particularly movement. Movement determines the rhythm of the cutting as well, the shots' durations being carefully measured to generate not just one rhythm but several conflicting ones as well. Thus in the first section of *Ballet Mécanique*, as Standish Lawder has pointed out, the gentle to-and-fro tempo of a woman sitting on a swing is interrupted by brief fusillades of shots ranging in length from 110 frames to 1 frame. Later, the woman's swinging movement is picked up in the rush of wheels, a swinging metal sphere, and rhythmic shifting of prismatically altered images. At one point, shots will be cut in almost perfectly even rhythm (81 frames/94

Figure 6.53

Figure 6.54

Figure 6.55

Figure 6.56

frames/93 frames/92 frames). But immediately, the shots will be quite irregularly measured (225/78/11/37/32/121 frames). At another moment, a straw hat, a chair, numerals, triangles, circles, wine bottles, and mannikins' legs engage in a stunning cinematic dance, thanks to very fast cutting (the average shot here is three frames long) and careful shifts in the graphic arrangement of each shot (see Fig. 6.52). Through such a complex juxtaposition of editing rhythms and an attention to the play of purely graphic configurations, *Ballet Mécanique* suggests the range of dimensions which the continuity style seldom explores.

Important as the graphic and rhythmic possibilities of editing have been to the nonnarrative film, their powers have not been wholly neglected in the narrative film. Although the continuity style seeks an overall graphic continuity, this is usually subordinated to the concern with mapping narrative space and tracing narrative time. Some narrative filmmakers, however, at times subordinate narrative concerns to graphic pattern. The most famous examples are probably the films for which Busby Berkeley choreographed elaborate dance numbers. In *42nd Street*, *Golddiggers of 1933*, *Footlight Parade*, *Golddiggers of 1935*, and *Dames*, the narrative periodically grinds to a halt and presents intricate dances that are arranged, shot, and edited with a concern for the pure configuration of dancers and background.

More complexly related to the narrative is the graphic editing of Yasujiro Ozu. Ozu's cutting is often dictated by a much more precise graphic continuity than we find in the classical continuity style. In *An Autumn Afternoon* Ozu cuts from one man drinking *sake* (Fig. 6.53) directly to another (Fig. 6.54) caught in almost exactly the same position, costume, and gesture. Later in the film, he cuts from one man to another (Figs. 6.55 and 6.56), keeping a beer bottle (a different one in each shot) in precisely the same position on frame left (including the position of the label). In *Ohayu* he uses color for the same purpose, cutting from laundry on a line to a domestic interior and matching on a red shape in the upper left of each shot (a shirt, a lamp). (See Plates 14 and 15.)

Figure 6.57

Figure 6.58

Graphic continuity is, of course, a matter of degree, and in narrative films the spectrum runs from Hollywood's general graphic continuity to Ozu's precise matching, with two shots like these from Eisenstein's *Ivan the Terrible, Part I* coming somewhere in the middle. (See Figs. 6.57 and 6.58.) The lighting (darkness on frame left, brightness on frame right) and the triangular shape on frame right of shot 1 are picked up in shot 2, with Anastasia's head and body now closely matching the tapering chair. If such graphic editing motivates the entire film's form, however, narrative will be dissolved, and the film will become more abstract in form.

Some narrative films have momentarily subordinated spatial and temporal editing factors to rhythmic ones. In the 1920s both the French "Impressionist" school and the Soviet avant-garde frequently made narrative secondary to purely rhythmic editing. In such films as Abel Gance's *La Roue,* Jean Epstein's *Coeur Fidèle* and *La Glace à Trois Faces,* and Ivan Mosjoukin's *Kean,* accelerated editing renders the tempo of an onrushing train, a whirling carousel, a racing automobile, or a drunken dance. In Epstein's *Fall of the House of Usher* a poetic sequence of Usher strumming a guitar and singing organizes the length of the shots in accord with a songlike pattern of verse and refrain. Kuleshov's *The Death Ray* and, as we shall see, Eisenstein's *October* occasionally make rhythm dominate narrative space and time. More recently, we can find rhythmic editing momentarily predominant in narrative films as varied as the Busby Berkeley musicals, Rouben Mamoulian's *Love Me Tonight,* René Clair's *Le Million,* several films of Ozu and Hitchcock, Resnais's *Last Year at Marienbad* and *Muriel,* and Godard's *Pierrot le Fou.* As we saw with graphics, rhythmic editing may override the spatial and temporal dimensions; when this happens, narrative becomes proportionately less important.

Spatial and Temporal Discontinuity.   Nonnarrative films, of course, implicitly attack the continuity style at its center, for that style is founded on the cogent presentation of a story. But what of *narrative* alternatives to the continuity system? How can one tell a story without use of the continuity rules? Let us sample some ways particular filmmakers have created distinct editing styles by use of what might be considered spatial and temporal discontinuities.

One obvious spatial discontinuity consists of violating the 180° system. Though many filmmakers have done this intermittently and unsystematically, at least two have replaced this system by one just as rigorous. The systems of filmmakers Jacques Tati and Yasujiro Ozu are based on what we might call 360° space. Instead of an axis of action that dictates that the camera be placed within an imaginary semicircle, these filmmakers work as if the action were not a line but a point at the center of a

Figure 6.59

Figure 6.60

circle and as if the camera could be placed at any point on the circumference. In *Mr. Hulot's Holiday, Playtime,* and *Traffic* Tati systematically films from almost every side; edited together, the shots present multiple spatial perspectives on a single event. Similarly, Ozu's scenes construct a 360° space that produces what the continuity style would consider grave editing errors. Ozu's films often yield no consistent background spaces and no consistent screen direction; the eyeline matches are out of joint and the only consistency is the *violation* of the 180° line. One of the gravest sins in the classical continuity style is to match on action while breaking the line, yet Ozu does this comfortably in *Early Summer* (see Figs. 6.59 and 6.60).

Explaining in more detail how Tati, Ozu, and others rigorously construct such 360° edited space would be out of place here. (See Part Four for further discussion of Ozu's *Tokyo Story.*) We can, however, pause to note a very important consequence of such spatially discontinuous editing. The defender of classical continuity would claim that spatial-continuity rules are necessary for the clear presentation of a narrative. But anyone who has seen a film by Ozu or Tati can testify that no narrative confusion arises from their continuity "violations." Though the spaces do not flow as smoothly as in the Hollywood style (this is indeed part of the films' fascination), the cause-effect chains remain intelligible. The inescapable conclusion is that the continuity system is only *one* way to render a narrative. Historically, this system has been the most dominant one, but aesthetically it has no priority over other styles.

There are two other noteworthy devices of discontinuity. In *Breathless* Jean-Luc Godard violates canons of spatial, temporal, and graphic continuity by his systematic use of the *jump cut.* Though this term is often loosely used, its primary meaning is this. When two shots of the

Figure 6.61

Figure 6.62

Figure 6.63

Figure 6.64

same subject are cut together but are not sufficiently different in camera distance and angle, there will be a noticeable jump on the screen. Classical continuity avoids such jumps by generous use of shot/reverse shots and by the "30° rule" (advising that every camera position be varied by at least 30° from the previous one). But an examination of shots from *Breathless* suggests the consequences of Godard's jump cuts. Between one shot of Michel and his girlfriend and another shot of them, they have moved several feet and some story time has elapsed (Figs. 6.61 and 6.62). Between the first shot of Patricia riding in the car and the second, the background has changed and some story time has elapsed (Figs. 6.63 and 6.64). These cuts, far from flowing smoothly, function to disorient the spectator.

A second prevalent violation of continuity is that created by the so-called *nondiegetic insert.* Here the filmmaker cuts from the scene to a metaphorical or symbolic shot that is not part of the space and time of the narrative. Clichés abound here. In *Deep Throat* a shot of orgasm cuts to a shot of a missile being launched. In Fritz Lang's *Fury* housewives gossiping are juxtaposed to shots of clucking hens. More complex examples occur in the films of Eisenstein and Godard. In Eisenstein's *Strike* the massacre of workers is intercut with the slaughter of a bull; in many of Godard's films shots of posters, magazine ads, and photographs disrupt the space and time of the scenes; these images construct a running "argument" by forcing the spectator to figure out their logical relationship to the scene's action.

Though both the jump cut and the nondiegetic insert can be utilized in a narrative context, both tend somewhat to weaken narrative continuity—the first by abrupt gaps, the second by suspension of story action altogether. It is no accident that both devices have been prominently used by the contemporary filmmaker most associated with the challenge to classical narrative—Jean-Luc Godard. In Part Four we shall examine the nature of this challenge.

There are still other alternatives to classical continuity, especially in the temporal dimension. Although the classical system may seem the most natural, it is only the most familiar. Story events do not *have* to be edited in a 1-2-3 order; not only flashbacks but also flashforwards are possible, as evidenced by films such as Resnais's *Je T'Aime, Je T'Aime,* Chris Marker's *La Jetée,* and Jean-Marie Straub's *Not Reconciled.* Editing can also play with variable frequency for narrative purposes; the same event may be shown repeatedly, as when Welles presents Susan's opera career three times in *Citizen Kane,* when Akira Kurosawa presents four incompatible versions of a rape and murder in *Rashomon,* or when Resnais depicts several hypothetical occurrences of the same funeral in *La Guerre Est Finie.*

Nor is narrative comprehension necessarily disturbed by alterations of duration. Although complete continuity and ellipsis are the most common ways of rendering duration, expansion—stretching a moment out, making screen time greater than story time—remains a distinct possibility. Truffaut uses such expansions in *Jules et Jim* to underscore narrative turning points (Catherine lifting her veil or jumping off the bridge). In Chabrol's *La Femme Infidèle*, when the outraged husband strikes his wife's lover with a statuette, Chabrol overlaps shots of the victim falling to the floor. On one hand, then, discontinuities of temporal order, duration, and frequency can become perfectly intelligible in a narrative context. On the other hand, in the jump cut and the nondiegetic insert, such temporal dislocations can also push away from traditional notions of "story" altogether. To explain how and to draw together in summary several of the alternatives to continuity we have mentioned, we may best examine one film: Sergei Eisenstein's *October*.

"To edit," writes the Soviet filmmaker Dziga Vertov, "means to organize pieces of film (shots) into a film, to 'write' a film with the shots, and not to select pieces for 'scenes.' " For Vertov, editing is a major means of organizing the entire form of the film; it does not simply serve the narrative progression, as in the continuity system. Sergei Eisenstein was a master of the kind of editing Vertov describes. His early films— *Strike, Potemkin, October, Old and New,* and the unfinished *Que Viva Mexico!*—all constitute attempts to make certain editing devices the fundamental principles in constructing his film. Rather than subordinate his editing patterns to the mapping out of a story, Eisenstein conceives of these films as editing constructions. As a Marxist, Eisenstein believed that the law of the dialectical *conflict and synthesis of opposites* could provide principles of dynamic editing. Thus he deliberately opposed himself to continuity editing; he sought out and exploited what Hollywood would call *dis*continuities. He staged, shot, and cut his films for the maximum *collision* from shot to shot, sequence to sequence, since he believed that only through being forced to synthesize such conflicts does the viewer participate in a dialectical process. Eisenstein sought to make the collisions and conflicts not only perceptual, but also emotional and intellectual; his aim was nothing less than to alter the audience's total consciousness.

To this end, Eisenstein did as Vertov described: He "wrote" his film by a juxtaposition of shots. No longer bound by conventional dramaturgy, Eisenstein's films roam freely through time and space to construct an intricate pattern of images calculated to stimulate the viewer's senses, emotions, and mind. This he called "intellectual montage." He dreamed of filming Marx's *Capital*, of writing an essay by means of film editing. Needless to say, the intricacy of Eisenstein's editing cannot be wholly

Figure 6.65

Figure 6.66

Figure 6.67

Figure 6.68

Figure 6.69

Figure 6.70

conveyed here; even a single sequence of an Eisenstein film is properly the subject of a chapter in itself. Let us, however, briefly indicate how Eisenstein uses editing discontinuities in a short sequence from *October*.

The sequence is the third one in the film (and comprises no fewer than 125 shots!). The story action is simple. The Provisional Government has taken power in Russia after the February Revolution, but instead of withdrawing from World War I, the government has continued to support the Allies. This maneuver has left the Russian people no better off than under the Czar. Now in classical Hollywood cinema, this story might be shown through a "montage sequence" of newspaper headlines smoothly linked to a scene wherein a protagonist complains that the Provisional Government has not changed a thing. *October's* protagonist, though, is not one person, but the entire Russian people, and the film does not usually use dialogue scenes to present its story points. Rather, *October* seeks to go beyond a simple presentation of story events by making the audience actively *interpret* those events. To this end, the audience is confronted with a disorienting and disjunctive set of images.

The sequence begins with shots showing the Russian soldiers on the front casting down their rifles and fraternizing freely with their German "enemies"—talking, drinking, laughing together (Fig. 6.65). Eisenstein then cuts back to the Provisional Government, where a flunky extends a document to an unseen ruler (Fig. 6.66); this document pledges the government to aid the Allies. The soldiers' fraternization is suddenly disrupted by a bombardment (Fig. 6.67). The soldiers run back to the trenches and huddle as dirt and bomb fragments rain down on them. Eisenstein then cuts to a series of shots of a tank being lowered off a factory assembly line and for a time crosscuts these images with the soldiers on the battlefield (Figs. 6.68 and 6.69). In the last section of the sequence, the shots of the tank are crosscut with hungry women and children standing in breadlines in the snow (Fig. 6.70). The sequence ends with two titles: "All as before . . . "/"Hunger and war."

What are the consequences of this editing construction? Rhythmi-

Figure 6.71

Figure 6.72

Figure 6.73

Figure 6.74

Figure 6.75

Figure 6.76

cally, the sequence is very interesting, especially in the bombing section, where the shots are only around 15 frames long. Of more interest here, however, are the various graphic, temporal, and spatial editing strategies used by Eisenstein.

Graphically, there are some continuities and many strong discontinuities. When the soldiers fraternize, many shots closely resemble one another graphically, and one shot of a bursting bomb is graphically matched in its movement with men bustling into a trench. But the graphic *discontinuities* are more noteworthy. Eisenstein cuts from a smiling German soldier facing right to a menacing eagle statue (swooping left) at the Government headquarters (Figs. 6.71 and 6.72). There is a bold jump cut from a flunky in one position to him in another (Figs. 6.73 and 6.74). A static shot of rifles stuck in the snow cuts to a long shot of a bursting shell (Figs. 6.75 and 6.76). When the soldiers race back to the trenches, Eisenstein often opposes their direction of movement from shot to shot. Moreover the cutting contrasts shots of the men crouching in the trenches looking *upward* with shots of the tanks slowly *descending* (Figs. 6.68 and 6.69). In the last phase of the sequence, Eisenstein juxtaposes the misty, almost completely static shots of the women and children with the sharply defined, dynamically moving shots of factory workers lowering the tank. Such graphic discontinuities recur throughout the film, especially in scenes of dynamic action, and stimulate perceptual conflict in the audience. To watch an Eisenstein film is to submit oneself to such percussive, pulsating graphic editing.

Eisenstein also makes vigorous use of temporal discontinuities. The sequence as a whole is opposed to Hollywood rules in its refusal to present the order of events unambiguously. Does the crosscutting of battlefield and government, factory and street indicate simultaneous action? (Consider, for example, that the women and children are seen at night, whereas the factory appears to be working in the daytime.) It is simply impossible to say if the battlefield events take place before or after or during the women's vigil. Eisenstein has sacrificed the delineation of

1-2-3 order so that he can control the shots as emotional and conceptual units.

Duration is likewise variable. The soldiers fraternize in relative continuity, but the Provisional Government's behavior is ellided drastically; this permits Eisenstein to identify the government as the unseen cause of the bombardment that ruptures the peace. At one point, Eisenstein utilizes one of his favorite devices, a temporal expansion: There is an overlapping cut as a soldier drinks from a bottle. (Later in *October*, such durational expansions create the famous bridge-raising sequence.) At another point, the gradual collapse of the women and children is ellided: We see them standing, then later lying on the ground. Even frequency is made discontinuous: It is difficult to say if we are seeing *several tanks* lowered off the assembly line or only one descending tank shown *several times*. Again, Eisenstein seeks a specific *juxtaposition* of elements, not obedience to a temporal chain. Order, duration, and frequency subordinate straightforward story time to specific logical relationships; Eisenstein creates these relationships by juxtaposing disparate lines of action through editing.

Spatially, the *October* sequence runs from rough continuity to extreme discontinuity. Although at times the 180° rule is respected (especially in the shots of women and children), never does Eisenstein start a section with an establishing shot. Reestablishing shots are rare indeed, and usually the major components of the locales are never shown in one shot. Moreover, these three locales are built up from close-ups (of the rifles, the tank, the women's feet). In all, then, the classical continuity of space is broken by the crosscutting of the different locales. To what end? By violating space in this manner, the film forces us to make emotional and conceptual connections. For example, crosscutting to the Provisional Government makes it the source of bombardment, a meaning reinforced by the way the first explosions are followed by the jumpcut of the government flunky.

More daringly, by cutting from the crouching soldiers to a descending tank, Eisenstein powerfully depicts the men visually crushed by the war-making apparatus of the Government. This is reinforced by a *false* "eyeline match" from the men looking upward, *as if* at the lowering tank—false because of course the two elements are in entirely separate settings (Figs. 6.68 and 6.69). By then showing the factory workers lowering the tank (Fig. 6.77), the cutting links the oppressed soldiers to the oppressed proletariat. Finally, as the tank hits the ground, Eisenstein crosscuts images of it with the shots of the starving families of the soldiers and the workers. They too are shown as crushed by the government machine; as the tank wheels come slowly to the floor, we cut to the women's feet in the snow, and the machine's heaviness is linked by titles

Figure 6.77

("one pound," "half a pound") to the steady starvation of the women and children. Although all of the spaces are in the story, such discontinuities push the sequence close to an essayistic commentary on the story by the plot.

In all, then, Eisenstein's spatial editing, like his temporal and graphic editing, constructs correspondences, analogies, and contrasts that *interpret* the story events. The interpretation is not simply handed to the viewer; rather, the editing discontinuities force the viewer to work out the interrelations. Like the rest of *October*, this sequence suggests that there are powerful alternatives to the principles of classical continuity.

Summary ■

When any two shots are joined, we can ask several questions:

1. How are the shots graphically continuous or discontinuous?
2. What rhythmic relations are created?
3. Are the shots spatially continuous? If not, what creates the discontinuity? (Crosscutting? Ambiguous cues?) If the shots are spatially continuous, how does the 180° system create the continuity?
4. Are the shots temporally continuous? If so, what creates the continuity? (For example, matches on action?) If not, what creates the discontinuity? (Ellipsis? Overlapping cuts?)

More generally, we can ask the same question we have asked of every film technique. How does this film's editing *function* with respect to the film's narrative or nonnarrative form? Does the film utilize editing to lay out the narrative space, time, and cause-effect chain in the manner of classical continuity? Or does the film utilize other editing patterns that enter into a different interplay with the narrative? If the film is not a narrative one, how does editing function to engage our formal expectations?

Some practical hints: You can learn to notice editing in several ways. Watch any film with the sole purpose of observing one editing aspect—say, the way space is presented or the control of graphics or time. Sensitize yourself to rhythmic editing by noting cutting rates; tapping out the tempo of the cuts can help. Watching 1930s and 1940s American films can introduce you to classical continuity style; try to predict what shot will come next in a sequence. (You will be surprised at how often you are right.) When you watch a film on television, try turning off the sound; editing patterns become more apparent this way. When there is a violation of continuity, ask what purpose it serves. When you see a film that doesn't obey classical continuity principles, search for its unique editing patterns. If it is feasible, sit down at an editor or viewer with a film sequence (almost any film will do) and analyze it as this chapter has done. Try making a film and executing cuts, fades, dissolves, etc., yourself. In such ways as these, you can considerably increase your awareness and understanding of the power of editing.

Notes and Queries ■

What Editing Is

An overview of the work of the film editor may be found in "Prime Cut," *Film Comment* **13**, 2 (March–April 1977): 6–29.

General discussions of film editing may be found in Rudolf Arnheim, *Film As Art* (Berkeley: University of California Press, 1967), pp. 87–102; Raymond Spottiswoode, *A Grammar of Film* (Berkeley: University of California Press, 1950), pp. 50–53; Erwin Panofsky, "Style and Medium in the Moving Pictures," in Daniel Talbot, ed., *Film: An Anthology* (Berkeley: University of California Press, 1970), pp. 15–32; Bela Balazs, *Theory of the Film* (New York: Dover, 1970), pp. 118–138; Ralph Stephenson and J. R. Debrix, *The Cinema as Art* (Baltimore: Penguin, 1969), pp. 63–138; Jean Mitry, *Esthétique et Psychologie du Cinéma*, Vol. I (Paris: Editions Universitaires, 1963), pp. 267ff; Gianfranco Bettetini, *The Language and Technique of the Film* (The Hague: Mouton, 1973), pp. 98–111, 128–180. We await an authoritative history of film editing, but at least one historical pattern has been sketched in André Bazin, "The Evolution of the Language of Cinema," in *What Is Cinema?* (Berkeley: University of California Press, 1967), Vol. I, pp. 23–40.

Editing has often been seen as an alternative to mise-en-scene and camera work. Instead of cutting to a close-up of the hero's face, we can have him come closer to the camera, or we can track into a close-up. Early film theory argued that editing was more inherently "cinematic" than the more "theatrical" technique of mise-en-scene; see in this connection Arnheim, Panofsky, and Balazs, cited above. But the aesthetic prominence of editing was disputed by the film theorist André Bazin, who argued that editing ruptures and falsifies the spatiotemporal continuum of reality. (See not only the Bazin essay cited above, but also "The Virtues and Limitations of Montage" on pp. 41–52 of the same volume.) Bazin claimed that concrete reality is better respected by cinematography and mise-en-scene techniques. This debate has been taken up by others. See Charles Barr, "Cinemascope and After," *Film Quarterly* **16**, 4 (Summer 1963): 4–24; David Thomson, *Movie Man* (New York: Stein and Day, 1967), pp. 84–91; Christian Metz, *Film Language*

(New York: Oxford University Press, 1974), pp. 31–91; Brian Henderson, "Two Types of Film Theory," *Film Quarterly* **24**, 3 (Spring 1971): 33–41.

Professional filmmakers' views of editing are invariably interesting. Roberto Rossellini and Jean Renoir, in a famous interview with André Bazin, minimize it ("Cinema and Television," *Sight and Sound* [Winter 1958–59]: 26–29). Alfred Hitchcock, in an equally famous interview with François Truffaut, swears by it (*Hitchcock*, New York: Simon and Schuster, 1967, *passim*). For Jean-Luc Godard, "editing can restore to actuality that ephemeral grace neglected by both snob and filmlover, or can transform chance into destiny" ("Montage My Fine Care," *Godard on Godard*, New York: Viking, 1972, p. 39). For V. I. Pudovkin, "Editing is the basic creative force, by power of which the soulless photographs (the separate shots) are engineered into living, cinematographic form" (*Film Technique*, New York: Grove, 1970, p. 25). An editor has recalled that John Ford shot so little footage that Ford would not have to involve himself in editing: "By and large, the film that an editor would get would almost *have* to go into the picture. After the shooting, [Ford] would often go off to his boat and not come back until after the picture was cut." (Peter Bogdanovich, *John Ford*, Berkeley: University of California Press, 1968, p. 9).

Dimensions of Film Editing

Very little has been written on graphic aspects of editing. See Vladimir Nilsen, *The Cinema as a Graphic Art* (New York: Hill and Wang, 1959); Sergei Eisenstein, "A Dialectic Approach to Film Form," in *Film Form*, New York: Harvest, 1963), pp. 45–63; and Jonas Mekas, "An Interview with Peter Kubelka," *Film Culture* 44 (Spring 1967): 42–47.

What we are calling rhythmic editing comprises the categories of "metric" and "rhythmic" montage discussed by Eisenstein in "Methods of Montage," *Film Form* (New York: Harvest, 1963), pp. 72–83. For a sample analysis of a film's rhythm, see Lewis Jacobs, *The Rise of the American Film* (New York: Teachers College Press, 1968), Chapter XI, "D. W. Griffith," pp. 171–201. Television commercials are useful to study for rhythmic editing, for their selection of highly stereotyped imagery permits the editor to cut the shots together in a rapid rhythm matched to the rhythm of the jingle on the sound track.

For a good discussion of spatial and temporal editing, see Noël Burch, *Theory of Film Practice* (New York: Praeger, 1973), especially pp. 3–16, 32–48; and Vladimir Nizhny, *Lessons with Eisenstein* (New York: Hill and Wang, 1962), pp. 63–92.

The Kuleshov experiments have been variously described. The two most authoritative accounts are in V. I. Pudovkin, *Film Technique* (New

York: Grove, 1970), *passim*, and *Kuleshov on Film: Writings of Lev Kuleshov*, tr. and ed. by Ronald Levaco (Berkeley: University of California Press, 1974), pp. 51–55. For attacks on the Kuleshov effect, see André Bazin, "The Virtues and Limitations of Montage," *op. cit.*, and Jean Mitry, *Esthétique et Psychologie du Cinéma*, Vol. I (Paris: Editions Universitaires, 1963), pp. 279–285.

The discussion of temporal possibilities of editing is adapted from Gerard Genette's remarks in *Figures III* (Paris: Seuil, 1972), pp. 77–182.

Continuity Editing

What is the history of continuity editing? Though research is lacking on the question, we do know that this system was embryonic in Edwin S. Porter's *Great Train Robbery* (1903) and Cecil Hepworth's *Rescued by Rover* (1905) and was refined by D. W. Griffith, Thomas Ince, Cecil B. DeMille, Mack Sennett, and others. By 1922 the continuity style seems to have become firmly established. Even today, needless to say, many films obey it. For historical accounts, see Kenneth MacGowan, *Behind the Screen* (New York: Delta, 1965), pp. 85–195; Arthur Knight, *The Liveliest Art* (New York: Mentor, 1957); and Noël Burch and Jorge Dana, "Propositions," *Afterimage*, 5 (Spring 1974): 40–66.

Since the continuity system was guided by explicit "rules," there are many sources which enumerate the principles of continuity. See Karel Reisz and Gavin Millar, *The Technique of Film Editing* (New York: Hastings House, 1973); A. J. Reynertson, *The Work of the Film Director* (New York: Hastings House, 1970); Arthur L. Gaskill and David A. Englander, *Pictorial Continuity: How to Shoot a Movie Story* (New York: Duell, Sloan, and Pearce, 1947): Terence St. John Marner, *Directing Motion Pictures* (New York: Barnes, 1972), pp. 66–96. Older but still informative sources include Sidney Cole, "Film Editor," in Oswell Blakeston, ed., *Working for the Films* (London: Focal Press, 1947), pp. 152–160; Anne Bauchens, "Cutting the Film," in Nancy Naumburg, *We Make the Movies* (New York: Norton, 1937), pp. 199–215; and Lewis Herman, *A Practical Manual of Screen Playwriting for Theater and Television Films* (New York: Meridian, 1974), pp. 93–165. Our diagram of a hypothetical axis of action has been adapted from Edward Pincus's concise discussion in his *Guide to Filmmaking* (New York: Signet, 1969), pp. 120–125.

Recent scholarship has begun increasingly to analyze the continuity style. See Raymond Bellour, "The Obvious and the Code," *Screen* 15, 4 (Winter 1974/5): 7–17; Stephen Heath, "Film and System: Terms of Analysis," *Screen* 16, 1 (Spring 1975): 7–77, and 16, 2 (Summer 1975): 91–113. A very difficult but interesting study of the psychological effects of the continuity style has been initiated by Jean-Pierre Oudart in "Cinema and Suture," *Screen* **18**, 4 (Winter 1977/78): 35–47. Oudart's ideas are discussed in Daniel Dayan, "The Tutor-Code of Classical Cinema," *Film Quarterly* **28**, 1 (Fall 1974): 22–31.

There are literally thousands of films which may be studied for their use of continuity editing, but here are a few familiar ones: *Bringing Up Baby* (Hawks, 1938); *Trouble in Paradise* (Lubitsch, 1932); *The Wizard of Oz* (Fleming, 1939); *Singin' in the Rain* (Donen-Kelly, 1952); *Mildred Pierce* (Curtiz, 1945); *Roaring Twenties* (Walsh, 1939); *White Heat* (Walsh, 1949); *Winchester 73* (Mann, 1950); *The Philadelphia Story* (Cukor, 1940); *The General* (Keaton, 1927); *Mr. Smith Goes to Washington* (Capra, 1939). In all of these films, watch for occasional violations of the continuity rules. The second scene of *Mr. Smith* is especially instructive in this regard; is there a pattern or reason behind Capra's frequent continuity breaks, or are they simply errors? Are the continuity rules obeyed in such non-American films as *Children of Paradise* (Carné, 1945); *The Blue Angel* (Von Sternberg, 1930); *M* (Lang, 1931); and *Persona* (Bergman, 1956)?

Alternatives to Continuity Editing

Eisenstein remains the chief source in this area. An exceptionally intro-spective filmmaker, he bequeathed us a rich set of ideas on the possibil-ities of nonnarrative editing; see the essays in *Film Form*. The writings of another Russian, Dziga Vertov, are of interest but are considerably less analytical; English translations may be found in Harry Geduld, ed., *Film Makers on Film Making* (Bloomington: Indiana University Press, 1969), pp. 79–105.

Experimental and avant-garde cinema have taken the largest steps toward constructing alternatives to the continuity style. David Curtis's *Experimental Cinema* (New York: Delta, 1971) and Jean Mitry's *Le Cinéma Experimental* (Paris: Seghers, 1974), provide general overviews of the history of experimental film. On the "New American Cinema" there are several sources: Gregory Battcock, ed., *The New American Cinéma* (New York: Dutton, 1967); Annette Michelson, ed., *New Forms in Film* (Montreux, 1974); P. Adams Sitney, *Visionary Film* (New York: Oxford University Press, 1974); and various essays in *Artforum*, 1971–1975. A continuing chronicle of the work of the New American Cinema is provided by the journal *Film Culture*, selections from which are collected in the *Film Culture Reader*, ed. P. Adams Sitney (New York: Praeger, 1970). A shot-by-shot analysis of *Ballet Mécanique*, from which material in this chapter is taken, may be found in Standish Lawder, *The Cubist Cinema* (Berkeley: University of California Press, 1975).

For further discussion of editing in *October*, see the essays by Annette Michelson, Noël Carroll, and Rosalind Krauss in the special "Eisenstein/Brakhage" number of *Artforum* 11, 5 (January 1973): 30–37, 56–65.

CHAPTER 7

SOUND IN THE CINEMA

The Powers of Sound ■

Many people tend to think of sound as simply an accompaniment to the real basis of cinema, the moving images. These viewers assume that the people and things pictured on the screen just produce an appropriate noise. But as we have seen, in the process of film production the sound track is created separately from the images and can be manipulated independently and flexibly.

Consider some of the advantages of sound for a film. First, it engages another sense mode: Our visual attention can be accompanied by an aural attention. (Even before recorded sound was introduced in 1926, the "silent" cinema recognized this by its use of accompaniment by orchestra, organ, or piano.) Second, sound can *actively shape how we interpret the image.* In one sequence of *Letter from Siberia,* Chris Marker demonstrates the power of sound to alter our perception of images. Three times Marker plays the same footage—a shot of a bus passing a car on a city street, three shots of workers paving a street. But each time the footage is accompanied by a completely different sound track. Compare the three versions tabulated alongside the sequence (Table 7.1). The verbal differences are emphasized by the sameness of the images; the audience will interpret the same images completely differently, depending on the sound track.

The *Letter from Siberia* sequence also demonstrates a third advantage of sound. Film sound can direct our attention quite specifically within the image. When the commentator describes the "blood-colored buses," we will look at the bus and not at the car. When Fred Astaire and Ginger Rogers are tapping out an intricate step, chances are that we watch their bodies and not the silent nightclub spectators looking on (see production still from *Swing Time,* Fig. 7.5). In such ways, sound can guide us through the images, "pointing" to things to watch. This possibility becomes even more complex when you consider that the sound cue for some visual element may *anticipate* that element and relay our atten-

189

Table 7.1 *Letter from Siberia* **Footage**

Images	First commentary	Second commentary	Third commentary
 Figure 7.1	Yakutsk, capital of the Yakutsk Autonomous Soviet Socialist Republic, is a modern city in which comfortable buses made available to the population share the streets with powerful Zyms, the pride of the Soviet automobile industry. In the	Yakutsk is a dark city with an evil reputation. The population is crammed into blood-colored buses while the members of the privileged caste brazenly display the luxury of their Zyms, a costly and uncomfortable car at best. Bending	In Yakutsk, where modern houses are gradually replacing the dark older sections, a bus, less crowded than its London or New York equivalent at rush hour, passes a Zym, an excellent car reserved for public utilities departments on account of its scarcity.
 Figure 7.2	joyful spirit of socialist emulation, happy Soviet workers, among them this picturesque denizen	to the task like slaves, the miserable Soviet workers, among them this sinister-looking Asiatic,	With courage and tenacity under extremely difficult conditions, Soviet workers, among them this Yakut
 Figure 7.3	of the Arctic reaches, apply themselves	apply themselves to the primitive labor	afflicted with an eye disorder, apply themselves to
 Figure 7.4	to making Yakutsk an even better place to live. Or else:	of grading with a drag beam. Or simply:	improving the appearance of their city, which could certainly use it.

Figure 7.5

tion to it. Suppose we have a close-up of a man in a room and we hear the creaking of a door opening; if the next shot shows the door, now open, the viewer will likely focus his or her attention on that door, the source of the offscreen sound. In an opposite way, if the next shot shows the door still closed, the viewer will likely ponder his or her interpretation of the sound. (Maybe it wasn't a door, after all?) Thus the sound track can clarify image events, contradict them, or render them ambiguous. In all cases, the sound track can enter into an *active* relation with the image track.

Moreover, as V. F. Perkins has pointed out, sound brings with it a new sense of the value of silence. "Only with colour as an available resource can we regard the use of black-and-white photography as the result of a conscious artistic decision. Only in the sound film can a director use silence for dramatic effect" (*Film as Film*, p. 54). In the context of sound, silence takes on a new expressive function.

A final advantage: Sound bristles with as many creative possibilities as editing. Through editing, one may join shots of any two spaces to create a meaningful relation. Similarly, the filmmaker can mix any sonic phenomena into a whole. With the introduction of sound cinema, the infinity of visual possibilities was joined by the infinity of acoustic events.

Fundamentals of Film Sound ■

Acoustic Properties

To pursue in detail the acoustic processes that produce sound would take us on a long detour (see Notes and Queries for reading on the subject). We should, however, isolate some qualities of sound as we perceive it. These qualities are familiar to us from everyday experience.

Loudness. Perceived sound results from vibrations in air; the amplitude of the vibrations produces our sense of volume. Film sound constantly manipulates volume. For example, in dozens of films a long shot of a busy street is accompanied by loud traffic noises, but when two people meet and start to speak, the loudness of the noise drops. Or, a dialogue between a soft-spoken character and a blustery one is characterized as much by the difference in volume as by the substance of the talk. Needless to say, loudness is also affected by perceived distance; often the louder the sound, the closer we take it to be. Some films exploit radical changes in volume for shock value, as when a quiet scene is interrupted by a very loud noise.

Pitch. The frequency of sound vibrations governs pitch, or the perceived "highness" or "lowness" of the sound. Pitch is the principal way we distinguish music from other sounds in the film, but it has more complex uses. When a young boy tries to speak in a man's deep voice and fails (as in *How Green Was My Valley*), the joke is based primarily on pitch. In the coronation scene of *Ivan the Terrible, Part I*, a court singer with a deep bass voice begins a song of praise to Ivan, and each phrase rises dramatically in pitch—which Eisenstein emphasizes in the editing, with successively closer shots of the singer coinciding with each change. When Bernard Herrmann obtained the effects of unnatural, birdlike shrieking in Hitchcock's *Psycho*, even many musicians could not recognize the source: violins played at extraordinarily high pitch.

Timbre. The harmonic components of a sound give it a certain "color" or tone quality—what musicians call timbre. When we call someone's voice nasal or a certain musical tone mellow, we are referring to timbre. Again, filmmakers manipulate timbre continually. Timbre can help articulate portions of the sound track; for instance, timbre differentiates musical instruments from one another. Timbre also "comes forward" on certain occasions, as in the clichéd use of oleaginous saxophone tones behind seduction scenes. More subtly, in the opening sequence of Rouben Mamoulian's *Love Me Tonight* people pass a musical rhythm from object to object—a broom, a carpet beater—and the humor of the number springs in part from the very different timbres of the objects.

As the fundamental components of film sound, loudness, pitch, and timbre usually interact to define the sonic texture of a film. At the most elementary level, loudness, pitch, and timbre enable us to distinguish among all of the sounds in a film; we recognize different characters' voices by these qualities, for example. But at a more complex level, all three interact to add considerably to our experience of the film. Both John Wayne and James Stewart speak slowly, but Wayne's voice tends to be deeper and gruffer than Stewart's querulous drawl. In *The Wizard of Oz* the disparity between the public image of the Wizard and the old charlatan who rigs it up is marked by the booming bass of the effigy and the old man's higher, softer, more quavering voice. *Citizen Kane* offers a wide range of sound manipulations: Echo chambers alter timbre and volume, and a motif is formed by the inability of Kane's opera-singing wife to hit accurate pitch. In *Citizen Kane* shifts between times and places are covered by continuing a sound "thread" and varying the basic acoustics: A shot of Kane applauding dissolves to a shot of a crowd applauding (shift in volume and timbre); Leland beginning a sentence in the street cuts to Kane finishing the sentence in an auditorium, his voice magnified by loudspeakers (shift in volume, timbre, and pitch). Such examples suggest that the elementary properties of sound afford a rich set of possibilities for the filmmaker to explore.

Selection and Combination

Sound in the cinema takes three forms: *speech, music,* or *noise* (also called *sound effects*). Occasionally a sound may share categories—is a scream speech or noise? is electronic music also noise?—and filmmakers have freely exploited these ambiguities. (In *Psycho,* when a woman screams, we expect to hear the human voice and instead hear "screaming" violins.) Nevertheless, in most cases the distinctions hold. Now that we have an idea of the role of acoustic properties, we must consider how speech, music, and noise are selected and combined for specific functions within films.

The creation of the sound track resembles the editing of the image track. Just as the filmmaker may select from several shots the best image, he or she may choose what exact bit of sound from this or that source will best serve the purpose. And just as the filmmaker may link or superimpose images, so may he or she join any two sounds end to end or one "over" another (as with commentary "over" music). Though we aren't usually as aware of the manipulation of the sound track, it demands as much selection and control as does the visual track.

Selection of the desired sound is a necessary step in the process. Normally, our perception filters out irrelevant stimuli and retains what is most useful at a particular moment. As you read this, you are attending to words on the page and (to various degrees) ignoring certain stimuli that reach your ears. But if you close your eyes and listen attentively to the sounds around you, you will become aware of many previously un-noticed sounds—distant voices, the wind, footsteps, a radio playing. As any amateur recordist knows, if you set up a microphone and tape recorder in a "quiet" environment, all of those normally unnoticed sounds suddenly become obtrusive. The microphone is unselective; like the camera lens, it does not automatically achieve the desired result. Sound studios, camera blimps to absorb motor noise, directional and shielded microphones, sound engineering and editing, and libraries of stock sounds all exist so that a film's sound track may be carefully controlled through selection. Unless a filmmaker *wants* to record all of the ambient noise of a scene, simply holding out a microphone while filming will rarely suffice.

Figure 7.6

Because normal perception is linked to our choices, the director's selection of the sounds in a film can control the audience's choices and thus guide the audience's perception. In one scene from Jacques Tati's *Mr. Hulot's Holiday* vacationers at a resort hotel are relaxing (Fig. 7.6). In the foreground guests quietly play cards; in the depth of the shot, Mr. Hulot is frantically playing ping-pong. Early in the scene, the guests in the foreground are murmuring quietly, but Hulot's ping-pong game is louder; the sound cues us to watch Hulot. Later in the scene, however, the same ping-pong game makes *no* sound at all, and our attention is drawn to the muttering card players in the foreground. The presence and absence of the sound of the ping-pong ball guides our expectations and perception, you will notice that filmmakers often use sound to shift our would not. If you start to notice how such selection of sound guides our perception, you will notice that filmmakers often use sound to shift our attention.

Such examples depend not only on selection, but also on the film-maker's *combining* of various sonic elements. It is the mixing of sounds in a specific pattern that constitutes the sound track as we know it. We have already seen that mixing is a careful and deliberate production procedure. What we must now notice is what functions the particular mix can have in the total film. Obviously the mix can range from very dense (e.g., a scene containing the babble of voices, the sounds of foot-steps, Muzak, and plane engines at an airport) to total silence, with most films falling in between. In addition, the filmmaker may create a mix in which each sound modulates and overlaps smoothly with the others, or one that is composed of much more abrupt and startling contrasts.

The possibilities of combining sounds are well illustrated by the final battle sequence of Akira Kurosawa's *Seven Samurai*. In a heavy rain, marauding bandits charge into a village defended by the villagers and the samurai. The torrent and wind form a constant background noise throughout the scene. Before the battle, the conversation of the waiting men, footsteps, and the sounds of swords being drawn are punctuated by long pauses in which we hear only the drumming rain. Suddenly distant horses' hooves are heard offscreen; Kurosawa cuts to a long shot of the bandits; their horses' hooves become abruptly louder. (This is typical of the scene: The closer the camera is to a sound source, the louder the sound.) When the bandits burst into the village, yet another sound element appears—the bandits' harsh battle cries, which increase steadily in volume as they approach. The battle begins. The muddy, storm-swept mise-en-scene and rhythmic cutting gain impact from the way in which the incessant rain and splashing are explosively interrupted by brief noises—the screams of the wounded, the splintering of a fence one bandit crashes through, the whinnies of horses, the twang of one samurai's bowstring, the gurgle of a speared bandit, the screams of women when the bandit chieftain breaks into their hiding place. The sudden intrusion of certain sounds marks abrupt developments in the battle. The scene climaxes after the main battle has ended: Offscreen horses' hooves are cut short by a new sound—the sharp crack of a bandit's rifle shot, which fells one samurai. A long pause, in which we hear only the driving rain, emphasizes the moment; the samurai furiously throws his sword in the direction of the shot and falls dead into the mud. Another samurai races toward the bandit chieftain, who has the rifle; another shot cracks out and he falls back, wounded; another pause, in which only the relentless rain is heard. The wounded samurai kills the chieftain. The other samurai gather. At the scene's end, the sobs of a young samurai, the distant whinnies and hoofbeats of now riderless horses, and the rain all fade slowly out. The relatively dense mix of this sound track (accomplished entirely without music) gradually introduces sounds to turn our attention to new narrative elements (hooves, battle cries) and then goes on to modulate these sounds smoothly into a harmonious whole. This whole is then punctuated by abrupt sounds of unusual volume or pitch associated with crucial narrative actions (the archery, women's screams, the gunshots).

Dimensions of Film Sound ■

We have now seen what sounds consist of and how the filmmaker can take advantage of the widely different kinds of sounds available. In addition, the way in which the sounds relate to other film elements gives them several other dimensions. First, because sound occupies a duration, it has a *rhythm*. Second, sound can relate to its perceived source with greater or lesser *fidelity*. Third, the sound relates to visual events that take place in a specific time, and this relationship gives sound a *temporal* dimension. And fourth, sound conveys a sense of the *spatial* conditions in which it occurs. These categories begin to reveal that sound in film is actually a very complex thing; let's look at each category briefly.

Rhythm

For our purposes, sounds can be considered to be organized *rhythmically* when strong and weak beats form a distinct pattern and move at a distinct pace. (This definition of rhythm combines features that musicians would distinguish as "meter," "rhythm," and "tempo.") But even this simple definition is complicated by the fact that the movements in the images themselves have a rhythm as well. In addition, the editing has a rhythm; as we have seen, a succession of short shots creates a fast rhythm, whereas shots held longer slow down the editing's rhythm. Moreover, all three types of sound on the sound track have their own rhythmic possibilities independent of one another. The gasping voice of a character who lies dying has a slower rhythm than the voice of a race-track announcer. Music obviously may have different rhythms in a film. Finally, sound effects also vary in rhythm (compare the plodding hooves of a farmhorse and a cavalry company riding at full speed).

But in most cases the rhythms of editing, of movement within the image, and of sound do not exist separately. Sound usually accompanies movements and often continues over cuts. Sound may motivate figure or camera movement. Thus there exists the potential for a considerable interplay among these three types of rhythm. No one "appropriate" combination exists.

Possibly the most common tendency is for the filmmaker to match visual and sonic rhythms to each other. An obvious example is the typical dance sequence in a musical; here the figures move about at a rhythm determined by the music. But variation is always possible. In the "Waltz in Swing Time" number in *Swing Time* the dancing of Astaire and Rogers moves quickly in time to the music. But no fast cutting accompanies this scene; indeed, there is no cutting at all within the dance, for the scene consists of a single long take from a long-shot distance. Another example of close coordination between screen movement and sound comes in the animated films of Walt Disney in the 1930s; Mickey Mouse and the other Disney characters often move in exact synchronization with the music, even when they are not dancing. (This nondance matching of movement with music in fact came to be known as "Mickey Mousing.")

The filmmaker may choose to create a disparity among the rhythms of sound, editing, and image. One way of accomplishing this is to keep the source of the sound offscreen and to show something else onscreen. Toward the end of John Ford's *She Wore a Yellow Ribbon*, the aging cavalry captain, Nathan Brittles, watches his troop ride out of the fort just after he has retired; he regrets leaving the service and desires to go with the patrol. The sound of the scene consists of the cheerful title song sung by the departing riders and the quick hoofbeats of their horses. Yet only a few of the shots show the horses and singers, who move at a rhythm matched to the sound. Instead, the scene concentrates our attention on Brittles, standing almost motionless by his own horse. (The moderate rate of cutting lies between these two rhythms.) The contrast of fast rhythm of sound with the shots of the solitary Brittles functions to emphasize his regret at having to stay behind for the first time in many years.

Several great directors have used music that might seem to have a rhythm inappropriate for the visuals. In *Four Nights of a Dreamer* Robert Bresson includes several shots of a large, floating nightclub cruising the Seine. The boat's movement is slow and smooth, yet the sound track consists of lively Calypso music. (Not until a later scene do we discover that the music comes from the boat.) The strange combination of fast music with the slow passage of the boat creates a langorous, mysterious effect. Jacques Tati does something similar in *Playtime*. In a scene outside a Parisian hotel, tourists climb aboard a bus to go to a nightclub; as they file slowly up the steps, raucous, jazzy music begins. The music again startles our expectations because it seems inappropriate to the images; in fact, it belongs with the next scene, in which some carpenters awkwardly carrying a large plate-glass window seem to be dancing to the music. By starting the fast music over an earlier scene of slower visual rhythm, Tati creates a comic effect and prepares for a transition to a new space.

Chris Marker has carried this contrast between image and sound rhythms to what may be its logical limit, in *La Jetée*. This film is made up almost entirely of still shots; except for one tiny gesture, all movement within the images is eliminated. Yet the film has a narrator, music, and sound effects of a generally dynamic rhythm. The result is not at all "uncinematic," but rather it has great effectiveness because of the originality of the concept and the care and consistency with which this juxtaposition of rhythms is carried through the whole structure of the film.

These examples suggest some of the ways in which rhythms may be combined. But of course most films also vary their rhythms from one point to another. A change of rhythm may function to shift our expectations. In a famous sequence Sergei Eisenstein develops the sound from slow rhythms to fast and back to slow: the battle on the ice in *Alexander Nevsky*. The first 12 shots of the scene show the Russian army prepared for the attack of the German knights. The shots are of moderate, even length, and they contain very little movement. The music is comparably slow, consisting of short, distinctly separated chords. Then, as the German army rides into sight over the horizon, both the visual movement and the tempo of the music increase quickly, and the battle begins. At the end of the battle Eisenstein creates another contrast with a long passage of slow, lamenting music and little movement.

Fidelity

By fidelity we don't mean "high-fi" in the sense of the quality of recording. Here we are speaking of whether the sound is faithful to the source as we conceive it. If a film shows us a barking dog and the sound track has a barking noise, that sound is faithful to its source—the sound maintains fidelity. But if the sound of a cat meowing accompanies the picture of the barking dog, there enters a disparity between sound and image—a lack of fidelity. Fidelity has nothing to do with what originally made the sound during filming. As we have seen, the filmmaker may manipulate sound independently of image; accompanying the image of a dog with the meow is no more difficult than accompanying the image with a bark. Note, however, that fidelity is purely a matter of our expectations. In production the bark or meow might be produced electronically or by an animal-imitator. Fidelity involves conventional expectations about sources, not knowledge of where the filmmaker actually obtained the sound.

A play with fidelity most commonly functions for comic effect. Jacques Tati is one of the directors most skillful at employing various degrees of fidelity. In *Mr. Hulot's Holiday* much comedy arises from the opening and closing of a dining-room door. Instead of simply recording a real door, Tati inserts a twanging sound like a plucked cello string each time the door swings; aside from being amusing in itself, this sound functions to emphasize the patterns in which waiters and diners pass through the door. Another master of comically unfaithful sound is René Clair. In several scenes of *Le Million* sound effects occur that are not faithful to their sources. When the hero's friend drops a plate, we hear not shattering crockery, but the clash of cymbals. Later, during a chase scene, when characters collide, the impact is portrayed by a heavy bass drum beat. Similar manipulations of fidelity commonly occur in animated cartoons.

But as with low- or high-angle framings, there is no recipe that will allow us to interpret every manipulation of fidelity as comic; some nonfaithful sounds have serious functions. In Hitchcock's *The Thirty-Nine Steps* a landlady discovers a corpse in an apartment. A shot of her screaming face is accompanied by a train whistle; then the scene shifts to an actual train. Though the whistle is not a faithful sound for an image of a screaming person, it provides a striking transition.

Finally, in some special cases fidelity may be manipulated by a change in volume. A sound may seem unreasonably loud or soft in relation to the other sounds in the film. Curtis Bernhardt's *Possessed* alters volume in ways that are not faithful to the sources. The central character is gradually falling deeper into mental illness; in one scene she is alone, very distraught, in her room on a rainy night. We begin to hear things as she does; the ticking of the clock and dripping of raindrops gradually magnify in volume. Here the shift in fidelity functions to suggest a psychological state.

Space

Sound has a spatial dimension because it comes from a *source*, and that source may be characterized by the space it occupies. If the source of a sound is a character or object in the story space of the film, we call the sound *diegetic.* The voices of the characters, sounds made by objects in the story, or music coming from instruments in the story space are all diegetic sound.

On the other hand there is *nondiegetic* sound, which does not come from a source in the story space. Familiar examples of such sound are easy to find. Much music added to enhance the film's action is nondiegetic; when a character is climbing a sheer cliff and tense music comes up, we don't expect to see an orchestra perched on the side of the mountain. Viewers understand that the movie music is a convention and doesn't issue from the space of the story. The same holds true for the so-called omniscient narrator, the disembodied voice that gives us information but does not belong to any of the characters in the film. Orson Welles speaks the nondiegetic narration in his own film *The Magnificent Ambersons,* for example. Nondiegetic sound effects are also possible. In *Le Million* various characters all pursue an old coat with a winning lottery ticket in its pocket. They converge backstage at the opera and begin racing and dodging around one another, tossing the coat to their accomplices. But instead of putting in the sounds coming from the actual space of the chase, Clair fades in the sounds of a football game; because the maneuvers of the chase do look like a football game, with the coat as ball, this enhances the comedy of the sequence. We hear a crowd cheering and a whistle's sound; yet we don't assume that the characters present are making these sounds (so this is not a manipulation of fidelity, as with the earlier examples from *Le Million*). The nondiegetic sounds create comedy by making a sort of audiovisual pun.

What are the possibilities of diegetic sound? We know that the space of the narrative action is not limited to what we can see on the screen at any given moment. If we know that several people are present in a room, we can see a shot that shows only one person without assuming that the

Figure 7.7

Figure 7.8

Figure 7.9

other people have dropped out of the story. We simply have a sense that those people are offscreen. And if one of those offscreen people speaks, we still assume that the sound is coming from part of the story space. Thus diegetic sound can be either *onscreen* or *offscreen,* depending on whether its source is within the frame or outside the frame.

Simple examples will illustrate this. A shot shows a character talking, and we hear the sound of his or her voice; another shows a door closing, and we hear a slam; a person plays a fiddle, and we hear its notes. In each case the source of the sound is in the story—diegetic—and visible within the frame—onscreen. But the shot may show only a person listening to a voice without the speaker being seen; another shot might show a character running down a street and the sound of an unseen door slamming; lastly, an audience is shown listening while the sound of a fiddle is heard. In all of these instances, the sounds come from within the story—again diegetic—but are now in a space outside the frame—offscreen.

This may seem a trivial distinction at first, but we know from Chapter 5 how powerful offscreen space can be. Offscreen sound can suggest space extending in various directions beyond the visible action. In *American Graffiti,* a film that plays heavily on the distinction between diegetic and nondiegetic music, offscreen sounds of car radios often suggest that all of the cars on a street are tuned to the same radio station. Offscreen sound may also control when we begin to formulate expectations about offscreen space. In *His Girl Friday* Hildy goes into the press room to write her final story. As she chats with the other reporters, a loud clunk comes from an unseen source. Hildy glances off left, and immediately a new space comes to our attention, though we haven't seen it yet. She walks to the window and sees a gallows being prepared for an execution. Here offscreen sound initiates the discovery of fresh space.

A brilliant use of a similar device comes in John Ford's *Stagecoach.* The stagecoach is desperately fleeing from a band of Indians; the ammunition is running out, and all seems lost until a troop of cavalry suddenly arrives. Yet Ford does not create the situation this baldly. He shows a medium close-up of one of the men, Hatfield, who has just discovered that he is down to his last bullet (Fig. 7.7); he glances off right and raises his gun (Fig. 7.8). The camera pans right to a woman, Lucy, praying. During all this, orchestral music, including bugles, plays nondiegetically. Unseen by Lucy, Hatfield's gun comes into the frame from the left, ready to shoot her to prevent her from being captured by the Indians (Fig. 7.9). But before he shoots, an offscreen gunshot is heard, and Hatfield's hand and gun drop down out of the frame (Fig. 7.10). Then the bugle music becomes somewhat more prominent, and Lucy's face changes as she says, "Can you hear it? Can you hear it? It's a bugle.

They're blowing the charge" (Fig. 7.11). Only then does Ford cut to the cavalry itself racing toward the coach. Rather than focusing on the mechanics of the rescue, Ford uses offscreen sound to restrict our vision to the initial despair of the passengers and their growing hope as they hear the distant sound. The sound of the bugle also emerges imperceptibly out of the nondiegetic music; only Lucy's line tells us that this is a diegetic sound which signals their rescue.

Figure 7.10

Are there other possibilities for diegetic sound? Often a filmmaker uses sound to represent what a character is thinking. We hear the character's voice speaking his or her thoughts even though that character's lips do not move; presumably other characters cannot hear these thoughts. A character may also remember words, snatches of music, or events as represented by sound effects. This device is so common that we need to distinguish between *internal* and *external* diegetic sound. External diegetic sound is that which we as spectators take to have a physical source in the scene. Internal diegetic sound is that which comes only from the mind of a character; it is subjective. (Nondiegetic and internal diegetic sounds are often called *sound over* because they do not come from the real space of the scene.)

Figure 7.11

In the Laurence Olivier version of *Hamlet*, for example, the filmmaker presents Hamlet's famous soliloquies as interior monologues. The character registers the appropriate emotion on his face, but does not move his lips while we hear his voice saying the words, "To be or not to be . . . ," and so on. Hamlet is the source of the thoughts we hear represented as speech, but the words are only in the character's mind, not in his physical space. Hence the words are simple diegetic, but internal.

To summarize: Sound may be diegetic (in the story space) or nondiegetic (outside the story space). If it is diegetic, it may be onscreen or offscreen, internal ("subjective") or external ("objective").

One characteristic of diegetic sound is the possibility of suggesting the *distance* of its source. Volume is one simple way to give an impression of distance. A loud sound tends to seem near; a soft one, more distant. The horses' hooves in the *Seven Samurai* battle and the bugle call from *Stagecoach* exemplify this.

In addition to volume, timbre may suggest the texture and dimensions of the space within which a sound supposedly takes place. In *The Magnificent Ambersons* the conversations that take place on the baroque staircase have an echoing effect, giving the impression of huge, empty spaces around the characters. The skillful filmmaker will pay attention to the quality of the sound, taking advantage of the possibilities of variation from shot to shot.

In recent years technical developments have added the possibilities of stereo, quadraphonic, and other multichanneled systems to the filmmaker's range. This means that the sound can suggest location not only in terms of distance (volume, resonance), but also by specifying *direction*. In stereo versions of David Lean's *Lawrence of Arabia*, for example, the approach of planes to bomb a camp is first suggested through a rumble occurring only on the right side of the screen. Lawrence and an officer look off right, and their dialogue identifies the source of the sound. Then, when the scene shifts to the besieged camp itself, the stereo sound slides from channel to channel, reinforcing the visual depiction of the planes swooping overhead. Multiple channels make it possible to delineate space precisely.

In general, the spatial relations of sounds in films are clearly diegetic or nondiegetic. But because film is such a complex art form, involving the combination of so many elements, some films blur the distinctions between diegetic and nondiegetic sound. Since we are used to placing the source of a sound easily, a film may cheat our expectations.

There is a moment in *The Magnificent Ambersons* when Welles creates an unusual interplay between the diegetic and nondiegetic sounds. A prologue to the film outlines the background of the Amberson family and the birth of the son, George. We see a group of townswomen gossiping about the marriage of Isabel Amberson, and one predicts that she will have "the worst spoiled lot of children this town will ever see." This scene has involved diegetic dialogue. After the last line, the nondiegetic narrator resumes his description of the family history. Over a shot of the empty street, he says: "The prophetess proved to be mistaken in a single detail merely; Wilbur and Isabel did not have *children*. They had only one." But at this point, still over the shot of the street, we hear the gossiper's voice again: "Only one. But I'd like to know if he isn't spoiled enough for a whole carload." After her line, a pony cart comes up the street, and we see George for the first time. In this exchange the woman seems to reply to the narrator, even though we must assume that she cannot hear what he says; after all, she is a character in the story and he is not. Here Welles playfully departs from conventional usage to emphasize the arrival of the story's main character.

This example from *The Magnificent Ambersons* juxtaposes diegetic and nondiegetic sounds in an ambiguous way. In other films a single sound may be ambiguous because it seems to fall with equal logic into either category. This is often true in the films of Jean-Luc Godard. He narrates some of his films, but sometimes he seems also to be present in the story space just offscreen. Godard does not claim to be a character in the action, yet the characters on the screen sometimes seem to hear him. In an early scene in *Two or Three Things I Know About Her* Godard's voice introduces the actress Marina Vlady and describes her, then does the same with the character that Vlady plays, Juliette Janson. He speaks in a whisper, and we are not sure whether she can hear him or not. Later in the scene she gives answers to questions seemingly asked by someone off-screen. Yet we do not hear the questions themselves and don't know if Godard is asking them from his position behind the camera as director. We are never sure whether Godard is nondiegetic narrator or diegetic character; in the latter case, his role would have to be something like "director/narrator of *Two or Three Things I Know About Her*." This uncertainty is important for Godard, since in some of his films an uncertainty as to diegetic or nondiegetic sound sources enables him to stress the conventionality of traditional sound usage.

The distinction between diegetic and nondiegetic sound is important not as an end in itself but as a tool for understanding particular films, as we shall see when we examine *A Man Escaped*.

Time

Sound relates temporally to filmic images in two ways: viewing time and story time. By *viewing time* we mean the physical length of the film—the time it takes the film to be projected. This usually differs from *story time*, that is, the time assumed to pass in the film's action. Events may cover a number of years in the characters' lives (story time), but most films we see in theaters take only about two hours to watch (viewing time). Viewing time becomes an instrument of the plot's manipulation of story time.

A sound may be juxtaposed in any temporal relationship with an image. The matching of sound with image in terms of our viewing time is called *synchronization*. When a sound is synchronized with the image, we hear it at the same time as we see the source produce the sound on the screen. Most dialogue between characters is matched so that the lips of the actors move at the same time that we hear the appropriate words.

When the sound does go out of synchronization during a viewing (e.g., through an error in projection), the result is quite distracting. But some imaginative filmmakers have obtained good effects by using out-of-sync, or *asynchronous*, sound. One such example occurs in a scene in the musical by Gene Kelly and Stanley Donen, *Singin' in the Rain*. The story is set in the early days of sound in Hollywood; a famous pair of silent screen actors have just made their first talking picture, *The Dueling Cavalier*. Their film company previews the film for an audience at a theater. In the earliest days of "talkies," sound was often recorded on a phonograph record to be played along with the film; hence the chances of the sound's getting out of synchronization with the picture were much greater than they are today. This is what happens in the preview of *The Dueling Cavalier*. As the film is projected, it slows down momentarily, but the record keeps running; from this point all the sounds come several seconds before their source is seen in the image. A line of dialogue begins, *then* the actor's lips move. A woman's voice is heard when a man moves his lips, and vice versa. The humor of this disastrous preview in *Singin' in the Rain* depends on our realization that the sound and image are supposed to be matched, but actually occur separately.

A lengthier example of a play with our expectations about synchronization comes in Woody Allen's film *What's Up Tiger Lily?* Allen has taken an Oriental spy film and dubbed a new sound track on, but the English-language dialogue is not a translation of the original; rather, it creates a new story in comic juxtaposition with the original images. Much of the humor results from our constant awareness that the words are not perfectly synchronized with the actors' lips. Allen has turned the usual problems of the dubbing of foreign films into the basis of his comedy.

Synchronization relates to *viewing* time. But what of *story* time? If the sound takes place at the same time as the image in terms of the story events, it is *simultaneous* sound; if the sound occurs earlier or later than the story events of the image, the sound is *nonsimultaneous*.

Most of the time a film's sound is simultaneous, with image and sound both in the present. We are familiar with this from countless dialogue scenes, musical numbers, chase scenes, and so forth. We shall call this simultaneous diegetic sound *simple diegetic*.

But scenes with nonsimultaneous sound are relatively familiar as well. Diegetic sound can occur in a time either earlier or later than the time of the image. In either case we shall call it *displaced diegetic* sound. As we saw earlier, both types of diegetic sound can have either an external or an internal source.

As these categories suggest, temporal relationships in the cinema are complex. To help distinguish them, Table 7.2 sums up the possible temporal and spatial relationships which may exist between image and sound.

Diegetic Sound

We have already discussed simple diegetic sound, both external and internal. This is the commonest kind of sound in films. Some concrete examples may help clarify the distinctions among the other categories.

1. *Sound earlier than image.* Displaced diegetic sound may recall an earlier scene through the repetition of sound from that scene while the images on the screen remain in the present. In a scene in Hitchcock's *Psycho* the repeated sounds are memories recalled by the central character, Marion Crane. In a previous scene Marion's boss has told her to deposit a large sum of money in the bank. Instead, she steals the money,

Table 7.2 Temporal Relationships of Sound in Cinema

	Space of source	
	Diegetic (story space)	**Nondiegetic** (nonstory space)
Temporal relation: 1. Sound earlier than image	Displaced diegetic: *External:* sound flash-back; image flash-forward *Internal:* Memories of character heard	Sound marked as past put over images (e.g., sound of a Winston Churchill speech put over images of Britain today)
2. Sound simultaneous with image	Simple diegetic: *External:* dialogue, effects, music *Internal:* thoughts of character heard	Sound, marked as simultaneous with images, put over images
3. Sound later than image	Displaced diegetic: *External:* Sound flash-forward; image flash-back with sound continuing in the present; character narrates earlier events *Internal:* Character's vision of future heard	Narrator in present speaks of events shown as being in past; sound marked as later put over images (e.g., reminiscing narrator of *The Magnificent Ambersons*)

and we see her driving away. The images show Marion in a medium close-up behind the wheel of her car. On the sound track, however, we hear an exact repetition of the lines spoken earlier by her boss; this sound is her memory of the earlier scene.

Less common but still possible is external sound that forms a sound flashback. Joseph Losey's *Accident* ends with a shot of a driveway gate. We hear a car crash, but the sound represents the crash that occurred at the *beginning* of the film. Since no one is remembering the scene and since the sound is from an earlier time than the image, we have an external sound flashback.

2. *Sound later than image.* Displaced diegetic sound may also occur at a later time than that of the images. Probably the most familiar use of

this category is the narrator who tells a story that has occurred in the past. In Ford's *How Green Was My Valley* the man Huw narrates the story of his boyhood in Wales. Aside from a glimpse at the beginning, we do not see him as a man, only as a boy; the words of the narration are spoken by a man's voice in a period long after that of the events we see on the screen.

An internal use of sound that is later than the images is rare, but there are a few cases. Later in the scene from *Psycho* described above, Marion begins to imagine what her boss *will* say on Monday when he discovers the theft. While the image of her driving the car remains on the screen, we hear internal displaced diegetic sound representing a *later* time: a character's premonition on the sound track.

Sound may belong to a later time than the image in another way. In some cases, particularly in films of the 1960s and 1970s, the sound from the next scene begins while the images of the last one are still on the screen. This is called a *sound bridge.* Sound bridges create transitions, since we see one image, say, of a person's face, but hear what seems an inappropriate sound, perhaps of a band playing. Then a cut reveals a new locale and time, and we see the band which was the source of the music. Since the sound belongs to the later scene, the moment before the cut uses nonsimultaneous sound.

Examples of sound flashforwards (external displaced diegetic) are rare, perhaps nonexistent, but such a use is logically possible in the cinema.

Nondiegetic Sound

Most nondiegetic sound has no relevant temporal relationship to the story. When "mood" music comes up over a tense scene, it would be irrelevant for us to ask if it is happening at the same time as the images, since the music has no relation to the space of the story. But occasionally the filmmaker may use a type of nondiegetic sound that does have a defined temporal relationship to the story. For example, Orson Welles's narration in *The Magnificent Ambersons* speaks of the action as having happened long ago, in a different era of American history.

Summary

All of these temporal categories offer us ways of making important distinctions in analyzing films. Fritz Lang's *Secret Beyond the Door,* for example, has an unusual combination of internal displaced diegetic and internal simple diegetic sound. In the first third of the film, the heroine's wedding is about to take place; her voice is heard recalling the circumstances that led to her marriage. This interior monologue is in the present tense. Over the scenes from the past, the monologue is internal displaced diegetic, but over the framing scenes of the wedding, her voice continues as internal simple diegetic. As a whole, the film depends on the contrast of two types of internal speech: The character's mind reacts to immediate situations (simple diegetic), and her mind reflects on past events (displaced diegetic). In such cases the various categories of sound help sharpen our awareness of the ways in which sound can combine with images.

Functions of Film Sound: <u>A Man Escaped</u> ■

Robert Bresson's *A Man Escaped (Un Condamné à Mort c'est Echappé)* shows how a variety of sound techniques can function throughout an entire film. The narrative takes place in France in 1943. Fontaine, a Resistance fighter arrested by the Germans, has been put in prison and condemned to die. But while awaiting his sentence, he works at an escape plan, loosening the boards of his cell door and making ropes. Just as he is ready to put his plan in action, a boy, Jost, is put into his cell. Deciding to trust that Jost is not a spy, Fontaine reveals his plan to him, and they are both able to escape.

Throughout the film, sound has many important functions. As in all of his films, Bresson emphasizes the sound track, rightly realizing that sound may be just as "cinematic" as the images. At certain points in *A Man Escaped*, Bresson even lets his sound techniques dominate the image; in ways we shall examine, we are compelled to *listen*. Indeed, Bresson is one of a handful of directors who create a complete interplay between sound and image.

A key factor in guiding our perception of the film is the commentary spoken over by Fontaine himself, which illustrates the category of external displaced diegetic sound. Fontaine's narration, which occurs in a time later than that of the images, has multiple functions.

First, the commentary helps develop the narrative. Certain temporal cues suggest how long Fontaine spends in prison. As we see him working at his escape plan, his voice-over tells us, "One month of patient work and my door opened." At other points he gives us additional indications of time. His commentary is particularly important during the final escape scene, where the action occupies only 15 minutes of viewing time and the lighting is so dim as to allow only glimpses of the action itself. Yet Fontaine's voice calmly tells us of the hours he and Jost spend on each stage of their progress.

We receive other vital information through the commentary. Sometimes the narration simply states facts: that the pin Fontaine obtains came from the women's wing of the prison or that certain prison officials' quarters were at various places in the building. More strikingly, Fontaine often tells what his thoughts had been. After being beaten and put in his first cell, he wipes the blood from his face and lies down; on the track we hear his voice say: "I'd have preferred a quick death." Often the actor does not register such thoughts visually. At some points the sound even corrects an impression given by the image. After Fontaine has been sentenced to death, he is led back to his cell and flings himself down on the bed. We might take him to be crying, but the commentary says, "I laughed hysterically. It helped."

Yet at first much of the commentary may seem unnecessary, since it often tells us something that we can also see in the image. In one scene Fontaine wipes the blood from his face, and his voice tells us, "I tried to clean up." Again and again in the film Fontaine describes his actions as we see him perform them or just before or after them. But this use of sound is not redundantly supporting the visuals. One major function of the commentary is to deflect the film's whole time scheme. Instead of simply showing a series of events in the present, the commentary (internal displaced diegetic) places the events in the past. Indeed certain phrases emphasize the fact that the commentary is a remembering of events. As we see Fontaine lie down in his cell after having been beaten, his commentary says, "I believe that I gave up and wept," as if the passage of time has made him uncertain. After meeting another prisoner, Fontaine narrates: "Terry was an exception; he was allowed to see his daughter. I learned this later." Again we sense that the meeting we see on the screen occurred at a point in the past.

Because of this difference in time between image and commentary, the narrative indicates to us that Fontaine will eventually escape rather than be executed. (The title also indicates this.) The final *effect* of the narrative cause-effect chain is known. As a result, our concentration is centered on the *cause*—not *whether* Fontaine will escape, but *how* he will escape. The film guides our attention, first of all, toward the minute details of Fontaine's work to break out of prison. The commentary and the sound effects draw our attention to tiny gestures and ordinary objects that become crucial to the escape. Second, the narrative stresses that work alone is not enough, that Fontaine and the other prisoners can survive, both mentally and physically, only through their mutual trust and efforts to help one another. Fontaine receives much aid from his fellow prisoners: His neighbor, Blanchet, gives him a blanket to make his ropes; another prisoner who also tries to escape, Orsini, provides vital information about how to get over the walls. Finally, Fontaine himself must extend trust and aid to his new cellmate, Jost, by taking him along in spite of suspicions that he may be a spy planted by the Germans.

The interplay between the sounds and images in *A Man Escaped* does not pertain solely to the commentary. The ability to focus our attention on details works with sound effects as well. In the long middle portion of the film, in which Fontaine works on breaking through his door and making the implements of escape, this focus on details becomes particularly prominent. A close-up shows Fontaine's hands sharpening a spoonhandle into a chisel; the loud scraping sound intensifies our perception of this detail. We also hear distinctly the rubbing of the spoon against the boards of the door, the ripping of cloth with a razor to make ropes, even the swish of a straw against the floor as Fontaine sweeps up slivers of wood.

Sound not only intensifies the attention we pay to small actions, but also at times controls *what* we see. As Fontaine looks around his cell for the first time, he names the items it contains—a slop bucket, a shelf, a window. *After* he mentions each, the camera moves to give us a glimpse of it. At another point Fontaine hears a strange sound outside his cell. He moves to the door, and we see what he sees in a point-of-view shot through the peephole in his door; a guard is winding the crank of a skylight in the hall. For the first time Fontaine becomes aware of the skylight, which eventually becomes his escape route. At another point Fontaine's neighbor, Blanchet, falls down during their daily walk to empty their slop buckets. We first hear the sound of his fall as the camera remains on a medium shot of Fontaine reacting in surprise; then there is a cut to Blanchet as Fontaine moves to help him up. Thus the sound anticipates and guides our perception.

At times, sound in *A Man Escaped* goes beyond controlling the image—sometimes it *replaces* it. Many of the film's scenes are so dark that sound must carry the burden of letting us know what the action is. After Fontaine falls asleep in prison for the first time, there is a fade-out; while the screen is still dark, we hear his voice-over saying: "I slept so soundly, my guards had to awaken me." This is followed by the loud sound of a bolt and hinge. The light let in by the door allows us to see a faint image of a guard's hand shaking Fontaine, and we hear a voice tell him to get up. The film contains many fade-outs in which the sound of the next scene begins before the image. By putting sound over a black screen or dark image, Bresson allows the sound track an unusually prominent place in his film.

The reliance on sound culminates in the final escape scene. During much of the last 15 or 20 minutes of the film, the action takes place in almost complete darkness. We get glimpses of gestures and settings, but often sound is our only guide to what is happening. Nor are there any establishing shots to give us a sense of the space of the roofs and walls Fontaine and Jost must scale. This has the effect of intensifying the spectators' perception greatly; we must strain to see and understand the action from what we can glimpse and hear. Sounds become paramount here. We judge the pair's progress from the church bells heard off tolling the hour; the train outside the walls serves to cover the noise they make; each strange noise suggests an unseen threat to the escape. In one remarkable shot Fontaine stands in almost total darkness by a wall, listening to the footsteps of a guard walking up and down offscreen. Fontaine knows that he must kill this man if his escape is to succeed; we hear his voice over discussing where the guard is moving and mentioning how hard his own heart is beating. All we see is his dim outline and a tiny reflection of light in his eye. Again, throughout this scene the sound concentrates our attention on the reactions and gestures of the characters rather than on the simple cause-effect sequence of the story action.

We have discussed how a filmmaker controls not only what we hear, but also the qualities of that sound. Bresson has achieved a considerable variety in *A Man Escaped.* Every object in the film is assigned a distinct pitch. The volumes of sounds range from very loud to almost inaudible, as the opening scene illustrates. The first few shots of Fontaine riding to prison in a car are accompanied only by the soft hum of the motor. But as a streetcar blocks the road, Fontaine seeks to use the streetcar's uproar to conceal his dash from the car. The moment Fontaine leaps from the car, Bresson eliminates the streetcar noise, and we hear running feet and gunshots off. Later, in the final escape, the film alternates sounds off (trains, bells, bicycle, and so on) with stretches of silence. The film's sparse mix effectively isolates specific sounds for our attention.

Certain sounds are not only very loud, but also have an echo effect added to give them a distinctive timbre. The voices of the German guards as they give Fontaine orders are reverberant and harsh compared to the voices of the other prisoners. Similarly, the noises of the handcuffs and bolts of the cell doors are magnified for the same echo effect. Thus our reactions to Fontaine's imprisonment are intensified through the manipulation of timbre.

These devices all help focus our attention on the details of Fontaine's prison life. But there are other devices that help unify the film and sustain its narrative and thematic development. These are the sound *motifs,* which come back at significant moments of the action; they often call attention to Fontaine's interactions with the other prisoners, since the men depend on one another.

One set of sound motifs emphasizes the space outside Fontaine's cell. We see a streetcar in the opening scene, and the bell and motor of a streetcar are heard offscreen every time Fontaine speaks to someone through his cell window; we are always aware of his goal of reaching the streets beyond the walls. During the second half of the film the sounds of trains also become important. When Fontaine is first able to leave his cell and walk in the hall unobserved, we first hear the whistle. It returns at other moments when he leaves his cell clandestinely, until the train provides the noise to cover the sounds Fontaine and Jost make during their escape. The daily gathering of the men to wash in a common sink becomes associated with running water; at first the faucet is seen, but later Bresson shoots the actions of the prisoners in closer shots, with the sound of the water offscreen.

Other sound motifs become associated with defiance of the prison rules. Fontaine uses his handcuffs to tap on the wall to signal his neighbors; he coughs to cover the sound of scraping (the coughs also become signals between the men); Fontaine defies the guards' orders and continues to talk to the other men.

Another motif involves the only nondiegetic sound in the film, passages from a Mozart mass. This music is motivated clearly enough; the film's narrative refers continually to religious faith. Fontaine tells another prisoner that he prays, but does not expect God to help him if he doesn't work for his own liberty. But the pattern of the actual uses of the music is less clear. After it is heard over the credits, the music doesn't return for some time. Its first use over the action occurs during the first walk Fontaine takes with the men to empty their slop buckets. As the music plays, Fontaine's commentary explains the routine: "Empty your buckets and wash, back to your cell for the day." The juxtaposition of ceremonial, baroque church music with the emptying of slop buckets in a prison is an incongruous one. Yet the contrast is not ironic. Not only are these moments of movement important to Fontaine's life in the prison, but they also provide his main means of direct contact with other prisoners. The music, which comes back seven more times, emphasizes the narrative development: Fontaine meets the other men, wins their support, and finally plans to share his escape. The music reappears whenever Fontaine makes contact with another prisoner (Blanchet, Orsini) who will affect his final escape. Later washing scenes have no music; these are scenes in which Fontaine's contact is cut off (Orsini decides not to go along). The music returns as Orsini attempts his own escape plan; he fails, but is able to give Fontaine vital information he will need in his own attempt. The music reappears when Blanchet, once opposed to Fontaine's plan, contributes his blanket to the rope making. Eventually the music becomes associated with the boy, Jost; it plays again as Fontaine realizes that he must either kill Jost or take him along. The final use of music comes over the very end of the film, as the two leave the prison and disappear into the night. The nondiegetic music has traced Fontaine's progress in his relations with the other men on whom his endeavor depends.

There are other sound motifs in the film (bells, guns, whistles, children's voices), but they share the different functions already noted: characterizing Fontaine's escape, calling our attention to details, and controlling what we see.

Let us look at a brief scene from *A Man Escaped* in order to see how silence and shifts between sounds that are internal and external, diegetic and displaced diegetic, guide our expectations. The four shots indicated by Figs. 7.12 through 7.22 constitute the scene in which the boy Jost is put into Fontaine's cell.

Shot	Voice	Effects	Action/camera
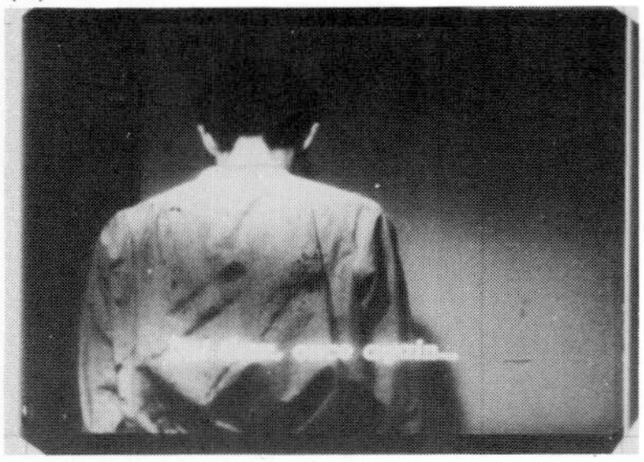 (1) 27 sec	F. (over): But then once again . . .	Lock rattles off	
		Rattle continues off	F. turns
Figure 7.12			
	. . . I thought I was lost.	Footsteps off	F. turns head left
			Watches off left, turning head
			Moves left and slightly forward
		Lock closing off	
		1 retreating footstep off	Catches door as it closes
Figure 7.13			
	(Over): In French and German uniform, he looked repulsively filthy.		
Figure 7.14			

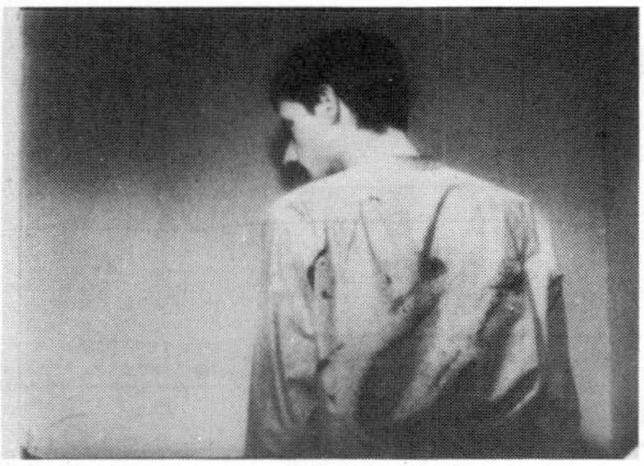

Figure 7.12

Figure 7.13

Figure 7.14

Shot	Voice	Effects	Action/camera
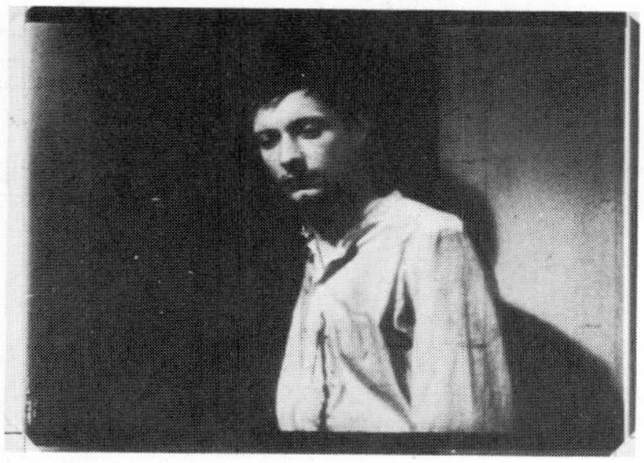 Figure 7.15	(Over): He seemed barely sixteen.	Echoing of locks and doors, off Two footsteps, off	
 Figure 7.16 (2) 10 sec	F. (aloud): Are you German?		
 Figure 7.17	French? What is your name?		Jost lifts head, looks off right
 Figure 7.18	Jost: Jost, François Jost. F. (over): Had they planted a spy?		

Shot	Voice	Effects	Action/camera

(3) 10 sec

Figure 7.19

F. (over): Did they think I was ready to talk?

F. lowers eyes

Figure 7.20

Sound of one footstep (F.'s) on cell floor

F. moves left and forward; camera pans to follow

Figure 7.21

F. (aloud): Give me your hand, Jost.

F. stretches right arm out

Shot	Voice	Effects	Action/camera
(4) 7 sec			
		Sound of Jost rising	Jost stands, they shake hands
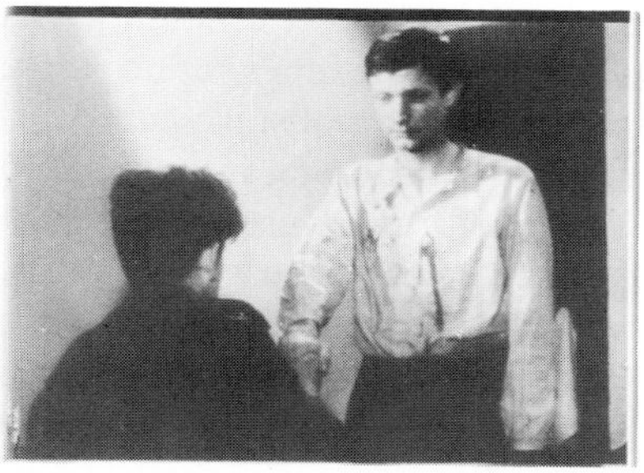	F. (aloud): There isn't much room.		F. looks right
		Shoes against floor	They both look around

Figure 7.22

Dissolve

The use of silence and the oscillations between Fontaine's internal and external speech dominate the scene. We have not seen Jost before and do not know what is happening as the scene begins. Fontaine's internal commentary tells us that a new threat has appeared; offscreen footsteps and Fontaine's gaze indicate that someone has entered the room, but the camera lingers on Fontaine; Bresson delays the cut to the newcomer for a surprisingly long time. (This first shot is as long as the other three shots combined.) The delay serves multiple functions. The fact that we wait to see Jost emphasizes the importance of his appearance; it also turns our expectations to Fontaine's reaction (conveyed largely through his displaced diegetic narration) rather than to the new character. By the time we actually see Jost, we know that Fontaine feels threatened by him and disturbed by his part-German uniform. The first words Fontaine speaks externally emphasize his doubt; rather than stating a decisive attitude, he simply seeks information. Again his internal commentary returns as he makes clear the dilemma he is in: Jost may be a spy planted by the prison officials. Yet his words to Jost contrast with this inner doubt as he shakes hands and begins to converse in a friendly fashion. Thus the interplay of external diegetic and internal displaced diegetic voice allows the filmmaker to present contrasting temporal and psychological aspects of the action.

The sound effects differentiate significant actions and develop the narrative progression. Fontaine's footstep is heard as he moves toward Jost after his initial reserve; Jost's rising accompanies their first gesture of trust, the handshake; finally, their shoes scrape against the floor as they relax and begin to speak of their situation.

This scene is very brief, but the combination of many different types of sound in a few shots indicates the complexity of the film's sound track. Regardless of whether we consider that sound track realistic or unrealistic, we can see it as a part of the entire film, functioning in interaction with other techniques and with narrative form. Bresson uses sounds that are recognizable to us but which come at carefully chosen moments. Through his control of what sounds we hear, what qualities these sounds have, and what relationships exist among those sounds and between sound and image, he has made this technique an important factor in controlling our perception throughout the film.

Summary ■

As usual, both extensive viewing and intensive scrutiny will sharpen your capacity to notice the functioning of film sound. You can get comfortable with the analytical tools we have suggested by asking:

1. What sounds are present—music, speech, noise? How are loudness, pitch, and timbre used? Is the mixture sparse or dense? Modulated or abruptly changing?
2. Is the sound related rhythmically to the image? If so, how?
3. Is the sound faithful or unfaithful to its perceived source?
4. *Where* is the sound coming from? In the story's space or outside it? Onscreen or offscreen?
5. *When* is the sound occurring? Simultaneously with the story action? Before? After?

Practice at trying to answer such questions will familiarize you with the basic uses of film sound. As always, though, it is not enough to name and classify; these categories and terms are most useful when we take the next step and examine how the types of sound we identify *function* in the total film.

Notes and Queries ■

For material on how sound is created in film production, see Notes and Queries to Chapter 1.

The Powers of Sound

As the *Letter from Siberia* example suggests, documentary filmmakers have experimented a great deal with sound. For other examples, see Basil Wright's *Song of Ceylon* and Humphrey Jennings' *Listen to Britain* and *Diary for Timothy*. Analyses of sound in these films may be found in Paul Rotha, *Documentary Film* (New York: Hastings House, 1952); Karel Reisz and Gavin Millar's *Techniques of Film Editing* (New York: Hastings House, 1968), pp. 156–170. Experimental and nonnarrative films also exploit unusual powers of sound; see Norman McLaren's "Notes on Animated Sound," *Film Quarterly* **7**, 3 (Spring 1953): 223–229 (an article on hand-*drawn* sound tracks); Robert Russell and Cecile Starr, *Experimental Animation* (New York: Van Nostrand, 1976), especially pp. 163–177; and P. Adams Sitney, *Visionary Film* (New York: Oxford University Press, 1974), *passim*.

Silent Film versus Sound Film

Some film aestheticians protested against the coming of "talkies," feeling that sound film spoiled a pristine mute art. In the bad sound films, René Clair claimed, "the image is reduced precisely to the role of the illustration of a phonograph record, and the sole aim of the whole show is to resemble as closely as possible the play of which it is the 'cinematic' reproduction. In three or four settings there take place endless scenes of dialogue which are merely boring if you do not understand English but unbearable if you do" (*Cinema Yesterday and Today* [New York: Dover, 1972], p. 137). Rudolf Arnheim, who saw the artistic potential of cinema as its inability to reproduce reality perfectly, asserted that "the introduction of the sound film smashed many of the forms that the film artists were using in favor of the inartistic demand for the greatest possible 'naturalness' (in the most superficial sense of the word)" *(Film As Art* [Berkeley: University of California Press, 1957], p. 154).

It is easy to find such beliefs anachronistic, but we must recall that many early sound films relied simply on dialogue for their novelty; both Clair and Arnheim welcomed sound effects and music but warned against talkiness. In any event, the inevitable reaction eventually came. André Bazin constructed a lengthy, influential argument in favor of the greater realism of both sound and image possible in the sound cinema. See his essays "The Evolution of the Language of Cinema," "In Defense of Mixed Cinema," and "Theatre and Cinema," all to be found in *What Is Cinema?* Vol. I (Berkeley: University of California Press, 1967). See also V. F. Perkins, *Film as Film* (Baltimore: Penguin, 1972); Erwin Panofsky, "Style and Medium in the Motion Pictures," in Gerald Mast and Marshall Cohen, eds., *Film Theory and Criticism* (New York: Oxford

University Press, 1974), pp. 151–169; and Siegfried Kracauer, *Theory of Film* (New York: Oxford University Press, 1965), wherein Kracauer remarks: "Films with sound live up to the spirit of the medium only if the visuals take the lead in them" (p. 103). As we have seen, however, the creation of realism is only one of many functions sound can perform in a film.

Film Music

Of all the kinds of sound in cinema, music has been most extensively discussed. The literature is voluminous, and with a recent surge of interest in film composers, many more recordings of film music have become available. A survey of the field, with bibliography and discography, may be found in Harry Geduld, "Film Music: A Survey," *Quarterly Review of Film Studies* 1, 2 (May 1976): 183–204. Basic introductions to music useful for film study include William S. Newman, *Understanding Music* (New York: Harper, 1961); Leonard B. Meyer, *Emotion and Meaning in Music* (Chicago: University of Chicago Press, 1956); and Deryck Cooke, *The Language of Music* (New York: Oxford University Press, 1962). Classic studies of film music are William Johnson, "Face the Music," *Film Quarterly* 22, 4 (Summer 1969): 3–19; Roger Manvell, *The Technique of Film Music* (New York: Hastings House, 1957); Kurt London, *Film Music* (New York: Hastings House, 1970); Aaron Copland, "Film Music," *What to Listen for in Music* (New York: Signet, 1957), pp. 152–157; and Hanns Eisler's attack on Hollywood film scoring, *Composing for the Films* (London: Dobson, 1947). A more recent work is Tony Thomas, *Music for the Movies* (New York: Barnes, 1973). See also Chuck Jones, "Music and the Animated Cartoon," *Hollywood Quarterly* 1, 4 (July 1946): 364–370. Music for silent films is discussed in Charles Hofmann, "Sounds for Silents," *Film Library Quarterly* 2, 1 (Winter 1968–1969): 40–43.

Despite the bulk of material on film music, there have been fairly few analyses of music's functions in particular films. The most famous (or notorious) is Sergei Eisenstein's "Form and Content: Practice," in *The Film Sense* (New York: Harvest, 1942), pp. 157–216, which examines sound/image relations in a sequence from *Alexander Nevsky*. Recent analysis of film music has been done by Claudia Gorbman in such detailed studies as "Music as Salvation: Notes on Fellini and Rota," *Film Quarterly* 28, 2 (Winter 1974–1975): 17–25; "Clair's Sound Hierarchy and the Creation of Auditory Space," *Purdue Film Studies 1976*, 113–123, and "Vigo/Jaubert," *Ciné-Tracts* 1, 2 (Summer 1977): 65–80.

Dimensions of Film Sound

The categories of sound suggested in the chapter conform to the distinctions most film analysts currently make, but the overall system and some of the terms are of our devising. Many other schemes for understanding film sound have been proposed. See Siegfried Kracauer, *Theory of Film* (New York: Oxford University Press, 1965), 102–156; Claudia Gorbman, "Teaching the Sound Track," *Quarterly Review of Film Studies* 1, 4 (November 1976): 446–452; Bela Balazs, *Theory of the Film* (New York: Dover, 1970), pp. 194–241; Raymond Spottiswoode, *A Grammar of the Film* (Berkeley: University of California Press, 1962): 173–197; Noël Burch, *Theory of Film Practice* (New York: Praeger, 1973): pp. 90–104. Each of these schemes offers tools for analyzing how sound interacts with the image.

Stereophonic and other complex sound systems are discussed in Michael Z. Wygotsky, *Wide-Screen Cinema and Stereophonic Sound* (New York: Hastings House, 1971).

Dubbing and Subtitles

People beginning to study cinema may express surprise (even annoyance) that films in foreign languages are usually shown with subtitled captions translating the dialogue. Why not, some viewers ask, use "dubbed" versions of the films, i.e., versions in which the dialogue has been translated into the audience's tongue and recorded on prints of the films? In many countries dubbing is very common. (Italy has a tradition of dubbing almost every film imported.) Why, then, do most people who study movies prefer subtitles?

There are several reasons. Dubbed voices usually have a bland "studio" sound. Elimination of the original actors' voices wipes out an important component of their performance. (Partisans of dubbing ought to look at dubbed versions of English-language films to see how a performance by Katherine Hepburn, Orson Welles, or John Wayne can be hurt by a voice that doesn't fit the body.) With dubbing, all of the usual problems of translation are multiplied by the need to synchronize specific words with specific lip movements. Most important, with subtitling viewers still have access to the original soundtrack; by eliminating the original voice track, dubbing simply destroys part of the film.

CHAPTER 8

STYLE AS A FORMAL SYSTEM: SUMMARY

At the beginning of Part Two, we saw how the different parts of a film relate to one another within the dynamic system we call its *form*. We have already examined one major aspect of a film's form: its organization into a categorical, rhetorical, abstract, or narrative structure. Now, having examined each category of techniques of the film medium, we may go on to see how these techniques interact to create another formal system of the film, its *style*. These two systems—style and narrative/ nonnarrative form—in turn interact within the total film.

Not all films use every technique that we have discussed. For many years in the early stages of film history, for example, filmmakers did not have the choice of using sound. Other techniques introduced over the years have broadened the range of possibilities. But usually the filmmaker limits his or her use of techniques not simply because of historical necessity, but through choice. The filmmaker selects certain techniques, then repeats and varies them in the course of a film; the result is a unique style in which the viewer perceives these techniques as they return and assimilates their functions.

Often when we speak of a filmmaker's style, we are referring to the particular techniques that person typically employs and the unique ways these techniques relate to one another in his or her films. When we discussed sound in *A Man Escaped*, we characterized Bresson as a director who makes sound particularly important in his films; we analyzed several important ways in which sound related to image in *A Man Escaped*. This use of sound is one aspect of Bresson's unique style. Similarly, we looked at *Our Hospitality* in terms of how its comic mise-en-scene is organized around a consistent use of long shots; this is part of Keaton's style. Both Bresson and Keaton have distinctive filmmaking styles, and we can become familiar with those styles by analyzing the way in which they utilize techniques within whole filmic systems.

Let us return to our original example of narrative form, *Citizen Kane*, and go on to look at its style—that is, *its characteristic and significant use of specific film techniques*. Now that we have all of the tools for

Figure 8.1

an analysis of a film's overall form, we should be able to examine how narrative and style interact.

In looking at *Citizen Kane*'s narrative, we discovered that the film is organized as a search; a detectivelike figure, the reporter Thompson, tries to find the significance of Kane's last word, "Rosebud." But even before Thompson appears as a character, we the spectators are invited to ask questions about Kane and to seek their answers. The very beginning of the film sets up a mystery. The fade-in reveals a "No Trespassing" sign; in a series of craning movements upwards, the camera travels over a set of fences, all matched graphically in the slow dissolves that link the shots. There follows a series of shots of a huge estate, always with the great house in the distance (Fig. 8.1). (This sequence depends largely on special effects; the house itself is a model, or perhaps a picture, combined through back projection with real objects in the foreground.) The gloomy lighting, the deserted setting, and the ominous music give the opening of the film the eerie quality that we associate with mystery stories. These shots are connected by dissolves; the camera gradually seems to shift closer to the house, though there is no camera movement. From shot to shot the foreground changes—from a golf course to a dock, and so forth—yet the single lighted window remains in almost exactly the same position on the screen. Graphically matching the window from shot to shot already focuses our attention on it; we assume (rightly) that whatever is in that room will be important in initiating the story.

This pattern of our penetration into the space of a scene returns at other points in the film. Again and again the camera moves toward things that might reveal the secrets of Kane's character. In the scene in which Thompson goes to interview Susan Alexander, the camera begins not on the reporter, but on the poster of Susan on the nightclub wall; then in a spectacular crane shot the camera moves up the wall, over the roof, through the "El Rancho" sign, and over to the skylight. At that point a dissolve and a crack of lightning shift the scene inside to another craning movement down to Susan's table. These two scenes have some striking similarities. Each begins with a sign ("No Trespassing" and the publicity poster), and each moves us into a building to reveal a new character. The first scene uses a series of shots, whereas the second depends more on camera movement; but these different techniques are working in similar directions to create a pattern that becomes part of the film's style. Thompson's second visit to Susan repeats the crane shots of the first. The second flashback of Jed Leland's story begins with another movement into a scene; the camera is initially pointed at the wet cobblestones of a street, then tilts up and tracks in toward Susan coming out of a drugstore; only then does the camera pan right to reveal Kane standing, splashed with mud, on the curb. This pattern of movement into the space of scenes carries through the narrative's search pattern.

As we have seen, films' endings often contain variations of their beginnings. Toward the end of *Citizen Kane*, Thompson gives up his search for Rosebud. But after the reporters leave the huge storeroom of Xanadu, the camera begins to move over the great expanse of Kane's collections. It cranes forward high above the crates and piles of objects (Fig. 8.2), then moves down to center on the sled from Kane's childhood. Then there is a cut to the furnace, and the camera again moves in on the sled as it is tossed into the fire. At last we are able to read the word "Rosebud" on the sled. The ending continues the pattern set up at the beginning; the film techniques create a penetration into the story space, probing the mystery of the central character. But after our glimpse of the sled, the film reverses the pattern. A series of shots linked by dissolves leads us back outside Xanadu, the camera travels down to the "No Trespassing" sign again, and we are left to wonder whether this discovery really provides a resolution to the mystery about Kane's character.

Figure 8.2

But *Citizen Kane* is not simply a mystery story, and the ominous gloom of the opening and closing contrasts with many other scenes of widely varied tone. Let us pick out some other stylistic patterns that have specific narrative functions.

One of the most famous devices in the film is its use of deep focus. A number of important scenes combine deep space and great depth of field with camera movement and the long take so as to make the dramatic situation of the characters visually apparent. The shot in which Kane's mother signs her son over to Thatcher is a good example of this. Several shots precede this one, introducing the young Kane. Then there is a cut to what at first seems a simple long shot of the boy (Fig. 8.3). But the camera tracks back to reveal a window; Kane's mother appears at the left of the frame, calling to him (Fig. 8.4). Then the camera continues to track

Figure 8.3

Figure 8.4

Figure 8.5

Figure 8.6

back, into another room (Fig. 8.5). Mrs. Kane and Thatcher sit at a table in the foreground to sign the papers, while Kane's father remains standing further away at the left, and the boy plays in the distance (Fig. 8.6). Welles eliminates cutting here. The shot becomes a complex unit unto itself, like the opening of *Touch of Evil* discussed in Chapter 5. Most Hollywood directors would have handled this scene in shot/reverse shot, but Welles keeps all of the implications of the action simultaneously before us. The boy, who is the subject of the discussion, remains framed in the distant window through the whole scene; his game leads us to believe that he is unaware of what his mother is doing. The tensions between the father and mother are conveyed not only by the fact that she excludes him from the discussion at the table, but also by the overlapping sound; his objections to signing his son away to a guardian mix in with the dialogue in the foreground—even the boy's shouts (ironically, "The Union Forever!") can be heard in the distance. The framing also emphasizes the mother in much of the scene. This is her only appearance in the film; the suggestion of her tenseness and controlled emotions helps motivate the many effects that follow from her action here. We have had little introduction to the situation prior to this scene, but the combination of sound, cinematography, and mise-en-scene conveys the complicated action quickly and clearly.

The "combinatory" method of arranging the action within a shot recurs in other parts of the film. A later sequence presents Kane's financial losses in the Depression; he is forced to sign over his newspaper to Thatcher's bank. The scene opens on a close-up of Kane's manager, Bernstein, reading the contract; he lowers the paper to reveal Thatcher, now much older, seated opposite him. We hear Kane's voice off, and Bernstein moves his head slightly (the camera reframes slightly); we see that Kane is pacing beyond them in a huge room (see Fig. 5.10). The scene is a single take in which the dramatic situation is created by the arrangement of the figures and the image's depth of field. The lowering of the contract recalls the previous scene, in which we first get a real look at the adult Kane as Thatcher puts down that newspaper that has concealed him. There Thatcher had been annoyed, but Kane had the power to defy him. Now Thatcher has gained control and Kane paces restlessly, still defiant, but stripped of his power over the *Inquirer* chain. The use of a similar device to open these two scenes sets up a contrasting parallel between them. Other effective moments that use deep space and deep focus are: the scene of Susan's suicide attempt, in which we see the poison bottle, glass, and spoon looming in the foreground and hear Kane's frantic pounding at the door; the *Inquirer* banquet at which Leland and Bernstein discuss whether the new staff will change Kane's approach to journalism, while Kane dances with the chorus in the background; the scene in which Kane sits typing, finishing Leland's review, while Leland comes toward him from the distant office; and the scenes in Xanadu where Kane and Susan shout conversation at each other from opposite sides of a gigantic room (Fig. 8.7). Within this variety of uses of deep space and deep focus, Welles consistently creates spatial arrangements that channel our understanding of the scene's narrative situation.

Figure 8.7

In looking at the development of the narrative form of *Citizen Kane*, we saw how Kane changes from an idealistic young man to a friendless recluse. The film sets up a contrast between Kane's early life as an editor and his later withdrawal from public life after Susan's opera career fails. This contrast is most readily apparent in the mise-en-scene, particularly the settings of the *Inquirer* office and Xanadu. The *Inquirer* office is initially an efficient but cluttered place. When Kane takes over, he creates a casual environment by moving in his furnishings and living in his office. The low camera angles tend to emphasize the office's thin pillars and low ceilings, which are white and evenly, brightly lit.

Xanadu, on the other hand, is huge and sparsely furnished. The ceilings are too high to be seen in most shots, and the few furnishings stand far apart. The lighting often strikes figures strongly from the back or side (such as the shot of Kane descending a great staircase, in Fig. 4.20), creating a few patches of hard light in the midst of general darkness.

The contrast between the *Inquirer* office and Xanadu is also created by the sound techniques associated with each. Several scenes at the newspaper (Kane's initial arrival and his return from Europe) involve a dense sound mix with a babble of overlapping voices; the timbre of these sounds is comparatively "flat." In Xanadu the conversations are very different. Kane and Susan speak their lines to each other slowly, with pauses between; their voices have an echo effect that combines with the setting and lighting to convey a sense of vast, empty spaces.

The transition from Kane's life at the *Inquirer* to his eventual seclusion at Xanadu is suggested by a change in the mise-en-scene at the *Inquirer*; while Kane is in Europe, the statues he sends back begin to fill up his little office. This hints at Kane's growing ambitions and declining interest in working personally on his newspaper.

This change culminates in the last scene in the *Inquirer* office, Leland's confrontation with Kane. The office is being used as a campaign headquarters; with the desks pushed aside and the employees gone, the room looks larger and emptier than it had in earlier scenes there. Welles emphasizes this by placing the camera at floor level and shooting from a very low angle (see Fig. 5.48). The Chicago *Inquirer* office, with its vast, shadowy spaces, also picks up this pattern; deep-focus photography with wide-angle lenses exaggerates the depth of the scene, making the characters seem very far apart (as in later conversation scenes in the huge rooms of Xanadu).

Contrast the Kane-Leland scene with one near the end of the film. The reporters invade Kane's museumlike storeroom at Xanadu. Though the echo of Xanadu reminds us of its cavernous quality, the reporters transform the setting briefly by the same sort of dense, overlapping dialogue that characterized the early *Inquirer* scenes and the scene after the newsreel. By bringing together these reporters and Kane's later environment, the film creates one final strong contrasting parallel that points up the change Kane underwent in his career.

In addition to Kane's gradual abandonment of his youthful resolve to serve the public with his newspapers, another major narrative concern of the film is Kane's attempt to gain public respect and popularity. Welles uses film techniques to create parallels between two scenes in which Kane makes a major effort to win popular support. In the first, Kane is running for governor and makes a speech at a mammoth rally; the main organizational principle of this scene involves editing that shows one or two shots of Kane speaking, then one or two close shots of small groups of characters in the audience (Emily and their son, Leland, Bernstein, Gettys), then back to Kane. The cutting establishes the characters who are important for their hopes for Kane and their eventual reactions to his coming disgrace; Boss Gettys is the last to be shown in the scene, and we

Figure 8.8

Figure 8.9

sense him as a threat to all of the other characters we have just seen. After his defeat, Kane sets out to make Susan an opera star and thus justify his interest in her to the public. In the scene which parallels Kane's election speech, Susan's debut, the organization of shots is similar to that of the political rally. Again the figure on the stage, Susan, serves as a pivot for the editing; one or two shots of her are followed by a few shots of the various listeners (Kane, Bernstein, Leland, the singing teacher), then back to Susan, and so on (Figs. 8.8 and 8.9). General narrative parallels and specific stylistic techniques articulate two stages of Kane's power quest: first, on his own, then with Susan as his proxy.

As we saw in examining *Citizen Kane*'s narrative, the newsreel is a very important sequence; it provides a "map" to the upcoming plot events. Because of its importance, Welles sets off the style of this sequence from the rest of the film by using distinctive techniques here which do not appear elsewhere in *Citizen Kane*. Also, we need to believe that this is a real newsreel in order to motivate Thompson's search for the key to Kane's life. The realistic newsreel sequence also helps establish Kane's power and wealth, which will be the basis of much of the upcoming action.

Welles uses several techniques to achieve the look and sound of an actual newsreel of the period. Some of these are fairly simple: The music used is that of actual newsreels, and the insert titles, outmoded for regular narrative films, were still a convention in newsreel films. But beyond this, Welles employs a number of subtle cinematographic techniques to achieve a "documentary" quality. Since some of the footage in the newsreel is supposed to have been taken in the silent period, he uses several different film stocks to make it appear that the different shots have been assembled from widely different sources. Some of the footage has been printed so as to achieve the jerkiness of silent film run at sound speed; Welles has also scratched and faded this footage to give it the look of old, worn film. This, combined with the makeup work, creates a remarkable impression of documentary footage of Kane with Teddy Roosevelt, Adolf

Figure 8.10

Figure 8.11

Hitler (Fig. 8.10), and others. In the later scenes of Kane being wheeled around his estate, the handheld camera, the slats and barriers (Fig. 8.11), and the high angle (from a tree?) imitate the effects of a newsreel reporter surreptitiously filming Kane. All of these "documentary" conventions are enhanced by the use of a narrator whose booming voice also mimics the commentary typical in the newsreels of the day.

Aside from the newsreel, the rest of the music for the film was written by one of the great cinema composers, Bernard Herrmann. The film uses a great deal of music, both diegetic and nondiegetic. For example, Susan's singing is central to the narrative. Her elaborate aria in the opera *Salammbo* contrasts sharply with the other main diegetic music, the little song about "Charlie Kane." Yet in spite of the differences between the songs, there is a parallel between them, in that both relate to Kane's ambitions. The "Charlie Kane" song seems silly, but its lyrics clearly show that Kane intends it as a political song, and it does turn up later as campaign music. In addition, the chorus girls who sing the song wear costumes with Rough Rider hats and boots, and they carry toy rifles; Kane's desire for war with Spain has shown up even in this apparently simple farewell party for his departure to Europe. When Kane's political ambitions are dashed, he tries to create a public career for his wife instead, but she is incapable of singing grand opera. Again, the songs create narrative parallels between different actions in Kane's career.

The film has a considerable range of nondiegetic music. The opening has ominous, solemn music over, setting up the air of mystery around Kane that will become a major motif in the film. The orchestra states a brief "Kane" theme at the shot of the house with a large cat statue in the foreground; this theme becomes a motif that returns at significant dramatic moments in Kane's life. The breakfast table sequence, which elliptically presents the collapse of Kane's first marriage, begins with a lilting waltz. At each transition to a later time, the music changes. A comic variation of the waltz follows its initial statement, then a tense one; then horns and trumpets restate the Kane theme. The final portion of the scene, with a stony silence between the couple, is accompanied by a slow, eerie variation on the initial theme. The dissolution of the marriage is stressed by this theme-and-variations accompaniment.

A few other examples must serve to indicate the characteristic and significant functions of *Citizen Kane*'s music. In the scene in which the young Kane bitterly unwraps his new sled at Christmas, the sound track has a high-pitched sound, probably a single, sustained note played by violins; this enhances the uncomfortable, strained relations which the scene suggests exist between Charles and his guardian. The subsequent montage sequence of Thatcher's annoyed reactions to Kane's various newspaper campaigns has comic music over, which helps to make Thatcher look silly. A similar effect comes in the scene in which Thompson visits the Thatcher library. A low-angle shot of Thatcher's statue is accompanied by comically pompous chords; the music, echoing voices, huge, empty rooms, and strong light rays falling on the manuscript, all combine to mock the pretensions of the Thatcher library.

The sound track of the entire film is a rich one, with frequent and extensive musical passages, as well as effects and voice. One scene is set off from all the others because it is the only one to use silence to any extent. This is the scene just after Susan leaves Kane. He stands uncertainly in her room; after a pause, he begins to hurl the contents of the room about in a rage. But instead of dramatic music, the only sound in the scene is the smashing of furniture and bric-a-brac. As a result, Kane's actions take on an unsettling quality: The clumsiness of his gestures and the impotence that is implicit in his rage are all the more apparent for the lack of music.

Sound is central to one device that recurs several times in the film: the so-called shock cut. This is a cut that creates some jarring juxtaposition—usually both a sudden shift to a higher sound volume and a considerable graphic discontinuity. Several examples are found in *Citizen Kane:* the abrupt beginning of the newsreel after the deathbed shot, the shift from the quiet conversation in the newsreel projection room to the lightning and thunder outside the El Rancho, and the sudden appearance of a screeching cockatoo in the foreground as Raymond's flashback begins. These make for dramatic transitions, of course, but if you look back at the sections into which we divided the film's narrative form (pp. 60–69), you can see that these shock cuts come right at the beginning of several major portions of the film's narrative. This shows how the film may use stylistic devices to help delineate its overall form.

This brief examination of *Citizen Kane*'s style has pointed out only a few of the major patterns in the film. You will be able to find others: the "K" motif appearing in Kane's costumes and in Xanadu's settings; the characterization of Kane's attitude toward Susan through the decor of her cluttered room at Xanadu; the changes in the acting of individuals as their characters age in the course of the story; and the playful photographic devices, such as the photos that become animated or the many superimpositions during montage sequences. *Citizen Kane* is rich in such formal patterns.

In this section we have suggested how one can analyze all of the various elements that go into creating the formal relationships within an entire film. Initially we looked at *Citizen Kane*'s narrative system;

now we have analyzed its stylistic system as well. But, as we have emphasized, there is no firm set of rules that will allow you to understand every film automatically. Any film sets up a unique formal system, and each individual element (each narrative event or stylistic technique) functions according to its place within that system. Finding the nature of that formal system and the functions of individual devices is the goal of the critic; Part Four of this book consists of a series of analyses showing how a critic may approach a widely differing range of narrative films.

Part Four
Critical
Analysis
of Films

Criticism is not an activity limited to those people who write articles or books about films. Any person who seeks actively to understand a film he or she sees is engaged in a process of criticism. You may be unsure why one scene was included in a film; your search for the function of that scene in the context of the whole is a first step in a critical examination. People who discuss a film they have all seen are participating in criticism.

Up to this point, we have looked at concepts and definitions that should enable a filmgoer to analyze a film systematically. The critic approaches a film already knowing that formal patterns, such as repetitions and variations, will likely be important and should be examined. In a narrative film the critic can trace through the series of causes and effects, the characters' goals, the principles of development, the degree of closure, and the other components of narrative.

The critic must know a series of formal principles to watch for in analyzing a film. After all, claims about films can be more or less plausible; not every critic's analysis of the same film will be equally enlightening. That critic best able to point to clear evidence from the film will make the most convincing case.

So far, we have looked at all of the techniques that constitute a film; we have laid out the basic principles that govern a film's formal system. Many detailed examples and an analysis of *Citizen Kane* have shown how elements of a film function in an overall system. But the only way to gain an ability to analyze films critically is through practice—in both viewing films critically and reading analyses by other critics. For this reason, we conclude our look at films as formal systems with a series of brief sample essays on individual films.

These analyses do not exhaust the films; you might study any one of them and find many more points of interest than we have been able to present here. Indeed, whole books can be and have been written about single films without exhausting the possibilities for enriching our experience of those films.

CHAPTER 9
FILM CRITICISM: SAMPLE ANALYSES

Each of the five major sections of this chapter emphasizes different aspects of different films. First, we discuss three classical narrative films: *His Girl Friday, The Man Who Knew Too Much,* and *Stagecoach.* This type of film is very familiar to most viewers; for this very reason, it is important to look at that which we take for granted and see how it works to affect us.

The narrative films of many countries utilize the classical narrative form and style of the Hollywood film; *The Man Who Knew Too Much* is a British film, but it operates with the same formal unity and economy at work in *His Girl Friday* or *Stagecoach.* Next, we move to films that create an ambiguous effect; the films in this second section do not have as clearcut a narrative chain of cause and effect as do the more classical films; they also tend to leave their endings more open. Our examples of films that use ambiguity as a formal principle are *Day of Wrath* and *Last Year at Marienbad.*

An individual filmmaker may create his or her own particular alternative to the classical narrative style. The third section of this chapter examines Yasujiro Ozu's *Tokyo Story,* which has noncontinuity style and which avoids tight, fast-paced narrative progression.

Many films strive to be unified, and for them unity is a virtue. We may evaluate them on the basis of their success at integrating all of their elements smoothly. But some films go in the other direction, creating a systematic disunity. Such films are relatively rare, but have become especially important in the last few decades. In the fourth section of the chapter we discuss *Innocence Unprotected* to show how disunity may be a positive feature of a film's system.

Finally, we move to analyses that emphasize social ideology. Our first example, *Meet Me in St. Louis,* is a film that accepts a dominant ideology and reinforces its audience's belief in that ideology. *The Crime of M. Lange,* in contrast, takes a fairly popular, but new, ideological position and presents it in such a way as to lead people to accept it.

233

Finally, a film that was very radical in its time, *La Chinoise,* takes a political position far removed from the ideologies of most of its spectators.

The application of these categories is not limited to the films we chose to put in them. *Meet Me in St. Louis,* for example, is a classical narrative film and could have been analyzed in that category. *La Chinoise* involves ambiguities (as its subtitle, "A Film in the Making," suggests); it also includes many disunified elements. Any film represents an ideological position which can be analyzed. Our choices suggest certain possibilities; your own critical activities will discover many more.

Narrative Unity ■

His Girl Friday

> 1940. Columbia. Directed by Howard Hawks. Script by Charles Lederer from the play *The Front Page* by Ben Hecht and Charles MacArthur. Photographed by Joseph Walker. Edited by Gene Harlick. Music by Morris W. Stoloff. With Cary Grant, Rosalind Russell, Ralph Bellamy, Gene Lockhart, Porter Hall.

The dominant impression left by *His Girl Friday* is that of speed: It is often said to be the fastest sound comedy ever made. Let us therefore "slow it down" analytically. By breaking the film into parts and seeing how the parts relate to one another logically, temporally, and spatially, we can suggest how classical narrative form and specific film techniques are used to create this unique, whirlwind experience.

His Girl Friday is built on the common unit of classical narrative cinema: the "scene." Typically marked off by editing devices such as the dissolve, fade, or wipe, each scene presents a distinct segment of space, time, and narrative action. We can locate 13 such scenes (or parts) in *His Girl Friday,* set in the following locales: (1) the *Morning Post* offices; (2) the restaurant; (3) the Criminal Courts pressroom; (4) Walter's office; (5) Earl Williams's cell; (6) the pressroom; (7) a precinct jail; (8) the pressroom; (9) the sheriff's office; (10) the street outside the prison; (11) the pressroom; (12) the sheriff's office; (13) the pressroom. All of these scenes are marked off by dissolves.

But within these scenes, smaller units of action occur. Note, for example, that scene 1, occupying almost 14 minutes of screen time, introduces almost all of the major characters and sets two plot lines in motion. Or, consider scene 13: Almost every major character appears in it, and it runs for no less than 33 minutes! We can, then, conveniently break several long scenes into smaller parts on the basis of groupings of character interactions. Thus scene 1 comprises: (a) the introduction to the newspaper office; (b) the first conversation between Hildy and Bruce; (c) Walter's discussion of the past with Hildy; (d) Walter's conference with Duffy about the Earl Williams case; (e) Hildy's telling Walter that she's remarrying; and (f) Walter's introduction to Bruce. To grasp the construction of such lengthy scenes, you may divide them into similar segments. It may be, in fact, that the somewhat "theatrical" feel of the film comes from its practice of segmenting its scenes by character entrances and exits (rather than, say, by frequent shifts of locale). In any event, the developing patterns of character interaction contribute a great deal to the hubbub and speed of the film.

The scenes function, of course, to advance the narrative action. As we saw in Chapter 3, classical Hollywood cinema often constructs a narrative around characters with definite traits who want to achieve specific goals; the clash of these characters (via contrasting traits and conflicting goals) propels the story forward in a step-by-step process of cause and effect. In *His Girl Friday* there are two such cause-effect chains:

1. *The romance.* Hildy Johnson wants to quit newspaper reporting and settle down with Bruce Baldwin. (This is her initial goal.) But her editor and ex-husband, Walter Burns, wants her to continue as his reporter and to remarry him (his goal). Given these two goals, the characters enter into a conflict in several stages. First, Walter lures Hildy by promising a nest egg for the couple in exchange for her writing one last story. But since Walter also plots to have Bruce robbed, Hildy tears up her story. Walter continues to delay Bruce, however, and eventually wins Hildy through her renewed excitement in reporting; she changes her mind about marrying Bruce and stays with Walter.

2. *Crime and politics.* Earl Williams is to be hanged for shooting a policeman, and the political machine of the city is relying on the execution to ensure its members' reelection (the goal of the mayor and sheriff). But Walter's goal is to induce the governor to reprieve Williams and thus unseat the mayor's party at the polls. Through the sheriff's stupidity, Williams escapes and is concealed by Hildy and Walter. In the meantime, a reprieve does arrive from the governor, but the mayor bribes the messenger into leaving. Williams is discovered, but the messenger returns with the reprieve in time to save Williams from death and Walter and Hildy from jail. Presumably the mayor's machine will be defeated at the election.

The crime-and-politics line of action is made to depend on events in the romance line at several points: Walter uses the Williams case to lure Hildy back to him, Hildy chases the Williams story instead of returning to Bruce, Bruce's mother reveals to the police that Walter has concealed Williams, etc. More specifically, the interplay of the two lines of action alters the goals of various characters. In Walter's case, inducing Hildy to write the story fulfulls his goals of embarrassing the politicos and of tempting Hildy back. Hildy's goals are more greatly altered: After she destroys her article, her decision to cover Earl Williams's jailbreak marks her acceptance of Walter's goal, and her later willingness to hide Williams and her indifference to Bruce's plea firmly establish her goals as linked to Walter's. In this way the interaction of the two plot lines reinforces Walter's goals but radically alters Hildy's.

Within this general framework, the cause-effect sequencing is very complex and deserves a closer analysis than space permits here. But consider, for example, the various ways in which Walter's delaying tactics (involving his confederates Duffy, Louie, and Angie) set up short-term chains of cause and effect in themselves. Also interesting is the way Bruce is steadily shouldered out of the romance plot, becoming more and more passive as he is shuttled in and out of precinct jails. In this regard Earl Williams undergoes a similar experience as he is manipulated by Hildy, the sheriff, the psychologist, and Walter. We could also consider the function of the minor characters, such as Molly Malloy (Williams's platonic sweetheart), Bruce's mother, the other reporters, and especially Pettibone, the delightful emissary from the governor. Perhaps most important, note how the scenes "hook into" each other. That is, an event at the end of scene 1 (Walter offers to take the couple to lunch) is seen as a cause leading to an effect, i.e., the event that begins scene 2 (the trio arrives at the restaurant). Diagrammed, it might look like this:

Events in cause-effect chain

Scene 1	ABC
Scene 2	C'DEF
Scene 3	F'GHI etc.

Hence the famous "linearity" of classical narrative: Almost every scene ends with a "dangling cause," the effect of which is shown at the beginning of the next scene.

The cause-and-effect logic of the film illustrates yet another principle of classical narrative structure: closure. No event is uncaused. (Even Pettibone's arrival is no *deus ex machina,* for we know that the governor is under pressure to decide about the case.) And, more important, both lines of action are clearly resolved, closed. Williams is saved and the politicians are disgraced; Bruce, having gone home with mother, leaves Walter and Hildy preparing for a second honeymoon no less hectic than their first.

So much for causality. What of narrative time? Classical Hollywood cinema typically subordinates time to the narrative's cause-effect relations, and one common way is to set a deadline for the action. Thus a temporal goal is wedded to a causal one, and the time becomes charged with cause-effect significance. The deadline is, of course, a convention of the newspaper genre, already adding a built-in time (and suspense) factor. But in *His Girl Friday* each of the two plots has its own deadlines as well. The mayor and sheriff face an obvious deadline: Earl Williams must be hanged before next Tuesday's election and before the governor can reprieve him. In his political strategizing Walter Burns faces the other side of the same deadline: He wants Williams reprieved. What we might not expect is that the romance plot has deadlines as well. Bruce and Hildy are set to leave on a train bound for Albany (and for marriage) at four o'clock that very day. So Walter's machinations keep forcing the couple to postpone their departure. Add to this the fact that when Bruce comes to confront Hildy and Walter, he leaves with the defiant ultimatum: "I'm leaving on the nine o'clock train!" (Hildy misses that train as well.) The temporal structure of the film, then, depends on the cause-effect sequence. If Earl Williams were to be hanged next month, or if the election were two years off, or if Bruce and Hildy were planning a marriage at some distant future date, the sense of dramatic pressure would be entirely absent. The numerous and overlapping deadlines under which all of the characters labor have the effect of squeezing together all the lines of action and sustaining the breathless pace of the film.

Another aspect of *His Girl Friday*'s patterning of time reinforces this pace. Though the film presents events in straightforward chronological order, it takes remarkable liberties with duration. Of course, since the action consumes about nine hours (from around 12:30 P.M. to around 9:30 P.M.), we expect that certain portions of time *between scenes* will be eliminated. And so they have been. What is unusual is that the time *within* scenes has been accelerated. At the start of the very first scene, for example, the clock in the *Post* office reads 12:36; after 12 minutes of screen time have passed, the clock in the *Post* office reads 12:57. It's important to note that there have been no editing ellipses in the scene; the narrative duration has simply been compressed. If you clock scene 13, you will find even more remarkable acceleration; people leave on long trips and return in less than ten minutes. Again, the editing is continuous: It is story time that "goes faster" than screen time. Add to this temporal compression the frenetically rushed dialogue and the occasionally accelerated rhythmic editing (e.g., the reporters' cries just before Williams's capture), and we have a film that often proceeds at breakneck pace.

Space, like time, is here subordinate to narrative cause and effect. Hawks's camera moves unobtrusively to reframe the characters symmetrically in the shot. (Watch any scene silent to observe the subtle "balancing act" that goes on during the dialogue scenes.) Straight-on camera angles predominate, varied by an occasional high-angle shot down on the prison courtyard or on Williams's cell. Lighting is generally high key, except for the morbid Gothic silhouettes of the gallows and of Earl Williams's cell bars. (Why, we might ask in passing, does the prison receive this visual emphasis in the camera angle and the lighting?) The restriction of the action to very few locales might seem a handicap, but the patterns of character placement are remarkably varied and functional: Walter's persuading of Hildy to write the story is interesting from this standpoint, as the two pace in a complete circuit around the desk and Walter assumes the most dynamic and comic postures. And spatial continuity in the editing anticipates each dramatic point by judiciously cutting to a closer shot or smoothly matching on action so that we watch the movements and not the cuts. (Apart from the many superb matches on action in the film, there is one deliberate mismatch which stretches out time; this occurs when Hildy returns to the pressroom after the newsmen's torment of Molly and remarks, in softly scathing tones: "Gentlemen of the press. . . . " Upon her entry, the pressroom door is shown swinging open *twice*. What functions does this overlapping cut perform in the context of this particular scene?) Virtually every scene, especially the restaurant episode and the final scene, offer many fine examples of classical continuity editing. In all, space is used to delineate the flow of the cause-effect sequence.

We might highlight for special attention one specific item of both sound and mise-en-scene. It is "realistic" that newspapermen in 1939 should use telephones, but *His Girl Friday* makes the phone integral to the narrative. Walter's duplicity demands phones: At the restaurant he pretends to be summoned away to a call; he makes and breaks promises to Hildy via phones; he directs Duffy and other minions by phone. More generally, the pressroom is equipped with a veritable flotilla of phones, enabling the reporters to contact their editors. And, of course, Bruce keeps calling Hildy from the various police stations in which he continually finds himself. The telephones thus constitute a communications network that permits the narrative to be relayed from point to point.

But Hawks also "orchestrates" visually and sonically the characters' use of the phones. There are many variations. One person may be talking on the phone, or several may be talking *in turn* on different phones, or several may be talking *at once* on different phones, or a phone conversation may be juxtaposed with a conversation elsewhere in the room, etc. In scene 11, there is a "polyphonic" effect of reporters coming in to phone their editors, each conversation overlapping with the preceding one. Later, in scene 13, while Hildy frantically phones hospitals, Walter screams into another phone. And when Bruce returns for Hildy, there arises a helter-skelter din that eventually sorts itself into three "sound-lines": Bruce begging Hildy to listen, Hildy obsessively typing her story, and Walter yelling into the phone for Duffy to clear page one ("No, no, leave the rooster story—that's human interest"). Like much in *His Girl Friday*, the telephones warrant close study for the complex and various ways in which they are integrated into the narrative.

The Man Who Knew Too Much

1934. Gaumont British Pictures, Great Britain. Directed by Alfred Hitchcock. Script by A. R. Rawlinson, Charles Bennett, D. B. Wyndham Lewis, Edwin Greenwood, from an original idea by Charles Bennett and D. B. Wyndham Lewis. Photographed by Curt Courant. Edited by H. St. C. Stewart. Music by Arthur Benjamin. With Leslie Banks, Edna Best, Peter Lorre, Frank Vosper.

Like *His Girl Friday*, *The Man Who Knew Too Much* presents us with a model of narrative construction. Its plot composition and its motivations for action contribute to making the film what a scriptwriter would call "tight." Moreover, the film also offers an object lesson in the use of cinematic style for narrative purposes.

Our analysis may begin by noting the obvious. The film belongs to the international intrigue genre, one in which Hitchcock has often worked (recall *Sabotage, The Thirty-Nine Steps, The Lady Vanishes, North By Northwest, Topaz*). Like other films in this genre, *The Man Who Knew Too Much* builds its narrative around flights and pursuits, mysteries, and assassinations, both accomplished and thwarted. What we should consider is how these familiar elements of the genre are treated in the film's unique narrative pattern.

We have seen in our analysis of *Citizen Kane* that a narrative built around a mystery demands that the plot (the order and duration of events as they are presented to us) omit or delay many important events which occur in the story (the causal-chronological series of events). Often a mystery in a narrative occurs when the plot withholds important events from our knowledge. *The Man Who Knew Too Much* contains such a mystery: What is the plan of the spy ring headed by Abbott? Not until far into the film do we learn that the spies plan to assassinate a foreign minister during a concert at the Albert Hall. What occupies our interest before this revelation is the couple Bob and Jill Lawrence, whose daughter, Betty, is kidnapped by the spy ring in order to prevent the parents from telling the police what they know. The plot follows Bob and Jill in their investigation and search for Betty, delaying the information about the assassination until Bob learns of it. When the mystery is solved, plot interest shifts to whether or not the assassination will succeed.

It is instructive to observe how the narrative's three major sections smoothly link plot events together. The beginning of the film gains its unity primarily through following the family on vacation in Switzerland.

Figure 9.1

As the family participates in various sports (skiing, skeet shooting) and relaxation (the dance), the major spies are introduced: the leader Abbott, Nurse Agnes, and the rifleman Ramon. The plot abruptly shifts when Louis is shot on the dance floor and Bob runs to his room. There Bob finds the mysterious slip of paper in Louis's shaving brush (Louis has been a British spy trailing Abbott's gang). When it is evident that Bob also "knows too much," Ramon kidnaps Betty.

A rising sun, "Wapping G. Barbour Make Contact A. Hall March 21st"—the code of Louis's message—becomes a "map" for the second major portion of the plot, guiding Bob and Uncle Clive in their search for Betty in London (Fig. 9.1). As in *His Girl Friday*, each scene leaves a cause dangling at its end, which the next scene hooks into and continues. In Wapping they find George Barbour, the dentist, and while there Bob sees Abbott and Ramon. Bob and Clive follow the spies to the Tabernacle of the Sun (decorated with the sun symbol on Louis's note), where Bob notices a ticket for the Albert Hall (the "A. Hall" of Louis's note) and Clive escapes to phone Jill. Thus Louis's note functions as a narrative device to unify the investigation section of the film.

The final portion of the film resolves the two major narrative issues: the assassination and the kidnapping. At the Albert Hall, Jill thwarts the assassination attempt. At the gang's hideout in the Tabernacle, the shootout between police and spies culminates in the recovery of Betty. All mysteries are solved, all issues resolved; with the death of Abbott the plot is completed.

To the conventional pattern of spy films, though, is added another line of action: that of family unity broken and restored. In Switzerland the Lawrences are already an uneasy group: Jill and Bob both playfully threaten Betty; Jill calls Betty Bob's "brat" and teases him with remarks about her "other man," Louis. But when Betty is kidnapped, the family is thrown into genuine turmoil—best presented by Jill's swirling subjective vision before she faints. The plot now gains *two* complementary protagonists, Bob and Jill. The moment Louis is killed, they begin to cooperate: The dying Louis whispers, "In the brush . . . " to Jill; she relays the message to Bob, who goes to search Louis's room. Early in the investigation Jill's role is passive (she waits by the phone), while Bob, with Clive's help, searches for Betty. But after Bob is captured by the gang, he occupies the passive role, and Jill goes to the Albert Hall to thwart the assassination. By the end of the film, Bob and Jill cooperate in saving Betty. Bob frees Betty and leads her onto the roof, and from across the street Jill's rifle bullet saves Betty from Ramon. The final shot of the film appropriately shows Betty lowered from the roof into her parents' arms: an image of the reunified family. The presence of two protagonists here should remind us that a narrative's hero is less a single character than a functional *role* that can be filled by one or more characters. (Hitchcock seems fond of this pattern; in *Psycho* different characters at one point or another occupy the role of the inquiring protagonist.)

The unity of the plot of *The Man Who Knew Too Much* is enhanced as well by more specific devices of motivation, narrative balance, and closure. Actions are motivated by characters making appointments that forward our interest to subsequent scenes or (as in *His Girl Friday*) by the establishing of deadlines; Louis's note names a specific date for the visit to Barbour's dentist office, and even the assassination of Ropa must be executed at precisely the right moment. The forward drive of the plot is also enhanced by Hitchcock's abrupt but functional (and motivated) transitions. A mention of Ramon leads to a cut to Ramon in the next scene. The word "kidnapped" propels us into a shot of a train, a toy belonging to Betty; her uncle plays with the train as he discusses the kidnapping with Betty's mother.

A web of more specific motifs also holds the film together. Betty is identified with the little skier pin that her mother gives her, so that at the Albert Hall, Ramon can remind Jill of Betty's danger simply by giving the pin to her. Barbour is associated with the spies' activities by the tooth image; Betty says of Ramon: "He has many too many teeth," and the first shot of the sequence outside Barbour's office shows us a huge row of teeth in close-up. Characters are tagged by repeated motifs, so that Hitchcock can obliquely suggest the presence of a character: Ramon is associated with his sleek, slicked-down hair; Abbott, with his pocket watch and its chiming tune.

Finally, it is worth paying attention to the careful paralleling of events. The most outstanding examples involve the shifting relations between Jill and Ramon. In Switzerland, when she competes with him in the skeet shoot, Abbott's well-timed watch chimes distract her and she loses the match. But this loss is compensated for in two parallel scenes. In the Albert Hall Jill's scream shakes Ramon's aim, and he merely wounds the ambassador. She is thus "paid back" for the match. And in the final shootout, when the police dare not fire at Ramon for fear of hitting Betty, it is Jill who snatches the rifle and with a single well-placed shot kills him. This last scene is a superb example of a unifying narrative device: It depends on the Switzerland scene (which establishes Jill as a crack shot); it parallels that scene (Jill gets the second shot she should have had at the match); and it resolves the major issue (Jill's marksmanship saves Betty). Such tidy narrative construction is surpassed only by the *very* neat echo between the film's first and last lines of dialogue: At the ski match, Bob asks, "Are you all right?" and in the final scene, Jill tells Betty, "It's all right . . . it's all right."

Such unity is worth looking at microscopically, if only briefly. The most celebrated scene in the film is the aborted assassination in the Albert Hall, for here editing, camera work, and sound function to present and withhold crucial narrative information. Here we cannot analyze in detail the 90 shots in the scene; we shall simply point out some features which we hope will tease the viewer into closely examining this very instructive bit of cinema.

Narratively, the sequence operates on two levels. First, it juxtaposes what is happening during the Albert Hall concert with the gang's listening to that concert over the radio. Here, the familiar technique of crosscutting functions efficiently; shots of the concert are juxtaposed with shots of the gang listening in their hideout. Moreover, the presence of the radio permits the sound of the concert (the "Storm Cloud Cantata") to continue over each spatially discontinuous cut, so that continuity of duration is maintained and the momentum of the music is allowed to build. We know that Ramon is to assassinate Ropa at a *fortissimo* passage in the piece (earlier, Abbott "rehearsed" the climactic portion for us and Ramon with the aid of a phonograph). But the gang, like ourselves, constantly expects the *fortissimo* to come; only Abbott and Ramon know the exact moment. Thus editing and sound, which juxtapose the gang with the Hall, increase our suspense as to when the shot will be fired.

Around Jill inside the Albert Hall, though, Hitchcock constructs another point of narrative interest. Here film style and narrative form seek to present her growing awareness of the assassination attempt through *subjective* devices. Hitchcock rigorously presents only what Jill can see or know, and he externalizes Jill's thought by means of cutting and cinematography. For example, eyeline-match editing and subjective or point-of-view camera position inform us when she is scanning the Hall, watching Ropa or the police, and thinking of Betty (in the latter case, we get this series: a shot of her looking down/shot of the little skier pin in her palm/shot of Jill looking up).

As the sequence approaches its climax—emphasized by more rapid rhythms of music and editing—Hitchcock boldly begins to play with the

Figure 9.2

Figure 9.3

Figure 9.4

image through shifts of focus. Jill looks up through her tears (Fig. 9.2); then the blur (Fig. 9.3) fades to white (Fig. 9.4), and the muzzle of a rifle pokes into the shot (Fig. 9.5). The series closes with Jill's new knowledge of the situation, registered by her looking across to Ropa's box seat (Fig. 9.6 and 9.7). The dissolving of the blur to a white background for the rifle represents the optical and mental movement of Jill's attention at the very moment that she realizes what is to happen in the Albert Hall. These shots climax the sequence's attempt to present the action through Jill's eyes and mind. (Compare this with *His Girl Friday*, which seldom utilizes subjective techniques.)

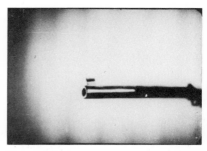

Figure 9.5

But this is not yet the climax of the sequence. After presenting Jill's realization that the assassination is about to occur, Hitchcock cuts very rapidly among Jill looking, Ropa's box, the gun muzzle, and instruments of the orchestra poised for the *fortissimo* passage. Hitchcock now postpones revealing crucial narrative information: He cuts back to the gang at the Tabernacle, Jill's scream continuing over the cut (just as the concert had at earlier moments). Then, while we are still watching the spies listening to the radio, we hear the crucial *fortissimo* chord that was to conceal Ramon's shot. By showing us the gang, Hitchcock momentarily delays our learning the outcome of Jill's action. A few shots later, we see Ropa wounded in the arm, but it is not until the next scene that we learn that Ramon's aim had been shaken by Jill's scream. In this climactic moment, then, editing and sound have worked together to keep us in suspense as to the outcome of the action.

Figure 9.6

Almost every scene in the film repays this kind of scrutiny. Other important instances of sound, camera work, and editing in relation to narrative occur in the scene of Louis's death and the final shootout. The visit to George Barbour makes remarkable use of silence and unbalanced compositions for narrative effect, and in the tabernacle scene an old woman amusingly uses the sound of the organ to drown out the din of a fistfight. In such ways *The Man Who Knew Too Much* remains a model of narrative and style working smoothly and economically together.

Figure 9.7

Stagecoach

1939. Walter Wanger Productions (released through United Artists). Directed by John Ford. Script by Dudley Nichols, from the short story "Stage to Lordsburg," by Ernest Haycox. Photographed by Bert Glennon. Edited by Dorothy Spencer and Walter Reynolds. Music by Richard Hageman, W. Franke Harling, John Leipold, Leo Shuken, Louis Gruienberg. With John Wayne, Claire Trevor, Thomas Mitchell, Andy Devine, George Bancroft, Donald Meek, Louise Platt, John Carradine, Berton Churchill.

Film theorist André Bazin has written of John Ford's *Stagecoach*: "*Stagecoach* (1939) is the ideal example of the maturity of a style brought to classic perfection. . . . *Stagecoach* is like a wheel, so perfectly made that it remains in equilibrium on its axis in any position." This classicism and perfection result from the film's concentration on the creation of a tight narrative unity, with all of its elements serving that goal.

As in *His Girl Friday*, the plot of *Stagecoach* takes place over a short time—two days. Ford's narrative takes the word "stagecoach" (a coach traveling in stages, stopping along the way) literally and makes this the basis of his narrative divisions. Thus the film's action is the progression of a stagecoach from its starting point to its destination, with the major scenes occurring at the places where the coach stops for meals and rest. Here is an outline of the major segments of the film's narrative form:

Day 1 Cavalry		Fades	Fades	Fades Fades
Town— boarding	First part of journey	First stage stop—	Second part of journey	Second stage stop —evening
		noon dinner		
1 2	3	4	5	6

Day 2				On road
Morning— departure	Third part of journey	Third stage stop— burned ferry	Lordsburg	
		Attack and chase		
7	8	9	10	11

The perfect balance of one part against another is apparent in this outline. At the very beginning and end, short scenes take place among the buttes of Monument Valley: Initially we see the cavalry riding and bringing the news that Geronimo is on the warpath; at the end, a single shot shows Ringo and Dallas riding through the valley toward their new life together. The film's second sequence takes place in the town of Tonto, where the passengers board the coach. The journey ends in sequence 10, which reverses the second sequence; here the passengers disembark in Lordsburg, their destination. Here also the various goals these characters had set up for themselves are resolved.

Between these two points of departure and arrival, there are three sequences of travel along the road (sequences 3, 5, and 8), each culminating in the arrival at one of the three stages, or stops, along the way. During the first stop, at Dry Fork, the passengers eat their noon meal. At the second, Apache Wells, they spend the night. The departure the next morning parallels the previous day's departure from the town; the pattern of sequences 5–6 repeats that of sequences 3–4.

As before, the departure scene leads to a new traveling phase, sequence 8. But after two repetitions of the travel-stage-stop pattern, the narrative introduces a major variation. When the coach arrives at the outpost for the third and final stage, East Ferry, the characters find it burnt by the Indians. The coach crosses the river and goes on toward Lordsburg, but our expectation of a major scene at this point is not disappointed. In the formal position of the third stage stop, the Indian attack occurs. After the chase and rescue, an ellipsis moves the narrative directly to Lordsburg, eliminating the last part of the journey.

The initial departure from Tonto establishes the goals of most of the characters. Lucy Mallory is traveling to join her husband, who is in the cavalry. Mr. Peacock, a whiskey salesman, is on his way home to join his wife in Kansas City. The two leaders of the group are the driver, Buck, who also is going home to his family in Lordsburg, and the marshal, Curley, who goes along as guard to try to capture the Ringo Kid.

Two "undesirables" leave town on the same stagecoach, driven out by the "respectable" elements of the town: Doc Boone, the local drunk, and Dallas, a prostitute. These two have no definite goal, except to find a place where they will be allowed to stay. The gambler Hatfield also joins the group with no definite goal of his own; he seeks to protect Lucy Mallory on her journey.

The narrative marks two characters off by having them board the coach later. Having stolen the payroll money deposited in his bank, Gatewood hails the coach on the street and gets in. Gatewood's goal is to escape undetected. A short while after the coach leaves Tonto, it meets

Ringo, who seeks to get to Lordsburg to avenge himself on the Plummer brothers. He joins the group, under arrest by Curly.

Most of the significant causal developments in the plot come in the scenes at the two stage stops. In the first the seating pattern at the table defines the social relationships. Within the group, Ringo and Dallas are both shunned as outcasts and hence thrown together. Mr. Peacock defines himself as the weakling of the group by being the only one to vote to return to Tonto when they discover that no cavalry escort will be available beyond that stop.

The second stage stop is the most important scene during the journey for its development of character relationships. Doc Boone and Dallas, the two outcasts of the original group, earn the admiration of the others by helping deliver Lucy's baby; at this point Ringo proposes marriage to Dallas.

Between the major sequences in the towns, the stages, and the Indian attack come three sequences of traveling through Monument Valley (sequences 3, 5, and 8), each consisting of a number of similar short scenes. Each scene begins with a long shot or extreme long shot of the coach; most of these are accompanied by the distinctive "stagecoach" musical motif. Several times, especially early in each sequence, this long shot is followed by a medium shot of the driver's seat, with Curly and Buck talking. These shots give snatches of exposition: We learn that Curly is sympathetic to Ringo's revenge motives and that he is suspicious of Gatewood.

Each short scene also contains a shot or shots inside the coach, with the passengers making conversation or exchanging glances. These interchanges tend to reestablish character traits and relations rather than move the action forward. Gatewood complains constantly; Boone filches drinks from Peacock's sample bag; Hatfield does courteous little favors for Lucy's comfort. Several motifs enter into these characterizations: Boone's liquor contrasts with the canteen the women drink from, and the two valises belonging to Gatewood and Peacock also set up a contrast. The development of the characters' attitudes toward one another is also apparent. Before the birth of Lucy's baby, the other characters ignore Dallas; in later scenes they are relatively kind to her.

These numerous short scenes, strung together within the travel sequences, function to give a sense of the coach's progression; dissolves link most of them, indicating the passage of time and space. Unlike *His Girl Friday* and *The Man Who Knew Too Much*, *Stagecoach* has almost no scenes that end with dangling causes that "hook" over into the beginning of the next scene. Causes are introduced, but these tend to disappear for long stretches of the action. Thus early in the film Curly mentions that he sympathizes with Ringo's desire for revenge; this sympathy recurs only in the final scene, in which Curly lets Ringo go have his shootout with the Plummers. Because most or all of the nine characters are present in almost every scene of the journey, *Stagecoach* has little need for dangling causes; there are few transitions from one set of characters in one locale to another set in another locale. The coach's journey itself provides the forward development of the narrative causes.

Much of the richness of *Stagecoach*'s narrative comes from the mixing of numerous characters with separate, sometimes contradictory goals. The rapid resolutions of the characters' goals on the arrival at Lordsburg gives a strong sense of closure. Lucy learns that her husband, reported to have been wounded by Indians, is safe; Peacock survives his wound; Gatefield is arrested. Thus most of the strongly positive and negative characters are taken care of.

Other characters have had to prove their worth in the course of the action. Hatfield has been a notorious gambler, but proves himself to be "a gentleman" by protecting Lucy and dying in the battle with the Indians. Doc Boone has delivered Lucy's baby, but also stands up to the Plummers in the tavern before the shootout. At the end of the film the marshal offers Boone a drink; he replies, "Just one," suggesting that even he has been reformed somewhat by his experiences on the trip.

The last part of the narrative focuses primarily on the fates of Dallas and Ringo. Ringo had entered the action last of all the passengers; now his goal of revenge comprises the last portion of the plot, after most of the other characters have gone their ways. Dallas, who had no definite goal of her own, has gained one in her love for Ringo. His victory over the Plummers and the marshal's decision not to send him back to jail lead to the final resolution; both Dallas and Ringo go free to start their new life together. The final long shot of their wagon moving along the road through Monument Valley recalls the beginning and the many long shots of the coach.

The style of *Stagecoach* helps create the repetitions and variations of this narrative action. We have indicated the repeated pattern of establishing long shots of the coach, interspersed with closer shots within the coach; these latter shots pick up the eyelines and gestures of the characters' conversations. We have already analyzed one outstanding use of offscreen sound in *Stagecoach*, in Chapter 7; you might examine other uses of sound in the film, along with their functions.

One aspect of the film's style is particularly outstanding: its use of deep space and deep focus. As we shall see in more detail in Chapter 10, the style of filming in Hollywood during the 1930s was generally a shallow-, or "soft-," focus style. (*His Girl Friday* provides an excellent example.) A few American films in the late 1930s began to experiment with deep focus, and *Stagecoach* was one of them. A number of shots in

Figure 9.8

Figure 9.9

Figure 9.10

Figure 9.11

the second stage-stop sequence use deep focus along the corridor outside Lucy's room, as when Ringo watches Dallas go out into the yard (Fig. 9.8) or outside when he follows her (Fig. 9.9). Welles claims to have watched *Stagecoach* many times before making *Citizen Kane*, the film usually credited with having introduced deep-focus photography; the similarities of lighting, mise-en-scene, and camera manipulations are apparent from these stills. These deep-focus shots make use of strong back lighting, which picks out Dallas and Ringo in the dark hallway and yard. This lighting is very different from the flat lighting used in most other scenes. This pattern of patches of light in darkness returns again in the Lordsburg sequence, when the plans the two have made in the sequence at the stage stop are finally made possible.

Stagecoach breaks several rules of classical continuity editing. The Indian attack violates screen direction; at times the coach and Indians move across the screen from left to right, at others they move right to left. Sometimes Ford uses a heads-on or tails-on shot to cross the line, in the accepted manner, but at other times he does not. At one point Ringo starts to leap down onto the horses' backs to retrieve a lost rein, for example; his leap begins in medium-long shot, from right to left. In the next shot he is going left to right (Figs. 9.10 and 9.11). But in spite of these "mistakes," Ford's editing style generally remains within the Hollywood continuity system.

These deviations show that violations of continuity rules don't always confuse the audience. The narrative context tells us that there is only one coach and one set of Indians chasing it in a straight line across a flat desert. As long as the filmmaker has sufficiently established the space and the moving elements, changes in screen direction should not be perplexing. It is usually only when we are uncertain about who is present and where the figures are in relation to one another that the violation of screen direction becomes confusing.

Stagecoach is our final example of classical films in which tight narrative unity is the overriding formal goal. We shall be looking at one more Hollywood film, *Meet Me in St. Louis*, to see how the formal and stylistic aspects of a classical film can generate an ideological stance. But from this point on, we shall concentrate on films that create alternative formal approaches to that of Hollywood.

Ambiguity ■

Day of Wrath (Vredens Dag)

1943. Palladium Film, Denmark. Directed by Carl Dreyer. Script by Dreyer, Mogens Skot-Hansen, and Poul Knudsen; based on the play *Anne*

Pedersdotter by Hans Wiers-Jenssen. Photographed by Karl Andersson. Edited by Edith Schluessel and Anne Marie Petersen. Music by Poul Schierbeck. With Lisbeth Movin, Thorkild Roose, Sigrid Neiiendam, Preben Lerdorff Rye, Anna Svierkier.

The films analyzed so far pose few difficulties for viewers who like their movies staightforward and easy to digest. But several films we will be examining from this point onward are not so clear in their form and style. In these films our uncertainty becomes central. In films like *Day of Wrath*, the questions we ask often do not get definite answers; endings don't tie everything up; film technique is not always functioning to "invisibly" advance the narrative. When analyzing such films, we should restrain ourselves from trying to answer all of the film's questions and to create neatly satisfying endings. Instead of ignoring peculiarities of technique, we should seek to examine how film form and style create uncertainty—seek to understand the cinematic conditions that produce ambiguity. *Day of Wrath*, a tale of witchcraft and murder set in seventeenth-century Denmark, offers a good test case.

As a narrative film, *Day of Wrath* depends on cause-and-effect relations, but what strikes us immediately is its unusual number of parallels. The first half of the film centers on the fate of Herlofs Marthe, the old woman accused of witchcraft. In the course of this half, Herlofs Marthe's progress toward the stake is constantly paralleled to action involving the pastor Absalon, his new wife, Anne, his mother, Merete, and his son, Martin. After Herlofs Marthe is burned (in a scene whose use of offscreen sound is of outstanding interest), the second part of the film is concerned primarily with Absalon's family and especially with the growing love affair between Anne and Martin. Crosscutting parallels the young couple's idyll in nature with Absalon's solitude or his consolation of a dying friend. The crosscutting conveys minute similarities of gesture and difference of mood between these pairs of actions. When Absalon dies, apparently killed by Anne, Dreyer again uses crosscutting to parallel old Merete, sitting by the coffin, with Anne and Martin wrapped in the fog.

Among all the parallels in the film, one stands out particularly. Herlofs Marthe, the "witch" of the first part, is constantly compared to Anne, the "witch" of the second. From the start, Dreyer uses crosscutting to parallel Herlofs Marthe, fleeing from the mob, with Merete and particularly with Anne. In the course of the film, most of what we see of Herlofs Marthe's progress—the interrogations, torture, and execution—is seen through Anne's eyes. (The privileging of Anne as the point-of-view character merits close study.) The Dies Irae musical motif, associated with Herlofs Marthe's immolation, is scored in a brighter key when Anne and Martin are wandering through the forests. A motif of lighting repeats the parallel: Often a shadow passes across Anne's face,

Figure 9.12

Figure 9.13

exactly as the shadows of leaves tremble on Herlofs Marthe's face before she is burned (compare Figs. 9.12 and 9.13). Thus not only narrative form, but also editing, sound, and lighting guide us to compare and contrast the old "witch" with the young one.

However clear such parallel relations may seem, the chains of narrative cause and effect lead us straight to ambiguities. The uncertainty revolves around the problem of witchcraft. The official whose hand writes and signs documents throughout the first third of the film assumes that witchcraft exists and threatens society. We are tempted to see this belief as simple superstition, the Church's means of oppression in this society. But things are not so simple. In the first sequence, a woman has sought out Herlofs Marthe for a potion. "This is sure to work," says Marthe. "It is herbs from under the gallows." And she adds, "There is power in evil." So perhaps she *is* a witch after all. Yet after she is captured and tortured, Dreyer's mise-en-scene in the torture chamber depicts her as only a victimized old woman. And yet again, she curses her inquisitor, Laurentius, and he soon dies; she predicts that Anne will go to the stake, and Anne eventually does. Herlofs Marthe's "power" puts us in doubt as to whether certain narrative events have a natural or a supernatural cause.

An even stronger ambiguity hovers over the causes for crucial events involving Anne. In the course of the film, she displays the ability to summon Martin from a distance, to make Absalon fear for his life, to kill Absalon by saying, "I wish you dead." What causes such events? Supernatural powers? The narrative does not explain how Anne could have acquired them. (There is the suggestion that her mother was a witch and "could call the quick and the dead," but this hardly constitutes a clear explanation of Anne's abilities.) Is, then, the cause sheerly psychological? Does Anne merely *believe* herself to be a witch? As we shall see, her entire behavior does change as she becomes more deeply in love with Martin. Yet again, psychological states don't explain her power to call or kill from a distance. Up to the very end, the film refuses to specify the exact causes of Anne's actions—supernatural, psychological, or social. (Compare, in this regard, the very explicit causes that determine the characters' action in *His Girl Friday, The Man Who Knew Too Much*, or *Stagecoach*.) "Is Anne a witch?" is a question that *Day of Wrath* does not answer clearly.

The ambiguity surrounding witchcraft and its effects is stressed in Dreyer's concept of mise-en-scene as well. We have already seen how facial lighting compares Anne with Herlofs Marthe; we ought also to notice how lighting functions to cast an uncertain aura over Anne. When she first sees Martin, she steps into a patch of shadow; when she swears that she did not kill Absalon, a shadow falls across her face. Such light-

Figure 9.14

Figure 9.15

Figure 9.16

Figure 9.17

ing reminds us of the possibly supernatural sources of her power, even at moments when she seems most innocent.

Other aspects of mise-en-scene reinforce Anne's ambiguous status. Her deepening love for Martin is expressed through changes in her bodily movements—at first constrained, somewhat rigid, but later more sinuous, even catlike. We first see her wearing a prim, rectangular cap; later, with Martin, she wears a softly curving lace bonnet; still later, she simply lets her hair hang free. Props such as her embroidery pattern (depicting a young woman with a baby) and her drawing of an apple tree (Martin's poem had described a "young maiden in an apple tree") also convey her sexual blossoming.

Yet all of these motifs cut two ways: Anne may be impelled by desire or by sorcery. The most obvious manifestation of the ambiguity may be seen in her changing facial expressions, at once cunning and inviting. At one point, both Absalon and Martin seek to read her essence in her eyes, and they come to exactly opposite conclusions. To the old man, Anne's eyes are "childlike and innocent, so clear"; to Martin, they are "fathomless and mysterious . . . in the bottom, a trembling, quivering flame." Dreyer's mise-en-scene brings the ambiguity to the viewer's notice, compelling us to ask at almost every moment what motivates Anne's actions and how we are to understand her.

Figure 9.18

Day of Wrath's final scene only partly dispels the uncertainties that run throughout the film. Absalon's funeral is beginning, and Martin has sworn to stand by Anne. Dreyer creates yet another narrative parallel by opening the scene with a very stressed lengthy circular tracking shot. Following the choirboys' treading through the death room (Fig. 9.14) permits Dreyer to establish, in a long take, the entire space and all of the relevant characters' positions: the church elders (Fig. 9.15), the judge, Merete (Fig. 9.16), the coffin (Fig. 9.17), and Anne and Martin (Fig. 9.18). The attentive viewer will recall that a similar circular tracking shot previously introduced the torture-chamber scene and later the death of Laurentius as well; Dreyer uses the camera movement to parallel three

Figure 9.19

Figure 9.20

somber interiors, all associated with the repressive power of the Church. In contrast to the "invisible" camera movements of *His Girl Friday*, Dreyer emphasizes the camera movements as a motif, calling our attention to the parallel situations.

In the course of this scene, Merete publicly accuses Anne of witchcraft. Martin abandons her, and Anne breaks down, confessing to having been in the service of "the Evil One." Does this, then, settle the matter of her witchcraft?

We know that in analyzing a film, it is useful to contrast the beginning with the ending. *Day of Wrath* begins with the image of a scroll unrolling, over which the medieval church melody "Dies Irae" plays nondiegetically. The scroll depicts and describes the terrible events that befall the sinful earth on Judgment Day (the "Day of Wrath" of the title). (See Fig. 9.19). After Anne confesses, she looks upward—for help, for mercy? The scroll now returns to the screen, accompanied by the sweet solo voice of a choirboy, describing how the "bruised soul" will be lifted to heaven. In the eternal context of the scroll, Anne is apparently forgiven. Yet *what* she is forgiven for—seducing Martin, practicing witchcraft, accepting her society's definition of herself *as* a witch—is never stipulated. The scroll seems not to resolve the ambiguity so much as to postpone it. The final image of the film is a cross, but the cross is slowly transformed into the witch motif we saw earlier, during Herlofs Marthe's execution (Fig. 9.20). Presumably, the parallel with Herlofs Marthe is now complete: Anne will be burnt. But the causes of certain events, the nature of witchcraft, the desires that motivate Anne—these remain, like her eyes, "fathomless and mysterious." *Day of Wrath* illustrates how a film may fascinate us not by its clarity but by its obscurity, not by fixed certainties but by teasing questions.

Last Year at Marienbad (L'année dernière à Marienbad)

> 1961. Précitel and Terrafilm, a French-Italian coproduction. Directed by Alain Resnais. Script by Alain Robbe-Grillet. Photographed by Sacha Vierney. Edited by Henri Colpi and Jasmine Chasney. Music by Francis Seyrig. With Delphine Seyrig, Giorgio Albertazzi, Sacha Pitoeff.

When *Last Year at Marienbad* was first shown in 1961, many critics offered widely varying interpretations of it. With most films, these critics would have been looking for what they took to be the meaning behind the plot. But faced with *Marienbad*, their interpretations were attempts simply to describe the events that take place in the film's story. These proved difficult to agree on. Did the couple really meet last year? If not, what really happened? Is the film one of the characters' dreams or a mad imagining?

Typically, a film's plot—however simple or difficult—allows the spectator to construct the causal and chronological story mentally. But *Marienbad* is different; its story is impossible to determine. The film has only a plot, with no single consistent story for us to infer. This is because *Marienbad* carries the strategy of *Day of Wrath* to a great extreme: It works entirely through ambiguities. As we watch the opening of the film, the events seem to be leading us toward a story, complicated though it might be. But then contradictions arise: One character says that an event occurred, specifying the time and place, but another character denies it. Because such contradictions are never resolved, we have no way of choosing which events are part of a causal series that would make up a potential story.

Figure 9.21

Marienbad creates its ambiguity through contradictions on many different levels—the spatial and temporal as well as the causal. Within the same shot, impossible juxtapositions may occur in the mise-en-scene. At one point a track forward through a door reveals the shrub-lined promenade that is (sometimes) situated in front of the hotel. The people scattered across the flat expanse in the center cast long, dark shadows, yet the pointed trees that line the promenade cast none (Fig. 9.21); the sun is apparently simultaneously shining and not shining. Later in the film, there is a shot of the woman. (As none of the characters have names, we shall call her the Heroine, the lead male the Narrator, and the tall man the Other Man.) There are three images of her within the frame; apparently two must be mirror reflections, yet the three images are facing in directions that make an arrangement of mirrors impossible (Fig. 9.22).

Figure 9.22

Settings shift in inconsistent ways between different segments of the film as well. The statue to which the couple frequently returns appears sometimes to be directly outside the French windows of the hotel (as in the fast track right as the Heroine leaves the Narrator and runs through these windows); at other times the statue is at a great distance. In some scenes the statue faces a lake; in others, the lake is behind it. In still other scenes the tree-lined promenade forms the background in shots of the statue. (Compare Figs. 9.23 and 9.24.) Within the hotel, things change as well, as the decoration of the Heroine's room becomes progressively more cluttered. New pieces of furniture appear, the gilded molding on the walls becomes more elaborate, and the decoration over the mantle is sometimes a mirror and sometimes a painting. The Narrator's frequent descriptions of the "vast hotel . . . baroque, dismal" and the "hallways crossing hallways" point up these impossible changes. His words cannot pin down the appearances of things, which frequently shift (as do the descriptions themselves, which the Narrator repeats many times, with different combinations of phrases).

Figure 9.23

Figure 9.24

Figure 9.25

Figure 9.26

Figure 9.27

Temporal relations are similarly problematic. In one shot the Heroine stands by the window to the left of the bed in her room; the darkness of a nighttime exterior is visible, and the lights by the bed are lit. But when she moves left, with the camera panning, she reaches another window through which sunlight is visible; the type of lighting inside the room is also different in this new portion of the setting, yet no cut or ellipsis has occurred (Fig. 9.25).

The temporal sequence of events is unclear across the film. Supposedly the Narrator has returned to take the Heroine away after an agreed-upon year's separation following their initial meeting. Yet in the scene at the end when they do leave together, the Narrator's voice is still describing this event as if it had taken place in the past—as if it were one of the things he is trying to recall to her mind. At the beginning of the film (which apparently coincides fairly closely with the Narrator's arrival at the hotel) the Heroine is watching a play called *Rosmer*; at the end, she stays away from the same performance in order to leave with the Narrator. (The actions of the Heroine and Narrator in this scene also duplicate those in the scene from *Rosmer* as we see it near the beginning of the film.) The play occurs only once, yet supposedly all of the events of the Narrator's attempt to convince the Heroine to leave take place between the two presentations of *Rosmer* in the plot. The temporal status of all of the events of the film becomes undeterminable.

Marienbad presents many varied combinations of ambiguous space, time, and causality. An action may carry from one time and space to a different time and space. This happens several times when editing "matches on action" occur with a change in locale. The first such "match" gives us our first really contradictory cue in the film. A series of shots after the *Rosmer* performance shows small groups of guests standing around the hotel lobby; one medium shot frames a blond woman beginning to turn away from the camera (Fig. 9.26). In the middle of her turn, there is a cut to a different setting; the woman is dressed identically, and her position in the frame is matched precisely (Fig. 9.27). This cut also uses a device common throughout the film—a sudden start or cessation of loud organ music. The abrupt changes on the soundtrack accentuate the film's discontinuities and startling juxtapositions. A similar "match" on action occurs later as the Heroine walks with the Narrator down a hallway. In the first shot there are several people in the background; after the cut, the couple are alone in a different hallway—yet converse without a break.

The opposite of this pattern also occurs; that is, the space and time may remain constant, while different actions occur that contradict each other. Several times the camera begins a shot on one or more characters, moves away from them across considerable space, and picks up the same characters in a different locale. This happens as the Narrator confronts the Heroine after the first pistol-range segment; they stand in medium shot as he talks. Then the camera tracks away right, past a series of other people; it reaches the Narrator, who is now standing at the other end of the room, looking off right. A pan right reveals the Heroine coming in a door at the top of a flight of stairs. At several other points, characters slip out one side of the frame as the camera moves, only to appear elsewhere at a later stage of the same shot.

Marienbad combines contradictions of space, time, and causality in many variations. The Narrator's voice-over account of events seems at first to make sense, but soon it comes into conflict with the image. In one shot (the night/day segment mentioned earlier), we see a "flashback," apparently illustrating the Narrator's account of a night he had seduced the Heroine. At first the images and his internal past-tense narration tally closely. But then discrepancies begin to creep in; he says that she went to the bed, yet in the image she remains standing by a wall made of mirrors near the door. He concedes, "It's true, there was a large mirror by the door . . . a huge mirror which you avoided"; yet the Heroine continues to move along the mirror, pressing herself closely to it. At other times the Narrator declares that entire sequences are false. We see the Other Man shoot the Heroine, apparently in jealousy over her affair with the Narrator; in the "present," the Narrator continues to describe the scene to the Heroine, trying to get her to remember it. But then he says, "That's not the right ending. It's you alive I must have." At other points he describes having entered the Heroine's bedroom and raped her, then denies that he had used force to seduce her. The images present several versions of the scene, with the Heroine sometimes cringing in fear, sometimes opening her arms in welcome. The Narrator's descriptions of the supposed events "last year" are unreliable, since he several times offers incompatible versions of scenes.

The film is careful not to give us clues to help establish clear connections. The title itself is purely arbitrary. It seems to imply that an important narrative event has occurred at a specific time and place. But in fact, the Narrator states several times that he had met the Heroine a year ago at Friedrichsbad. Only when she denies ever having been there does he reply, "Perhaps it was elsewhere . . . at Karlstadt, at Marienbad, or Baden-Salsa, or in this very room." Nor can we tell what the relationships among the characters are. The Narrator says that the Other Man is "perhaps" the Heroine's husband. He may also be her brother, friend, or lover, but we have no way of determining which. All of the characters invariably use the formal *vous* (you) to one another rather than the more intimate *tu*. As a result, we never get a sense of how close the Heroine's relationship to either of the two men is supposed to be.

In addition to these unclarities, *Marienbad* uses several devices that are simply incongruous. For example, when the Narrator and Heroine attend a concert in the hotel's music room, the two musicians on the stage play a violin and cello, yet only loud organ music is audible (a good example of lack of fidelity between image and sound track). At a later point a solid stone balustrade collapses as the Narrator climbs over it to avoid meeting the Other Man; although this alarms the Heroine very much at the time, the incident is never referred to or explained in relation to other events.

Marienbad teases us on to try to fit its parts into a coherent whole, yet at the same time it provides several indications that such a constructed unity is impossible. First, there is the statue beside which the couple often stands. The Narrator describes how they had discussed the figures of the man and woman in the statue, offering different interpretations: He says that the man is trying to keep the woman back from something dangerous, whereas she believes that the woman is pointing something out to the man. Each hypothesis is equally reasonable as an explanation for the gestures of the stone figures (as are still other explanations). The Narrator's voice-over says, "Both were possible," but goes on immediately to elaborate on his own explanation. Finally, he tells how the Heroine had insisted on identifying the statues: "You . . . began naming them—haphazardly, I think. Then I said, they might just as well be you and I or anyone. Leave them nameless, with more room for adventure." Yet the Heroine still persists in trying to interpret the statue and invent a story to go with it. Later, the Other Man offers a precise explanation of the statue as an allegorical figure representing Charles III. Here we have an apparently correct interpretation, for the Other Man seems to have special information that the others lack. But by this point in the film we are suspicious of everyone—perhaps he is only making it up. The statue resembles the film as a whole in several ways: Its temporal and spatial situation shifts without explanation, and its meaning ultimately remains elusive.

The ending of the film leaves the Heroine lost in the gardens of the hotel with the Narrator. The mazelike hotel and gardens suggest the windings of the narrative itself. The space, both inside and outside, is impossible; we can never reconstruct it. The Narrator's voice is heard over the ending, describing the locale: "The gardens of this hotel were in the French manner, without trees, without flowers, without plants, nothing. Gravel, stone, marble, straight lines setting rigid patterns of space, surfaces without mystery." The space as he describes it is stable and unambiguous; yet, as we have seen, contradictions abound in this apparently stable space. The Narrator goes on: "It seemed impossible— at first—to lose one's way there. At first. Among the stones, where you were, already, losing your way forever, in the quiet night, alone with me." This ease of losing one's way in a deceptively straightforward path applies to the spectator's attempts to construct the film's story as well. "At first" it seems possible to piece events together in a chronological fashion; only gradually do we realize that the task is hopeless.

A major motif in the film is the game that the Other Man plays against several opponents, always winning easily. The game is not a symbol in the sense of representing some hidden meaning, but it does present another image of impossibility. It is impossible to win the game without knowing the key. One onlooker suggests that perhaps the one who starts the round wins—but the Other Man wins whether he goes first or second. The Narrator struggles to learn the key, but the film offers no solution. Instead, the game helps to suggest to the spectator the nature of the film he or she is watching. The narrative, too, has no key that will enable us to find its hidden coherence; it is a game that we must lose. The whole structure of *Marienbad* is a play with logic, space, and time which does not offer us a single, complete story as a prize for winning this "game."

This is why *Marienbad* fascinates some people but frustrates others. Those who go expecting a comprehensible story and refuse to abandon that expectation may come away baffled and discouraged, feeling that the film is "obscure." But *Marienbad* broke with conventional expectations by suggesting, perhaps for the first time in film history, that a film could base itself entirely on a gamelike structure of ambiguity. Critics have too often tried to find a thematic key to the film while ignoring this formal play. Much of *Marienbad*'s fascination for the spectator rests in the process of discovering its ambiguity. The film's Narrator gives us good guidance when he resists interpreting the statue; of the film's characters and other devices we might also say, "Leave them nameless, with more room for adventure."

A Nonclassical Approach to Narrative, Space, and Time ■

Tokyo Story (Tokyo Monogatari)

1953. Shochiku/Ofuna, Japan. Directed by Yasujiro Ozu. Script by Ozu and Kogo Noda. Photographed by Yuharu Atsuta. With Chishu Ryu, Chieko Higashiyama, So Yamamura, Haruko Sugimura, Setsuko Hara.

We have seen how the classical Hollywood approach to filmmaking created a stylistic system ("continuity") in order to establish and maintain a clear narrative space and time. The continuity system is a specific set of guidelines which a filmmaker may follow. But some filmmakers do not use the continuity system; they develop an alternative set of formal guidelines, which allows them to make films that are quite distinctive from classical narratives. Japanese director Yasujiro Ozu is one such director; his approach to the interrelationships of time, space, and narrative logic differs greatly from that of most if not all other filmmakers. Although he is one of the greatest of all filmmakers, Ozu is less well known than some others because his films were seen only in Japan for many years; *Tokyo Story* was the first Ozu film to make a considerable impression in the West.

Ozu's approach to the creation of a narrative differs from that used in more classical films like *His Girl Friday* or *The Man Who Knew Too Much*. Instead of making narrative events the central organizing principle, Ozu tends to decenter narrative slightly; spatial and temporal structures come forward and create their own interest. Sometimes we learn of important narrative events only indirectly; an ellipsis occurs at a crucial moment. The last portion of *Tokyo Story*, for example, involves a series of events surrounding the sudden illness and death of the grandmother of a family. Although the grandparents are the film's two central characters, we do not see the grandmother falling ill; we hear about it only when her son and daughter receive telegrams with the news. Similarly, the grandmother's death occurs between scenes; in one scene her children are gathered by her bedside, and in the next scene they are mourning her.

Yet these ellipses are not evidence of a fast-paced film such as *His Girl Friday*, which must cover a lot of narrative ground in a hurry. On the contrary, the sequences of *Tokyo Story* often linger over details: the sad conversation between the grandfather and his friends in a bar as they discuss their disappointment in their children, or the grandmother's walk on a Sunday with her grandchild. The result is a shift in the balance of more classical narratives. Key narrative events are deemphasized by means of ellipsis, whereas narrative events that we do see in the plot are simple and understated.

Accompanying this shift away from a presentation of the "dramatic" events of the narrative is a sliding away from narratively significant space. Scenes do not begin and end with shots that frame the most important narrative elements in the mise-en-scene. Instead of the usual transitional devices, such as dissolves and fades, Ozu typically employs a series of separate transitional shots linked by cuts. And these transitional shots often show spaces not directly connected with the action of the scene; the spaces are usually *near* where that action will take place. The opening of the film, for example, has five shots of the port town of Onomichi—the bay, schoolchildren, a passing train—before the sixth shot reveals the grandparents packing for their trip to Tokyo. Although a couple of important motifs make their first appearances in these first five shots, no narrative causes occur to get the action under way. (Compare the openings of *His Girl Friday* and *Stagecoach*.) Nor do these transitional shots appear only at the beginning. Several sequences in Tokyo start with shots of factory smokestacks, even though no action ever occurs in these locales.

Figure 9.28

These transitions have only a minimal function as establishing shots. Sometimes the transitions do not establish space at all, but tend to confuse the space of the upcoming scene. After the daughter-in-law, Noriko, gets a phone call at work telling her of the grandmother's illness, she goes and sits sadly at her desk. This scene ends on a medium shot of her; the only diegetic sound is the loud clack of typewriters. A nondiegetic musical transition comes up in this shot. Then there is a cut to a low-angle long shot of a building under construction; riveting noises replace the typewriters, with the music continuing. The next shot is another low angle of the construction site. A cut changes the locale to the clinic belonging to the eldest son, Dr. Hirayama. The sister, Shige, is present. The music ends and the new scene begins. (See Figs. 9.28 through 9.31.) In this segment, the two shots of the construction site are not necessary to the action. The film doesn't give us any indication where the building under construction is. We might assume that it is outside Noriko's office, but the riveting sound is not audible in the interior shots.

Figure 9.29

These transitional spaces do not always involve outdoor locales. Some shots of spaces are within the characters' homes and do not involve any characters. Early in the film Mrs. Hirayama, the doctor's wife, argues with her son, Minoru, over where to move his desk to make room for the grandparents. This issue is dropped, and there follows a scene of the grandparents' arrival. This ends on a conversation in an upstairs room; transitional music again comes up over the end of the scene. The next shot frames an empty hallway downstairs that contains Minoru's schooldesk, but no one is in the shot. An exterior long shot of children running along a ridge near the house follows; these children are not characters in the action. Finally, a cut back inside reveals Minoru at his father's desk in the clinic portion of the house, studying. Here the editing creates a very indirect route between two scenes, going first to a place where the character should be (at his own desk), but is not; then the scene moves completely away from the action, outdoors. Only then, in the third shot, does a character reappear and the action continue.

Figure 9.30

But Ozu's style does not result in a random approach to editing; he does not simply cut to any point in space or time. (Such extremes of discontinuity are more characteristic of Jean-Luc Godard's style, as we shall see in analyzing *La Chinoise*.) Ozu's editing patterns are as systematic as those of Hollywood, but they tend to be almost exactly the opposite of the continuity rules.

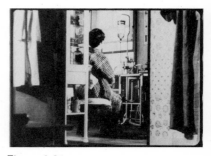

Figure 9.31

Figure 9.32

Figure 9.33

Figure 9.34

Figure 9.35

Figure 9.36

For example, Ozu does not observe the 180° line, or axis of action. Nor is his "violation" of these rules occasional, as Ford's is in *Stagecoach*. Ozu frequently cuts 180° across the line to frame the scene's space from the opposite direction. This, of course, violates rules of screen direction, since characters or objects on the right in the first shot will appear on the left in the second, and vice versa. At the beginning of a scene in Shige's beauty salon, the initial interior medium shot frames Shige from opposite the front door (Fig. 9.32). Then a 180° cut reveals a medium long shot of a woman under a dryer; the camera now faces the rear of the salon (Fig. 9.33). Another cut 180° presents a new long shot of the room, viewed toward the door again, and the grandparents come into the salon (Fig. 9.34). Rather than being an isolated violation of continuity rules, this is Ozu's typical way of framing and editing a scene.

Ozu is a master of matching on action, but unlike the Hollywood continuity style, his style often matches on a cut that crosses the axis of action. As Noriko and the grandmother walk toward the door of Noriko's apartment to leave, there is a 180° cut that matches their action of walking (Figs. 9.35 and 9.36).

Ozu in fact uses a completely circular shooting space instead of the semicircular space on one side of the axis of action. He cuts in a full circle around the action, usually in segments of 90° or 180°. This means that backgrounds change frequently, as is apparent in both previous examples. In a Hollywood film, backgrounds remain roughly consistent throughout much of the action, because the camera doesn't cross the axis of action to look at the fourth wall. Because surroundings change more frequently in *Tokyo Story*, they become more prominent in relation to the action; the viewer must pay attention to setting or become confused.

In these ways Ozu draws our attention away from the strictly narrative functions of space and makes space important in its own right. He does the same with the flat graphic space of the screen as well. Chapter 6 contained examples of graphic matches from Ozu films. This stylistic

Figure 9.37

Figure 9.38

device is characteristic of Ozu; he seldom uses the graphic match for any narrative purpose. In *Tokyo Story* a conversation situation leads to a shot/reverse/shot pattern, but again with cuts 180° across the axis of action. The two men speaking are framed so that each looks off right. (In Hollywood upholders of the continuity system would claim that this implies that both are looking off toward the same thing.) Because they are positioned similarly in the frame, the result is a strong graphic carry-over from one shot to another—a graphic match (Figs. 9.37 and 9.38).

A scene that displays Ozu's characteristic use of framing and editing occurs in the sequence when the grandparents visit a spa at Atami. The scene begins with a long shot along a hallway (Fig. 9.39); Latin-style dance music plays offscreen, and several people walk through the hall. The next shot (Fig. 9.40) is a long shot of another hallway upstairs, with a maid carrying a tray; two pairs of slippers are just visible by a doorway at the lower left. Next comes a medium long shot of a hallway by a court-yard (Fig. 9.41); more people bustle through. A medium shot of a mah-jongg game follows (Fig. 9.42); there is a loud sound of talking and moving pieces about. Then Ozu cuts 180° across the axis, framing another mah-jongg table (Fig. 9.43); the first table is now in the back-gound, viewed from the opposite side. The next cut returns to a long shot along the courtyard hallway (Fig. 9.44), but with a slightly different framing. (Ozu often varies his set-ups slightly between shots of the same space.) In all of these shots, we have not yet seen the grandparents, who are the only major characters present at the spa. Finally, there is a medium shot of the two pairs of slippers by the door in the upper hall-way (Fig. 9.45), suggesting that this is the grandparents' room; the panes of glass in the wall reflect the lively movement of the offscreen party, and the loud music and talk are still audible. A medium shot of the Hirayamas in bed, trying to sleep through the noise, finally reveals the narrative situation of the scene, and a conversation begins between the couple (Fig. 9.46). For seven shots the film slowly explores the space of

Figure 9.39

Figure 9.40

Figure 9.41

Figure 9.42

Figure 9.43

Figure 9.44

Figure 9.45

Figure 9.46

the scene, gradually letting us discover the situation. The presence of the slippers in the second shot is almost unnoticeable; it hints that the grandparents are there, but the revelation of their whereabouts is then put off for several more shots.

The use of space and time in *Tokyo Story* is not willfully obscure, nor does it play a symbolic function in the narrative. Rather, it suggests a different relationship among space, time, and narrative logic than exists in the classical film. Space and time no longer simply function unobtrusively to create a clear narrative line; Ozu brings them forward and makes them into prominent aesthetic elements in their own right. Ozu does not eliminate narrative, but he opens it out; *Tokyo Story* and his other films allow other stylistic devices to exist independently alongside narrative. The result is that the viewer is invited to look at his films in a new way, to participate in a play of space and time.

Disunity ■

Innocence Unprotected (Nevinost Bez Zastite)

> 1968. Avala Film, Yugoslavia. Directed by Dusan Makavejev, incorporating a film directed by Dragoljub Aleksic. Script by Makavejev. Photographed by Branko Perak and Stevan Miskovic. Edited by Ivanka Vukasovic. Music by Vojislav Dostic. With Dragolijub Aleksic, Ana Miloslavljevic, Vera Jovanovic, Bratoljub Gliforijviec, Ivan Zivkovic, Pere Milslavljevic.

Like *Last Year at Marienbad*, Dusan Makavejev's *Innocence Unprotected* (more correctly translated as *Innocent Unprotected*) presents us with the problem of a film that seems radically disunified—willfully fragmentary and chaotic, full of interruptions and loose ends. In analyzing the film stylistically and formally, it is useful to think of the film's form as a *collage*—an assemblage of materials taken from widely different sources that does not blend these materials into a perfectly smooth unity, but that emphasizes the heterogeneity of its components. This is not a defect in the film. Rather, the collage principle permits Makavejev to use film techniques and film form in fresh and provocative ways. The result is a film that examines the nature of cinema—particularly, cinema in a social and historical context.

The collage aspect of *Innocence Unprotected* stands out most strikingly in its use of a wide range of materials. In one sense it is a compilation film. There are at least four different sources. At the core is the original fiction film, "Innocence Unprotected," made by the Yugoslav acrobat Aleksic and his collaborators in 1942, under the German occupation. (Since we are dealing with two films of the same name, let us put Aleksic's film "Innocence Unprotected" in quotation marks and Makavejev's film *Innocence Unprotected* in italics.) A second source is the mass of social-political documentation from the same period: newsreels of Yugoslavian current events, German propaganda films, footage of contemporary newspaper headlines, and footage of contemporary posters. Third, there appear excerpts from another fiction film, the Soviet feature *Circus* (Grigori Alexandrov, 1936). Finally, there is present-day footage of Aleksic and the surviving participants in the original production. The last three types of footage permit Makavejev to imbed

Aleksic's original film in a complex context, justifying Makavejev's subtitle: "A New Version of a Very Good Old Film."

The four strands—original film, documentary footage, other fiction footage, and present-day footage—function initially to compare several different styles and modes of filmmaking. We are forced to compare Aleksic's technically crude "Innocence Unprotected" (with its academically incorrect continuity editing and flat lighting) with the Hollywood norms of "technical perfection." By inserting newsreel footage into fictitious scenes, Makavejev also impels us to contrast fiction film with documentary. (When Nada, the heroine of "Innocence Unprotected," looks out a window, an eyeline match cut suggests that she "sees" the rubble of a bombed Belgrade.) The digressions in *Innocence Unprotected* often come from Makavejev's habit of breaking off one kind of footage to juxtapose it with another—a fictional scene with attack maps or animated cartoons, an interview interrupted by a fictional scene.

Perhaps most complicated of all are the comparisons we draw between Aleksic's old film, "Innocence Unprotected," and the "new version," which Makavejev has "prepared, decorated, and supplied with comments." Aleksic's original was a fictional narrative shot in black and white; Makavejev has juggled sequences, inserted new footage, added commentative titles, toned the black and white in several hues, and even hand-colored parts of certain shots. (See Plate 13 for example of blue-black toning and hand-coloring.) Thus we always see Aleksic's film at one remove, *through* Makavejev's interpretive framework. Moreover, in the present-day sections, which Makavejev has shot, the differences between the original and the new versions function to contrast the past and the present. The participants are frantically energetic in the 1942 film; now, though still vital, they are elderly. The disparity of past and present is perhaps most amusingly indicated when we see Aleksic as a young man dangling from a plane by his teeth, and then, while the plane noise continues over the image, Makavejev's camera in the present tracks through a house to find Aleksic dangling by his teeth in his cellar.

Yet it would be rash to stress only the differences between the original "Innocence Unprotected" and the new version. The original film itself was something of a collage, drawing on newsreel footage of Aleksic's stunts. And Makavejev often imitates the editing discontinuities and musical effects found in Aleksic's 1942 original. At times Makavejev even hesitates to keep the two films separate, as when the credits for *Innocence Unprotected* include names of people who worked only on the original. In *Innocence Unprotected*, then, the juxtaposition of various strands of source material contrasts and likens various uses of film technique.

The strands do weave together, but not in conventional ways. We have little trouble in demarcating the separate scenes in films like *His*

Girl Friday, but *Innocence Unprotected* (again like *Last Year at Marienbad*) is difficult to segment into scenes or sequences. This is because Makavejev has chopped into collage fragments whatever narrative unity Aleksic's first version had. But *Innocence Unprotected* does have a form, often more categorical than narrative. Here is the breakdown we propose:

Part 1:	Introduction	Credits; explanatory prologue; introduction of surviving cast and crew
Part 2:	"Innocence Unprotected" begins its narrative	Scene 1 of "Innocence Unprotected"; newsreel footage of German attack; Aleksic is introduced, now and then
Part 3:	Production background	Financing; the film's success and the censorship; Serbia's place in Yugoslavia; the Occupation; credits of "Innocence Unprotected"
Part 4:	"Innocence Unprotected" narrative continues	Scenes 2–8 of "Innocence Unprotected," interspersed with newsreels
Part 5:	Souvenirs of Youth	(to be analyzed)
Part 6:	Aleksic's strength	Scene 9 of "Innocence Unprotected" (Aleksic rescues Nadia); Aleksic's stunts today; Scene 10 of "Innocence Unprotected" (Aleksic escapes from police)
Part 7:	Innocence protected	"Innocence Unprotected" narrative resolved (dance in cafe, lovers united); Aleksic cleared of criminal charges

The outline shows that this is no ordinary narrative film. Parts 2, 4, 6, and 7 emphasize the original narrative, but parts 1, 3, and 5 function principally to put the film into historical contexts. And every part is riddled with jokes, interruptions, and digressions. In this connection we might recall Eisenstein's notion of intellectual montage. (See the *October* example in Chapter 6.) By cutting freely from one kind of footage to another, Makavejev's collage form creates discontinuities that "free the action from time and space," as Eisenstein said of intellectual montage, in order to make abstract, ironic points. *Innocence Unprotected* presents us with a skeletal narrative form interrupted by parts that are organized categorically, around topics or concepts.

As a concrete example, consider part 5. We label this "Souvenirs of Youth" because that is the concept binding together a varied collection of material. The sequence begins in the present, with the original participants reflecting on their pasts. First, Aleksic and two collaborators stand on a roof used in the filming (Fig. 9.47). Next, Vera, the actress who portrayed the stepmother, recalls the beauty of her legs and performs a vaudeville song (Figs. 9.48 and 9.49). Then Pera, who played the butler

Figure 9.47

Figure 9.48

Figure 9.49

Figure 9.50

Figure 9.51

Figure 9.52

Figure 9.53

Figure 9.54

Figure 9.55

in the original, sings a song about political fence sitting during the Occupation while standing before a memorial to heroism (Fig. 9.50).

The film now moves into the past, showing a newsreel of the boy King Peter reviewing his troops (Fig. 9.51). (Although a king, he had little power; Prince Paul actually ran the country before turning Yugoslavia over to Germany and fleeing.) Back to the present, with Aleksic bending a bar. ("This is a souvenir of my youth"; see Fig. 9.52.) Now shots from *Circus* show a young woman shot from a cannon (Fig. 9.53). We learn that this film inspired Aleksic to build a similar cannon for one of his stunts (Fig. 9.54). Finally, news stories report how someone was killed by Aleksic's contraption (Fig. 9.55).

The sequence's sources—songs, newsreels, a Russian musical—and the different periods discussed are not unified by narrative principles (cause-effect, temporal progression). Instead, a *concept* pulls the fragments loosely together; souvenirs from the youth of the participants in the film and from a period when their country was ruled by a child.

The "Souvenirs of Youth" segment also illustrates how the concepts derived from the collage form tend to be overtly political ones. Makavejev's prologue announces: "This first Yugoslav talkie is not mentioned in our film histories because it was made during the Occupation." Makavejev situates Aleksic's "Innocence Unprotected" firmly within the ferment of Serbian nationalism. The success of Aleksic's film at the time is held to be a triumph for Serbian rights. More subtly, Makavejev's "decoration and commentary" turn Aleksic's film into an allegory of Yugoslav resistance to the Germans. When the Uncle lunges toward Nada, Makavejev cuts in animated newsreel maps showing the German invasion: Nada, the unprotected innocent, becomes identified with native Yugoslavia, the Uncle with the Nazis. By the same token, Aleksic emerges as a heroic, politicized figure. "We can all be proud of him," says Nada, "but we underrate what is our own." While Aleksic breaks his chains in a stunt, Makavejev plays the Communist anthem *The Internationale*. In part 6 Aleksic's prowess is celebrated in mock-heroic shots of him as a statue or a god. Here, as elsewhere, the nationalist allegory becomes ironic, but it nevertheless functions to make Makavejev's "decoration and commentary" overtly political.

Though this analysis has barely scratched the film's surface, we might end by posing the question of the title. Who is the innocent without protection? In Aleksic's 1942 film, it is the orphan Nada, rescued by Aleksic. But by comparing film styles, working out a unique form, and making general political points, Makavejev's "collage" strategy also suggests that Aleksic, the strong man who made the film, is something of an innocent, too. Over newsreel footage of blasted bodies we hear the characters in Aleksic's film singing a café tune. By situating the film in a political context, Makavejev suggests that Aleksic and his crew were dangerously innocent, oblivious to the concrete political situation. All involved insist that they had no subversive intent, that they made the film only to get rich. They risked death at the hands of the Nazis to make a silly romance about an acrobat.

Yet despite the lack of political purpose, Makavejev makes the original "Innocence Unprotected" emerge as a genuinely subversive film. In the original, Aleksic's rescue of Nada culminates in a victory dance at a café ("our national dance"), and Makavejev hand-colors one woman's dress the colors of the Serbian flag. No wonder Makavejev calls the original "a very good old film." The Germans banned it. The closing moments of *Innocence Unprotected* linger over the question of "innocence"; we are told that many participants in the film fought in the Resistance and that Aleksic was exonerated after the war, since his film "had not told a single lie." The fiction film has become a document; the apolitical project has become political. Makavejev's use of style and form has revised the old film in ways that make us rethink cinema and its functions in history.

Form, Style, and Ideology ■

Meet Me in St. Louis

> 1944. MGM. Directed by Vincente Minnelli. Script by Irving Brecher and Fred F. Finklehoffe, from the book by Sally Benson. Photographed by George Folsey. Edited by Albert Akst. Music by Hugh Martin and Ralph Blane. With Judy Garland, Margaret O'Brien, Mary Astor, Lucille Bremer, Leon Ames, Tom Drake.

Just over half way through *Meet Me in St. Louis*, the father, Alonzo Smith, announces to his assembled family that he has been transferred and that they must move to New York City. "I've got the future to think about—the future for all of us. I've got to worry about where the money's coming from," he tells the dismayed group. These ideas of family and future, central to the form and style of the film, are used to create an ideological stance.

All of the films we have already analyzed could be examined for their ideological standpoints; any film combines form and stylistic elements in such a way as to create an ideological stance, whether overtly stated or implicit. We have chosen to stress the ideology of *Meet Me in St. Louis* because it provides a clear example of a film that does not seek to change people's ways of thinking; instead, it tends to reinforce certain aspects of a dominant social ideology. In this case *Meet Me in St. Louis*, like most Hollywood films, seeks to uphold values of family unity and home life conceived of as "American."

The film was released during 1944, late in World War II. The audience for this film would have consisted largely of women and children whose adult male relatives had been absent for extended periods, often overseas. It was also a time of rationing. In short, families were often forced apart, and the people who remained behind had to make considerable sacrifices for the war effort. In this context *Meet Me in St. Louis* appeared as a nostalgic look back at America in 1903; parents of young fighting men in a 1944 audience would remember this as the period of their own childhoods. It suggested an ideal of family unity for the future.

Meet Me in St. Louis is set during the preparations for the Louisiana Purchase Exposition in St. Louis; the fair itself becomes the culmination of the action. The film displays its form in a straightforward way, with a title card announcing each of its four sections with a different season, beginning with "Summer, 1903." In this way the film simultaneously suggests the passage of time (equated with the fair, which will bring the fruits of progress to St. Louis) and the unchanging cycle of the seasons.

The Smiths, living in a big Victorian house, form a large and closely knit family. The seasonal structure allows the film to show the Smiths at the traditional times of family unity, the holidays; we see them celebrating Halloween and Christmas. At the end, the fair becomes a new sort of holiday, the celebration of the Smiths' decision to remain in St. Louis.

The opening of the film quickly introduces the idea of St. Louis as a city on the boundary between tradition and progress. The fancy "candy-box" title card for Summer forms a vignette of white and red flowers around an old-fashioned black-and-white photo of the Smiths' house. As the camera moves in on the photo, color fades into the photo, and it "comes to life." Slow, subdued chords over the title card give way to a bouncy tune more in keeping with the onscreen movement. Horse-drawn beer wagons and carriages move along the road; but an early-model automobile (a bright red, which draws our eye) passes them. Already the motif of progress and inventions becomes prominent; it will develop quickly into the emphasis on the upcoming fair.

The Smith son, Lon, arrives home by bicycle; a dissolve inside to the kitchen continues the process of introduction. One by one we meet the family members as they go about their daily activities through the house. The camera follows the second youngest daughter, Agnes, as she goes upstairs singing "Meet Me in St. Louis." She encounters Grandpa, who takes up the song; the camera follows him for a brief time. The passage of the characters from room to room involves several very close matches on action as they pass through doors, yielding a smooth flow of movement that presents the house as full of bustle and music. Grandpa hears voices singing the same song; he moves to a window, and a high-angle shot from over his shoulder shows the second oldest sister, Esther, stepping out of a buggy. Her arrival brings the sequence full circle back to the front of the house.

The house remains the main image of family unity throughout most of the film. Inside, the mise-en-scene is lush, colorful, cluttered with bric-a-brac. In the opening sequence, the family members return home one by one, until they all gather around the dinner table. We see few other locations than the house. Every section of the film begins with a similar candy-box title card and a move in toward the house. Aside from the expedition of the young people on the trolley to see the construction of the fair, the Christmas dance, and the final fairground sequence, the entire action of the film takes place in or near the Smith house. In the film's ideology the home appears to be a self-sufficient place; other social institutions seem peripheral.

This vision of the unified family within an idealized household places the women at the center of importance. (Recall here that in 1944 many women became the sole heads of households while their husbands were away.) Women are portrayed as the agents of stability; the action constantly returns to the kitchen, where the mother and maid Katie work calmly in the midst of small crises. The men, on the other hand, present the threat to the family's unity. Mr. Smith wants to take them to New York, thereby destroying their links with the past. (The grandfather, as representative of the older generation, sides with the women in their desire to stay in St. Louis.) Even Lon goes away to "the East," to college at Princeton. In general, the narrative's causality makes any departure from the home a threat—an example of how narrative generates an ideological stance.

Within the family there are minor disagreements, but the members cooperate among themselves. The two older sisters, Rose and Esther, help each other in their flirtations. Esther is in love with the boy next door, John Truitt; marriage to him poses no threat to the family unity. Several times in the film she sits and watches him or gazes across at his house, without having to leave her own home. First she and Rose go out onto the porch to try to attract his attention; then she sits in the window to sing, "The Boy Next Door." Finally, much later, she sits in a darkened bedroom upstairs and sees John pull his shade just after they have become engaged. The romantic involvements of the older girls and the pranks of the younger pair become part of the pleasant round of small occurrences that make up the everyday life of the Smith family (notice also their plain, ordinary name). The idea that girls might want to travel is not considered; similarly, education is presented as secondary to marriage.

Many stylistic devices build up a picture of a happy existence for the family. Their life is so perfect that any change becomes unthinkable; by the time Mr. Smith announces his decision to leave, it has been thoroughly motivated that we see the move to New York as a threat. The color contributes greatly to the lushness of the mise-en-scène. (See Plates 10 and 11.) The characters wear bright clothes. Esther is often in blue. She and Rose wear red and green, respectively, to the Christmas dance; this strengthens the association of the family unity with holidays and incidentally makes the sisters easy to pick out in the swirling crowd of pastel-clad dancers. (Note in the shot from the trolley scene that Esther is conspicuous because she is the only woman in black amidst the generally bright-colored dresses; a color need not be brighter than others to stand out.) The film was shot in Technicolor, which in the 1940s could render colors with extreme intensity and brightness. As a result, the hues of the costumes, the wallpaper of the house, Rose and Esther's red hair, and many other visual elements are conspicuous and attractive.

Meet Me in St. Louis is a musical, and music plays a large part in the family life. Songs come at moments of romance or at gatherings. Rose and Esther sing "Meet Me in St. Louis" in the parlor before dinner; the father is initially characterized as he returns from work and snaps at them: "For heaven's sake, stop that screeching!" At once we see him as both anti-music and anti-fair ("I wish everyone would meet at the fair and leave me alone"). Esther's other songs show that her romance with John Truitt is a safe and reasonable one; a woman does not have to leave home to find a husband—she can find him in her neighborhood ("The Boy Next Door") or by riding the trolley ("The Trolley Song"). Other songs accompany the two dances. Finally, Esther sings "Have Yourself a Merry Little Christmas" to Tootie, the youngest sister, after the Christmas dance. Here she tries to reassure Tootie that life in New York will be all right if the family can remain together.

But already there is a sense that such unity is impossible: "Someday soon we all will be together, if the Fates allow/Until then we'll have to muddle through somehow." Already we know that Esther has become engaged to John Truitt; she will have to decide between him and her family if they do move to New York. By this point, the story has reached an impasse; whichever way she decides, the old way of life will be destroyed. The narrative needs a resolution, and Tootie's hysterical crying in reaction to the song leads the father to reconsider his decision.

Tootie's destruction of the snow people after Esther's song is a striking image of the threat to family unity posed by the move to New York. As the winter season section had opened, the children were building the snow people (and a dog) in the yard. In effect they had created a parallel to their own family, with statues of different sexes and sizes. At first these snow people were part of the comic scene in which Esther and Katie persuade Lon and Rose to go to the Christmas dance together. But when Tootie becomes hysterical at the prospect of leaving St. Louis, she runs down in her nightgown to smash the snow people. The scene is almost shocking, since Tootie seems to be killing the doubles of her own family. This strong moment is necessary because it motivates the father's change of mind; he realizes that his desire to move to New York threatens the family's internal ties. This realization leads to his decision to stay in St. Louis.

Two other elements of the mise-en-scene are important because they present the comfortable life of the family; these motifs involve food and light. The Smiths live surrounded by food. In the initial scene the women are making ketchup, which is shortly served at the family dinner. After the scene in which Rose's boyfriend fails to propose to her by phone, the tensions are reconciled, and the maid serves large slices of corned beef.

The frequent holidays and parties involve more food. As Esther and her little sister Tootie dance during a gathering at the house, behind them the refreshments are visible, laid out on the table. In the Halloween scene the connection between the plentiful food and family unity becomes even more explicit. At first, the children gather around to eat cake and ice cream, but the father arrives home and makes his announcement about moving to New York. The family members depart without eating; only when they hear the mother and father singing at the piano do they gradually drift back to eat their cake. The words of the song, "Time may pass, but we'll be together," accompany their actions. The use of food as a motif associates the family's life in the house with plenty and with gatherings of the individuals into a group. At the fair in the last sequence, they decide to visit a restaurant together; the food motif returns at the moment of their reaffirmation of their life together in St. Louis. Again, the sumptuous Smith cuisine would have strong impact on a 1944 audience.

The house is also ablaze with light much of the time. As the family sits together at dinner, the low evening sun sends bright yellow light in through the transparent white curtains behind the father's chair. Later, one of the loveliest scenes involves Esther's request that John accompany her through the downstairs to help her turn out the lights. This action is primarily accomplished in one long take, with the camera moving at ceiling height from room to room with the characters. At each pause, the brightly lit chandelier is framed in the upper portion of the screen (Plate 10). As the rooms darken and the couple moves out to the hall, the camera moves down to a height level with their faces. The shot contains a remarkable shift of tone. It begins with Esther's comically contrived excuse ("I'm afraid of mice") to keep John with her and develops gradually toward a genuinely romantic tone.

The Halloween sequence takes place entirely at night and makes light a central motif; the camera initially moves in toward the house's brightly lit yellow windows. Tense, slightly eerie music makes the house seem an island of safety in the darkness. As Tootie and Agnes go out to join the other children in playing tricks, they are silhouetted blackly against the flames of the bonfire the group has gathered around. At first the fire seems threatening, contradicting the earlier associations of light with safety and unity, but this scene actually fits in with the previous uses of light. Tootie is excluded from the group activities because she is "too little." After she proves herself worthy, she is allowed to help feed the flames along with the others. Note particularly the long track-back as Tootie leaves the fire to play her trick; the fire remains in the background of the shot, appearing as a haven she has left behind. The first sequence of the Halloween section of the film becomes a sort of miniature working out of the entire narrative structure; Tootie's position as a part of the group is abandoned as she moves away from the fire, then triumphantly affirmed as she returns to it.

Similarly, light plays an important part in the resolution of the threat to the family's unity. Late on Christmas Eve, Esther finds Tootie awake; they look out the window at the snow people standing in the yard below. A strip of bright yellow light falls across the snow from a different window, suggesting the warmth and safety of the house they plan to leave. Tootie's hysterical crying, however, leads the father to reconsider his decision. As he sits thinking, he holds the match, with which he was about to light his cigar, unnoticed in his hand until it burns him; combined with the slow playing of the "Meet Me in St. Louis" theme over, the flame serves to emphasize his abstraction and his gradual change of mind. As he calls his family down to announce his decision not to move, he turns up all the lights; the dim, bleak halls full of packing boxes become again the scene of busy activity as the family gathers. The lamps' glass shades are red and green, identifying the house with the appropriate Christmas colors. The announcement of the decision coincides with the opening of the presents.

As night falls in the final fair sequence, the many lights of the buildings come on, reflected in lakes and canals. Here the film ends, with the family gazing in awe at the view; once more light signifies safety and family enjoyment. These lights also bring the other motifs of the film together. The father had originally wanted to move to New York as a provision for his family's future. In deciding to stay in St. Louis, he had told them, "New York hasn't got a copyright on opportunity. Why, St. Louis is headed for a boom that'll make your head swim. This is a great town." The fair confirms this; St. Louis allows the family to retain its unity and safety, and yet have all the benefits of progress. The film ends with the following comments by the characters:

Mother: There's never been anything like it in the whole world.

Rose: We don't have to come here in a train or stay in a hotel. It's right in our own home town.

Tootie: Grandpa, they'll never tear it down, will they?

Grandpa: Well, they'd better not.

Esther: I can't believe it. Right here where we live. Right here in St. Louis.

These lines do not *create* the film's ideology, which has been present in the narrative and stylistic devices throughout—the dialogue simply makes explicit what has been implicit all along.

The fair solves the problems of the future and family unity. The family is able to go to a *French* restaurant without going away from home. The ending also restores the father's position as at least the titular head of the family; only he is able to remember how to get to the restaurant and prepares to guide the group there.

The implication of all of these formal devices—motifs, songs, color, and the rest—for the 1944 audience is a reassuring one. If the women and others left at home can be strong and hold their families together against threats of disunity, harmony will eventually return. *Meet Me in St. Louis* espouses an essentially conservative ideology; its narrative form and use of film techniques uphold the virtues of small-town life, where sons and daughters marry and settle down near their parents. Eastern sophistication, equated with the big city and college degrees, is seen as a threat to this way of life. This view of home as a cornucopia in which all the things a person could possibly need are ready to hand is deeply ingrained in much of American thought. By setting forth this ideology at a time when so many people had been forced to leave home, *Meet Me in St. Louis* upholds dominant views instead of challenging them.

The Crime of M. Lange (Le Crime de M. Lange)

1936. Obéron, France. Directed by Jean Renoir. Script by Renoir and Jacques Prévert, adapted by Prévert from a story by Jean Castanier and Renoir. Photographed by Jean Bachelet. Edited by Marguerite Renoir. Music by Jean Wiener. With René Lefèvre, Jules Berry, Florelle, Nadia Sibirskaia, Sylvia Bataille, Henri Gyisol, Marcel Levèsque.

The Crime of M. Lange's narrative deals with the justification of the protagonist's murder of his boss; at the end, he goes free, and the film suggests that his crime was in fact a heroic action. Such a narrative would have been unthinkable in America at the time. In Hollywood a new code of self-censorship had been adopted in the early 1930s by the film industry; among many other regulations, this code stated that all criminal acts depicted in a narrative had to be punished by the end. A murderer had to die a just death.

But France had no such regulation to prevent Renoir from making *Lange*. The film was made during the brief, hopeful period of the mid-1930s, when the Popular Front government was in control. Big business was suffering, and the populist-oriented left wing gained political power; there was a short-lived belief that France's involvement in the impending world war could be averted. Renoir made *Lange* in support of the Popular Front and with the participation of many members of the French Communist Party (including his scriptwriter, Jacque Prévert).

The ideas in *Lange* were popular in France, but they were by no means uncontroversial. The Popular Front had many strong opponents and lasted only a short time. Renoir's film would not have simply reinforced beliefs that were held by most people; *Lange* would need to convince many French people about the benefits of socialist policies. In contrast, most Americans would probably take the ideas about the family in *Meet Me in St. Louis* for granted; that film would not need to persuade its audience. *The Crime of M. Lange* does; as a result, the filmmakers used new narrative and stylistic devices to force audiences to perceive in new ways.

The narrative concerns the firm of a villainous publisher, Batala, who exploits his workers and seduces women. After Batala flees his creditors and is reported dead in a train crash, the workers make the publishing house into a cooperative, which has a great success. Batala returns unexpectedly and threatens to take the firm back; Lange shoots him and flees with Valentine, his lover.

These events are told as flashbacks in a scene at a border inn as Valentine tries to justify Lange's crime to some workers who have recognized him and contemplate calling the police. The emphasis is on the judgment of Lange by his fellow workers rather than by an official jury. Valentine leads into her account by saying, "I know what it is to work for a living."

The justification for Lange's murder of Batala is that he has acted not for himself, but for others. The film does not make Lange into a strong hero who dominates the action, as is the case in most classical films. Rather, he is comic and weak. Surprisingly, in a story about exploitation and murder, the action is primarily fast-paced and funny. Lange appears first as a foolish fellow who spends his nights writing adventure stories about cowboys in Arizona, a place he has never visited. Batala easily tricks him out of the rights to his stories; Valentine taunts him as a dreamer and has to go to great lengths to seduce him, since he is too naive to see that she is in love with him. Even his name is strange; Valentine laughs at his first name, "Amédée." "Lange" is a pun on the French word *l'ange* ("the angel"). In general, he seems a strange character whose final action of killing Batala comes unexpectedly; Valentine and their friend Meunier have to take the initiative in arranging an escape for the dazed Lange.

Lange's lack of strong character traits makes him blend in with the rest of the characters rather than stand out as a markedly central protagonist. The film's emphasis thus falls on the workers in the publishing firm and in Valentine's laundry. These characters' concerns intersect partly because of their physical proximity; most of the film takes place in the setting of a building that surrounds a central courtyard. The second floor contains the publishing house, the first has Valentine's laundry, and other parts of the building contain apartments where several of the central characters live.

André Bazin has pointed out the importance of the concentric-circles pattern in the bricks that pave this building's central courtyard (on p. 45 of his important study, *Jean Renoir*, New York: Simon & Schuster, 1973). The film's style deemphasizes the separate spaces within the building, concentrating instead on the overlapping of different actions all taking place in relation to one another. The center of the courtyard is the core around which swirls a series of these actions; the life of the building comprises a small, bustling community, culminating in the formation of the cooperative upon Batala's "death."

Renoir is the cinema's master at creating a sense of unity among characters via his style. We have already seen this tendency in the camera work in *Grand Illusion*. In *Lange* the style frequently emphasizes actions that occur simultaneously in adjacent spaces. Conversations between several sets of people may occur in the same shot, with a long, fluid camera movement connecting these actions. This is particularly true in the crowded publishing office; Batala and other characters move rapidly through the crowd of employees at various points in the film, speaking to several in turn.

A particularly important camera movement comes at the moment just after the employees have formed their cooperative. Lange goes to take down a poster Batala has put up in the courtyard, covering the window of the concierge's son; the boy has broken his leg and languished in the sunless room behind the poster. As the shot begins, Lange and the concierge move into medium-long shot in a directly frontal view of the poster (Figs. 9.56 and 9.57). As Lange begins to pry it off, the camera leaves him to crane up and right to a second-floor window of the publishing house (Fig. 9.58); its workers lean out and watch enthusiastically (Fig. 9.59). The camera moves left to another window; here Meunier, Batala's heir, who has just agreed to the formation of the cooperative, joins the workers at the window (Fig. 9.60). Upon being told that Lange is the author of the "Arizona Jim" stories, Meunier leaves the window. The camera cranes back down to the initial medium-long framing of the poster (Fig. 9.61); shortly after the camera stops moving, Meunier dashes in from the left to greet Lange (Fig. 9.62); he has run down the offscreen stairs during the final phase of the craning movement.

This circular camera movement takes the emphasis off Lange as a single person removing the poster and places his action in the context of the group. They all participate in an action that will benefit the concierge's son, Charles. Even the cooperative itself becomes part of the

Figure 9.56

Figure 9.57

Figure 9.58

Figure 9.59

Figure 9.60

Figure 9.61

Figure 9.62

larger group, the inhabitants of the building. Although Charles, Valentine, and other characters are not employees of the publishing house, all form a community in support of one another.

The circular craning movement in this scene is part of a motif of sweeping camera movements that recur in other parts of the film. The news of Batala's "death" is heard on a radio at night while the camera cranes over the outside of the lighted apartments. Eventually it moves in on Lange's window, and we glimpse him in bed with Valentine, before a cut inside for a dialogue scene. But again the camera movement suggests the consequences of Batala's death for the community, rather than simply for Valentine and Lange.

Other instances of circular camera movement very much deserve analysis, but let us note the culminating ones during Lange's murder of Batala. Another crane shot over the outside of the building follows Lange as he moves through the publishing offices with Batala's gun; the camera moves down to meet him at the door. A cut closer in frames him in medium shot (Fig. 9.63) as he faces right and begins to move out of the frame toward Batala (Fig. 9.64). A conventional camera movement at this point would pan or track right to follow him as he moves across the courtyard. But instead, the camera pans and tracks left, *away* from

Figure 9.63

Figure 9.64

Figure 9.65

Figure 9.66

Figure 9.67

Figure 9.68

Lange; it moves over the lit windows of a room where the workers of the building are celebrating (Fig. 9.65), over the dark walls of the courtyard (Fig. 9.66), and finally moves in on Batala standing with Valentine. Now Lange comes into the frame from the left to shoot Batala (Figs. 9.67 and 9.68). Again, the movement of the individual character is deemphasized, and the camera presents an image of the courtyard and its inhabitants (whom we do not see, but can hear singing offscreen). The justification of Lange's crime comes from the fact that his actions are tied to the lives of all in the building.

Along with these camera movements, the film uses deep space, sometimes in combination with deep focus, to present several locales and actions at once. Many scenes take place near windows or doors, with other characters visible in the background. As Batala prepares to flee from Paris, he visits Valentine to try to get money from her. As he is leaving, they stand in medium shot before the door to the hallway. Batala opens it, then ducks back as we see the official who has just visited his office pass through the hall in the background. After he leaves, the old concierge comes down the stairs, and Batala takes up his suitcase and goes back to speak to the concierge as Valentine closes the door. Here there are three layers of action, with Valentine in soft focus close to the

Figure 9.69

Figure 9.70

camera, Batala in focus farther back, and the concierge in the hallway beyond (see Fig. 5.99).

Other notable instances of deep space occur when Charles is brought home with a broken leg in a taxi. The camera remains on the far side of the taxi, framing through the window as the family members and friends lean in to speak to Charles from the far side. Later, as Lange is taking the poster down, there is a shot from inside the bedroom (Fig. 9.69). The flat space of the room suddenly opens out as the poster disappears; the whole expanse of the courtyard is revealed in deep focus. The crowd fetches Charles's girlfriend, Estelle, from the laundry across the way (Fig. 9.70).

Along with the camera movement and deep space, Renoir employs sound overlap to create the spatial links within the little community. We have already mentioned the use of the radio in the announcement of Batala's "death" and the offscreen presence of the workers during the murder. In the first scene involving Batala, he speaks with a man on business; during their dialogue, the sound of a violin being practiced can be heard from another part of the building. Frequently in the scenes with groups of characters, snatches of dialogue overlap and blend together. Sound becomes an effective device for suggesting spaces beyond the ones visible and for reminding us of the interwoven lives of the characters within the building.

Ultimately *Lange*'s leftist ideological position is based on the fact that Lange's crime is justified. In order for it to be justified, his murder of Batala must be an action taken for the whole community's survival. That community among the various characters is created largely by the stylistic devices we have examined. Neither the ideology nor the style of *The Crime of M. Lange* is particularly radical, but the two do form an alternative to the classical norm we have examined in Hollywood films, and specifically in *Meet Me in St. Louis.* A more radical break with the classical norm takes place in the films of certain Marxist directors. One such director is Jean-Luc Godard, whose *La Chinoise* is the last film we shall analyze.

Figure 9.71

Figure 9.72

Figure 9.73

Figure 9.74

La Chinoise

1967. Coproduction of Productions de la Guéville, Simar Films, Anouchka Films, Athos Films, France. Directed by Jean-Luc Godard. Script by Godard. Photographed by Raoul Coutard. Edited by Agnès Guillemot, Delphine Desfons. Music by Karl-Heinz Stockhausen. With Anne Wiazemsky, Jean-Pierre Leaud, Michel Sémeniako, Lex de Bruijn, Juliet Berto, Omar Diop, Francis Jeanson.

Jean-Luc Godard's *La Chinoise* bases its formal system on a radical, Marxist political position. We have seen how an attempt to present a nondominant ideology implies that the filmmaker may seek new film forms; if the film is to set the audience thinking in new ways, it cannot be perceived with the viewers' old comfortable moviegoing habits.

Godard has been one of the most successful radical filmmakers, in that he has created an alternative approach to film form utterly opposed to the classical Hollywood style. This means that at first his films are difficult to watch and understand. We are used to unified narrative films, and little in our filmgoing experience prepares us to understand the formal system of a Godard film. This is the fault not of Godard, but of our own assumption that standardized habits constitute the *only* ways to make films. Thus an understanding and enjoyment of Godard's films often involves a willingness to learn and to build up new viewing skills. An understanding of some of Godard's formal strategies can aid in this learning process, and *La Chinoise* provides examples of many of these strategies.

Godard has gone perhaps as far as any filmmaker in creating a stylistic system in opposition to Hollywood's continuity system. We have seen how the continuity system allows a filmmaker to set up a coherent space and flow of time so that the spectator can follow the narrative smoothly. But like Eisenstein, Ozu, Resnais, Makavejev, and other directors we have studied, Godard does not give narrative a privileged place in the formal systems of his films. Many of his techniques make the narrative *less* easy to follow.

The cutting in *La Chinoise* freely juxtaposes events in different times and spaces. Godard does not restrict himself to showing those things he can physically place in front of his camera; if he cannot film something, he shows a photograph of it. When the young actor, Guillaume, mentions Brecht and Shakespeare, the next two shots are a photo of Brecht and a picture of Shakespeare. These in turn are followed by a close-up of a book page. (See Figs. 9.71 through 9.74.) In each of these shots the picture or page fills the frame and is filmed straight-on, so that we do not see the space in which the picture is situated.

Figure 9.75

Figure 9.76

Figure 9.77

Indeed, many of these pictures do not exist in the space of the narrative. In Chapter 6 we called such shots *nondiegetic inserts*, for like the nondiegetic voice of a narrator, they do not exist as a part of the narrative. Godard uses many such nondiegetic inserts; they allow him to cut freely from anything to anything, without obeying the rules of continuity. Not all of these inserts are as clearly related to the action as the Brecht and Shakespeare shots are. One character speaks about painting and reality; his voice continues over a series of shots consisting of modernist paintings and an early photograph. Here the images do not literally depict the subject matter of the speaker, but help illustrate the ideas in the talk.

During his interview, Henri tells an anecdote about the ancient Egyptians, who, he claims, thought that "their language was the language of the gods." As he says this, there are cuts to two close-ups of gold relics from the tomb of King Tutankhamen (Figs. 9.75, 9.76, and 9.77). This juxtaposition creates an intellectual montage series similar to the kind used by Eisenstein in portions of *October*; specifically, the two shots form a reference to the celebrated "God and Country" sequence of that film. In another scene one of the characters refers to Eisenstein as the main figure who has worked to create a socialist cinema. Much of God-

Figure 9.78

Figure 9.79

Figure 9.80

ard's use of discontinuous nondiegetic inserts attempts to continue and develop Eisenstein's montage style.

In general, Godard's uses of discontinuities differ from those of Resnais. Although we could analyze the ideology of *Last Year at Marienbad*, the film has no overt political goal; the discontinuities create ambiguities.

Within a scene as well, Godard systematically uses cutting of a type that would be considered incorrect by someone who adhered to views of classical continuity. During the "Mao" song, a series of cuts moves successively farther away from Véronique, seated writing at a table. Although the song continues over and Véronique seems to be engaged in a single action, the color of her sweater changes in every shot. In addition, the shelves behind her hold a greater number of Little Red Books in each shot, and the radio and Mao's picture change position. Note also that the object Véronique holds to her mouth in the first shot is a pen, whereas in the second it is a cigarette. (See Figs. 9.78, 9.79, and 9.80.) The interview with Yvonne takes place with her framed in medium close-up in front of a blue surface with two printed pages tacked on it. Yvonne's voice then continues over a shot of a separate action of Véronique painting a sign on a wall. We might take this to be another part of the apartment, seen in temporal continuity; yet the blue door with its tacked-up papers is visible in the background of the shot, and Yvonne is not in front of it. At other points, Godard intercuts shots of characters in one situation with shots of the same characters in another situation. Such discontinuities occur almost constantly.

The refusal to create clear spatial and temporal relationships between actions is one of Godard's strategies for creating a difficult, nonclassical narrative. He also avoids the repetition which we have seen is typical of Hollywood-style story telling. Far from being repetitious, Godard's films contain too much information for the spectator to absorb in one viewing. Sometimes there are multiple channels of information at work simultaneously. A character may speak while a printed page is on

Figure 9.81

the screen. Not only must the spectator read and listen to two different discourses, but usually the shot is not held long enough for him or her to read the entire passage. At some points, the frame of the image cuts off the edges of the printing, so that the words do not make sense even if one does read them (as with the inserted pages on theater during Guillaume's interview; see Figs. 9.71–9.73 above).

This density of material has several effects. First, it runs counter to the traditional treatment of films as artworks that are given only one casual viewing. Godard films encourage multiple viewings, since there is so much to absorb; hence he encourages analysis of his films. Second, by using such a dense weave of perceptual material, the film puts its emphasis on language and other media in general rather than on each specific bit of information. People are often frustrated because they cannot absorb every statement or image of Godard's films. What they fail to notice is that the film itself works to frustrate a complete, unified "reading" of its narrative and meanings.

Innocence Unprotected showed how one of the strongest characteristics of the classical Hollywood cinema is the tendency toward unity. Ideas of unity lead us to think that the film we are watching will be one kind of film throughout: If it is a documentary, it will not suddenly introduce a fictional story; if it is a historical drama set in the Renaissance, people will not drive up in an automobile. But like *Innocence Unprotected, La Chinoise* does not adhere to these classical assumptions about unity; it mixes its formal components freely in a "collage" fashion. At one moment it may seem to be a fictional narrative, with two characters, Guillaume and Véronique, in a dialogue. Then abruptly, Guillaume faces the camera in close-up and answers inaudible questions directed to him by someone offscreen. Now the film seems to be a documentary; yet we are not able to tell if this is still Guillaume the character speaking, or Jean-Pierre Leaud, the actor who plays Guillaume. He refers to the fact that he is being filmed, and there follow shots of the cameraman (Fig. 9.81) and sound recordist of *La Chinoise*. At other points in the film,

Figure 9.82

photos of historical personages are inserted; the film takes on an essay-like quality, with the characters arguing their various positions on subjects such as political art. In a later scene, Francis Jeanson, a French philosopher, plays himself and has a long discussion with the fictional character Véronique. Late in the film, one character even appears dressed in a costume of the French Revolutionary period—an unexplained inclusion of a convention from historical drama within this contemporary narrative (Fig. 9.82). Throughout *La Chinoise* the mixture of film styles forces the spectator to keep switching assumptions and modes of perception to accommodate the disunity. This frequent shift leads the viewer to be aware of the process of perception and the different habits of viewing we employ in watching films.

Another strategy of disunity that works against the creation of a smooth series of narrative events is the refusal to conceal the filmmaking process. Most films, especially those made in the continuity style, do not include devices that will remind the spectators that what they are watching is a construct. The camera is not shown; we do not hear the director speaking to the actors; if a mistake occurs, the scene will be shot again to allow the filmmakers to eliminate the problem. But *La Chinoise*, as we have seen, shows the cameraman (filming himself in a mirror) and the sound recordist. The person seated offscreen interviewing the characters is apparently Godard himself, but he speaks so softly as to be inaudible in most scenes. In the train conversation between Véronique and Francis Jeanson, the camera's reflection is visible in the window at several points.

Another formal device that reveals the filmmaking process is the appearance at intervals of a clapboard at the beginning of a scene. As we saw in Chapter 1, a clapboard is used at the beginning of each take to identify it for the editor; when assembling the shots, the editor usually cuts the clapboard portion of the shot out. Godard leaves a few in—just enough to be startling to the spectator. (Each clapboard shot also has a white X across one frame—the mark used to allow the synchronization of the sound of the clapboard to the image. See Fig. 9.83.)

Figure 9.83

These reminders of the filmmaking process, like the spatiotemporal discontinuities and the frequent insertion of titles between shots of action, help break up the spectator's concentration on the linear development of the narrative. In most classical narratives the spectator's attention is limited primarily to *following* the story. Hollywood's ideology of film as mere entertainment implies that the spectator need not question why the narrative is the way it is. The ideological implications of narratives are suppressed or glossed over, since entertainment films seem to have nothing to do with everyday reality. But as we saw with *Meet Me in St. Louis,* a musical comedy may have a very definite ideological stance. *La Chinoise* strives to acknowledge its own ideology; it invites the spectator to keep a distance on it—not to become absorbed in narrative, but to think about and critique this film *as* a film, and as a *political* film at that.

Although *La Chinoise* is a Marxist film, it does not simply support Marxism in a straightforward, propagandistic fashion. Instead, the film presents a critique of a group of young Maoist revolutionaries living and studying in a Paris apartment. The students are naive in their approach to terrorism and class struggle, but to varying degrees and with varying viewpoints on individual issues. These students make speeches on topics such as terrorism and the function of revolutionary art; these speeches too are often undercut. Godard invites us to analyze and evaluate the characters' actions and beliefs. The philosopher Jeanson, in his conversation with Véronique, argues that her terrorist techniques are useless without a broad base of support among the populace—which she and her group do not have. The group spends the whole summer studying language, the arts, and the media in preparation for their revolutionary activities. Yet the irony comes when Véronique is chosen to assassinate a visiting Soviet dignitary. She goes to his hotel, but makes a mistake when reading the room number upside down; her command of language has not enabled her to carry out this one basic task. So at the end the group breaks up, realizing to various degrees that their summer has been a small beginning rather than a major event in their careers. *La Chinoise* declares at its opening that it is "a film in the making"; at the end, a title declares: "End of a beginning."

The film, like the characters, offers a tentative exploration of some questions of ideology, but no final solution. *La Chinoise* marks a shift in Godard's career toward a more radical ideological practice; since then, he has continued to create Marxist films that challenge the conventions of the classical narrative cinema and the perceptual habits that it has fostered in us.

Inevitably people who do not admire Godard's films ask how he can make films that will create a Marxist revolution if only a small number of people see them. Godard's films cannot of themselves effect major changes in society. But for us to change our ways of thinking involves a difficult process. Learning to watch and understand Godard's films is similarly difficult. But if we do learn to change our viewing habits to the degree where we can analyze and enjoy a film like *La Chinoise*, we can hardly remain unchanged in our ways of thinking and perceiving in general. Films that can change our ways of looking at the world are few and therefore significant; *La Chinoise*, for many, is such a film.

Part Five
Film
History

CHAPTER 10
FILM FORM AND FILM HISTORY

Introduction ■

"Everything is not possible at all times." This aphorism of art historian Heinrich Wölfflin might serve as a slogan for the final chapter of this book. So far, our survey of film art has examined various formal and stylistic possibilities, and we have drawn our examples from the entire range of film history. But film forms and techniques do not exist in a realm outside human history; in particular historical circumstances, certain possibilities will be present while others are not. Griffith could not make films as Godard does, nor could Godard make films as Griffith did. This chapter asks: What are some ways in which film art has been treated in some particular historical contexts?

These contexts will be defined, first, by period and by nation. Although there are other equally good tools for tracing change, period and nation are standard ways of organizing historical problems. Second, in all of our cases but one (early cinema), we shall look for what are typically called *film movements*. A film movement consists of:

1. films that are produced within a particular period and/or nation and that share significant traits of style and form; and

2. filmmakers who operate within a common production structure and who share certain assumptions about filmmaking.

There are other ways of defining a historical context (e.g., biographical study, genre study), but the category of *movement* corresponds most closely to the emphasis of this book. The concepts of formal and stylistic systems permit us to liken films within a movement and to contrast them with films of other movements. So what follows seeks to identify and distinguish film movements by period and nation. Finally, we shall be concerned with Hollywood and selected alternatives; we shall trace the development of the commercial narrative cinema while contrasting to it other approaches to style and form.

Since a film movement consists of not only films, but also the activities of specific filmmakers, we must go beyond noting stylistic and formal qualities. For each period and nation, we shall also sketch relevant factors that impinge on the cinema. These factors include the state of the film industry, artistic theories held by the filmmakers themselves, pertinent technological features, and elements of the socioeconomic context of the period. Such factors necessarily help explain how a particular movement began, what shaped its development, and what affected its decline. However brief, such material will also provide a context for particular films we have already discussed; for example, the following section on early cinema situates Lumière and Méliès in the work of their period.

Needless to say, what follows is drastically incomplete. The writing of serious film history is just beginning, and we must often rely on secondary sources that will eventually be superseded. This chapter reflects only current states of knowledge; there are doubtless important films, filmmakers, and movements that await discovery. (A list of further readings may be found at the end of this chapter.) Moreover, there are many unfortunate omissions. Important filmmakers who do not relate to a movement (e.g., Tati, Bresson, Kurosawa) are absent. So too are certain important film movements (e.g., French populist cinema of the 1930s, current "structuralist" and underground cinema, and the materialist cinema of Godard, Straub, and Oshima). What follows simply seeks to show how the categories of film form and style could be applied to a few typical and well-known historical movements.

Early Cinema (1893–1903) ∎

Because moving images depend on individual still pictures' appearing in rapid succession, the invention of films was not possible until certain technological developments had occurred. The invention of photography in 1820 began a series of discoveries that gradually made possible the creation of an illusion of movement. Early photographs required lengthy exposures (initially hours, later minutes) for a single image; this made photographed motion pictures, which need 12 or more frames per second, impossible. Faster exposures, of about 1/25 second, became possible by the 1870s, but only on glass plates. Glass plates were not usable as a base for motion pictures, since there was no practical way to move them through a camera or projector. In 1879 Eadweard Muybridge, an American photographer, did make a series of photographs of a running horse by using a series of cameras with glass plate film and a fast exposure, but he was interested in freezing phases of an action, not recreating the movement by projecting the images in succession.

In 1882 another scientist interested in analyzing animal movement, the Frenchman Étienne-Jules Marey, invented a camera that recorded 12 separate images on the edge of a revolving disc of film. This was a step closer to the motion picture camera. Later, in 1888, Marey built the first camera to use a long strip of flexible film, this time on paper. Again, the purpose was only to break down movement into a series of stills; the movements photographed lasted a second or less.

In 1889 Kodak introduced a flexible film stock, celluloid (one type of which still forms the base of film stock today). With this base, and camera mechanisms to draw the film past the lens and expose it to light, the creation of lengthy series of frames became possible.

Projectors had existed for many years and had been used to show slides and other shadow entertainments. These "magic lanterns" were modified by the addition of shutters, cranks, and other devices to become early motion picture projectors.

One final device was needed if films were to be projected. Since the film stops briefly while the light shines through each individual frame, there had to be a mechanism to create an *intermittent* motion of the film. Marey used a Maltese cross gear on his 1888 camera, and this became a standard part of early cameras and projectors.

The combination of a flexible, transparent film base, fast exposure time, a mechanism to pull the film through the camera, an intermittent device to stop the film, and a shutter to block off light was achieved by the early 1890s. After several years, inventors working independently in several countries had developed several different film cameras and devices for showing films. The two most important firms were Edison in America and Lumière in France.

Thomas A. Edison's assistant, W. K. L. Dickson, developed a camera by 1893 that made short 35-mm films. Interested in exploiting these films as a novelty, Edison hoped to combine them with his phonograph to show sound movies. He had Dickson develop a peep-show machine to show these films to individual viewers, the *kinetoscope* (Fig. 10.1).

Since Edison believed that movies were a passing fad, he did not develop a system to project films onto a screen. This was left to the Lumière brothers, Louis and Auguste. They invented their own camera independently; it also served as a developing machine and projector (see Fig. 10.2). On December 28, 1895, the Lumière brothers held the first public showing of motion pictures projected on a screen, at the Grand Café in Paris. Thus, although the Lumières did not invent cinema, they largely helped to determine the specific form the new medium was to take. (Edison himself was soon to abandon kinetoscopes and form his own production company to make films for theaters.)

The first films were extremely simple in form and style. They usually consisted of a single shot with a fixed frame. A single action would occur, usually at long-shot distance. In the first film studio, Edison's

Figure 10.1

Figure 10.2

Figure 10.3

Figure 10.4

Black Maria (Fig. 10.3), vaudeville entertainers, famous sports figures, and celebrities (e.g., Annie Oakley) performed for the camera. The Lumières, on the other hand, took their cameras out to parks, gardens, beaches, and other public places to film everyday activities or news events, as in their *Workers Leaving the Factory*, filmed on the street outside their own factory (see Fig. 10.4).

Although most films until 1908 were such simple documentaries, narrative form quickly entered the cinema. Edison staged comic scenes, like one copyrighted 1893 in which a drunken man struggles briefly with a policeman. The Lumières made a popular success with *Arroseur Arrosé* (*The Waterer Watered*, 1895), also a comic scene, in which a boy tricks a gardener into squirting himself with a hose (see Fig. 4.6).

After the initial success of the new medium, filmmakers had to find more complex or interesting formal properties to keep the public's interest. The Lumières sent camera operators all over the world to show films and to photograph important events and exotic locales. But after making a huge number of films in their first few years, the Lumières diminished their output, and they ceased filmmaking altogether in 1905.

In 1896 Georges Méliès purchased a projector from the British inventor Robert William Paul and soon modified it for use as a camera as well. Méliès' first films resembled the Lumières' shots of everyday activities. But as we have seen, Méliès was also a magician, and he discovered the possibilities of simple special effects. In 1897 Méliès built his own studio; unlike Edison's Black Maria, Méliès's studio was fashioned like a greenhouse, allowing the filming to utilize sunlight (Fig. 10.5).

Méliès also began to build elaborate settings to create fantasy worlds within which his magical transformations could occur. From the simple filming of a magician performing a trick or two in a traditional stage setting, Méliès progressed to longer narratives with a series of "tableaux" (each consisting of one shot). He adapted old stories (e.g., *Cinderella*, 1899) or wrote his own. We have already seen how Méliès thereby became the first master of mise-en-scene technique (see Figs. 4.1–4.5).

Figure 10.5

Méliès's films were extremely popular and were widely imitated. During this early period, films circulated freely from country to country. Pioneers in Germany, Russia, and other countries all obtained or built cameras similar to those of Lumière and soon were making their own films of everyday scenes or fantasy transformations. Once the Lumières and Georges Méliès had blazed the trail, the early cinema became a worldwide phenomenon. Later World War I was to block the free flow of films from country to country, and Hollywood was to emerge as the dominant industrial force in world film production. These factors contribute to the creation of distinct differences in the formal traits of individual national cinemas.

The Development of the Classical Hollywood Cinema (1903–1927) ■

Edison's determination to exploit the money-making potential of his company's invention led him to try to force competing filmmakers out of business by bringing patents-violation suits against them. Several other companies, notably Biograph, managed to survive by inventing cameras that differed from Edison's patents. In 1908 Edison brought these other companies under his control by forming the Motion Picture Patents Company (MPPC), a group of ten firms, based primarily in New York and New Jersey; Edison and Biograph were the only stockholders and licensed other members to make, distribute, and exhibit films.

The MPPC never succeeded in eliminating its competition. Numerous independent companies were formed throughout this period. Biograph's most important director from 1908 on, D. W. Griffith, formed his own company in 1913, as did other filmmakers. One independent distributor, William Fox, brought suit against the MPPC in 1913; in 1915 it was declared a monopoly.

After about 1910, film companies began to move out to California (although some went to Chicago and other cities); eventually Hollywood, a small town on the outskirts of Los Angeles, became the site of much of the film production. Some historians claim that the independent companies moved west to avoid the harrassment of the MPPC, but a few MPPC companies also made the move. Some advantages of Hollywood were the climate, which permitted shooting year-round, and the great variety of terrains—mountains, ocean, desert, city—available for location shooting.

The demand for films was so great that no one studio could meet it. This was one of the factors that had led Edison to accept the existence of a group of other companies (although he tried to control them as much as possible through his licensing procedure). Before 1920, the American industry assumed the structure which would continue for years: a number of individual studios with individual artists under contract. In Hollywood the studios developed a "factory" system, with each production under the control of the producer, who usually did not work on the actual making of the films. Even an independent director like Buster Keaton, with his own studio, had a business manager and distributed his films through a larger company, Metro.

Gradually through the 1920s the smaller studios merged to form the large firms which still exist today. Famous Players joined with Jesse Lasky's company, which in turn merged with Paramount. By the late 1920s, most of the major companies existed—MGM (a merger of Metro, Goldwyn, and Mayer), 20th Century-Fox (another merger), Universal, Paramount. Though in competition with one another, these studios tended to cooperate to a degree, realizing that no one studio could supply the market.

Within this system of factorylike studios, and for reasons that are not yet clear, the American cinema became definitively oriented toward narrative form. One of Edison's directors, Edwin S. Porter, made some of the first films to utilize principles of narrative continuity and development (as opposed to the series of tableaux or the filmed vaudeville-style skits which made up early, preclassical narrative films). The first of these was *The Life of an American Fireman* (1903), which showed the race of firefighters to rescue a mother and child from a burning house. Although this film utilized several important classical narrative elements (a fireman's premonition of the disaster, a series of shots of the horse-drawn engine racing to the house), it still had not worked out the logic of temporal relations in cutting. Thus we see the rescue of the mother and child twice, from both inside and outside the house; Porter had not realized the possibility of intercutting the two locales within the action or matching on action to convey narrative information to the audience.

Later in 1903, Porter made *The Great Train Robbery*, an early prototype for the classical American film. Here the action develops with a clear linearity of time, space, and logic. We follow each stage of the robbery, the escape, and the final defeat of the robbers. In 1905 Porter also worked with a simple parallel narrative in *The Kleptomaniac*, contrasting the fates of a rich woman and a starving woman who both are caught stealing.

At about the same time, British filmmakers in Brighton were working along similar lines. The most famous film of this group was Cecil Hepworth's 1905 film, *Rescued By Rover*, which treated a kidnapping in a linear fashion similar to that of *The Great Train Robbery*. After the kidnapping, we see each stage of Rover's journey to fetch the child's father, and then of Rover and the father retracing the route to the kidnapper's lair.

In 1908 D. W. Griffith began his directing career. In the next five years, he was to make hundreds of one- and two-reelers (running around 10 and 20 minutes, respectively). These films created relatively complex narratives in short spans. Griffith probably was not the initiator of all the devices with which he has been credited, but he did give many techniques strong narrative motivation. For example, Griffith sometimes used fades and irises to create smooth transitions between scenes. He was also among the first to develop an analytical cutting style, inserting closer shots within scenes. (Many films up to this point had used one shot per scene.) Again, although other filmmakers had used last-minute rescues, Griffith is famous for having developed parallel cutting between the rescuers and victims. By the time he made *The Birth of a Nation* (1915) and *Intolerance* (1916), Griffith could cut between several different locales for lengthy portions of his films. His impressive developments of editing patterns were to exert considerable influence on the Soviet montage style of the 1920s.

The refinement of narratively motivated cutting occurs in the work of a number of important filmmakers of the period. One of these was Thomas Ince, a producer and director responsible for many films between 1910 and the end of World War I. He devised a "unit system," whereby a single producer could oversee the making of numerous films. He also emphasized tight narratives, with no digressions or loose ends. *Civilization* (1915) and *The Italian* (1915) are good examples of films personally directed by Ince; he also supervised the popular Westerns of William S. Hart.

Another prolific filmmaker of this period (and later periods as well) was Cecil B. DeMille. Not yet engaged in the creation of historical epics,

Figure 10.6

Figure 10.7

Figure 10.8

Figure 10.9

DeMille made a series of short-feature-length dramas and comedies. His *The Cheat* (1915) reflects important changes occurring in the studio style between about 1914 and 1917. During that period, the glass-roofed studios of the earlier period began to give way to studios dependent on artificial lighting rather than mixed daylight and electric lighting. *The Cheat* used spectacular effects of *chiaroscuro*, using only one or two bright sources of light and eliminating fill light. DeMille justified this effect to his nervous producers as "Rembrandt" lighting. This so-called Rembrandt, or "north," lighting was to become part of the classical repertoire of lighting techniques. *The Cheat* also greatly impressed the French Impressionist filmmakers, who occasionally used similar stark lighting effects.

The Cheat also uses a linear pattern of narrative. The first scene (Fig. 10.6) introduces the stark lighting, but also quickly establishes the Burmese businessman as a ruthless collector of objects; we see him burning his brand onto a small statue. This initial action motivates a later scene in which the businessman brands the heroine, who has fallen into his power by borrowing money from him (Fig. 10.7). *The Cheat* was evidence of the growing formal sophistication of the Hollywood film.

The period 1914–1917 saw the development of the basic continuity principles. No extensive and systematic survey has yet determined when these rules became standard practice. The match on action was definitely in use by 1916; it appears in such Douglas Fairbanks films as *The Mystery of the Leaping Fish* (1916) and *Wild and Woolly* (1917). Shot/reverse shot was not used extensively at this point, but isolated instances occur in such films as *The Cheat*, *The Narrow Trail* (a William S. Hart Western of 1917), and Griffith's *A Romance of Happy Valley* (1918).

By the 1920s, the continuity system had become a standardized style that directors in the Hollywood studios used almost automatically to create coherent spatial and temporal relations within narratives. A match on action could provide a cut to a closer view in a scene, as in *The Three Musketeers*, with Fairbanks (Figs. 10.8 and 10.9; Fred Niblo, 1921). A

Figure 10.10

Figure 10.11

Figure 10.12

Figure 10.13

Figure 10.14

three-way conversation around a table would not be handled in a single frontal shot, as would have been the case a dozen years earlier; note the clear spatial relations in Figs. 10.10 through 10.14, shots from *Are Parents People?* (Malcolm St. Clair, 1925). Screen direction was usually respected, as in these cases. When an awkward match might have resulted from the joining of two shots, the filmmakers could cover it by inserting a dialogue title.

Keaton's *Our Hospitality* (1923), which we examined in Chapter 4, provides another example of a classical narrative. Keaton's mastery of classical form and style are evident in the carefully motivated recurrences of the various narrative elements and in the straightforward causal development from the death of Willie McKay's father in the feud to Willie's final resolution of the feud.

By the end of the silent period, in the late 1920s, the classical Hollywood cinema had developed into a sophisticated movement; the Hollywood "product" was, however, remarkably standardized. All of the major studios used the same production system, with a similar division of labor at each. Independent production became difficult. Keaton gave up his small studio in 1928 to go to MGM under contract; there his career declined, due partly to the incompatibility of his old working methods with the rigid production patterns of the huge studio. Griffith, Mary Pickford, Fairbanks, and Charles Chaplin were better off; forming a distributing corporation of their own, United Artists, in 1919, they were able to continue independent production at small companies under their umbrella corporation.

There were alternative kinds of films being made during these years—most of them in other countries. After examining these alternative movements, we shall return to a brief examination of the classical Hollywood cinema after the coming of sound.

German Expressionism (1919–1924) ∎

At the start of World War I, the output of the German film industry was relatively insignificant, both within the country and internationally. Germany's 2000 movie theaters were playing mostly French, American, and Danish films. Although America and France banned German films from their screens immediately, Germany was not even in a solid enough position to ban French and American films—the theaters would have had little to show.

In order to combat imported competition, as well as to create its own propaganda films, the German government began to support the film industry. Production increased rapidly; from a dozen small companies in 1911, the number grew to 131 by 1918. But government policy encouraged these companies to band together into cartels.

The war was unpopular with many in Germany, and rebellious tendencies increased after the success of the Russian Revolution in 1917. Widespread strikes and antiwar petitions were organized during the winter of 1916–1917. In order to promote prowar films, the Deutsches Bank and large industrial concerns formed UFA in 1917; backed by the essentially conservative interests of major industrialists, UFA was a move toward a control of not only the German market, but the postwar international market as well.

With this huge financial backing, UFA was able to gather superb technicians and build the best-equipped studios in Europe. These studios later attracted even foreign filmmakers (including the young Alfred Hitchcock). This led to coproductions in the 1920s between Germany and other countries, which helped break down the stigma against the German industry.

In late 1918, with the end of the war, the need for overt militarist propaganda disappeared, and the German film industry concentrated on three types of films. One was the internationally popular genre that had appeared in the early teens, the adventure serial, featuring spy rings, clever detectives, or exotic settings. Second was a brief sex exploitation cycle, which dealt "educationally" with such topics as homosexuality and prostitution. Finally, UFA set out to copy the popular Italian historical epics of the prewar period.

This last type of film proved financially successful for UFA. In spite of continued bans and prejudice against German films in America and France, UFA finally was able to break into the international market. In September 1919 Ernst Lubitsch's *Madame DuBarry*, an epic of the French Revolution, inaugurated the magnificent UFA Palatz theater in Berlin. This film reopened the world film market to Germany. Released as *Passion* in the United States, this film was extremely popular; it was less well received in France, but still prepared the way for future film showings there. Other Lubitsch historical films were soon exported, and in 1923 he became the first German director to be hired by Hollywood.

Some small companies remained independent briefly; among these was Erich Pommer's Decla-Bioscop. In 1919 Pommer decided to take a chance on an unconventional script offered him by Carl Mayer and Hans Janowitz; these young writers wanted the film to be made in an unusually stylized way. Pommer assigned the film to three designers—Hermann Warm, Walter Reimann, and Walter Rohrig; these three suggested that the film be done in an *Expressionist* style. As an avant-garde movement, Expressionism had first been important in painting (starting about 1908) and had been quickly taken up in theater, then in literature, and in architecture. Now Pommer consented to try it in the cinema, believing that this might be a selling point in the international market.

He was proved right when the inexpensively made film, *The Cabinet of Dr. Caligari*, created a sensation in Ameria, France, and other countries. Because of its success, imitations in Expressionist style soon followed; the film started a stylistic movement in cinema that lasted several years.

The success of *Caligari* and other Expressionist films meant that Germany's avant-garde remained largely within the industry. A few experimental filmmakers made abstract films, like Viking Eggeling's *Diagonal-symphonie* (1923), or Dada films influenced by the international art movement, like Hans Richter's *Ghosts Before Breakfast* (1928). Big firms such as UFA (which absorbed Decla-Bioscop in 1920) as well as smaller companies invested in Expressionist films because these films could compete with those of America. Indeed, by the mid-1920s, the German films were widely looked on as among the best in the world.

The first film of the movement, *Caligari*, is also one of the most typical examples. One of its designers, Warm, claimed: "Films must be drawings brought to life." *Caligari*, with its extreme stylization, was indeed like a moving expressionist painting. In contrast to French

Figure 10.15

Figure 10.16

Impressionism, which bases its style primarily on cinematography and editing, German Expressionism depends heavily on mise-en-scene. Shapes are distorted and exaggerated unrealistically for expressive purposes. Actors often wear heavy makeup and move in jerky or slow, sinuous patterns. Most important, all of the elements of the mise-en-scene interact graphically to create an overall composition; characters do not simply exist within a setting, but rather form a visual element that merges with that setting. We have already seen an example of this in Fig. 4.32; the character Cesare collapses in a stylized forest, with his body and outstretched arms echoing the shapes of the trees' trunks and branches.

In *Caligari* the Expressionist stylization functions to convey the distorted viewpoint of a madman; we see the world as the hero does. This narrative function of the settings becomes explicit at one point, as the hero enters an asylum in his pursuit of Caligari. As he pauses to look around, he stands at the center of a pattern of radiating black and white lines that go across the floor and up the walls (Fig. 10.15); the world of the film is literally a projection of the hero's vision.

Later, as Expressionism became an accepted style, filmmakers did not motivate Expressionist style as the narrative point of view of mad people. Instead, Expressionism functioned to create stylized situations for horror and fantasy stories (as with *Waxworks*, 1924, and *Nosferatu*, 1922) or historical epics (as with *The Nibelungen*, 1924). Some Expressionism became less graphic and took on a more plastic, architectural style (see Fig. 10.16, from *Siegfried*, Part I of *The Nibelungen*). Both graphic and plastic varieties of Expressionism depended greatly on their designers. In the German studios a film's designer received a relatively high salary, third only after the director and the individual stars; a famous designer might even receive more money than the star of the film, a practice very different from that of other countries.

A combination of circumstances caused the disappearance of the movement. The rampant inflation of the early 1920s drove many of the small firms out of business, although UFA and other major firms were little affected at first. In 1924 the Dawes plan led American firms to begin investing in the German film industry. American money provided welcome support, but also allowed Hollywood companies to lure the best of the German filmmakers to America. Producers (e.g., Pommer), directors (e.g., F. W. Murnau and E. A. Dupont), actors (e.g., Emil Jannings and Conrad Veidt), and camerapersons (e.g., Karl Freund) left the German industry. Some, such as Fritz Lang, stayed on, only to be driven into exile at the beginning of the Nazi regime.

In addition to the emigration of personnel and the eventual Nazi control of the industry, the Germans also faced stiffer competition from the Americans after 1924. In a desire to imitate the American product, many filmmakers diluted the unique qualities of the Expressionist style. As a result, Expressionism as a movement died out in about 1924. But as Georges Sadoul has pointed out, an Expressionist tendency lingered on in many of the German films of the late 1920s and even into such 1930s films as Lang's *M* (1930) and *Testament of Dr. Mabuse* (1932). And because so many of the German filmmakers came to America, Hollywood films also displayed Expressionist tendencies; horror films such as *Son of Frankenstein* (1939) and *films noirs* have strong expressionist touches in their settings and lighting. Although the German movement lasted only five years, expressionism has never entirely died out as a film style.

French Impressionism and Surrealism (1917–1930) ■

In France during the silent era, several film movements posed major alternatives to classical Hollywood narrative form. Some of these alternatives—abstract cinema, Dada filmmaking—are not specifically French and so will be discussed shortly as part of an international avant-garde. But two alternatives to the American mode remained quite localized. The first, Impressionism, was an avant-garde style that nonetheless operated within the film industry; Impressionist filmmakers were independent, yet able to utilize studio facilities. The second alternative movement, Surrealism, lay utterly outside the film industry; allied with the Surrealist movement in other arts, these filmmakers relied on their own means and private patronage. France in the 1920s thus offers a striking instance of how different film movements can coexist at the same time and place.

Impressionism

World War I struck a serious blow to the French film industry, as personnel were conscripted, much export was halted, and film factories were shifted to wartime duties. Yet since the two major firms, Pathé Brothers and Léon Gaumont, also controlled circuits of theaters, there was a need to fill vacant screens, and so in 1915 American films began to flood into France. Represented by Pearl White, Douglas Fairbanks, Chaplin and Ince films, DeMille's *The Cheat*, and William S. Hart (affectionately named "Rio Jim" by the French), the Hollywood cinema soon dominated the market. After the war, French filmmaking never recovered: In the 1920s, French audiences saw eight times more Hollywood footage than domestic footage. The film industry tried in several ways to recapture the market—through imitation of Hollywood production methods and genres—but the most significant move was the firms' encouragement of younger French directors: Abel Gance, Louis Delluc, Germaine Dulac, Marcel L'Herbier, and Jean Epstein.

These directors differed from their predecessors. The previous generation had regarded filmmaking as a commercial craft. More theoretical and ambitious, the younger filmmakers wrote essays proclaiming cinema to be an art comparable to poetry, painting, and (especially) music. Cinema should, they said, be purely itself and owe nothing to the theater or literature. (Here the Impressionists drew heavily on Symbolist poetic theory to define an art of suggestion and fleeting sensation.) Impressed by the verve and energy of the American cinema, the young theorists compared Chaplin to Nijinsky and the films of "Rio Jim" to *The Song of Roland*. Cinema should, above all, be (like music) an occasion for the artist to express feelings. Gance, Delluc, Dulac, L'Herbier, and Epstein would seek to put this aesthetic into practice as filmmakers.

Between 1917 and 1928, in a series of extraordinary films, the younger directors experimented with cinema in ways that posed an alternative to the dominant Hollywood formal principles. Given the centrality of emotion in their aesthetic, it is no wonder that the intimate psychological narrative dominated their filmmaking practice. The interactions of a few characters—often a love triangle (as in Delluc's *L'Inondation*, Epstein's *Coeur Fidèle* and *La Belle Nivernaise*, and Dulac's *The Smiling Mme. Beudet*)—would serve as the basis for the filmmakers' exploration of fleeting moods and shifting sensations.

As in the Hollywood cinema, psychological causes were paramount, but the school gained the name "Impressionist" because of its interest in making narrative form represent as fully as possible the play of a character's consciousness. The interest falls not on external physical behavior but on *inner* action. To a degree unprecedented in international filmmaking, Impressionist films manipulate plot time and subjectivity. To depict memories, flashbacks are common; sometimes the bulk of a film will be a flashback. Even more striking is the films' insistence on registering characters' dreams, fantasies, and mental states. Dulac's *The Smiling Mme. Beudet* consists almost entirely of the main character's fantasy life, her imaginary escape from a dull marriage. Despite its epic length (over four hours), Gance's *La Roue* rests essentially on the erotic relations among only four people, and the director seeks to trace every development of each character's feelings. On the whole, then, Impressionism's emphasis on personal emotion gives the films' narratives an intensely psychological focus.

The "Impressionist" movement earned its name as well for its use of film style. The filmmakers experimented with ways of rendering mental states by new uses of cinematography and editing. In Impressionist films, irises, masks, and superimpositions function as traces of characters'

Figure 10.17

thoughts and feelings. In *Coeur Fidèle,* a young man envisions the face of his lover over the foul jetsam of a waterfront (Fig. 10.17). In *La Roue* the image of Norma is superimposed over the smoke from a locomotive. To intensify the subjectivity, the Impressionists' cinematography and editing present characters' perceptual experience, their optical "impressions." These films use point-of-view cutting—showing a shot of a character looking at something, then a shot of that thing, from an angle and distance replicating the character's vantage point. When a character in an Impressionist film gets drunk or ill or dizzy, the filmmaker renders that experience through out-of-focus or filtered shots or vertiginous camera movements. Finally, the Impressionists began experimenting with pronounced rhythmic editing to suggest the pace of an experience as a character "feels" it, moment by moment. During scenes of violence or emotional turmoil, the rhythm accelerates—the shots get shorter and shorter, building to a dynamic climax, sometimes with shots only a few frames long. In *La Roue* a train crash is presented in accelerating shots ranging from thirteen frames down to two. In *Coeur Fidèle* lovers at a fair ride in whirling swings, and Epstein presents their giddiness in a series of shots four frames, then two frames long. Several Impressionist films use a dance to motivate a markedly accelerated cutting rhythm. (Indeed, their comparison of cinema to music encouraged the Impressionists to explore rhythmic editing.) In such ways subjective shooting and editing patterns function within Impressionist films to reinforce the narrative treatment of psychological states.

Impressionist film form created certain demands on film technology. Gance, the boldest innovator in this respect, used his epic *Napoléon* as a chance to try new lenses (even a 275-mm telephoto), multiple frame images (called "Polyvision"), and widescreen ratio (the celebrated triptychs; see Fig. 5.21). The most influential Impressionist technological innovation was the development of new means of frame mobility. If the camera was to represent a character's eyes, it should be able to move with the ease of a person. Impressionists strapped their cameras to cars, carousels, and locomotive cowcatchers. For Gance's *Napoléon*, the camera manufacturer Debrie perfected a handheld model that let the operator move on roller skates. Gance put the machine on wheels, cables, pendulums, and bobsleds. In *L'Argent* L'Herbier had his camera gliding through huge rooms and even swooping along ceilings.

Such formal, stylistic, and technological innovations had given French filmmakers the hope that their films could win the popularity granted to Hollywood's product. During the 1920s the Impressionists had in fact operated somewhat independently; they had formed their own small production companies and had leased studio facilities from Pathé and Gaumont in exchange for distribution rights. But by 1929, audiences had not taken to Impressionism; its experimentation was attuned to elite tastes. Moreover, although production costs were rising, the Impressionists (especially Gance and L'Herbier) became even more prodigal; as a result, filmmakers' companies either went out of business or were absorbed by the big firms. The two behemoth productions of the decade, *Napoléon* and *L'Argent*, failed and were recut by the producers. With the arrival of the sound film, the French industry tightened its belt and had no money to risk on experiments. Thus Impressionism as a distinct movement may be said to have ceased by 1928. But the influences of Impressionist form—the psychological narrative, subjective camera work and editing—continued to operate in the work of Alfred Hitchcock and Maya Deren, in Hollywood "montage sequences," and in certain American genres and styles (the horror film, *film noir*).

Surrealism

Whereas the French Impressionist filmmakers worked within the commercial film industry, the Surrealist filmmakers relied on private patronage and screened their work in small artists' gatherings. Such isolation is hardly surprising, since Surrealist cinema was a more radical movement, producing films that perplexed and shocked most audiences.

Surrealist cinema was directly linked to Surrealism in literature and painting. According to its spokesperson, André Breton, "surrealism" was "based on the belief in the superior reality of certain forms of association, heretofore neglected, in the omnipotence of dreams, in the undirected play of thought." Influenced by Freudian psychology, Surrealist art sought to register the hidden currents of the unconscious, "in the absence of any control exercised by reason, and beyond any aesthetic and moral preoccupation." "Automatic" writing and painting, the search for bizarre or evocative imagery, the deliberate avoidance of rationally explicable form or style—these became features of Surrealism as it developed in the period 1924–1929. From the start, the Surrealists were attracted to the cinema, especially admiring films that presented untamed desire or the fantastic and marvelous (e.g., slapstick comedies, *Nosferatu*). In due time, painters such as Man Ray and Salvador Dali and writers such as Antonin Artaud began dabbling in cinema, while young Luis Buñuel, drawn to Surrealism, became its most famous filmmaker.

Surrealist cinema is overtly antinarrative, attacking causality itself. If rationality is to be fought, causal connections among events must be dissolved. *The Seashell and the Clergyman* (1928; scripted by Artaud, filmed by the Impressionist Germaine Dulac) begins with the protagonist pouring liquids from flasks and then systematically breaking each one. In Dali-Buñuel's *An Andalusian Dog* (1928) the hero drags a piano, stuffed with dead donkeys, across a parlor. In Buñuel's *L'Age d'Or* (1930) a woman obsessively begins sucking the toes of a statue. Like *Last Year at Marienbad*, many Surrealist films tease us to find a narrative logic that is simply absent. Causality is as evasive as in a dream. Instead, we find events juxtaposed for their disturbing value: The hero gratuitously shoots a child *(L'Age d'Or)*, a woman closes her eyes only to reveal eyes painted on her eyelids (Ray's *Emak Bakia*, 1927), and—most famous of all—a man strops a razor and deliberately slits the eyeball of an unprotesting woman (*An Andalusian Dog*, Fig. 10.18). An Impressionist film would motivate such events as a character's dreams or hallucinations, but in these films character psychology is all but nonexistent. Sexual desire and ecstasy, violence, blasphemy, and bizarre humor furnish events that Surrealist film form combines with a disregard for conventional narrative principles. The hope was that the free form of the film would arouse the deepest impulses of the viewer. Buñuel called *An Andalusian Dog* "a passionate call to murder."

Figure 10.18

The style of Surrealist films is eclectic. Mise-en-scene is often influenced by Surrealist painting: The ants in *An Andalusian Dog* come from Dali's pictures, whereas the pillars and city squares of *The Seashell and the Clergyman* hark back to the Italian painter de Chirico. Surrealist editing is an amalgam of some Impressionist devices (many dissolves and superimpositions) and some devices of the dominant cinema. The shocking eyeball-slitting at the start of *An Andalusian Dog* relies on some principles of continuity editing (and indeed on the Kuleshov effect). On the other hand, discontinuous editing is also commonly used to fracture any organized temporal-spatial coherence: In the same film, the heroine locks the man out of one room only to turn to find him already there with her. On the whole, Surrealist film style refused to canonize any particular devices, since that would order and rationalize what had to be an "undirected play of thought."

The fortunes of Surrealist cinema shifted with changes in the art movement as a whole. By late 1929, when Breton joined the Communist party, Surrealists were embroiled in internal dissension about whether communism was a political equivalent of Surrealism. Buñuel left France for a brief stay in Hollywood and then returned to Spain. The chief patron of Surrealist filmmaking, the Vicomte de Noailles, supported Jean Vigo's *Zéro de Conduit* (1932), a film of Surrealist ambitions, but then no longer sponsored the avant-garde. Thus as a unified movement, French Surrealism was no longer viable after 1931. Individual Surrealists continued to work, however—the most famous being Buñuel, who has continued to work in his own brand of the Surrealist style for 50 years. His recent films, such as *Belle de Jour* (1967) and *The Discreet Charm of the Bourgeoisie* (1972), continue the Surrealist tradition.

Soviet Montage (1924–1930) ∎

In spite of the success of the Russian Revolution in 1917, the new Soviet government faced the difficult task of controlling all sectors of life. Like other industries, the film production and distribution systems took years to develop to a point where they could achieve a substantial output that served the aims of the new government.

Although the pre-Revolutionary Russian film industry had not figured prominently in world cinema, there were a number of private production companies operating in Moscow and Petrograd. These companies resisted the move made directly after the Revolution to nationalize all property, including private companies. These film companies simply refused to supply films to theaters operating under the control of the government. In July 1918 the government's film subsection of the State Commission of Education put strict controls on the existing supplies of raw film stock. As a result, producers began hoarding their stock; many took all the equipment they could and fled to other countries. Some companies made films commissioned by the government, while hoping that the Reds would lose the Civil War and that things would return to pre-Revolutionary conditions.

In spite of the shortages of equipment and the difficult living conditions, a few young filmmakers made tentative moves that would result in the development of a national cinema movement. Dziga Vertov began working on documentary footage of the war; at age 20, he was placed in charge of all newsreels. Lev Kuleshov, teaching in the newly founded State School on Cinema Art, performed a series of experiments by editing footage from different sources into a whole that creates an impression of continuity. (In this sense, Kuleshov was perhaps the most conservative of the young Soviet filmmakers, since he was basically trying to systematize principles of editing similar to the continuity practices of the classical Hollywood cinema.) Even before they were able to make films, the young filmmakers were working at the first film school in the world and writing theoretical essays on the new art form. This grounding in theory would be the basis of the montage style.

In 1920 Sergei Eisenstein worked briefly in a train carrying propaganda to the troops in the Civil War; he returned that year to Moscow to work in the new workers' theater, the Proletkult. In May 1920 Vsevolod Pudovkin made his acting debut in a play presented by Kuleshov's State Film School. He had been inspired to go into filmmaking by seeing Griffith's *Intolerance*, which was finally shown in Russia in 1919. American films, particularly those of Griffith, Douglas Fairbanks, and Mary Pickford, were a tremendous influence on the filmmakers of the emerging Soviet movement.

None of the important filmmakers of the montage style were veterans of the pre-Revolutionary industry. All came from other fields (e.g., Eisenstein from engineering, Pudovkin from chemistry) and discovered the cinema in the midst of the Revolution's ferment. Those established filmmakers who did make films in Russia in the 1920s tended to stick to older traditions. One popular director of the Tsarist period, Yakov Protazanov, went abroad briefly, but returned to continue making films whose style and form owed almost nothing to the theory and practice of the new filmmakers.

Protazanov's return coincided with a general loosening of government restrictions on private enterprise. In 1921 the country was experiencing tremendous difficulties, including a widespread famine. In order to facilitate the production and distribution of goods, Lenin instituted the New Economic Policy (NEP), which for a few years permitted private management of business. For film, this meant a sudden reappearance of film stock and equipment belonging to the producers who had not emigrated. By 1923 the government was able to create a Soviet monopoly on film production by nationalizing the industry permanently.

"Of all the arts, for us the cinema is the most important," Lenin stated in 1922. Since Lenin saw film as a powerful tool for education, the first films encouraged by the government were documentaries and newsreels such as Vertov's newsreel series *Kino-Pravda*, which began in May 1922. Fictional films followed eventually. A Georgian film of 1923, *Red Imps*, was the first Soviet film to compete successfully with the predominantly foreign films on Russian screens. (In 1924 only 28.5 percent of all films shown in the Soviet Union were of Soviet origin; one year later this figure had inched up to 30 percent.)

The Soviet montage style became a full-blown movement in 1924, with Kuleshov's class from the State Film School filming *The Extra-*

Figure 10.19

Figure 10.20

Figure 10.21

Figure 10.22

ordinary Adventures of Mr. West in the Land of the Bolsheviks. This delightful film, along with Kuleshov's next film, *The Death Ray* (1925), showed that Soviet directors could apply montage principles and come up with amusing satires or exciting adventures comparable to the Hollywood product.

Eisenstein's first feature, *Strike* (1924) was released early in 1925. This film and *Potemkin*, released later in 1925, drew the attention of other countries to the new movement. In the next few years Eisenstein, Pudovkin, Vertov, and the Ukrainian Alexander Dovzhenko created a series of films that are classics of the montage style.

Eisenstein has written: "We all came to the Soviet cinema as something not yet existent. We came upon no ready-built city." The theoretical writings and filmmaking practice of these directors were based on editing. They all declared that a film does not exist in its individual shots, but only in their combination through editing into a whole. We should remember here that since the primitive cinema, no national film style had yet appeared that depended on the long take; the great films that inspired these Soviet filmmakers, like *Intolerance*, were based largely on editing juxtapositions.

Not all of the young theoreticians agreed on exactly how this editing was to be done. Pudovkin, for example, believed that shots were like bricks, to be joined together to build a sequence. Eisenstein disagreed, saying that the maximum effect would be gained if the shots did not fit together perfectly, if they created a jolt for the spectator; he also favored the juxtaposition of shots to create a concept, as we have already seen with his technique of "intellectual montage." Vertov disagreed with both theorists, favoring a "cinema-eye" approach to recording and shaping documentary reality.

We have already seen examples of Soviet montage in our examination of a sequence from *October* (1928) in Chapter 6. Pudovkin's *Storm Over Asia* (1928) provides a comparison. In one scene a British officer (fighting against the Reds in the Civil War) and his wife dress in elegant clothes to attend a ceremony at a Buddist temple. Pudovkin intercuts shots of the couple and their accessories (Figs. 10.19 and 10.20) with shots of the preparations at the temple (Figs. 10.21 and 10.22). By the use of montage, Pudovkin creates a parallelism that points up the absurdity of the British rituals. Other famous examples of Soviet montage style in this film are the moment when the hero knocks over a fishtank (rendered with many close shots of various phases of the action) and the "storm" finale, with fast cutting to convey the relentless sweep of the Mongolian troops.

The Soviet approach to form set it apart from the cinemas of other countries. Soviet narrative films tended to downplay character psychology as a cause; instead, social forces provided the major causes. Characters were interesting for the way these social causes affected their lives. We have already mentioned (in Chapter 3) that films of the Soviet montage movement did not always have a single protagonist; large groups could form a collective hero, as in Eisenstein's films before *Old and New*. In keeping with this deemphasis of individual personalities, Soviet filmmakers often avoided well-known actors, preferring to cast parts by searching out nonactors. This practice was called *typage*, since the filmmakers would search out an individual whose appearance seemed at once to convey the "type of character he or she was to play. Except for the hero, Pudovkin used nonactors to play all of the Mongols in *Storm Over Asia*.

By the end of the 1920s, each of the major figures of this movement had made about four important films. The decline of the movement was not caused primarily, as in Germany and France, by industrial and economic factors. Instead, government political pressures exerted a strong control which discouraged the use of the montage style. By the late 1920s, Eisentein and Dovzhenko were being criticized for their excessively formal and "esoteric" approaches. In 1929 Eisentein went to Hollywood to study the new technique of sound; by the time he returned in 1932, the attitude of the film industry had changed. The Soviet authorities, under Stalin's direction, encouraged filmmakers to create simple films that would be readily understandable to all audiences; any stylistic experimentation or nonrealistic subject matter was criticized or censored.

This trend culminated in 1934, when the government instituted a new artistic policy called Socialist Realism. This dictated that all artworks must depict Revolutionary development while being firmly grounded in "realism." The great Soviet directors continued to make films, occasionally masterpieces, but the montage experiments of the 1920s had to be discarded or modified. Eisenstein managed to continue his work on montage, but occasionally incurred the wrath of the authorities up until his death in 1948. As a movement, the Soviet montage style can be said to have ended by about 1930, with the release of Dovzhenko's *Earth* and Vertov's *Enthusiasm*.

Summary: International Stylistic Trends of the Late Silent Cinema ■

So far we have treated the three major alternative movements of the silent period—French, German, and Russian—as largely separate from one another. This is how they began, but filmmakers in each country quickly became aware of the other movements. We have seen how German companies worked to break down bans and prejudices against their films in other countries. Soon German films were shown frequently in France and Russia. Russian films were exported later. (*Strike,* for example, opened in Berlin in 1927.) Often Soviet films had to be shown at private cinema clubs in France and England, due to political resistance to things Soviet; there grew up, however, an international film culture that would have been aware of the major formal and stylistic traits of all three movements.

As a result, the filmmakers of each movement began to be influenced by the films of the other movements. Impressionism began in 1917 and German Expressionism in 1920; by 1923–1924, there were definite signs that the two groups of filmmakers had seen each other's work. Expressionist elements crop up in the mise-en-scene of French films, such as L'Herbier's *Don Juan et Faust* (1923) and *L'Inhumaine* (1924).

In turn, the Germans began to employ the subjective camera style developed by the French. F. W. Murnau created a sensation by rendering the hero's drunkenness in *The Last Laugh* (1924) with a handheld camera, yet the French had already been doing this sort of thing for several years. Fritz Lang followed suit by mounting his camera on a swing for his 1926 *Metropolis,* subjectively rendering an explosion's impact on the hero.

The Russians were also seeing German films. One team of filmmakers, Kozintsev and Trauberg, was influenced by them; their films stand out from the majority of the Soviet films by their use of stylized sets, lighting, and acting. More important, several French Impressionist films reached Russia by 1925. These included Jean Epstein's *Coeur Fidèle* (1923) and excerpts from Gance's *La Roue* (1922). The latter film's most spectacular sequences involved fast rhythmic editing, some with series of single frame shots. Direct influence is difficult to prove, but Eisenstein's editing changes considerably between *Potemkin* (1925) and *October* (1928); in the latter film, the editing is much faster, including series of two-frame shots. Pudovkin uses very fast montage in the last sequence of *Storm Over Asia* (1928) as well.

By the late 1920s, the stylistic traits of German mise-en-scene, French cinematography and editing, and Soviet montage were being freely used by filmmakers of various countries. Dreyer's *La Passion de Jeanne d'Arc,* made in France in 1928, exemplifies this perfectly (Fig. 10.23, a production still). The film's set designer was Hermann Warm, who had collaborated on the designs of *Caligari* and other German films. Dreyer used elaborate swinging camera movements of the French style and assembled his scenes from close shots of parts of the action, somewhat in Soviet montage fashion. Other films that combine two or more of these stylistic tendencies are the German film *Überfall* (1928) and the French *Fall of the House of Usher* (1928).

The international style even made its way to Hollywood. Since so many filmmakers, particularly Germans, were hired by the American

Figure 10.23

studios, the European traits began to show up in American films. F. W. Murnau's *Sunrise* (1927) was written by *Caligari's* scriptwriter, Carl Mayer; it was an elaborate studio production for 20th Century-Fox, but aside from its familiar American stars, it might have been made in Germany.

One aspect of the European cinema that completely avoided national boundaries was the extreme avant-garde. The Dada movement, an anarchist antiart group, began in Switzerland in the early 1920s and quickly spread to France and Germany. France's René Clair made one of the most important Dada films, *Entr'acte* (1924), to be shown in the intermission of a Dada ballet. Other Dada films included Marcel Duchamp's *Anemic Cinema* (1926) and Hans Richter's German film *Ghosts Before Breakfast* (1927–1928). These films resembled the Surrealist films, but carried their illogic to an even greater degree. If the Surrealist films had a dreamlike, mystical quality, the Dada films showed objects in an anarchic revolt against conventional society. In *Entr'acte* a camel pulls a hearse in a chase through the streets of Paris; in *Ghosts Before Breakfast* bowler hats fly off the heads of their respectable owners and cavort in the air.

Overall, the various national and international trends of the silent cinema had developed the film art to a highly sophisticated level by the end of the 1920s. Since then, the introduction of sound and color have provided new stylistic possibilities, but no filmmakers have ever surpassed the intense theoretical study and variety of experiment which existed during this period.

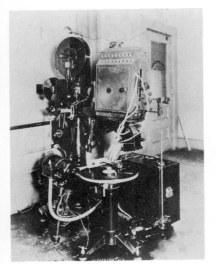

Figure 10.24

The Classical Hollywood Cinema
After the Coming of Sound ■

Contrary to accounts in most film histories, the introduction of sound technology was not a last-ditch gamble by a bankrupt Warner Brothers studio; nor did sound burst unexpected onto the scene. In fact, Warner Brothers was on firm financial ground and was in the process of investing a great deal of money to expand its facilities and holdings. One of these expansions was the investment (totaling only about one-fifth of the over-all expansion by the studio) in a sound system using records in synchronization with film images. (Fig. 10.24 shows an early projector with sound attachment.)

By means of the release of *Don Juan* (1926) with orchestral accompaniment and sound effects on disc and a series of sound vaudeville shorts, Warner Brothers began to popularize the idea of sound films. In 1927, *The Jazz Singer* (a part "talkie" with silent scenes) had a tremendous success, and the Warner Brothers investment began to pay.

The success of *Don Juan* and the shorts convinced other studios that sound contributed to profitable filmmaking. Unlike the early period of filmmaking and the Motion Pictures Patents Company, there was now no fierce competition within the industry. Instead, firms realized that whatever sound system the studios finally adopted, it would have to be compatible with the projection machinery set up in any theater. Eventually a sound-on-film rather than a sound-on-disc system became the standard and continues so to the present. By 1930 virtually every theater in America was wired for sound.

For a few years, sound created a setback for Hollywood film style. The camera had to be put inside a sound booth so that its motor noise would not be picked up by the microphone. Figure 10.25 is a publicity still showing a setup for a dialogue scene in a 1928 MGM film. The camera operator can hear only through his earphones; obviously the camera cannot move except for short pans to reframe. The bulky microphone, on the table at the right, also did not move; the actors had to stay within a limited space if their speech was to register on the track. The result of such restrictions was a short period of static films resembling stage plays.

But soon solutions were found for these problems. Smaller cases, which enclosed only the camera body, replaced the cumbersome booths. These *blimps* (Fig. 10.26) permitted camerapersons to place the camera on movable supports. Early sound films such as Rouben Mamoulian's *Applause* (1929) and René Clair's *Under the Roofs of Paris* (1930) demonstrate that the camera soon regained a great flexibility of movement. Similarly, microphones mounted on booms and hanging over the heads of the actors could also follow moving action without a loss of recording quality.

Figure 10.25

Figure 10.26

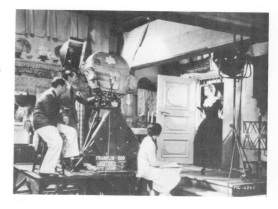

The introduction of sound coincided with and contributed to a change in the photographic style of classical Hollywood films. The need for silence on the set made necessary the use of incandescent Mazda lights, replacing the earlier mercury vapor and arc lamps of the silent period, which had produced a noticeable hiss. Mazda lights were softer and more appropriate to the new, faster panchromatic film stock, which became the standard in the late 1920s. (For a comparison of ortho-chromatic and panchromatic film stocks, see Chapter 4.) The overall effects of the different lighting and film stocks were softer, more diffused tonalities combined with shallow-focus photography. The soft-focus effect was strengthened by the placement of diffusion gauzes over the camera lens. An early sound film (with musical track only) such as Frank Borzage's *Seventh Heaven* (1927) uses this style a great deal; the softened textures of this film set it apart from films of just a few years before. These earlier films had used hard-edged lighting with the slower orthochromatic stock.

Once camera movement and subject movement were restored to the sound films, filmmakers continued to use many of the stylistic characteristics developed in Hollywood during the silent period. Diegetic sound provided a powerful addition to the system of continuity editing; a sound overlap could establish spaces outside the frame and could create temporal continuity.

Within the overall patterns of continuity style and classical narrative form, each of the various large studios developed a distinctive approach of its own. Thus MGM, for example, became the prestige studio, with a huge number of stars and technicians under long-term contract. MGM lavished money on settings, costumes, and special effects, as in *The Good Earth* (1937), with its locust attack, or *San Francisco* (1936) in which the great earthquake is spectacularly recreated. Warner Brothers, in spite of its success with sound, was still a small studio and specialized in less expensive genre pictures. Its series of gangster films *(Little Caesar, Public Enemy)* and musicals *(Forty-Second Street, Gold-diggers of 1933)* were among the studio's most successful products. Even lower on the ladder of prestige was Universal, which specialized in low-budget, atmospheric horror films such as *Frankenstein* (1931) and *The Old Dark House* (1932).

One major genre, the musical, became possible only with the introduction of sound. (Indeed, the original intention of the Warners when they began their investment in sound equipment was the cheap circulation of vaudeville acts, which had previously toured the country live.) The form of most musicals involved separate numbers inserted into a linear narrative (although a few "review" musicals simply strung together a series of numbers, with virtually no connecting narrative.) One of the major studios, RKO, made a series of musicals starring Fred Astaire and Ginger Rogers; *Swing Time* (George Stevens, 1936) illustrates how a musical can be a classically constructed narrative. Like *Our Hospitality*, *Swing Time* contains a set of causally important motifs that recur to create a tight narrative. Fred comes from a family of gamblers, and his skill allows him to win a night club away from its owner—a band leader who is also a gambler. Thus Fred wins Ginger, who works for the bandleader. As a gambler, the hero has a "lucky" quarter, the loss of which causes his initial meeting with Ginger. Thus the musical numbers are motivated by the narrative. Initially Ginger works in a dancing school; although Fred is a professional dancer, he pretends to be a beginner to get to know her. When Ginger decides to marry the bandleader, Fred persuades her to dance one last romantic dance with him; this helps to motivate the final scene, in which Ginger chooses Fred instead of the bandleader. Stylistically, the musical numbers are set apart from the other scenes by a change in the rhythm of the editing; shots within musical numbers tend to be longer.

During the 1930s, color film stocks became widely used for the first time. Photographic color had been around in various forms since 1908. In the 1920s, a few films had Technicolor sequences, but the process was too costly to use extensively. But by the mid-1930s, Technicolor was more economically feasible, and studios used it for big productions, such as Mamoulian's *Becky Sharp* (1935), the first all-color feature-length film. (See Plates 10 and 11, from *Meet Me in St. Louis*, for examples of Technicolor.)

Technicolor needed a great deal of light on the set, and the light had to favor certain hues. The incandescent Mazda lights did not suffice, so arc lamps, improved to eliminate their noise, were reintroduced. These brighter lights, combined with the fast film stocks, made it easier for camerapersons to achieve greater depth of field by using more light and a smaller aperture. Many cinematographers stuck to the old soft-focus style, but others began to experiment.

By the late 1930s, there was a definite trend toward a deep-focus style. We have already seen an example in Ford's *Stagecoach* (1939; see Figs. 9.8 and 9.9). William Wyler's *Jezebel* (1938) and Alfred L. Werker's *The Adventures of Sherlock Holmes* (1939) also utilized deep focus to some degree. But it was *Citizen Kane* that in 1941 brought deep focus strongly to the attention of spectators and filmmakers alike. Welles placed the foreground figures very close to the camera and the background figures deep in the space of the shot. This was so impressive that *Citizen Kane* helped make the tendency toward deep focus a major part of classical Hollywood style in the next decade. Many films using the technique soon appeared. *Citizen Kane*'s cinematographer, Gregg Toland, worked on some of them, such as *The Little Foxes* (William Wyler, 1941).

With deep focus came a corresponding emphasis on the long take. Rather than setting up a conversation scene with the actors close together, but in separate reverse shots, the filmmaker might now place them in depth in a single framing. The brightness of the light necessary for deep focus also tended to lend a hard-edged appearance to objects. Gauzy effects were largely eliminated, and much 1940s cinema became visually quite distinct from that of the 1930s. But the insistence on the clear narrative functioning of all these techniques remained strong. The classical Hollywood narrative modified itself over the years, but did not change radically.

The same has remained true until the present day. In the 1950s Hollywood responded to the invention of television (which competed with it for audiences) by introducing a series of technical innovations. Some of these (stereo, wide screen) have remained with us in one form or another. Others (3-D, Cinerama) have been used only sporadically in recent years. With the dwindling of the film audience, Hollywood has tended toward specialization. Where once it tried to lure the "family" audience, now it makes films specifically for children, others specifically for college students, still others to be shown only in drive-ins.

But in spite of these technical innovations and fashions in types of narrative form, the basic style of the classical Hollywood cinema remains. Continuity editing is still assumed to be the norm. The scene in *Jaws* (1975) where the young scientist visits the Brodys at home is handled very similarly to the restaurant sequence in *His Girl Friday*; both have three characters at a table and present the dialogue in a series of reverse shots. Clear, linear narrative remains the dominant factor in this type of filmmaking.

Italian Neorealism (1942–1951) ■

The term "neorealism" was coined by the Italian film critic Umberto Barbaro in referring to four films made in 1942. Why was this a "new" realism? Under Mussolini, the film industry—run by Mussolini's brother—had concentrated on colossal historical epics and sentimental upper-class melodramas (nicknamed "white telephone" films). Staying comfortably within the lavish Cinecitta studios, filmmakers did not venture out to document contemporary life. But Barbaro hoped that these four films (the most famous was Luchino Visconti's *Ossessione*) would inaugurate a trend toward realism. After Mussolini's fall in 1943, as several filmmakers began to make films with the goal of revealing contemporary social conditions, the trend became the Neorealist movement.

Economic, political, and cultural factors helped Neorealism survive. Nearly all of the major Neorealists—Roberto Rossellini, Vittorio De Sica, Luchino Visconti, and others—came to the movement as experienced filmmakers. They knew one another, frequently shared scriptwriters and personnel, and gained public attention in the journals *Cinema* and *Bianco e Nero*. Government subsidy and American aid helped sustain Neorealist production, and before 1948 the movement had enough friends in the government to be relatively free of censorship. Small, independent production companies blossomed. There was even a curious correspondence between Neorealism and an Italian literary movement of the same period modeled on the *verismo* of the previous century. Visconti's *Ossessione* (1942) and *La Terra Trema* (1947); Rossellini's *Open City* (1945), *Paisan* (1946), and *Germany Year Zero* (1947); De Sica's *Shoeshine* (1946) and *Bicycle Thieves* (1948); and other works of Lattuada, Blasetti, De Santis, and Germi—the major Italian films of the 1940s were supported by a particular combination of historical factors.

Because of these factors, the Neorealist movement created a distinct approach to film style. By 1945 the fighting had destroyed most of Cinecitta, and sound equipment was rare. As a result, Neorealist mise-en-scene relied on actual locales, and its photographic work tended toward the raw roughness of documentaries. Rossellini has told of buying bits of negative stock from street photographers, so that much of *Open City* was shot on different qualities of film stock.

Shooting on the streets and in private buildings made Italian camerapersons adept at available-light cinematography which avoided the "three-point" lighting system of Hollywood. Although Noeorealist films often featured famous stage or film actors, they also made use of nonactors, recruited for their realistic looks or behavior. For the adult "star" of *Bicycle Thieves*, De Sica chose a factory worker: "The way he moved, the way he sat down, his gestures with those hands of a working man and not of an actor . . . everything about him was perfect." There had been a long tradition of dubbing in the Italian cinema, and the ability to postsynchronize dialogue permitted the filmmakers to work on location with smaller crews and to move the camera. With a degree of improvisational freedom in the acting and setting went a certain flexibility of framing and camera movement, well displayed in the death of Pina in *Open City*, the final sequence of *Germany Year Zero*, and the magnificent panning and tracking shots in *La Terra Trema*. The tracking shots through the open-air bicycle market in *Bicycle Thieves* illustrate the possibilities which the Neorealist director found in returning to location filming (Fig. 10.27).

No less influential was the Neorealist sense of narrative form. Reacting against the intricately plotted white-telephone dramas, the Neorealists tended to loosen up narrative relations. The earliest major films of the movement, such as *Ossessione*, *Open City*, and *Shoeshine*, contain relatively conventionally organized plots (albeit with unhappy endings). But the most formally radical Neorealist films tend to allow the intrusion of noncausally motivated ("accidental") details, such as the famous scene in which the hero encounters a group of priests during a rain shower, in *Bicycle Thieves*. Although the causes of characters' actions are usually seen as concretely economic and political (poverty, unemployment, exploitation), the effects are often fragmentary and inconclusive. Rossellini's *Paisan* is frankly episodic, presenting five anecdotes of life in Italy during the Allied invasion; often we are not told the outcome of an

Figure 10.27

event, the consequence of a cause. *Bicycle Thieves* ends with the worker and his son wandering down the street, their stolen bicycle still missing, their future uncertain. Although ending with the defeat of the Sicilian fishermen's revolt against the merchants, *La Terra Trema* does not cancel the possibility that a later revolt will succeed. Neorealism's tendency toward a slice-of-life plot construction gave many films of the movement an open-ended quality quite opposed to the narrative closure of the Hollywood cinema.

As economic and cultural forces had sustained the Neorealist movement, so they were prime causes of its cessation. When Italy began to prosper after the war, the government looked askance at films so critical of contemporary society. After 1949, censorship and state pressures began to constrain the movement. Large-scale Italian film production began to reappear, and Neorealism no longer had the freedom of the small production company. Finally, the Neorealist directors, now famous, began to pursue more individualized concerns: Rossellini's investigation of Christianity and Western history, De Sica's sentimental romances, Visconti's examination of upper-class milieux. Most historians date the end of the Neorealist movement with the public attacks on De Sica's *Umberto D* (1951). Nevertheless, Neorealist elements are still quite visible in the early works of Fellini (*I Vitelloni*, 1954, is a good example) and of Antonioni (*Cronaca di un Amore*, 1951); both directors had worked on Neorealist films. The movement has exercised a considerable influence on individual filmmakers such as Satyajit Ray and on groups such as the French New Wave.

The New Wave (1959–1964) ■

In the mid-1950s a group of young men who wrote for the Paris film journal *Cahiers du Cinéma* made a habit of attacking the most artistically respected French filmmakers of the day. "I consider an adaptation of value," wrote François Truffaut, "only when written by a *man of the cinema*. Aurenche and Bost [the leading scriptwriters of the time] are essentially literary men and I reproach them here for being contemptuous of the cinema by underestimating it." Addressing 21 major directors, Jean-Luc Godard asserted: "Your camera movements are ugly because your subjects are bad, your casts act badly because your dialogue is worthless; in a word, you don't know how to create cinema because you no longer even know what it is." Truffaut and Godard, along with Claude Chabrol, Eric Rohmer, and Jacques Rivette, championed certain directors considered somewhat outdated (Jean Renoir, Max Ophuls) or esoteric (Robert Bresson, Jacques Tati). More important, the young men saw no contradiction in rejecting the French filmmaking establishment while loving blatantly commercial Hollywood. The young Turks of *Cahiers* claimed that in the works of certain directors—certain *auteurs* (authors)—artistry existed in the American cinema. An *auteur* managed to stamp his or her personality on genre and studio products, transcending the constraints of a mass-production system. Howard Hawks, Otto Preminger, Samuel Fuller, Vincente Minnelli, Nicholas Ray, Alfred Hitchcock—these were more than craftsmen: Each person's total output constituted a coherent world. Truffaut quoted Giraudoux: "There are no works, there are only *auteurs*."

Writing criticism did not, however, satisfy these young men. They itched to make films. Borrowing money from friends and filming on location, each started to shoot short films. By 1959 they had become a force to be reckoned with. In that year Rivette filmed *Paris Nous Appartient (Paris Belongs to Us)*; Godard made *A Bout de Souffle (Breathless)*; Chabrol made his second feature, *Les Cousins*; and in April Truffaut's *Les Quatre Cent Coups (The 400 Blows)* won the Grand Prize at the Cannes Festival. Godard treated it as a victory: "We won the day in having it acknowledged in principle that a film by Hitchcock, for example, is as important as a book by Aragon. Film *auteurs*, thanks to us, have finally entered the history of art."

The novelty and youthful vigor of these directors led journalists to nickname them *la nouvelle vague*—the "New Wave." Their output was staggering. All told, the five directors made 32 feature films between 1959 and 1966; Godard and Chabrol made 11 apiece! So many films must of course be highly disparate, but there are enough similarities of narrative form and cinematic style for us to identify a "New Wave" movement.

The most obviously revolutionary quality of the New Wave films was their casual look; to proponents of the carefully polished French "cinema of quality," the young directors must have seemed hopelessly sloppy. The New Wave directors had admired the Neorealists (especially Rossellini), and in opposition to studio filmmaking, took as their mise-en-scene actual locales in and around Paris. Shooting on location became the norm. Similarly, glossy studio lighting was replaced by what Raoul Coutard called "light of day." The New Wave encouraged its actors to improvise their lines, even if that might slow down the plot; *Breathless*'s bedroom scene was startling for many reasons, but partly because of its rambling, repetitive dialogue. Given such mise-en-scene, cinematography changed too. In general, the New Wave camera moves a great deal; it is often panning (sometimes 360°, as in *Jules et Jim*) and tracking, following characters or tracing out relations within a locale. Furthermore, shooting cheaply on location demanded flexible, portable equipment; fortunately, Eclair had recently developed a lightweight camera

Figure 10.28

that could be handheld. (That the Eclair had been used primarily for documentary work accorded perfectly with the "realistic" mise-en-scene of the New Wave.) New Wave films were intoxicated with the new freedom offered by the handheld camera. In *The 400 Blows* the camera explores a cramped apartment and rides a carnival centrifuge. *Paris Belongs to Us* also contains handheld-camera scenes within apartment locations; in *Breathless* the cinematographer held the camera while seated in a wheelchair to follow the hero along a complex path in a travel agency's office.

Along with the handheld camera went an interest in the long take, which the New Wave directors admired in American filmmakers such as Minnelli and Otto Preminger and in Japanese directors such as Kenji Mizoguchi. Figure 10.28 is from a long-take shot in *Breathless*; the handheld camera moves back (again, Coutard held the camera while seated in a wheelchair) as the characters chat and stroll along a Paris street. The casual style of the New Wave resulted in occasional accidental intrusions by passersby, as with the man at the right, who glances at the actors.

One more quality of the New Wave style should be mentioned: its humor. These young men deliberately played with the medium. In Godard's *Band of Outsiders* the three main characters resolve to be silent for a minute, and Godard dutifully shuts off *all* the diegetic sound. In Truffaut's *Shoot the Piano Player* a character swears that he's not lying: "May my mother drop dead if I'm not telling the truth"; cut to a shot of an old lady keeling over. But most often the humor lies in intricate references to other films, Hollywood or European. These are homages to admired *auteurs*: Godard characters allude to *Johnny Guitar* (Ray), *Some Came Running* (Minnelli), and "Arizona Jim" (from *The Crime of M. Lange*). In *Les Carabiniers* Godard parodies Lumière, and in *Vivre sa*

Vie he "quotes" *La Passion de Jeanne d'Arc*. Hitchcock is frequently cited in Chabrol's films, and Truffaut's *Les Mistons* recreates a shot from a Lumière short; compare Fig. 10.29 with the frame from *Arroseur Arrosé* (Fig. 4.6). Such homages even became in-jokes, as when New Wave actors Jean-Claude Brialy and Jeanne Moreau "walk on" in *The 400 Blows* or when a Godard character mentions "Arizona Jules" (combining names from *M. Lange* and *Jules et Jim*). Such gags, the New Wave directors felt, took some of the solemnity out of filmmaking and film viewing.

Figure 10.29

New Wave films were narrative films, but as a group they were perhaps the most perplexing, discontinuous narratives that film viewers had seen since Surrealist filmmaking. In general, causal connections became quite loose. Why does Michel, the hero of *Breathless*, behave as he does? In *Shoot the Piano Player* the first sequence consists mainly of a conversation between the hero's brother and a man he accidentally meets on the street; the latter tells of his marital problems at some length, even though he has nothing to do with the film's narrative. Is there actually a political conspiracy going on in *Paris Belongs to Us*? Why is Nana shot at the end of *Vivre sa Vie*?

Moreover, the films lack goal-oriented protagonists. The heros drift aimlessly, engage in actions on the spur of the moment, often spend their time talking and drinking in a café or going to movies. New Wave narratives often introduce startling shifts in tone, jolting our expectations. In *Breathless* Michel's comic monologue in the first scene as he drives along a road leads directly into his brutal murder of a policeman. When two gangsters kidnap the hero and his girlfriend in *Shoot the Piano Player*, the whole group begins a comic discussion of sex. Discontinuous editing—seen at its limit in Godard's jump cuts—further disturbs narrative continuity. Perhaps most important, the New Wave film typically ends ambiguously. In *Breathless* Michel dies cursing his girlfriend, Patricia; looking out at us, her response is to rub her lip in the same Bogart-inspired gesture Michel himself has used, then to turn abruptly away. Antoine in *The 400 Blows* reaches the sea in the last shot, but as he moves forward, Truffaut zooms in and freezes the frame, ending the film with the question of where Antoine will go from here. In Chabrol's *Les Bonnes Femmes* and *Ophelia*, in Rivette's *Paris Belongs to Us*, and in nearly all of the work of Godard and Truffaut, the looseness of the causal chain leads to endings that remain defiantly open and uncertain.

Curiously, despite the demands that the films place on the viewer and despite the critical rampages of the filmmakers, the French film industry was not hostile to the New Wave. The decade 1947–1957 had been good to film production: The government supported the industry through enforced quotas, banks had invested heavily, and there was a flourishing business of international coproductions. But in 1957 cinema attendance fell off drastically (chiefly because television became more widespread). By 1959 the industry was in a crisis. Into this vacuum many directors, New Wave or not, stepped (Alain Resnais, Agnès Varda). The New Wave method of independent financing of low-budget films seemed to offer a good solution. New Wave directors shot films much more quickly and cheaply than did reigning directors. Moreover, the young directors helped one another out and thus reduced the financial risk by the established companies. Thus the French industry supported the New Wave through distribution, exhibition, and eventually production. Indeed, it is possible to argue that by 1964, although each New Wave director had his own production company, the group had become absorbed into the French film industry: Godard made *Le Mépris (Contempt)* for a major commercial producer, Carlo Ponti; Truffaut made *Fahrenheit 451* in England for Universal; and Chabrol began turning out parodies of James Bond thrillers. Dating the exact end of the movement is difficult, but most historians select 1964, when the characteristic New Wave formal system had already become diffused and imitated (by, for instance, Tony Richardson in *Tom Jones*). Certainly, after 1968 the political upheavals in France drastically altered the personal relations among the directors. As of this writing, Chabrol, Truffaut, and Rohmer remain firmly entrenched in the French film industry, whereas Godard has challenged that practice with films such as *Tout va bien,* and Rivette has experimented with narratives of unprecedented complexity and length (such as *Out One,* originally about 12 hours long!).

Bibliography ■

General

Huaco, George, *The Sociology of Film Art* (New York: Basic Books, 1965).

Knight, Arthur, *The Liveliest Art* (New York: Signet, 1957).

MacGowan, Kenneth, *Behind the Screen* (New York: Delta, 1965).

Nowell-Smith, Geoffrey, "Facts About Films and Facts of Films," *Quarterly Review of Film Studies* I, 3 (August 1976): 272–275.

Rotha, Paul, *The Film Till Now* (London: Spring, 1967).

Sadoul, Georges, *Histoire Générale du Cinéma*, Vols. 1–6 (Paris: Denoel, 1973–1977).

Early Cinema

Card, James, "Problems of Film History," *Hollywood Quarterly*, **4, 3** (Spring 1950): 279–288.

Ceram, C. W., *Archaeology of the Cinema* (New York: Harcourt, Brace, 1965).

Hammond, Paul, *Marvelous Méliès* (New York: St. Martin's Press, 1975).

Hendricks, Gordon, *The Edison Motion Picture Myth* (Berkeley: University of California Press, 1961).

Pratt, George, ed., *Spellbound in Darkness* (Greenwich: New York Graphic Society, 1973).

Spehr, Paul C., *The Movies Begin* (Newark, N.J.: Newark Museum, 1977).

Classical Hollywood Cinema (1903–1927)

Balio, Tino, ed., *The American Film Industry* (Madison: University of Wisconsin Press, 1976).

Brownlow, Kevin, *The Parade's Gone By* (New York: Bonanza, 1968).

Hampton, Benjamin, *History of the American Film Industry* (New York: Dover, 1970).

Jacobs, Lewis, *The Rise of the American Film* (New York: Teachers College Press, 1968).

Koszarski, Richard, "Maurice Tourneur: The First of the Visual Stylists," *Film Comment* **9**, 2 (March–April 1973): 24–31.

Pratt, George, *Spellbound in Darkness* (Greenwich: New York Graphic Society, 1973).

Salt, Barry, "Film Style and Technology in the Forties," *Film Quarterly* **31**, 1 (Fall 1977): 46–57.

————, "Film Style and Technology in the Thirties," *Film Quarterly* **30**, 1 (Fall 1976): 19–32.

Wagenknecht, Edward, *Movies in the Age of Innocence* (New York: Ballantine, 1971).

German Expressionism

Bucher, Felix, ed., *Germany* (New York: Barnes, 1970).

Eisner, Lotte, *F. W. Murnau* (Berkeley: University of California Press, 1973).

————, *Fritz Lang* (New York: Oxford University Press, 1977).

————, *The Haunted Screen* (Berkeley: University of California Press, 1969).

Kracauer, Siegfried, *From Caligari to Hitler* (Princeton, N.J.: Princeton University Press, 1969).

Miesel, Victor H., ed., *Voices of German Expressionism* (Englewood-Cliffs, N.J.: Prentice-Hall, 1970).

Myers, Bernard S., *The German Expressionists* (New York: Praeger, 1963).

Selz, Peter, *German Expressionist Painting* (Berkeley: University of California Press, 1957).

Titford, John S., "Object-Subject Relationships in German Expressionist Cinema," *Cinema Journal* **13**, 1 (Fall 1973): 17–24.

Tudor, Andrew, "Elective Affinities—the Myth of German Expressionism," *Screen* **12**, 3 (Summer 1971): 143–150.

Willett, John, *Expressionism* (New York: McGraw-Hill, 1970).

French Impressionism and Surrealism

Abel, Richard, "Louis Delluc: The Critic as Cinéaste," *Quarterly Review of Film Studies* **1**, 2 (May 1976): 205–244.

Blumer, Ronald, "The Camera as Snowball," *Cinema Journal* **9**, 2 (Spring 1970): 31–39.

Brownlow, Kevin, *The Parade's Gone By* (New York: Bonanza, 1968).

Clair, René, *Cinema Yesterday and Today* (New York: Dover, 1972).

Martin, Marcel, *France* (New York: Barnes, 1971).

Milne, Tom, "The Real Avant-Garde," *Sight and Sound* **32**, 3 (Summer 1963): 148–152.

Sadoul, Georges, *The French Cinema* (London: Falcon Press, 1952).

Tate Gallery, *Léger and Purist Paris* (London: Tate Gallery, 1970).

Soviet Montage

Bordwell, David, "The Idea of Montage in Soviet Art and Film," *Cinema Journal* **11**, 2 (Spring 1972): 9–17.

Bowlt, John, ed., *Russian Art of the Avant-Garde* (New York: Viking, 1973).

Carynnyk, Mario, ed., *Alexander Dovzhenko: Poet as Filmmaker* (Cambridge, Mass.: M.I.T. Press, 1973).

———, "The Vertov Papers," *Film Comment* **8**, 1 (Spring 1972): 46–51.

Eisenstein, S. M., *Film Form* (New York: Harcourt Brace, 1949).

Fischer, Lucy, "Enthusiasm: From Kino-Eye to Radio-Eye," *Film Quarterly* **21**, 2 (Winter 1977–78): 25–36.

Fuelop-Miller, René, *The Mind and Face of Bolshevism* (New York: Harper & Row, 1965).

Henderson, Elizabeth, "Shackled by Film; The Cinema in the Career of Mayakovsky," *Russian Literature Triquarterly,* 7 (Winter 1974): 297–320.

Hunt, Ronald, "The Constructivist Ethos," Pt. 1, *Artforum* **6,** 1 (Sept. 1967): 23–29; Pt. 2, *Artforum* **6, 2** (Oct. 1967): 26–32.

Kuleshov, Lev, *Kuleshov on Film* (Berkeley: University of California Press, 1974).

Leyda, Jay, *Kino* (New York: Colliers, 1973).

Michelson, Annette, "Man with a Movie Camera: From Magician to Epistemologist," *Artforum* **10,** 7 (March 1972): 60–72.

Nilssen, Vladimir, *Cinema as a Graphic Art* (New York: Hill & Wang, 1959).

Pudovkin, V. I., *Film Technique and Film Acting* (New York: Grove, 1960).

Schnitzer, Luda, Jean Schnitzer, and Marcel Martin, eds. *Cinema and Revolution* (New York: Hill and Wang, 1973).

The Classical Hollywood Cinema After the Coming of Sound

Balio, Tino, ed., *The American Film Industry* (Madison: University of Wisconsin Press, 1976).

Gomery, J. Douglas, "Writing the History of the American Film Industry: Warner Bros. and Sound," *Screen* **17,** 1 (Spring 1976): 40–53.

Ogle, Patrick, "Technological and Aesthetic Influences upon the Development of Deep Focus Cinematography in the United States," *Screen* **13,** 1 (Spring 1972): 45–72.

Italian Neorealism

Armes, Roy, *Patterns of Realism* (New York: Barnes, 1970).

Bazin, André, "Cinema and Television," *Sight and Sound* **28,** 1 (Winter 1958–1959): 26–30.

Cannella, Mario, "Ideology and Aesthetic Hypotheses in the Criticism of Neo-Realism," *Screen* **14,** 4 (Winter 1973/4): 5–60.

Gough-Yates, Kevin, "The Destruction of Neo-Realism," *Films and Filming* **16,** 12 (Sept. 1970): 14–22.

Leprohon, Pierre, *The Italian Cinema* (New York: Praeger, 1972).

Pacifici, Sergio J., "Notes Toward a Definition of Neorealism," *Yale French Studies* 7 (Summer 1956): 44–53.

The New Wave

Armes, Roy, *The French Cinema Since 1946,* Vol. II (New York: Barnes, 1970).

Brown, Royal S., ed., *Focus on Godard* (Englewood Cliffs, N.J.: Prentice-Hall, 1972).

Burch, Noël, "Qu 'est-ce que la Nouvelle Vague?" *Film Quarterly* **13,** 2 (Winter, 1959): 16–30.

Godard, Jean-Luc, *Godard on Godard* (New York: Viking, 1972).

Graham, Peter, ed., *The New Wave* (New York: Doubleday, 1968).

Monaco, James, *The New Wave* (New York: Oxford University Press, 1976).

Mussman, Toby, ed., *Jean-Luc Godard* (New York: Dutton, 1968).

CREDITS

Many of the frame enlargements and production stills used in the text are in the public domain; the others were obtained from a variety of sources. In the following listing, the boldface numbers are the figure references. In addition, the following abbreviations are used: WCFTR (Wisconsin Center for Film and Theater Research) and MOMA (Museum of Modern Art Film Stills Archive).

1.1 From the collection of the authors; **1.9** courtesy WCFTR; **1.10** British Lion/Columbia; **1.11** from the Collection of MOMA; **1.12–1.15** courtesy WCFTR; **1.16** from the Collection of MOMA; **1.17** courtesy WCFTR.

3.1 From the Collection of MOMA.

4.7–4.10 From the Collection of MOMA; **4.11** courtesy Images, Inc.; **4.12** courtesy Palladium Films, Copenhagen, and MOMA; **4.16** courtesy WCFTR; **4.17** courtesy New Yorker Films; **4.19** copyright 1958, Universal; **4.20–4.22** courtesy WCFTR; **4.23** copyright 1958, Universal; **4.24** courtesy WCFTR; **4.26** courtesy WCFTR; **4.27** copyright 1954, Toho; **4.28** courtesy WCFTR; **4.29** copyright 1950, Universal; **4.30** copyright 1932, Paramount; **4.33** courtesy MacMillan Audio-Brandon; **4.34** courtesy Norman McLaren; **4.35** courtesy Palladium Films, Copenhagen, and MOMA; **4.36** courtesy WCFTR; **4.37** courtesy New Yorker Films; **4.38–4.39** courtesy Palladium Films, Copenhagen, and MOMA; **4.40** courtesy New Yorker Films; **4.41** courtesy WCFTR; **4.43–4.56** courtesy MacMillan Audio-Brandon.

5.1 copyright, Rome-Paris Films; **5.2** courtesy MacMillan Audio-Brandon; **5.3** courtesy Palladium Films, Copenhagen, and A. J. Films; **5.5** copyright 1958, Universal; **5.7–5.8** courtesy Ernie Gehr; **5.9** courtesy MacMillan Audio-Brandon; **5.10** courtesy WCFTR; **5.11–5.12** courtesy MacMillan Audio-Brandon; **5.13–5.14** from the Collection of MOMA; **5.15** courtesy New Yorker Films; **5.16** courtesy MacMillan Audio-Brandon; **5.19–5.20** courtesy WCFTR; **5.21** from the Collection of MOMA; **5.22–5.23** copyright 1963, Toho; **5.24** from the Collection of

MOMA; **5.25–5.31** courtesy WCFTR; **5.36** courtesy New Yorker Films; **5.39–5.46** courtesy WCFTR; **5.47** courtesy Palladium Films, Copenhagen, and MOMA; **5.48** courtesy WCFTR; **5.49** copyright 1959, MGM; **5.51** courtesy WCFTR; **5.53–5.55** courtesy WCFTR; **5.56** courtesy New Yorker Films; **5.57** courtesy WCFTR; **5.58** courtesy Palladium Films, Copenhagen, and MOMA; **5.59–5.60** courtesy Palladium Films, Copenhagen, and A. J. Films; **5.61–5.62** courtesy WCFTR; **5.65** courtesy Pennebaker, Inc.; **5.66–5.68** courtesy WCFTR; **5.69–5.72** courtesy MacMillan Audio-Brandon; **5.76–5.81** courtesy MacMillan Audio-Brandon; **5.82** from the Collection of MOMA; **5.83–5.116** courtesy Janus Films; **5.117–5.119** courtesy Michael Snow; **5.120–5.125** courtesy MacMillan Audio-Brandon; **5.126–5.137** copyright 1958, Universal.

6.1–6.3 courtesy WCFTR; **6.4** copyright 1954, Toho; **6.5–6.8** copyright 1963, Universal; **6.9–6.14** copyright 1954, Toho; **6.15–6.16** copyright 1958, Universal; **6.17–6.27** copyright 1963 Universal; **6.28–6.50** courtesy WCFTR; **6.51** from the Collection of MOMA; **6.52–6.55** courtesy New Yorker Films; **6.58–6.63** courtesy MacMillan Audio-Brandon.

7.1–7.4 courtesy New Yorker Films; **7.5** from the Collection of MOMA; **7.7–7.11** copyright 1939, United Artists; **7.12–7.22** courtesy New Yorker Films.

8.1–8.11 courtesy WCFTR.

9.8–9.11 copyright 1939, United Artists; **9.12–9.20** Palladium Films, Copenhagen, and MOMA; **9.28–9.46** courtesy New Yorker Films; **9.47–9.55** courtesy Grove Press Films; **9.56–9.70** courtesy MacMillan Audio-Brandon; **9.71–9.83** courtesy Pennebaker, Inc.

10.1 courtesy WCFTR; **10.3–10.4** courtesy WCFTR; **10.6–10.16** courtesy WCFTR; **10.17** from the Collection of MOMA; **10.18–10.22** courtesy WCFTR; **10.24** from the Collection of MOMA; **10.25–10.27** courtesy WCFTR; **10.28** courtesy MacMillan Audio-Brandon; **10.29** courtesy WCFTR.

Plates 1–2 courtesy Pennebaker, Inc.; **3–4** copyright Walter Reade, 1972; **7–9** courtesy New Yorker Films; **10–11** from the MGM release *Meet Me in St. Louis* © 1944 Loewe's Incorporated. Copyright renewed in 1971 by Metro-Goldwyn-Mayer Inc., courtesy MGM, Inc.; **12** courtesy MacMillan Audio-Brandon; **13** Grove Press Films; **14** courtesy MacMillan Audio-Brandon; **15–16** courtesy MacMillan Audio-Brandon.

For terms and concepts, italic numbers indicate the most significant mention; thus "Narrative form" will be discussed in most detail on pp. 50–57. For titles of films, an abbreviation indicates the rental source. (See Film Rental Key below.) An asterisk by a film title indicates that the film is available for purchase. (See Film Purchase Sources below.)

Film Rental Key

In this index, rental sources for films are designated by the following abbreviations.

Film Purchase Sources

Films that are available for purchase may be obtained from one or more of the following sources:

Blackhawk Films, Inc.
Davenport, IA 52808

Festival Films
4445 Aldrich Ave. S.
Minneapolis, MN 55409

Reel Images
465 Monroe Turnpike
Monroe, CT 06468

Thunderbird Films
PO Box 65157
Los Angeles, CA 90065

Names and Subjects

Thème et Variations (1928), 174
*The Third Man (1949), Bud; 116–117
30° rule, *178*
*The Thirty-Nine Steps (1935), Bud,
  Jan, KP; 198, 239
Thomas, Tony, 218
Thompson, Kristin, 71
Thomson, David, 150, 184
The Three Musketeers (1921), AB,
  MOMA; 296
Three-point lighting, *84*
THX 1138 (1971), AB; 81
Tilt (frame movement), *122*, 123
Timbre, *192*, 193, 201
Time, in *Citizen Kane*, 62–65
  in editing, 161–163, 171–173, 185–186
  and frame mobility, 128–129
  in French Impressionism, 302
  in *His Girl Friday*, 236–237
  in *Last Year at Marienbad*, 254–255
  and mise-en-scene, 89–90
  in narrative, *52–54*, 59
  in *October*, 181–182
  of sound, 196, 203–207
  in *Tokyo Story*, 258, 262–263
Time-lapse cinematography, 103
Tinting, *101*
Titford, John S., 324
Todorov, Tzvetan, 69
TohoScope, 111
Tokyo Story (1953), NY; 177, 233,
  257–263
Toland, Gregg, 11, 18, 23, 315
Tom Jones (1963), UA; 322
Tom Tom the Piper's Son (1971), FMC,
  MOMA; 104
Tomashevsky, Boris, 70
Tonalities, *99–102*
Toning, *101*
Topaz (1969), Univ; 239
Touch of Evil (1958), Univ; 71, 82, 83,
  105, 129, 141, 156, 224
Toulmin, Stephen, 69
Tout va Bien (1971), NY; 322
Tracking shot, *122*, 123, 124–125
  in *Day of Wrath*, 251–252
Traffic (1971), Swank; 177
Transitional shot, in *Tokyo Story*,
  258–259
Trauberg, Leonid, 310
Treatment, *10*
Trevor, Claire, 244
Triptych, 110
*Triumph of the Will (1936), AB,
  MOMA; 97
Trouble in Paradise (1932), MOMA,
  Univ; 85, 187
Trucking shot, *see* Tracking shot

Truffaut, François, 12, 22, 59, 147, 148,
  179, 185, 318, 319, 320, 321, 322
Tudor, Andrew, 324
Turim, Maureen, 71
Twentieth Century-Fox, 294, 311
*Two or Three Things I Know About
  Her* (1966), NY; 202–203
2001 (1968), FI; 53, 108, 121, 146, 173
Typage, *309*

*Überfall (1928), Bud, KP, MOMA; 310
UFA, 146, 298–300
Umberto D (1951), Jan; 318
Underlighting, 83
Under the Roofs of Paris (1930), Cor;
  312
Unit production manager, *10*
United Artists, 244, 298
Unity, in film form, *43*, 55, 56, 74, 233
  in *The Man Who Knew Too Much*,
  239–242
  in *Stagecoach*, 244–248
Universal, 294, 314, 322

Varda, Agnes, 322
Variable area, 7
Variable density, 7
Variation, in film form, *41–42*, 46,
  55–56
  in *Our Hospitality*, 95
  in *Stagecoach*, 247
*Variety (1925), AB, KP, MOMA; 148
Veidt, Conrad, 85, 300
Venanzo, Giovanni di, 12
Vertigo (1958), 127
Vertov, Dziga, 48, 103, 104, 142, 148,
  160, 179, 187, 306, 308
Victory at Sea, 17
Vierney, Sacha, 252
Viewing time, 203
Vigo, Jean, 218, 306
Visconti, Luchino, 12, 316
I Vitelloni (1954), Cor; 318
Vivre sa Vie (1962), Cor; 320–321
Vlady, Marina, 202
Von Sternberg, Josef, 12, 82, 97, 187
Von Stroheim, Erich, 79, 81
Vorkapich, Slavko, 173
Vosper, Frank, 239
Vukasovic, Ivanka, 263

Wagenknecht, Edward, 323
Walker, Joseph, 234
Walsh, Raoul, 187
Wanger, Walter, 244
Warhol, Andy, 10, 16, 59, 138, 139, 151
Warm, Hermann, 18, 299, 310
Warner Brothers, 312, 314

Warren, Austin, 45
Watching for the Queen (1973), CFD; 90
Wavelength (1967), Can, FMC, Grove;
  105, 136
Waxworks (1924), AB; 300
Wayne, John, 193, 219, 244
Wellek, Rene, 45
Welles, Orson, 10, 11, 23, 65, 71, 82,
  83, 98, 105, 112, 122, 129, 138, 141,
  149, 156, 162, 173, 178, 199, 206,
  219, 224, 226–227, 248
Werker, Alfred L., 315
Wertheimer, Max, 19–20
Western History (1972), Can; 174
*What's Up Tiger Lily (1966), AB, Bud;
  204
White Heat (1949), UA; 84, 187
White, John, 145
White, Pearl, 301
White Shadows in the South Seas
  (1928), FI; 16
Whitney, John, 90
Wiazemsky, Anne, 280
Wide-angle lens, *104–105*
Wiener, Jean, 274
Wiers-Jenssen, Hans, 249
*Wild and Woolly (1917), AB, EG,
  MOMA; 296
Will Success Spoil Rock Hunter? (1957),
  FI; 173
Willett, John, 324
Williams, Alan, 71
Winchester 73, 85, 187
Winterwind (1969), Grove; 138
Wipe, *152*
The Wizard of Oz (1939), FI; 27–28,
  31–36, 39–44, 54, 56, 58, 59, 81,
  143, 187, 193
Wölfflin, Heinrich, 289
Wollen, Peter, 23, 72
Wood, Robin, 71
Woodstock (1970), WB; 97
The World at War, 17
Wright, Basil, 217
Wygotsky, Michael Z., 147, 219
Wyler, William, 84, 87, 98, 113, 149,
  170, 315

Yamamura, So, 257
*Young and Innocent (1937), Bud, KP;
  127

Zero de Conduit (1932), AB; 306
Zinneman, Fred, 23
Zivkovic, Ivan, 263
Zoetrope, 3
Zoom lens, *105–106*, 124–125, 148–149
  in *Wavelength*, 136